Unification Through Division

Unification Through Division

Histories of the Divisions of the American Psychological Association

VOLUME I

EDITED BY

Donald A. Dewsbury

AMERICAN PSYCHOLOGICAL ASSOCIATION
WASHINGTON, DC

Published by
American Psychological Association
750 First Street, NE
Washington, DC 20002

Copies may be ordered from
APA Order Department
P.O. Box 92984
Washington, DC 20090-2984

In the UK and Europe, copies may be ordered from
American Psychological Association
3 Henrietta Street
Covent Garden, London
WC2E 8LU England

Typeset in Goudy by PRO-Image Corporation, Techna-Type Div., York, PA

Printer: TechniGraphix, Reston, VA
Cover Designer: Minker Design, Bethesda, MD
Production Manager: Debbie K. Hardin, Reston, VA

Library of Congress Cataloging-in-Publication Data
Unification through division : histories of the divisions of the
   American Psychological Association / Donald A. Dewsbury, editor.
      p.   cm.
   Includes bibliographical references and index.
   ISBN 1-55798-379-8 (v. 1 : alk. paper)
   1. American Psychological Association—History.   I. Dewsbury,
Donald A., 1939–   .
BF11.U55 1996
150'.6073—dc20   96-41480
                                                                        CIP

British Library Cataloguing-in-Publication Data
A CIP record is available from the British Library.

Printed in the United States of America
First edition

CONTENTS

2

A HISTORY OF DIVISION 6 (BEHAVIORAL NEUROSCIENCE
AND COMPARATIVE PSYCHOLOGY): NOW YOU SEE IT, NOW
YOU DON'T, NOW YOU SEE IT 41
Donald A. Dewsbury

8

A HISTORY OF DIVISION 39 (PSYCHOANALYSIS) 233
Murray Meisels and Robert C. Lane

CONTRIBUTORS

Rodney R. Baker, Audie L. Murphy Memorial Veterans Hospital, San Antonio, Texas.

Jan L. Culbertson, Child Study Center, Oklahoma City

Thomas C. Dalton, California Polytechnic State University, San Luis Obispo

Donald A. Dewsbury, University of Florida

Thomas K. Fagan, The University of Memphis

Raymond D. Fowler, American Psychological Association, Washington, DC

Ernest R. Hilgard, Standford University

D. Brett King, University of Colorado at Boulder

Robert C. Lane, Nova Southeastern University

Murray Meisels, Independent Practice, Ann Arbor, Michigan

Donald K. Routh, University of Miami

James T. Todd, Eastern Michigan University

Michael Wertheimer, University of Colorado at Boulder

Michael G. Wessells, Randolph-Macon College

FOREWORD

As we approach the landmark 50th anniversary of the American Psychological Association divisions, it is appropriate to stop and reflect on the histories of these divisions and what they have contributed both to the APA and to the development of psychology itself. Looking at the list of APA divisions today and the variety of fields and perspectives that it holds, it is exciting to see the fruits of the division structure begun 50 years ago. I was part of those early discussions of how the division structure was to take shape, and everyone who was there remembers the pressures of this time. I recap here some of the major events of the founding of the divisions.

The APA, as we know it today with its divisional structure, began with what was called the Intersociety Constitutional Convention, held at the Pennsylvania Hotel in New York City, May 29 to 31, 1943, under the chairmanship of E. G. Boring.

The name "Intersociety" depended on the growing influence of the American Association of Applied Psychology, the Psychometric Society, the Society for the Psychological Study of Social Issues, and a number of other scientific and professional societies made up primarily of psychologists. All were invited to send delegates. The decision was made to retain the APA as the parent organization, so that the legal procedure became that of modifying the bylaws of the APA. The bylaws were drastically revised by providing a diverse divisional structure to recognize the plurality of psychological interests, scientific and professional.

A draft of the new bylaws included provisions for the divisions and methods by which to create new ones, for a Council of Representation as a legislative body selected from the divisions, a small Board of Directors, a Policy and Planning Board to provide for regular reviews to keep the structure functional and to include procedures for electing officers.

The necessary actions for modifying the APA were completed in 1945, although the war lasted until September 1945. The first APA convention under the new bylaws was held in Philadelphia in 1946, by which time the largest competing organization, the American Association for Applied Psychology, had disbanded.

The new bylaws provided for a full-time, paid officer as executive secretary and a central office. The transition was well managed by Dael L. Wolfle, who as the first executive secretary organized the central office, created the machinery for fulfilling the intentions under the new bylaws, and set high standards for the journal the *American Psychologist*. He negotiated for a new APA building and represented psychology well vis-à-vis other scientific societies and agencies of government.

The division structure evolved under a Division Organization Committee, given the assignment of selecting temporary chairs and secretaries for each of the proposed divisions to become operative at the time of the APA meeting in 1945. (For details, see Hilgard (1945). Temporary chairmen and secretaries for proposed APA divisions. *Psychological Bulletin, 42*, 294–296.)

In the text that follows, you will be presented with the results of this new organizational structure. I hope that this series will engender a new appreciation for how the division structure, which these events fostered, has helped to hold psychology's many voices under one roof.

— Ernest R. Hilgard
Stanford University

PREFACE

The interests of members of the American Psychological Association (APA) are broad and highly varied. Psychology embraces the entire range of behavior and experience, so it is not surprising that the APA is similarly broad and differentiated. The diverse concerns of its members are reflected in the APA's 49 divisions.

Divisions were included in the structure of the APA to, in the words of the APA's first executive officer, "give greater recognition to the individual interests, both scientific and professional, of specialized subgroups within the total membership."[1] The establishment of divisions was seen as a way to promote psychology as a unified science and profession, as well as a way to involve the maximum number of members in the affairs of the association.

BACKGROUND

Divisions have been part of the APA structure for only about half of its 105 years. They became a formal aspect of the APA in 1945 as a part of a general reorganization. The purpose of establishing divisions was to promote the diverse areas of psychology and to ensure that all the legitimate interests of APA members were recognized and accommodated. A half century later, the divisions still serve that purpose.

In the early years of the APA, nearly all members were academicians. The association was unified and mostly homogenous. By 1910, the increasingly diverse interests of psychologists were expressed first in the organization of convention program sessions under distinctive topics and then by

---

[1]Wolfle, D. (1946). The reorganized American Psychological Association. *American Psychologist, 1*, 3–6.

the evolution of three major interest groups. The first group, known originally as the "Experimentalists" and later as the Society of Experimental Psychologists, were university professors interested in encouraging more fundamental research activities. At about the same time, Lightner Witmer led a group that was interested in promoting clinical psychology while Hugo Münsterberg and his group of applied psychologists were establishing the foundations of industrial psychology.

The tensions that developed between the academic and applied members of the association led to the formation of the American Association of Clinical Psychologists (AACP) in 1917. This threat to the APA's organizational cohesion aroused such concern among members that they conceded to providing three new sections within the APA to address clinical, industrial, and educational interests. AACP members were admitted as members of the APA, and the AACP was then formally dissolved.

By 1939, one third of APA members were employed outside of academia, primarily in applied positions. The continued dissatisfaction of applied psychologists eventually led to the formation of the Association of Consulting Psychologists around 1925. This group, augmented by several newly formed state psychological associations, became the American Association of Applied Psychology (AAAP) in 1937, and the sections on clinical, industrial, and educational psychology within the APA became inactive. Other psychologists, dissatisfied with the APA's lack of involvement with social issues, formed the Society for the Psychological Study of Social Issues (SPSSI). Most members of AAAP and SPSSI continued to be members of the APA as well, and by 1938 both groups had become affiliates of the APA.

With the beginning of World War II, the National Research Council formed the Emergency Committee for Psychology and initiated meetings between the APA and the AAAP to effect a reconsolidation. The AAAP agreed to merge with the APA, contingent on a number of changes that would encourage the participation of applied members, including the establishment of a divisional structure. Membership standards were changed, and applied psychologists who had been associate members were granted full membership and the right to vote and hold office. The establishment of a central office with a director and staff members enabled the APA to provide the kinds of services that the practitioners needed. In 1944, the membership approved the changes to the bylaws that established the new APA, and those changes became effective in 1945.

In order to determine which divisions were needed to represent the full range of its membership, the APA surveyed its members in 1944 with a questionnaire that proposed 19 possible divisions and provided spaces for members to write in additional divisions. After analyzing the primary and secondary interests of the members as reflected by the survey results, the APA combined some of the divisions that had large overlaps. Others were combined in order to reach a membership of 50, the minimum required to form a division. The final list contained 19 divisions.

Among the 19 charter divisions listed in the first bylaws, 5 (Divisions 12, 13, 14, 15, and 19) had been sections of the AAAP and 2 were independent groups (SPSSI and the Psychometric Society). SPSSI became Division 9, but the Psychometric Society, which was to become Division 4, never became a division. The members of Division 11 (Abnormal and Psychotherapy) decided after a year to combine with Division 12 (Clinical) to form a single division. Positions 11 and 4 have remained vacant.

It was generally assumed at the outset that the initial array of divisions would change as weaker divisions died out and were replaced by new ones reflecting current interests. In fact, the charter divisions have proved quite hearty. Some regrouping and name changing has occurred, but except for two vacant slots, all of the charter divisions and all that were formed subsequently are still active.[2]

ARE THERE TOO MANY DIVISIONS?

APA members, especially those in positions of leadership, frequently express concern about the steady increase in the number of APA divisions. The current list of 49 divisions seems bewilderingly large to many members. Some doubt that there are really that many interest areas in psychology and suspect that there may be duplications and overlap. Some members have suggested that smaller divisions be combined to form larger ones or be absorbed by other divisions. Such suggestions have been strongly rejected by leaders of the smaller divisions, who point out that the fact that the numbers are small in some areas of psychology is not an indication that these areas are unimportant. The Council of Representatives has frequently discussed proposals for a moratorium on new divisions and imposed one for a brief period (January 1982 to January 1984), but they later lifted it and admitted two more divisions.

In fact, the growth in APA membership has far exceeded the growth of divisions. In 1946, there were about 260 members for each division, but by 1996, there are about 1,800 members for each division. Since 1980, APA membership has increased from 51,000 to 84,000 (a 65% increase), and the number of divisions has increased from 47 to 49 (an increase of 4%). Several divisions now have over 5,000 members, more than the total number of APA members in 1946. If the numerical relationship between membership and the number of divisions had remained constant,

---

[2]In 1949, Division 3 (Theoretical and Experimental Psychology) and Division 6 (Physiological and Comparative Psychology) combined, leaving 6 vacant and changing the name of Division 3 to Experimental Psychology. In 1962, the council approved a new Division 6 with the old name, which was subsequently changed to Behavioral Neuroscience and Comparative Psychology.

there would now be more than 300 divisions. Conversely, if the number of divisions had remained constant and an ever larger membership was distributed among them, we might well have divisions with 25,000 members or more. Because divisions exist partly to promote more direct communication among members with common interests, having divisions so large would defeat their purpose.

About half of the total division memberships are in the postcharter divisions. The newer divisions are not, as some believe, mostly practice divisions. They are less likely than the original divisions to represent fundamental subject matter areas (e.g., experimental, developmental, social, or clinical), but they are quite diverse. Some divisions reflect public interest concerns (e.g., Psychology of Women, Lesbian and Gay Issues, and Ethnic Minority Interests), new areas of application (e.g., Consumer Psychology, Psychology–Law, and Health Psychology), and subject matter areas that were small or nonexistent in 1945 (such as Experimental Analysis of Behavior and Psychopharmacology and Substance Abuse).

As the number of psychologists involved in clinical and health care services has grown, several divisions have formed to represent areas that might formerly have been encompassed by the Division of Clinical Psychology. Some, like Psychotherapy (Division 29) and Group Psychology and Group Psychotherapy (Division 49), began as sections of Division 12; others evolved from interest groups—that is, Psychologists Interested in Private Practice became Psychologists in Independent Practice (Division 42) and Psychologists Interested in the Study of Psychoanalysis became the Division of Psychoanalysis (Division 39). Others, such as Family Psychology (Division 43), evolved independently of Division 12.

It is not surprising that new divisions have emerged over the past 50 years and that they continue to emerge at a rate of one every year or so. Divisions have representation on the Council of Representatives and thereby influence the APA's policies and activities, and they can facilitate the growth of an interest area through journals, convention programs, and communication. By bringing members together and encouraging their interactions, divisions continue to fulfill the purposes for which they were established.

GROWTH OF DIVISIONS

Individual APA members may belong to as many divisions as they wish, or they may belong to none. The total number of division memberships (93,900) exceeds the total number of APA members (84,000) because many members belong to more than one division. About 44% of APA members do not belong to any division. Some divisions are growing, a few are shrinking, and many are keeping pace with the growth of the APA.

Some that are decreasing may be the victims of changes in specialization by members. When all divisions are examined, it does not appear that the loss of division members is primarily attributable to division members leaving the APA, because the percentage of members leaving has remained fairly stable over the years. There is no doubt, however, that the establishment of a large number of specialized societies, such as the Society for Neuroscience and the Animal Behavior Society, has affected the membership of divisions in those areas. A preliminary analysis suggests that most members who leave a division remain in the APA. It is interesting to note that some people who leave the APA continue to be actively involved in the APA divisions. Overall, participation in divisions has remained strong.

What makes one division grow, another shrink, and another remain stable in size? Surely some of the variation is random. Most divisions have good years and bad years. A particularly energetic membership chair may increase a division's membership by a large percentage in 2 or 3 years, but if some of those members are only marginally interested in the division's areas of concern, they may drift away over the next few years, causing concern on the part of the division that is experiencing a downward trend.

Changing patterns of self-identification may also play a part in the ebb and flow of divisions. Some people who might have referred to themselves as educational psychologists in the past now self-identify as cognitive psychologists and may, as a result, be less likely to join the Division of Educational Psychology. In the same way, general clinical psychologists who have some interest in neuropsychology may specialize in the area and thus join the Division of Clinical Neuropsychology in preference to the Division of Clinical Psychology.

Changes in employment patterns obviously play a major part in division growth. The increased employment opportunities in the private sector for health service providers has resulted in rapid growth for the Division of Independent Practice and related growth in some of the other practice-oriented divisions. Funding patterns are also influential. As in all disciplines, various subareas may be hot for a time and then lose some of their attraction. The 1960s and 1970s saw great support for community psychology, the study of mental retardation, and environmental psychology and the relevant APA divisions grew accordingly. Reduced funding opportunities have been paralleled by reductions in division membership.

The tendency of some divisions (such as Educational or Personality and Social) to gradually shrink in size is a matter of some concern, because they represent fundamental areas of the discipline. The smaller numbers attracted to those divisions in recent years may reflect a complex mix of factors. Employment patterns are certainly one of those factors. Almost no *Monitor* advertisements, for example, specify such broad areas as experimental psychology, although they often did in the past. The fact that psychologists in academic settings are somewhat less likely to join the APA than are practicing psychologists also affects the numbers available for division membership, as does the issue of self-identification. Sixty years ago, most psychologists identified themselves as experimental psychologists. Now fewer see themselves in such a broad category. The expansion of part-time practice opportunities for academicians may have led some personality psychologists to affiliate with more practice-oriented divisions.

COMMUNICATIONS[3]

One of the important functions of divisions is to facilitate communication to and among members. The APA communicates in a variety of ways, especially through the *Monitor*, but because the target audience is so large the message is somewhat generic in nature. Divisions provide more direct and specific communications with members through their newsletters, journals, and meetings.

Division newsletters range from several pages photocopied and stapled together to printed volumes of 40 pages or more. Our 49 divisions publish two to six newsletters a year, and quite a few divisions have sections that also publish newsletters. Common newsletter features include columns by the president or other officers, updates on APA council activities from the division's representative, reprints of presidential or invited addresses, research or opinion articles submitted by members or others, updates on current division activities, recommendations to members on how to vote in APA elections, announcements of coming events, and letters to the editor.

Editors of division newsletters generally invest a lot of time in producing quality newsletters. Some attract such excellent articles that they eventually evolve into division journals, only to be replaced by another newsletter to carry out the original function of communication among the members. For example, the Division 12 (Clinical) newsletter evolved into a division journal that subsequently became a major APA journal (*Professional Psychology: Research and Practice*).

Divisions start journals for a variety of reasons. Sometimes, when the area represented by the division is relatively new, there is no journal that is directly relevant. Even when journals exist in the area, division leaders may feel that they are overloaded, not oriented to their interests, too narrow in their scope, or otherwise not as useful as a new journal might be. Of the 49 divisions, 19 publish their own journals. The earliest journal published by a division is the *Journal of Social Issues*, which was published by SPSSI even before it became Division 9 in 1946. SPSSI also develops

---

[3]This section draws heavily from material prepared by Gary VandenBos, PhD, APA's executive director for communications. It is presented here with his permission.

papers on social issues. The journal published by the Division of Teaching of Psychology (Division 2), *The Teaching of Psychology*, evolved from the *Teaching of Psychology Newsletter* in 1974. The journal for Section 1 of Division 12, the *Journal of Clinical Child Psychology*, started as a newsletter, became a journal in 1971, and was recognized as a division journal by the Council of Representatives in 1977. Ownership of the *Journal of Family Psychology* was transferred to the APA by Division 43 and it became an APA journal. Because there is currently no journal of the history of psychology, Division 26 (History of Psychology) is currently developing one in cooperation with the APA Communications Office. It may eventually become an APA journal.

The APA's Board of Publications and Communications is vested by the APA bylaws with the responsibility of supervising the managing and editing of division journals. Believing that the editors of division journals should have editorial freedom, the Publications and Communications (P&C) Board delegates its management responsibility in full to the relevant division and vests the general responsibility for the journal in the executive committee of the division. The divisions report their journal activities to the P&C Board by including in their annual reports a statement of editorial operations comparable to the statements prepared by APA journal editors for the P&C Board.

The bylaws require that the Council of Representatives approve any new journal proposed by a division. Because the intent of the P&C Board is to foster scientific communication, it will normally recommend to the council that a new journal be authorized.

Because a division is a constituent part of the APA, any publishing arrangement for a division that involves a contract with a non-APA publisher requires review and approval by the P&C Board prior to signing a contract. Because division journals are official APA publications, the council requires that they participate in the APA liability insurance program; but the APA currently pays the insurance premiums for all divisions. Division journal editors are encouraged to seek advice from the APA Central Office and the P&C Board on matters of mutual concern, such as printers and printing costs, postal regulations, advertising, accounting systems, copyrights, and permission practices.

SERVICES PROVIDED BY THE APA TO ITS DIVISIONS

The APA has always provided support for its divisions through an allocation from APA membership dues and through services offered by the Central Office. Initial financial support given to divisions was $1 for each member's first division membership. In the early 1960s, that amount was raised to $2. The APA historically has done billing and collection for divisional dues and assessments, offered assistance with division officer elections by including division slates on the APA election ballot, and provided divisions with information on prospective members as a result of information gathered annually from the APA membership.

In August 1986, the Council of Representatives approved the establishment of an Office of Divisional Affairs in the Central Office to further assist divisions in handling their administrative tasks, facilitate interdivisional communications, and act as an interface between the APA and its divisions. It was staffed initially on a part-time basis, and a full-time person was hired to staff the Division Services Office in 1988.

Division Services has grown over the past 10 years to its current complement of two full-time and one part-time staff persons. The office is now well equipped to handle a wide range of division-related questions on division officers, membership information and application procedures, meetings, benefits, publications, activities at convention, and so forth.

In October 1989, the first contract between the APA and a division (Division of School Psychology) for the provision of administrative services was signed. These contractual arrangements permit the Division Services Office to act as the division's central office, offer additional services beyond those normally provided to divisions, and collect and maintain information on non-APA division members. Currently, the APA has contractual agreements with 13 divisions for provision of administrative services through the Division Services Office.

In September 1989, the APA secured group tax-exempt status for those divisions that had not received an exemption independently. Thirty-eight divisions were originally covered under this exemption, and new divisions are now being added as they are established. This beneficial status allows divisions to enjoy the same tax benefits as the parent organization and requires them to file financial information with the Internal Revenue Service on an annual basis. The APA Financial Affairs Office assists those divisions involved in the group tax exemption by preparing the annual group tax return.

The APA provides many other services to its divisions. Some of the most significant include publisher's liability coverage for division journals and newsletters; assistance with publishing contracts and copyright and permission practices for division journals; director's and officer's insurance for division officers and volunteers; legal consultation; financial review of division contracts and grants; and optional bookkeeping, accounting, and investment services.

RELATIONSHIP OF DIVISIONS TO THE APA

What is the appropriate relationship between the APA and its divisions? According to the APA's first executive officer, Dael Wolfle, the relation of the divisions to the reorganized APA was to be similar to the relation of the states of the union to the federal government—that is, the divisions would retain a high degree of internal autonomy yet they would concede certain authority to the central organization. Changes to give the divisions more or less autonomy have been considered, and minor changes have been made, but the federal model that grants considerable autonomy to the divisions in managing their own affairs has prevailed.

The divisions were founded to help promote psychology as a unified science and profession, and they have continued to play a major role in keeping the APA together as an organization and psychology together as a discipline. Just as the founding of the APA created a critical mass of scholars who then established the discipline, the founding of a division creates a critical mass of specialists who work together to develop that area of interest. An equally important function of the divisions is to bring together, through common interest in a specific area, researchers, teachers, and practitioners who otherwise might not make contact. This is particularly true of those divisions that are almost equally devoted to scientific, applied, and public interest concerns, but almost all divisions contain an element of diversity.

After the reorganization vote, some divisions expressed serious concerns that their autonomy might be restricted or even that the APA might confiscate their assets. APA leadership has never made such a proposal. The initial bylaws required divisions to return unused dues to the APA treasury each year, but this was changed at the urging of the divisions, and the divisions currently retain all surpluses for their own use. The assets of the divisions belong to the divisions.

The substantial number of APA members who are also members of the American Psychological Society (APS) has led some divisions to establish informal affiliation with that organization and to encourage APS members, whether or not they are APA members, to become division members. Some divisions have become separately incorporated, and a few manage their own mailing lists, elections, and finances. The APA bylaws and association rules permit the divisions considerable flexibility in these matters. Divisions, regardless of their corporate status, remain an integral part of the APA. They may carry the name "Society of _____," as many do, but they continue to carry, in addition, the designation, "A division of the American Psychological Association." Occasionally, particularly in the days following the failed reorganization vote in 1988, various division leaders have talked of "leaving APA" and establishing a division as a separate organization or as an affiliate of APS. However, no division has taken such a step or come close to doing so. Because divisions are an integral part of the APA's corporate structure, a division could not "leave" the APA without the permission of the Council of Representatives. Individual members or groups of members could choose to resign from the APA and establish a new organization with the same purposes as those served by the division, but the division would remain a part of the APA until it was terminated by the Council of Representatives.

The divisional structure was an experiment that worked. Some divisions have renamed themselves, merged with others, or changed their focus, but no division has ever failed. The Division Services Office is being given additional resources to provide assistance where it is needed and requested by the divisions, and plans are being developed for a major membership recruitment campaign in which the divisions will be invited to participate. The APA has a large stake in the health of its divisions, and the divisions have a similar stake in the continued health of the APA. Although their working relationship has occasionally required fine-tuning, on the whole it has been harmonious.

— Raymond D. Fowler
APA Chief Executive Officer

INTRODUCTION

DONALD A. DEWSBURY

Some 50 years ago the American Psychological Association (APA) was reorganized around a set of divisions structured to represent the diverse interests of constituent groups of psychologists within the organization at that time. Although the number of divisions has grown since then, the basic structure remains intact today. It is through these divisions that the unity of the APA was reestablished. By providing homes for groups with similar interests in research, practice, and policy, the divisions can work more effectively on many problems of local interest than can the APA as a whole, which must deal with broader issues. Further, because the divisions are smaller, they are more flexible and can change more readily as fields change. So effective have these divisions been that some psychologists identify more closely with these interest groups than with the APA. It is fitting, therefore, that as we celebrate 50 years of the divisional structure, we consider the histories of these core units so critical to the overall functioning of the APA.

This is the first volume in a series that will include the histories of as many of the APA's 49 divisions as possible. In Volume 1 we present the first nine division histories of the series. The project began with a survey of existing division histories, some of which had just been written for the 1992 APA centennial. From that survey, and word of mouth, we have located authors for chapters that cover many of the divisions. The first volume includes chapters whose authors could meet the first possible deadline for inclusion. We considered the possibility of holding chapters in order to publish a set of volumes with coherent themes, rather than the mix of diverse divisions as in the present volume. However, the advantages of such coherence seemed outweighed by the disadvantages of holding some chapters for several years as other authors work and the original chapters grow stale. The diversity of each volume will be characteristic of the wonderful and mystifying complexity of the field of psychology.

Some chapters were prepared from scratch; others are adaptations of material originally prepared for inclusion in other venues. In at least one case, Wight and Davis's (1992) excellent history of Division 2 (Teaching of Psychology), it was decided not to rewrite or reprint the chapter, as an appropriate and current version already has been published by the APA. That chapter can be regarded as a part of the present set of division histories.

We hope that these chapters will be of interest to diverse readerships. Division members should be aware of the histories of their divisions and understand where they stand in the webs and cascades of developing psychology. Historians of psychology and nonpsychologists will find much information with which to help understand the evolving fabric of the discipline of psychology. The hope is that any reader interested in understanding the complexity of this very complex field will benefit from these chapters.

THE APA BEFORE WORLD WAR II

The APA was founded in G. Stanley Hall's living room at Clark University in July 1892 and held its first annual convention in Philadelphia in December of that year. Throughout its history, the APA has been the primary organization of psychologists in North America (see Evans, Sexton, & Cadwallader, 1992). However, throughout its history various interest groups of psychologists, on the sides of both basic research and practice, have formed their own organizations either inside or outside of the APA. Beginning in 1904 Edward B. Titchener's Experimentalists, later known as the Society of Experimental Psychologists, was one such alternative organization for experimental psychologists (Boring, 1967). During the 1920s another group of experimental psychologists formed to conduct round tables within the framework of the APA.

From the practice side, the American Association of Clinical Psychologists was founded in 1917 and became a section of the APA 2 years later. When the American Association of Applied Psychology (AAAP) was founded in 1937, the APA clinical section was disbanded and joined sections on consulting, educational, and industrial psychology as the clinical section of the AAAP.

Thus, when World War II broke out psychology lacked a unified presence. The Emergency Committee in Psychology was formed by the Division of Anthropology and Psychology of the National Research Council in 1940 to help mobilize psychologists for the war effort. It was from the Subcommittee on Survey and Planning of the Emergency Committee that Robert M. Yerkes and other psychologists began a push to reunify the APA, the AAAP, and various other smaller organizations into a single voice for psychology. An Intersociety Constitutional Convention was convened on May 29, 1943, in New York City to effect the reorganization. The result was a revised constitution and set of bylaws for the APA, which became an organization whose stated purpose was not only to advance psychology as a science but also as a practice that could be used in the promotion of human welfare. Membership requirements were changed in order to accommodate practitioners whose efforts often did not lead to publication. Most important for our purposes, the divisional structure was conceived as a way to maintain diverse interest groups within the broader structure of the new APA. Both the APA and the AAAP officially approved the reorganization in September 1944, and the new APA was inaugurated on September 6, 1945.

Psychologists were canvassed for their division interests with a preliminary list of 19 proposed divisions (Recommendations, 1943) and the results used to modify the proposed list into a revised set of 19 charter divisions arranged in a modified hierarchy (Doll, 1946; Hilgard, 1945a). Temporary division chairs and secretaries were appointed (Hilgard, 1945b) and elections of the first officers were held in 1945. The divisions were up and running.

This basic structure has seen minor modification over the past 50 years but has remained largely intact. Perhaps the greatest challenge to the integrity of the APA has come with the formation in 1988 of the American Psychological Society (APS), a group of academic, applied, and experimental psychologists that has challenged the hegemony of the APA. One can only hope that another unification will soon come to pass.

FROM 1945 TO THE PRESENT

Psychology in North America has changed dramatically in the 50 years since the division structure was adopted. I would summarize the changes as follows:

1. *Growth*. The membership has grown from approximately 3,200 in 1943 to more than 80,000 50 years later.

2. *Specialization.* Psychology has become more specialized, with few general psychologists and many psychologists limiting their interests to relatively narrow areas.

3. *Fractionation.* With increased specialization there have emerged many smaller societies and organizations that vie with the larger, umbrella groups for psychologists' loyalties.

4. *Professionalization.* There has been a dramatic shift from a dominance of basic science in psychology to an overwhelming numerical dominance of those with practice interests.

5. *External politization.* Psychologists have become more involved with matters of policy outside of the APA and psychology in general, including interactions with governmental agencies at all levels.

6. *Internal politization.* There has been an increase in the political structure and activity within the APA.

7. *Feminization.* There has been a substantial increase in the number of women in psychology and in the roles they play within the APA.

8. *Diversification.* There has been an increase in representation and activity from members of diverse racial and ethnic groups.

9. *Internationalization.* There is increased recognition of the importance of psychology as it is developing outside of North America.

10. *Cognitivization.* The field has become more cognitively oriented.

11. *Expansion.* Psychologists have expanded their spheres of activity into areas not previously covered, as in the increased conduct of therapy and the drive for prescription privileges.

12. *Legalization.* Both the practice and science of psychology have, like many functions in the United States, become more entwined with the courts, litigation, and lawyers.

The divisions have evolved in synchrony with these broader trends, both helping to effect the changes and being affected by them. The themes just elaborated should stand out as one reads the chapters of this volume. There are many problems for divisions created by the growth, specialization, and fractionation of psychology over this period. Most of these problems have affected all divisions to some degree, but some are more apparent in the histories of some. As will be apparent, these problems have led to conflict within divisions, among divisions, and with groups outside of psychology.

The shifting balance between science and practice can be seen in the dominance of practice orientations in the formation of many of the higher numbered divisions and in the evolution of some of the older divisions, such as Division 25 (Experimental Analysis of Behavior). The increased presence of psychologists in policy matters is especially apparent in the formation of the Divisions of Child, Youth, and Family Services and of Peace Psychology. The expansion of psychology is especially apparent as the members of the Division of Psychoanalysis interact with physicians in defining appropriate spheres of activity.

AN OVERVIEW OF THE CHAPTERS

We are fortunate to have a Foreword written by Ernest R. Hilgard, one of the foremost U.S psychologists and a person who was there when the divisional structure was adopted some 50 years ago. Indeed, Hilgard was one of the seven members of the Subcommittee on Survey and Planning chosen by Robert Yerkes in 1942 to work under the auspices of the Emergency Committee in Psychology to do the long-range planning that led to the reorganization of the APA, and he served as vice chair of the critical 1943 Intersociety Constitutional Convention. Further, it was Hilgard (1945a) who published the article in which the results of a survey of psychologists regarding the emerging divisional structure first appeared in print.

In the Preface, Raymond D. Fowler, the APA's chief executive officer and past president, provides an overview of the founding and evolution of divisions over the past 50 years. He emphasizes the flexibility of the divisions and the extent to which they can address the needs and interests of specific interest groups in psychology, while at the same time remaining a part of the overall larger structure.

In chapter 1, accomplished historians of psychology Michael Wertheimer and D. Brett King write about Division 1 (General Psychology). They begin with a section about the general issue of how to write a division history and, more critically, how to locate reliable information about pivotal events in a division's history. We see that psychologists' memories often are less than accurate and that there is a need for the archival preservation of documents that record historical events with accuracy—at least as perceived by those preparing the documents. This chapter will be helpful in encouraging other divisions and organizations to prepare good paper trails of significant events in their evolution.

Changes in divisions reflect both changes in the ways in which psychology itself is structured and the impact of events outside of psychology. These can be seen in the history of Division 6 (Behavioral Neuroscience and Comparative Psychology), about which I write in chapter 2. From its inception, there was a question of whether or not this division should be separate from Division 3 (Experimental Psychology). Division 6 was one of the original divisions that became amalgamated within Division 3 between 1948 and 1963, and later remerged. From my perspective as both historian of psychology and a comparative psychologist, I think that, more than most others, Division 6 has been affected by the membership realignments outside of the APA. This division, which was focal in the APA, is in danger of again disappearing—this time for different reasons.

The history of Division 7 (Developmental Psychology) is presented in chapter 3 by Thomas C. Dalton, a political scientist with strong interests in developmental processes. Like many divisions, Division 7 has one hand in basic research and one hand in matters of policy. Dalton provides a balanced treatment of the division's history in relation to both changing research trends and policy issues at the federal level. Further, he shows how historically shifting priorities affect the research questions deemed most worthy of study in developmental psychology, as reflected in the division's programs and other activities.

Thomas K. Fagan, who has worked and written extensively on the history of school psychology, provides the history of Division 16 (School Psychology) in chapter 4. Fagan clearly delineates the changing problems faced by the division as it evolved. In the early years, there was a struggle for existence and survival. During the middle years, the focus shifted to problems of more clearly defining its identity and of the credentialing and accreditation of practitioners. Recent years have seen substantial growth and emerging problems related to litigation and regulation. Fagan sees the division as "running twice as fast" in order to keep up with the level of professionalization seen in other groups of psychologists.

Chapter 5 on Division 18 (Psychologists in Public Service) is written by Rodney R. Baker, a psychologist working within a Veterans Hospital setting. Division 18 was a charter division, but there was so much concern over the large number of psychologists in public service and the fear that it might come to dominate the APA that restrictions were placed on its early activities. Again we see evolutionary change, with guild issues dominating the first 20 years. More academic and professional content issues came to the fore during the middle years; it was then that sections within the division were formed. In recent years, attention has been focused on such issues as the reorganization of the APA, health care, the furtherance of research, and the further development of organizational structures to aid in enabling psychologists better to fulfill their roles in public service.

James T. Todd, one of the leading historians of modern behaviorism, presents a history of Division 25 (Experimental Analysis of Behavior) in chapter 6. This is an unusual division in that it is largely devoted to the promulgation of a particular approach, behavior analysis, rather than to a specific content area of research or practice. As such, the division has struggled to avoid being perceived as dominated by the ideas and activities of one man—B. F. Skinner. The division's main function in the early years was to present a program at the annual convention. With time and growth, as well as the increased involvement of behavior analysts in applied work, issues of certification became critical and a new activism appeared. As other, non-APA organizations developed, the role of the division became less clear.

Chapter 7 on Division 37 (Child, Youth, and Family Services) was written by two of its past presidents, Donald K. Routh, a leading historian of clinical psychology, and Jan L. Culbertson. The primary missions of the division have been centered around advocacy and social policy issues concerning children, youth, and families. So controversial was a division devoted to advocacy that its founding could go forward only when the term *child advocacy* was removed from its proposed name; the division's primary function, however, remained unchanged. Division 37 has been effective in its chosen role.

Chapter 8 on Division 39 (Psychoanalysis) was written by two prominent past presidents of that division, Murray Meisels and Robert C. Lane. This is one of the more complex divisions, with major sections, local chapters, multiple publications, its own annual convention, and complex relationships with allied organizations, such as psychoanalytic institutes. Perhaps because of the broader controversies within psychoanalysis, this division appears more conflict-prone than others. The turf conflict between psychoanalytic psychologists and organizations dominated by medically trained psychiatrists was focal, but many conflicts, especially those related to membership standards, developed within the division as well. Despite the conflicts, the division thrives as a large, functioning organization effectively representing psychoanalytically oriented psychologists.

One might wonder why we should include a history of a division such as Division 48 (Peace Psychology), which has existed for just 5 years, in chapter 9. If we return to the history of Division 1, however, we can but wish that the early history of that division had been written while the record was fresh. Here, Michael Wessells, a prominent player in the development of the division, captures the major events involved with the founding and early history of this division.

CONCLUSION

An understanding of institutional structures and frameworks is essential if we are to obtain a complete understanding of the rich fabric of American psychology. The division histories included in this and subsequent volumes should help to fill many gaps in understanding the diversity and complexity in the field and thus facilitate a better grasp of where it has come from, where it is, and where it may be going.

REFERENCES

Boring, E. G. (1967). Titchener's Experimentalists. *Journal of the History of the Behavioral Sciences*, 3, 315–325.

Doll, E. A. (1946). The divisional structure of the APA. *American Psychologist*, 1, 336–345.

Evans, R. B., Sexton, V. S., & Cadwallader, T. C. (Eds.). (1992). *100 years of the American Psychological Association: A historical perspective*. Washington, DC: American Psychological Association.

Hilgard, E. R. (1945a). Psychologists' preferences for divisions under the proposed APA by-laws. *Psychological Bulletin*, 42, 20–26.

Hilgard, E. R. (1945b). Temporary chairmen and secretaries for proposed APA divisions. *Psychological Bulletin*, 42, 294–296.

Recommendations of the Intersociety Constitutional Convention of Psychologists: IV. Sample blank for survey of opinion on the proposed by-laws. *Psychological Bulletin*, 40, 646–647.

Wight, R. D., & Davis, S. F. (1992). Division in search of self: A history of APA Division 2, the Division of the Teaching of Psychology. In A. E. Puente, J. R. Matthews, and C. L. Brewer (Eds.), *Teaching psychology in America: A history* (pp. 365–384). Washington, DC: American Psychological Association.

1

A HISTORY OF DIVISION 1 (GENERAL PSYCHOLOGY)

MICHAEL WERTHEIMER and D. BRETT KING

How should one go about writing the history of an American Psychological Association (APA) division? Several different strategies could be considered. One way is to do an institutional history: How has creation of the division in 1945, and the ups and downs of its fate in the ensuing years, been influenced by social, political, and economic factors related to the APA, academia, and other settings that employ people to whom the division is—or should be—relevant? How has the division been affected by events in the nation and the world? Another approach is to focus on the human side: Who have been some of the significant figures in the history of the division, what did they try to do, what did they actually accomplish, and what were their apparent motives? Then there is the internal history of the division: What major events, crises, or changes in focus or perspective may have affected the division's purposes, programs,

Earlier versions of this essay were presented at the 1991 APA convention and appeared in Division 1's newsletter *The General Psychologist* in 1992. We thank several reviewers of a draft of this version, especially Donald A. Dewsbury, for their useful suggestions. Parts of this manuscript are directly based on remarks by Professor Dewsbury, who is the current historian for Division 1. He also managed to generate a much more complete list of the division's officers than we had succeeded in compiling and, with gratitude to him, we have used his list rather than our own in Table 1 in this chapter.

or routine procedures? A functional analysis might also be instructive: What functions have been served by the sheer existence of the division and by its various activities—both functions that the division and its prominent members explicitly intended it to fulfill and those that a dispassionate outsider might convincingly speculate the division was actually, if inadvertently, performing? Although thorough answers to such questions could yield a substantial monograph, we have summarized in brief a few highlights of Division 1's history in this chapter.

THE SEARCH FOR INFORMATION ABOUT THE HISTORY OF DIVISION 1

One might assume that the information needed for such a monograph, or even a brief account like this one, is readily available in substantial—and perhaps tedious—detail. The place to look for the raw material for the history of a division is in the division's files or archives, it would seem. The division's historian must have a bank of file drawers full of the division's archival documents. On the contrary, one author of this chapter was the division's official historian for a number of years and can assure the reader that no such archive exists. Having been a former president, council representative, and member-at-large of the division's executive committee as well, this author did ship some old files to the Archives of the History of American Psychology at the University of Akron a few years ago, but apparently that shipment did not contain any material on Division 1. (John Popplestone, the archivist of the Akron Archives, did locate copies of three Division 1 newsletters—Numbers 12, 13, and 14 for January, summer, and winter of 1972—in another place in his collection, and he kindly sent them to us.) For a time, this author had access to a box of papers from a former long-time secretary-treasurer of Division 1, Helen Warren Ross; that box contained an almost haphazard collection of mostly routine division correspondence from the mid-1970s and the early 1980s. Knowing that the APA has, off and on, shipped APA documents to the Library of Congress, in 1992 this author tried to find out whether those deposits contained any materials potentially useful for writing the division's history; unfortunately, much of that pile of papers has not yet been cataloged, and what has been cataloged cannot be retrieved simply by asking for documents relevant to Division 1: That is not the way the material is being indexed. A major find by Rick A. Sample, then the APA's head librarian (which was kindly photocopied for us by the APA's associate librarian at that time, Sandra C. Pisano), was a substantial but incomplete collection of Division 1 newsletters, from the first issue published in 1966 to those published 20 years later (1986) in the library of the new APA building next to Union Station in Washington. Also, Christine Cubby, then head of the APA Membership Office, found a large file of correspondence that the late Jane Hildreth—for decades the membership person in the APA Central Office—had exchanged with various members and officers of Division 1; these items were written from as early as 1953 to more than one third of a century later. Almost all of that file pertains to routine nominations for APA fellow through Division 1, along with some occasional sad stories about people who did not make it. Fortunately, the file contains a few tidbits about other matters as well, and Hildreth's letters are typically a delight to read, with their masterful diplomacy, sheer human warmth, and frequent flashes of humor. Tia Scales-Taylor and Sarah Jordan of the APA Membership Office kindly made us photocopies of that whole file in the summer of 1992.

Where else might appropriate information be available? We worked our way through selected issues of the *American Psychologist* from 1945 to the present, where we were able to find some relevant information. That search, and information provided by Division 1's current historian, Donald Dewsbury, allowed us to generate a list of Division 1 officers (see Table 1). Sleuthing in the University of Colorado's Norlin Library, we managed to find further relevant information in such journals as the *Psychological Review* and the *Psychological Bulletin* (e.g., Hilgard, 1945a, 1945b) during the 1940s and later, as well as in other sources such as Hilgard's (1987) *Psychology in America*. We also thumbed through an incomplete collection of APA directories and membership registers since 1948 and were able to generate a partial chart of Division 1 membership over the years (see Figure 1).

Another strategy was to write to former and current Division 1 presidents and other officers, which we did. A gratifying number of them replied, sometimes at length, to our plea for help, documents, suggestions, and relevant anecdotes.[1] Unfortunately, although they were prompt and friendly in their responses, very few were able to provide much information. That is not surprising; one author of this chapter, who has held various offices in the division since 1974, hardly remembers a thing that happened during that period—except that instead of a presidential address he arranged a symposium on psychology and the future for which he was lucky enough to obtain a number of illustrious participants, such as Allan G. Barclay, Stuart W. Cook, M. Brewster Smith, Charles A. Kiesler, Virginia L. Senders, and Sigmund Koch, who were so eloquent that the symposium ended up being published in the *American Psychologist* (1978).

---

[1]We would like to thank them all. In alphabetical order, they were Anne Anastasi, Charles L. Brewer, Meredith P. Crawford, Frank W. Finger, Ernest R. Hilgard, Edwin P. Hollander, Howard H. Kendler, Gregory A. Kimble, Wilbert J. McKeachie, and Robert Perloff (who, for a number of years, prepared a whimsical column titled "Standard Deviations" for the division's newsletter).

TABLE 1
Major Officers of Division 1: General Psychology

Year	President[a]	Secretary–Treasurer	Council Representatives	Members-at-Large	Newsletter Editor
1945–1946	Dashiell, John F. (Chair)	Wolfle, Dael	Bray, Charles W. Dennis, Wayne Muenzinger, Karl F. Seashore, Robert H.		
1946–1947	Munn, Norman L.	Dennis, Wayne	Bray, Charles W. Dennis, Wayne Muenzinger, Karl F. Seashore, Robert H.		
1947–1948	Tolman, Edward C.	Wickens, Delos D.	Bray, Charles W. Anastasi, Anne Dallenbach, Karl M. Munn, Norman L.		
1948–1949	Seashore, Robert H.	Wickens, Delos D.	Anastasi, Anne Munn, Norman L. Dennis, Wayne Leeper, Robert W.		
1949–1950	Heidbreder, Edna	Wickens, Delos D.	Anastasi, Anne Leeper, Robert W. Dennis, Wayne Seashore, Robert H.		
1950–1951	Dallenbach, Karl M.	Rexroad, Carl N.	Anastasi, Anne Seashore, Robert H. Dennis, Wayne Rexroad, Carl N.	Dallenbach, Karl M. (?) Flanagan, John C. Munn, Norman L.	
1951–1952	Fernberger, Samuel W.	Rexroad, Carl N.	Dashiell, John F. Dennis, Wayne Rexroad, Carl N. Dallenbach, Karl M.	Dallenbach, Karl M. Munn, Norman L. Leeper, Robert W.	

1952–1953	Tolman, Edward C.	Bitterman, Morton E.	Dennis, Wayne Bitterman, Morton E. Dallenbach, Karl M.	Munn, Norman L. Leeper, Robert W. Duffy, Elizabeth
1953–1954	Hovland, Carl I.	Prentice, W. C. H.	Dallenbach, Karl M. Tolman, Edward C. Hovland, Carl I.	Leeper, Robert W. Duffy, Elizabeth Crawford, Meredith P.
1954–1955	Dennis, Wayne	Prentice, W. C. H.	Tolman, Edward C. Hovland, Carl I. Wickens, Delos D.	Duffy, Elizabeth Crawford, Meredith P. Finger, Frank W.
1955–1956	Wickens, Delos D.	Prentice, W. C. H.	Hovland, Carl I. Wickens, Delos D. Anastasi, Anne	Crawford, Meredith P. Finger, Frank W. MacPhee, Halsey M.
1956–1957	Anastasi, Anne	Finger, Frank W.	Wickens, Delos D. Anastasi, Anne Leeper, Robert W.	Crawford, Meredith P. Finger, Frank W. Leeper, Robert W. (?)
1957–1958	Leeper, Robert W.	Finger, Frank W.	Anastasi, Anne Leeper, Robert W. Helson, Harry	Crawford, Meredith P. Waters, Rolland H. Pronko, N. H.
1958–1959	Helson, Harry	Finger, Frank W.	Leeper, Robert W. Helson, Harry Prentice, W. C. H.	Waters, Rolland H. Pronko, N. H. Bitterman, Morton E.
1959–1960	Prentice, W. C. H.	Stolurow, Lawrence M.	Helson, Harry Prentice, W. C. H. Berrien, F. Kenneth Finger, Frank W.	Pronko, N. H. Bitterman, Morton E. Wickens, Delos D.
1960–1961	Finger, Frank W.	Stolurow, Lawrence M.	Prentice, W. C. H. Berrien, F. Kenneth Finger, Frank W. Duffy, Elizabeth	Bitterman, Morton E. Wickens, Delos D. Russell, Roger W.
1961–1962	Duffy, Elizabeth	Stolurow, Lawrence M.	Berrien, F. Kenneth Finger, Frank W. Duffy, Elizabeth Solomon, Richard L.	Wickens, Delos D. Russell, Roger W. Razran, Gregory

Table 1 — continued

Year	President[a]	Secretary–Treasurer	Council Representatives	Members-at-Large	Newsletter Editor
1962–1963	Solomon, Richard L.	Razran, Gregory	Duffy, Elizabeth Solomon, Richard L. Flanagan, John C.	Russell, Roger W. Razran, Gregory Dennis, Wayne	
1963–1964	Flanagan, John C.	Meenes, Max	Solomon, Richard L. Flanagan, John C. Berrien, F. Kenneth Razran, Gregory	Dennis, Wayne Crook, Dorothea Gilmer, B. von Haller	
1964–1965	Razran, Gregory	Meenes, Max	Flanagan, John C. Berrien, F. Kenneth Razran, Gregory Meenes, Max	Dennis, Wayne Gilmer, B. von Haller Stolurow, Lawrence M.	
1965–1966	Meenes, Max	Voeks, Virginia W.	Berrien, F. Kenneth Razran, Gregory Meenes, Max Katz, Daniel	Gilmer, B. von Haller Stolurow, Lawrence M.	
1966–1967	Katz, Daniel	Voeks, Virginia W.	Meenes, Max Katz, Daniel Finger, Frank W. Kendler, Howard H.	Dallenbach, Karl M. Stolurow, Lawrence M.	Voeks, Virginia W.
1967–1968	Kendler, Howard H.	Voeks, Virginia W.	Finger, Frank W. Kendler, Howard H. Duffy, Elizabeth Russell, Roger W.	Dallenbach, Karl M. Kendler, Howard H. Dallenbach, Karl M. Helson, Harry McKeachie, Wilbert J.	Voeks, Virginia W.
1968–1969	Russell, Roger W.	Voeks, Virginia W.	Finger, Frank W. Kendler, Howard H. Russell, Roger W. Underwood, Benton J.	Helson, Harry McKeachie, Wilbert J. Scott, J. P.	Voeks, Virginia W.

Year					
1969–1970	Underwood, Benton J.	Voeks, Virginia W.	Russell, Roger W. Underwood, Benton J. Helson, Harry Lindzey, Gardner	McKeachie, Wilbert J. Scott, J. P. Berrien, F. Kenneth	Voeks, Virginia W.
1970–1971	Lindzey, Gardner	Voeks, Virginia W.	Underwood, Benton J. Helson, Harry Lindzey, Gardner Leeper, Robert W.	Scott, J. P. Berrien, F. Kenneth Sherif, Muzafer	Voeks, Virginia W.
1971–1972	Leeper, Robert W.	Voeks, Virginia W.	Helson, Harry Lindzey, Gardner Leeper, Robert W. Kendler, Howard H.	Sherif, Muzafer Walker, Edward L. Verplanck, Williams S.	Voeks, Virginia W.
1972–1973	McKeachie, Wilbert J.	Voeks, Virginia W.	Leeper, Robert W.	Sherif, Muzafer Walker, Edward L. Verplanck, William S.	Voeks, Virginia W.
1974	Berlyne, Daniel E.	Voeks, Virginia W.	Helson, Harry	Walker, Edward L. Verplanck, William S. Wickens, Delos D.	Voeks, Virginia W.
1975	Postman, Leo J.	Voeks, Virginia W.	Helson, Harry	Walker, Edward L. Wickens, Delos D. Deese, James E.	Voeks, Virginia W.
1976	Wertheimer, Michael	Voeks, Virginia W.	Campbell, Byron Little, Kenneth B. Kimble, Gregory A.	Wickens, Delos D. Deese, James E. Bevan, William	Voeks, Virginia W.
1977	Deese, James E.	Little, Kenneth B.	Kimble, Gregory A.	Deese, James E. (?) Bevan, William Campbell, Byron	Voeks, Virginia W.
1978	Wickens, Delos D.	Little, Kenneth B.	Kimble, Gregory A.	Bevan, William Campbell, Byron Senders, Virginia	Lynch, Mervin

Table 1 — continued

Year	President[a]	Secretary–Treasurer	Council Representatives	Members-at-Large	Newsletter Editor
1979	Koch, Sigmund	Little, Kenneth B.	Hollander, Edwin P. Koch, Sigmund Mandler, George	Campbell, Byron Senders, Virginia Reuder, Mary E.	Lynch, Mervin
1980	Bevan, William	Wylie, Ruth C.	Hollander, Edwin P. Koch, Sigmund Mandler, George	Senders, Virginia Reuder, Mary E. Ross, Helen Warren	Lynch, Mervin
1981	Hollander, Edwin P.	Wylie, Ruth C.	Koch, Sigmund Mandler, George	Reuder, Mary E. Ross, Helen Warren Barber, Theodore X.	Lynch, Mervin
1982	Kimble, Gregory A.	Ross, Helen Warren	Anastasi, Anne Zajonc, Robert B.	Barber, Theodore X. Wylie, Ruth C. Koch, Sigmund	Boneau, C. Alan
1983	Mandler, George	Ross, Helen Warren	Anastasi, Anne	Barber, Theodore X. Koch, Sigmund Little, Kenneth B.	Boneau, C. Alan
1984	Zajonc, Robert B.	Ross, Helen Warren	Hollander, Edwin P. Anastasi, Anne	McKeachie, Wilbert J. Koch, Sigmund Reuder, Mary E. Bevan, William Maddi, Salvatore R. Wertheimer, Michael	Boneau, C. Alan
1985	Little, Kenneth B.	Ross, Helen Warren	Hollander, Edwin P.	McKeachie, Wilbert J. Koch, Sigmund Boneau, C. Alan Bevan, William Maddi, Salvatore R. Wertheimer, Michael	Boneau, C. Alan

Year				
1986	Maddi, Salvatore R.	Ross, Helen Warren	Wertheimer, Michael Mandler, George	McKeachie, Wilbert J. Koch, Sigmund Park, Denise C. Lynn, Elizabeth Reuder, Mary E. Rumbaugh, Duane M.	Boneau, C. Alan
1987	Boneau, C. Alan	Ross, Helen Warren	Miller, James G. Wertheimer, Michael	Koch, Sigmund Park, Denise C. Lynn, Elizabeth Farley, Frank Rumbaugh, Duane M. White, Charlotte L.	Boneau, C. Alan
1988	Reuder, Mary E.	Ross, Helen Warren	Wertheimer, Michael Little, Kenneth B.	Denmark, Florence L. Rumbaugh, Duane M. Farley, Frank White, Charlotte L. Ross, Helen Warren Lynn, Elizabeth	Boneau, C. Alan
1989	Ross, Barbara C.	Lynn, Elizabeth	Kimble, Gregory A.	Boneau, C. Alan Farley, Frank Park, Denise C. Ross, Helen Warren White, Charlotte L. Lynn, Elizabeth	Boneau, C. Alan
1990	Denmark, Florence L.	Lynn, Elizabeth	Kimble, Gregory A.	Boneau, C. Alan Park, Denise C. Ross, Helen Warren Sexton, Virginia Staudt Sternberg, Robert J. Wertheimer, Michael	Boneau, C. Alan

Table 1 — continued

Year	President[a]	Secretary–Treasurer	Council Representatives	Members-at-Large	Newsletter Editor
1991	Gleitman, Henry	Lynn, Elizabeth	Kimble, Gregory A.	Boneau, C. Alan Park, Denise C. Ross, Helen Warren Halpern, Diane F. Wertheimer, Michael Wittig, Arno	Boneau, C. Alan
1992	Sexton, Virginia Staudt[b]	Lynn, Elizabeth	Halpern, Diane F.	Hasher, Lynn Perloff, Robert Platt, Jerome Ross, Helen Warren Wertheimer, Michael Wittig, Arno	Boneau, C. Alan
1993	Brewer, Charles L.	Lynn, Elizabeth	Halpern, Diane F.	Hasher, Lynn Perloff, Robert Platt, Jerome Wittig, Arno Hall, Judy Johnson, Neal F.	Boneau, C. Alan
1994	Sternberg, Robert J.	Lynn, Elizabeth	Halpern, Diane F.	Hasher, Lynn Perloff, Robert Platt, Jerome Ellis, Henry C. Hall, Judy Ross, Helen Warren	Boneau, C. Alan
1995	Johnson, Neal F.	Lynn, Elizabeth	Farley, Frank	Boneau, C. Alan Ceci, Stephen J. Ellis, Henry C. Hall, Judy Perloff, Robert Ross, Helen Warren	Boneau, C. Alan

Year				
1996	Halpern, Diane F.	Lynn, Elizabeth	Farley, Frank	Field, Tiffany M. Ellis, Henry C. Perloff, Robert Ross, Helen Warner Kimble, Gregory A. Bricklin, Patricia M.	Boneau, C. Alan
1997	Ceci, Stephen J.				

[a]All Presidents served as president-elect during the year preceding their presidency and as past president during the year following their presidency.
[b]Because Virginia Staudt Sexton was unable to serve during the year of her presidency, President-Elect Charles L. Brewer acted as president in her stead.
Note. Entries are labeled with a question mark if there is some doubt about them, such as in the list of members-at-large of the Executive Committee who were also listed in that same year as holding another elected office simultaneously in the division.

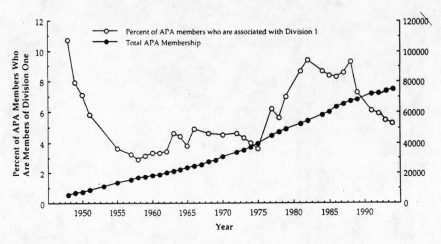

Figure 1. Percentage of APA members (Fellows, Members, Associates, and Life members) Who Are Members of Division 1.

Responses to Queries About the Division's History

Our query to the officers was dated May 18, 1992; answers to it were postmarked between May 22 and June 5. Our respondents were clearly efficient in answering their correspondence. Let us share a few excerpts from their letters, in the order in which they were received. These excerpts illuminate the kinds of information that such inquiries can provide, including not only the perhaps surprising paucity of personal recollections, but also their unreliability. To avoid unnecessary embarrassment, only a few of the respondents are identified in these excerpts.

The first respondent suggested contacting Division 1 members in the San Diego region and recommended that we all get together at the American Psychological Society's convention in California in June of 1992, but we did not get to that convention. The respondent added, "Nothing very juicy in the way of anecdotes comes to mind. Division 1, after all, is not a very juicy division."

The second respondent indicated no knowledge about Division 1's records and suggested that we ask various people, most of whom we had already asked. "If they are as ignorant as you and I on this matter," the respondent wrote, "then you may be out of luck. Having no recorded history must be frustrating for the historian." The letter closed with the observation that the then ongoing centennial celebration of the APA "may be the only one that some of us will see."

The third had this to say:

The only suggestion I can offer is to resort to speculation. After all, if they can speculate about the origins of the universe, one should have

20   MICHAEL WERTHEIMER AND D. BRETT KING

no difficulty with Division 1, e.g., the Big Bang theory of Division 1 and the consequent proliferation of other divisions.

In the fourth letter, Ernest R. Hilgard did offer interesting substantive points:

> I know very little about the history of Division 1 except that it has not done what it was originally supposed to do. It was supposed to be a residual division so that any member who could not find a specialized division to which he or she wanted to belong would be assigned to Division 1, at least as a voting Division member. It was no sooner organized than those who like to consider themselves as "generalists" tried to give substantive meaning to general psychology and attempted to find a niche for the Division comparable to that of other divisions.

Hilgard added that the Division of General Psychology is "one of the largest divisions" and suggested that "it would be of some interest to make some kind of analysis of the membership in the Division." It turns out that several such analyses have been made over the years, and they have typically concluded that the mix of academic and practice-oriented members has roughly paralleled the mix in the APA as a whole. Hilgard remarked, "The history that you . . . are preparing can be very enlightening." We hope our efforts will not make him feel too let down.

The fifth respondent, Anne Anastasi, was pessimistic about getting any help from the APA Central Office: "They do not even keep Board of Directors or Council of Representatives minutes" other than what is printed in the *American Psychologist*. Her own files are in the Akron archives, and she indicated that there might be some Division 1 material among her "unsorted papers." She did add a personal reminiscence that contrasts a bit with Hilgard's account:

> My recollection of how Division 1 started may be of some interest to you, although you have probably heard it from many others. When the divisional structure was proposed in the reorganized APA in the . . . 1940s, several of us objected strongly to such "fractionation" (!) and refused to join any division. Upon realizing that this would completely prevent us from voting on any matters that would influence [the] Council [of Representatives] . . . , we decided to form a nondivisive division of general psychology. Among the more vociferous members of that group were Norman Munn and I, who accordingly were elected as the two representatives of Division 1 to the first APA C/R [Council of Representatives].

The issue of fractionation or fragmentation clearly is not new to the 1980s and 1990s but already was salient a half century ago.

Which account, Hilgard's or Anastasi's, is more accurate? Both accounts are interesting. However, as their contrast illustrates, the well-known principle that memory is not purely passive but is an active, creative cognitive process applies to Anastasi and Hilgard just as much as it does to all other human beings. As for Anastasi's account, the 1945 *Psychological Bulletin* and the *American Psychologist* for the next few years indicate that Division 1's first president (actually referred to as its chair) was John F. Dashiell and its first council representatives were Charles W. Bray, Wayne Dennis, Karl Muenzinger, and Robert Seashore; in 1946, its president was Norman L. Munn and the council representatives were still Bray, Dennis, Muenzinger, and Seashore. By 1947, Edward Chace Tolman was president, and the four council representatives were Bray, Karl M. Dallenbach and, finally, Anne Anastasi and Norman L. Munn. As for the printed record on how and why the division was actually established, that exists in the *Psychological Bulletin*, the *American Psychologist*, and elsewhere, and we will get to that soon.

The next respondent penned a brief note directly on the letter of inquiry and sent it back to us. In its entirety, it read: "This stumps me, too. . . . The only suggestion I have—and it is laborious—is to call as many past presidents [as] you can get hold of. Sorry." We did not call them, but the mails may have been almost as effective in yielding information as the telephone would have been.

The seventh sent a handwritten note:

I wish I could be helpful on the Division 1 records, but I know of nothing beyond what you mentioned in your letter. When I served as president in [the early 1980s], there was no "archive," nor any repository known to me for files and the like. However, past (and current) Secretary–Treasurers may know about them. Sorry to say "no" also on . . . "anecdotes." None spring to mind.

Telephone calls to the current and the immediate past secretary–treasurer did not yield substantial amounts of additional useful information.

The eighth respondent wrote, "Unfortunately I don't recall ever receiving any sort of file for Division 1 when I was president and I'm not sure that I passed on anything to my successor." That respondent's files are in the APA archives at the Library of Congress, and may contain a folder or two on Division 1, "but I'm afraid I can't be of much help to you. Nor do I have any . . . anecdotes that come to mind." The letter suggested that we get in touch with two particular individuals who "have been active in the division over a long period of time," but added, "I imagine that you have already written them." Near the end of the letter was the perceptive observation, "I fear that most are like me in terms of being active for a period and then less active after having served on the executive committee and as an officer."

The next-to-last respondent sent a brief note: "I regret to say that I cannot help you in your search for Division 1 papers or other materials. I have no file on Division 1, and while I am a member, I have not been active in the Division." Here is another instance of the reconstructive processes in memory; the official record indicates that this person was indeed active in the division. To be sure, that activeness occurred long ago—this individual was an elected member-at-large of the division's executive committee during the 1950s.

The last response, lengthy and helpful, came from someone who had been secretary–treasurer of the division and then became president of the division soon thereafter. This respondent wrote, "I'm sorry to tell you that I know of no archives of Division 1. I inherited none from my predecessor. . . . Aside from my personal files, whatever I had . . . I turned over to my successor in the office of Secretary–Treasurer." The letter continued, "To help you reconstruct the list of officers, here they [are] in the early years, in order. I apologize for the gap, [which reflects the time] when I was out of the governance structure." The list of of presidents that was provided omitted some of the early ones and garbled the order of a few others, at least according to the list we received from Donald Dewsbury and the official record in the *American Psychologist*. Omitted from the list of early presidents were, for instance, John F. Dashiell, S. W. Fernberger, and Robert H. Seashore, and the order was mixed up for such illustrious past presidents as Edward C. Tolman, Edna Heidbreder, Karl M. Dallenbach, and Norman L. Munn. Table 1 is based on official printed sources and on the list of officers constructed by Dewsbury. Listed also in the letter were a few of the representatives to the APA Council of Representatives from the division. The lists that were provided for secretary–treasurer and for members-at-large of the executive committee also did not accord perfectly with the published lists of officers, but clearly the respondent had conscientiously attempted to provide us with the best information that the respondent had available. Incidentally, this informant's list of past members-at-large of the executive committee *included* the name of the next-to-the-last respondent, the one who claimed not to have been active in the division.

The letter continued:

I'm not sure what constitutes a [relevant] anecdote, but there are a couple of events that stand out in my mind. Around 1960 we found ourselves failing to spend all of our funds, so some reverted to the APA treasury. To avoid that unhealthy situation we decided to organize a program of traveling lecturers, who would visit small colleges for a day or two, giving formal and informal presentations and having conferences with promising undergraduates, hoping to convince them that research is exciting and encouraging them to try graduate school.

In parentheses, there followed the sentence, "There was a time when we were afraid that a shortage of experimental psychologists was imminent." Then the respondent offered this anecdote:

So in 1960–61 [Karl M.] Dallenbach went to Wabash College, [John F.] Dashiell to Hollins, [Robert W.] Leeper to Reed, and [W. C. H.]

Prentice to Gettysburg/Lebanon Valley. Well, we felt that it had been a resounding success, and we fully intended to continue it the following year, committing about $600 to the project. Instead, it turned out to be a sort of a pilot for the much more expansive program of visiting lecturers arranged by APA, with far more generous support by NSF [National Science Foundation], that continued in various forms for several years.

Until we received this letter, we were unaware that Division 1 had been involved in the predecessor to a substantial NSF-supported program of visiting lecturers that persisted not only "for several years" but for more than two decades. Dozens of psychologists and hundreds of colleges participated in that program during the 1960s and 1970s.

The letter continued by referring to

A note in my files, in which I complain bitterly to Jane Hildreth at Headquarters that the division secretaries' lunch at the convention in Chicago is an outrageous drain on the APA treasury—at $4.00 a pop. There has been a bit of inflation since 1956!

Clearly this respondent took extensive pains to ransack personal files in trying to provide us with relevant information. The next matter mentioned in the letter was

An exchange of correspondence I had with the U.S. Department of Labor, which was revising the *Dictionary of Occupational Titles* in 1959. The definition of "General Psychologist" included the information that we investigated psychological phenomena "for use by administrators, lawmakers, educators, and other officials engaged in predicting and controlling behavior in society." To be included under this title, among others, are "those who have an undergraduate degree in psychology but have no experience."

The next sentence asserted, "While I confess I never saw the finished product, the reply from the official in charge sounded as if my objections bore fruit."

The missive next made this claim:

There was a big increase in Division membership during 1957–58, resulting from a mailed invitation to Association members to use Division 1 as a home if there was reluctance to designate a specialty—one of the primary excuses during the 1946 reorganization for our existence (reiterated by President Roger [W.] Russell during 1969).

This argument, in various forms, was used on later occasions by Kenneth B. Little, among others, resulting in substantial increments from time to time in Division 1 membership. Paradoxically, the change in the number of Division 1 members, as given in APA registers and directories, does not corroborate the respondent's remark that membership increased in

1957–58. It *did* increase somewhat during the early 1960s, but between 1955 and 1958 it hovered at just under 500. Archival historical data frequently are not perfectly consistent with the convictions of people who are conscientiously and honestly trying to reconstruct the past.

The letter next stated that "The genesis of the Division newsletter appears to have been in 1965. [This was perhaps] another way of using our excess funds—a way that over the years has proven worthwhile." The first issue was dated Spring 1966. Virginia Voeks was its editor, and she continued to publish the newsletter for 10 years in succession, with issue Number 20 appearing in spring 1976. Mervin Lynch served as editor for the next ten issues. Number 31, the first issue edited by C. Alan Boneau, was dated winter 1981/82; Boneau edited the Division 1 newsletter for more years than did Dr. Voeks (and he edited more than half again as many issues).

The respondent offered to send us copies of revisions of the division's bylaws in 1959 and 1968, "largely to bring them into conformity with APA regulations and with our evolved practices."

Guidelines for Gathering Elusive Information

This was the outcome of our efforts to try to locate relevant material. Although we did not succeed in creating a full, formally documented record or a complete Division 1 archive, we did obtain a rich array of interesting, if occasionally somewhat haphazard, information. Indeed, much of the correspondence with former and current officers, as well as contacts with people working in APA's Central Office, did yield a host of details that, although not constituting a well-organized formal history of Division 1, clearly are part of that history and provide a perspective, sometimes with a bit of whimsy, on that history.

Although this introductory material may have been somewhat chatty and phenomenological, we hope that it is useful to others who have to cope with the problems of writing a history when no reliable and complete source of documentation for such a history exists. Emerging from our experience are a couple of general principles or admonitions that will alert others to the possible problems associated with such an undertaking. First, recognize that memories are fallible and that human cognition works in such a way that individuals, whether they are aware of it or not, construct versions of remembered events to suit their purposes, however innocent such purposes may be. Second, and far more important, divisions—and all other organizations that may wish some time to look back at their past—should make systematic efforts to preserve their historical documents. It may not always be easy to decide which documents are going to turn out to be historical, but it is prudent to err more on the side of overinclusiveness than on the side of overselectivity. Any document considered important at a particular point in time should be preserved in a systematic, constantly updated archive, and that archive should be housed in a safe, readily accessible location. Let future historians decide which among those documents are indeed historic.

ESTABLISHING THE DIVISION

Let us attempt to sketch a somewhat more systematic history of Division 1 (General Psychology) of the APA. Division 1 was 1 of 19 divisions—almost immediately reduced to 17— established formally when the APA was reorganized in 1945. That reorganization had been gestating for several years. As Hilgard described the process in 1974 (p. 148),

> A rift had been growing between the APA and the AAAP (the American Association of Applied Psychology). The applied psychologists, who had formed the new organization in 1937, felt that the APA was too much under control of academics, and threatened to withdraw.

Hilgard (1974, pp. 148–149) presented some of the details of the negotiations, in which he was intimately involved, that led to major revisions of the APA's bylaws so as to create a divisional structure that might accommodate the interests of a variety of specialized groups. The new bylaws were adopted in September 1944 to go into effect the next year. In the ballot that had gone to "all American psychologists, regardless of society affiliation, early in 1944," Hilgard wrote in 1945 (1945a, p. 20) that "attention was called to the provision of the proposed by-laws which stated: 'Members of the Association not expressing a preference for any special division . . . shall be members of a Division of General Psychology'" (p. 21). Thus the division was initially intended as a kind of default division-at-large. In spite of this provision, only 24% of the 3,680 who sent in their ballots selected general psychology as their division of first, second, or even later choice (p. 22). These data do indicate that Hilgard's recollection in his letter to us was reasonably accurate; yet Anastasi's concern has also continued to be a major theme of Division 1 over the decades—that is, the opposition to fractionation or fragmentation and a desire to see the whole discipline integrated or at least reunited. Division 1 has continued, in effect, as a microcosm of the entire earlier APA—including a sizable representation of clinical, child, and other applied practice fields, as well as academia.

With the adoption of the new bylaws, the AAAP voted to go out of existence as a separate body and to become part of the APA (Wolfle, 1946). Indeed, the earlier APA constitution formally had stated that the APA's objective was "the advancement of psychology as a science"; the new constitution expanded that statement to read, as it still does, "The object of the American Psychological Association shall be to advance psychology as a science, as a profession, and as a means of promoting human welfare." In the reorganized APA, the "relations between the APA and its divisions are something like those between the United States and its states," wrote Wolfle in 1946 (p. 5), but this left the Division of General Psychology in a somewhat anomalous position. Was it a division with a substantive focus, or was it a default division for those who did not choose to join any of the other divisions?

The list of divisions that was originally proposed by an intersociety constitutional convention, and that was used in the mail ballot, was alphabetical, with general psychology, it happens, falling out as Number 8. But the final list, after several surveys and deliberations by a number of bodies, made general psychology Division 1. Doll in 1946 (p. 339) mused that "the renumbering of the divisions from an alphabetical arrangement to the modified hierarchy reflects perhaps the historical evolution of psychology as a movement from scientific-academic background to professional service and applications." In his article, Doll (1946, p. 344) echoed a sentiment also expressed by Hilgard at about that time (and since) and heard at least annually since the reorganization took place when he wrote,

> No member of the Association can look forward with anything but apprehension to another schism between science and profession or between teaching and practice. . . . [T]hose interested in psychology as a profession are genuinely reluctant to become divorced from psychology as a science and discipline.

In 1974, Hilgard remarked that a rift somewhat different from the one that led to the reorganization of the APA and the demise of the AAAP occurred,

> as the Psychonomic Society asserts its autonomy from the APA for a reason symmetrical to, but opposite from, the reason for the creation of the AAAP: the members of the Psychonomic Society believe that the APA, instead of being too academic, as earlier charged, is now not academic enough! (p. 149)

A lively, informative account of the founding of the Psychonomic Society, incidentally, has been prepared by Dewsbury and Bolles (1995).

DEFINING THE PURPOSE OF DIVISION 1

Since its establishment, Division 1 has been concerned with keeping all of psychology in a single fold, if not a single mold. Almost every year, divisional program items have addressed whether psychology was, is, should be, or could be a single integrated endeavor or discipline, and separately started organizations, such as the Society for Uninomic Psychology, devoted to trying to reunify the field have in effect merged into Division 1.

But in recent years the centrifugal forces seem to have overcome the centripetal ones with the emergence, for instance, of a surprisingly strong American Psychological Society (APS), separate from the APA and explicitly devoted to the promotion of psychology as a science or an empirical endeavor, rather than as a practice or a profession. During this storm and stress, Division 1 has, explicitly as often as implicitly, had as one of its major goals the purpose of trying to hold the entire field together. That it still exists as a division attests to the attractiveness of that vision for a significant number of APA members; that it has not been unequivocally successful in this mission (any more than has the APA as a whole) is clear from its relatively small membership and its shrinking voice on the APA Council of Representatives, as well as from the health of other general associations such as the Psychonomic Society, the APS, and a plethora of specialized societies other than the APA or Division 1 to which tens of thousands of psychologists belong. Clearly not all psychologists think of themselves as *general psychologists*, whatever they consider that phrase to mean (and there have been endless debates on that subject) and whatever they believe that Division 1 stands for within APA—as well as whatever image they may have of the overall APA, of which the Division of General Psychology remains a part.

RISE AND FALL OF DIVISION 1 MEMBERSHIP

Figure 1 presents a rough sketch of the percent of APA members over the years who chose to become members of Division 1, in the context of overall growth of the APA. The pattern is interesting, but its interpretation is not obvious. The division's popularity among APA members was highest at the very beginning; perhaps it dwindled—and substantially so—as the ambiguity increased as to what "general psychology" is or should be. The percentage dropped from more than 10 to between 3 and 5, and stayed there for two decades. Then, as the rift identified by Hilgard and others between science and profession grew again during the 1970s and 1980s, perhaps more members were inspired by the vision of retaining both orientations within a single association; the percentage soared back to a level that had not been seen since the late 1940s. Perhaps the drop in the past few years may reflect the success of the APS, in that the few nonprofessional, nonpracticing psychologists who had maintained their membership in the APA finally decided that the APA's image no longer fit their own and left the association. Perhaps, also, the practitioners who in the past had joined the division to indicate that they really did think of themselves as generalists, as well as nonpracticing specialists, either no longer saw the need to do so, changed their self-image, or believed that the division's activities and programs were not really all that relevant to them. Some of the blips in the curve (such as the jump in division membership in the mid to late 1970s) are doubtless due to special mailings, such as one inviting all APA members who were not members of any division to join Division 1, noting that their lack of membership in other divisions must mean that they are generalists and, besides, membership in one division is free. This ploy was used successfully in 1974 and again in 1976, as well as earlier.

Your interpretation of the initial precipitous drop in proportional membership in Division 1, followed by its long flat period, then a significant increase again, and another downward slide during the past decade, may be different from ours, but the pattern does require explanation. How can one best account for the changing level of membership in the division? No particular interpretation seems to be inherently superior to another at this point. Because no formal record such as the newsletter existed before 1966 (for that matter, it is somewhat surprising that no formal, regular newsletter was published during the division's first two decades), it is difficult to pinpoint any specific events that might have been responsible for changes in membership during the division's first two decades.

The reorganization of the APA that created Division 1 occurred during the immediate postwar period, an era of ferment in many other aspects of the Western world than just psychology. In the same year in which Division 1 was born, the United Nations came into existence. The world was also on the brink of major technological changes, including the explosion in telecommunications, jet travel, and increasing world population; the computer revolution was just around the corner. Division 1 appeared on the scene at a time when the society that supports psychologists and psychology was undergoing a series of major upheavals.

DIVISION 1 OFFICERS

The division has become a focus for many people who were prominent in their time. The first president (or *chair*, in his case), John F. Dashiell, had been chair of the prestigious Society of Experimental Psychologists in 1938, edited *Psychological Monographs* from 1935 to 1947, was president of the Southwestern Psychological Association in 1961, and was the 1960 recipient of the American Psychological Foundation's Gold Medal Award (see Dashiell, 1967). The names of many past officers of the division are still well known, although others have passed into history and are no longer familiar to most present-day psychologists. That Division 1 is in a sense both the old and the new APA in microcosm is suggested by the observation that fully seven Division 1 presidents have also been presidents of the APA itself: Edward Chase Tolman in 1937, John F. Dashiell in 1938, Gardner Lindzey in 1967, Anne Anastasi in 1972, Wilbert J. McKeachie in 1976, Florence Denmark in 1980, and William Bevan in 1982.

The gender distribution of the division's main officers, unfortunately, does not reveal a special sensitivity to equity. All secretaries or secretary–treasurers during the division's first two decades were men, and during the past three decades all but one have been women. There was one female president each during the 1940s (Heidbreder), 1950s (Anastasi), and 1960s (Elizabeth Duffy); none in the 1970s; but three in the 1980s (Mary E. Reuder, Ross, and Denmark); and two so far in the 1990s (Virginia Staudt Sexton and Diane F. Halpern).

SOME HIGHLIGHTS IN THE DIVISION'S HISTORY

Let us next focus on a few points, in chronological order, gleaned from the division's newsletters, from Hildreth's correspondence, and from a few other sources. They may serve to highlight what the division has been about, what it has tried to do, and how its foci have both changed and stayed the same during the half century of its existence. Its history is unique, but it no doubt has features that parallel the histories of other APA divisions, indeed of other societies devoted to a discipline. A comparative analysis of the history of several APA divisions—and of these histories with the histories of other scientific, intellectual, and professional societies—has yet to be prepared.

Early Meetings and Convention Programs

The first formal Division 1 program was presented at the Boston convention of the APA in 1948. Chaired by Delos D. Wickens, a student of John Dashiell who was to hold various offices in the division later, it consisted of only two items, but the foci of the two items were prophetic of what later programs would be like. One paper, by W. A. Bousfield, presented an empirical study that crossed several different subfields in psychology; later pronouncements by division officers included the suggestion that the division should serve as a bridge across more specialized fields. Bousfield's paper was titled "The Relationship Between Mood and the Production of Affectively Toned Associates." The second paper, by Robert H. Seashore, addressed "The Role of a Psychologist as a Citizen," a broad theme that was to flourish much later in what was to become APA's concern with the public interest.

The 1959 revision of the Division 1 bylaws, in Article 1, Section 2, tried to define what "general psychology" means. It stated that

The Division shall concern itself with the general problems of psychology considered both as a science and as a profession. These include such problems as: (1) historical, systematic, and methodological aspects of psychology as a whole; (2) scientific and professional developments; (3) the relationship of psychology to other areas of human knowledge and other professions; and (4) the bearing of legislative and social action on psychology as a profession.

The minutes of the Division 1 business meeting in 1959 reported that up to $600 was authorized to be spent on the lectureships that had been mentioned by one of the respondents to our request for information about the division. Anne Anastasi made other members of the division aware at that meeting that the APA was planning to institute such a program with support from a source such as the National Science Foundation (NSF). What evolved from these modest beginnings was the long-lived, highly successful NSF-supported visiting psychologist program, which was mentioned previously.

Division 1 apparently followed a practice that somewhat differed from that of the other APA divisions in that it actively generated its convention programs (rather than depending primarily on spontaneous submissions) almost from the start. It usually sponsored only invited symposia and invited speakers, and it did not accept proposals for papers. A ballot sent to all members in late 1959 asked them to rank a number of suggested invited symposia and asked whether Division 1 should cosponsor symposia generated by other divisions but that were of general interest as well. In 1961, Division 1 sponsored 13 hours of APA program time, and these hours consisted of symposia only, some cosponsored with Divisions 3, 8, and 10.

In 1962, apparently unsolicited papers were considered for the annual convention; 3 of the 8 papers submitted were accepted, and 11 of the 16 symposia proposed were actually presented, most of them cosponsored with other divisions. The minutes indicate that the division had decided it "could accept long theoretical papers." The committee voted to include the following "official statement" in calls for future programs: "The program will consist of symposia, invited addresses, and theoretical papers. Papers (30–40 minutes) which summarize and organize particular fields are especially desired." The broad, integrative focus of the division was becoming more explicit.

Fellowship Procedures for Division 1

A recurring concern of the APA Membership Committee has been, and continues to be, whether nomination to become a fellow of the APA should be made in the absence of the nominee's knowledge or whether self-nominations or applications should be considered appropriate. For years the division has had a conscientious committee that took care of the extensive paperwork needed to make nominations to the Membership Committee of people to become fellows of the APA through the division. A letter to Lawrence Stolurow, chair at the time of Division 1's Fellows Committee, from Leo J. Postman, dated July 3, 1962, found its way into Jane Hildreth's file. That letter stated,

> Thank you very much for your letter of June 22 and also for your previous communication concerning my invitation to become a Fellow of Division 1. I have not responded because some time ago I decided that the application procedure for fellowship status is much too cumbersome, which I realize is not anything the division can control. I hope I don't sound petulant, but if the APA requires all that red tape for someone to become a Fellow, I am content to remain just a plain member. Many thanks for your interest.

Did Postman's letter lead to any changes in APA's procedures for electing fellows? Not to any that we know of.

Problems in the Use of Surplus Funds

In the same month, Division 1's president, Elizabeth Duffy, proposed using some of the division's "surplus funds . . . for bringing a young foreign psychologist to the International Congress," and asked Jane Hildreth whether that would be permissible according to the APA's policies and practices; Hildreth responded affirmatively, reporting that several other divisions (7, 8, and 12) had made the same proposal. However, correspondence between Duffy and Hildreth in late 1962 made it clear that, unfortunately, the use of surplus Division 1 dues to establish "a Division 1 Foundation for the purpose of furthering research and scholarship in general psychology" was not possible under then-current Rules of Council. The minutes of the September 1964 meeting of Division 1's executive committee indicated that there was once again a surplus; $200 was contributed "to the Furnishings and Appointments Committee of APA to help toward equipping the new building."

THE DIVISION 1 NEWSLETTER AND THE CONTROVERSIES IT EXPLORED

The first newsletter, dated spring 1966, included the minutes of the September 6, 1965, executive committee meeting. Part of the minutes was the item, "The Executive Committee voted to publish at least one copy of a newsletter. . . . A limit of $1,000 was placed on the cost." Another item, from the Council of Representatives, indicated that

The division was asked to vote on the petition to add a division on the History of Psychology. In spite of the feeling that the history of psychology should find a home in the Division of General Psychology, the Executive Committee voted to endorse the petition for the new Division of History in the APA.

Although the creation of a new division on the history of psychology was viewed as encroaching on Division 1's territory, the division nevertheless decided to support the new addition. But the purpose of Division 1 as stated in its bylaws was not changed; one focus of Division 1's concern still officially remained the "historical, systematic, and methodological aspects of psychology as a whole." The first newsletter also contained a brief article by the editor, Virginia Voeks, titled "A Bit of History," which emphasized the illustrious nature of the division's officers. It listed "men and women [who] have served as officers of [the] division," and indicated that "this is a notably distinguished group, and augurs well for the future." Voeks broke the list down into presidents, secretary–treasurers, members-at-large of the executive committee, and representatives to the council. Included in the long list of individuals she named were E. C. Tolman (president), Karl M. Dallenbach (president and member-at-large), Edna Heidbreder (president), Norman L. Munn (president and member-at-large), Carl I. Hovland (president), Wayne Dennis (president and secretary–treasurer), Delos D. Wickens (president, secretary–treasurer, and member-at-large), Anne Anastasi (president), Robert W. Leeper (president and member-at-large), Harry Helson (president), W. C. H. Prentice (president, secretary–treasurer, and council representative), Frank W. Finger (who at various times held each of the four positions), Elizabeth Duffy (president, member-at-large, and council representative), Richard L. Solomon (president and council representative), John C. Flanagan (president, member-at-large, and council representative), Gregory Razran (who, like Finger, at various times held each of the four offices), Morton E. Bitterman (member-at-large and council representative), Carl N. Rexroad and Lawrence Stolurow (both of whom had been secretary–treasurer), Max Meenes (secretary–treasurer and council representative), Halsey M. MacPhee, Meredith Crawford, Rolland H. Waters, N. H. Pronko, Roger W. Russell, Dorothea M. Crook, and B. von Haller Gilmer (all seven of whom had been members-at-large) and F. Kenneth Berrien (who had been a council representative). Over the entire history of the division, as indicated in Table 1, seven secretaries or secretary–treasurers were later elected as president (Wayne Dennis, Delos Wickens, W. C. H. Prentice, Frank W. Finger, Gregory Razran, Max Meenes, and Kenneth B. Little), three individuals (all women) held the office of secretary–treasurer for very long terms (Virginia Voeks for 11 years, Helen Warren Ross for 7 years, and Elizabeth Lynn for 8 years so far), and three served twice in the office of president (Edward C. Tolman, Delos D.

Wickens, and Robert W. Leeper). Many presidents-elect served as the division's representative to the council during the year before they became president, especially during the 1950s and consistently throughout the 1960s: Wickens, Helson, Prentice, Finger, Duffy, Solomon, Flanagan, Razran, Meenes, Daniel Katz, Kendler, Russell, Benton J. Underwood, Lindzey, Leeper, and Hollander. Serving as the division's representative no doubt helped them become knowledgeable about issues important to the APA and the division. It is not clear how this practice started, nor why it was abandoned.

The second issue of the newsletter, dated summer 1966, contained most of Gregory Razran's 1965 division presidential address on classical conditioning and summarized the 1966 convention program: planned were four symposia (on the measurement of emotion, hypnosis, drug effects, and punishment), as well as six papers, including Max Meenes' presidential address. For the third issue, winter 1966, then-president Daniel Katz wrote a lead article titled "Is a Division of General Psychology Necessary?" The division's identity crisis clearly had not been laid to rest. Among Katz's comments were that Division 1

> Stands alone as the one group which does not represent a specific set of substantive or professional interests. As such, its activities lack the force and focus of many other divisions. . . . [O]ur generalism generates good will but little in the way of an operational program. . . . Are we then an anachronism, an institutional survival, an organizational form without a function? Do we represent a hopeless gesture against the dominant forces of fractionation and fragmentation in research and theory?

Note that these words were written not in 1996, but in 1966; the rift that is still so salient today was already front and center 30 years ago. Katz argued, of course, that the division *did* still serve a function; it "is still a means through which individuals can maintain their self and group identification as general psychologists. It provides programs at APA meetings which other divisions would neglect." He also provided various other arguments that were stated before and were repeated by others, such as that "there is a continuing and urgent need within our bureaucratic structure for an organizational forum where psychologists of all persuasions can be psychologists first and specialists second."

The excerpt from Max Meenes' 1966 presidential address in the spring 1967 newsletter began with the closely related theme, "There was a time, not too long ago, when all psychologists were generalists." Meenes pointed out that back in "1948 Division 1 ranked third in membership among 17 divisions," but by 1965 it was "seventh among 23 divisions." Much of his address concerned the need for more psychologists with a generalist perspective. That newsletter also listed the Division 1 program for the September 1967 APA convention, consisting of five papers on a handful of unrelated topics; symposia on publishing in psychology, punishment research, and the general systems approach to psychology; as well as an invited address by James Deese on future directions in psychology; Katz's presidential address; and an invited symposium titled "Perspectives on American Psychology: Seventy-Five Years," clearly intended to commemorate the APA's 75th anniversary. The winter 1967 issue of the newsletter carried a lead message by president Howard H. Kendler titled "The Unity of Psychology: Reality or Illusion?"—still another variation on the old theme. President Robert Leeper sounded yet another variant in the January 1972 newsletter:

> With all this multiplication of Divisions within the APA, we should not feel there is some reduced function which a Division of General Psychology might serve. On the contrary, there is an increased need for a sub-organization within the APA which will seek more than ever to foster the idea that, as much as we possibly can, we psychologists must be as broadly and richly informed as possible—even though we may choose to work on very particular problems. Narrow specialization is stultifying.

During Virginia Voeks' long editorship, the newsletter typically carried brief messages from the president, minutes of business meetings, excerpts from presidential addresses, programs of upcoming conventions, lists of current officers, requests for nominations of division members for APA fellow status, notices of books written by division members, changes in members' addresses, and occasionally other brief items of news.

The minutes of the 1972 business meeting noted that $50 was contributed for the "maintenance of historical exhibits in the APA building," the same amount was budgeted for the same purpose in 1973, and $100 was budgeted in 1974. In 1975, the division decided to "donate up to $500 to APA for the purpose of setting up the APA historical exhibit (located in the APA Central Office) in some suitable location." The then-president, who happened to be Michael Wertheimer, was ordered to "write to the APA Executive Officer making this request and offer and . . . suggesting that the exhibit be devoted to the early founders of American psychology." Personal recollection recalls that the exhibits were to be called the Edwin G. Boring Museum, in honor of the late dean of historians of psychology, and a glass display case, with an occasionally changing exhibit, did in fact exist for a while in the lobby of the APA building at 1200 17th Street, N.W.; there were four- to six-page descriptions of the exhibits for the interested passersby to take away with them as handouts. Division 1 can take credit for having started the ball rolling about a quarter of a century ago on a project that came to fruition in a somewhat different form, and a magnificent scope, as the Traveling Psychology Exhibit that was first shown in the Smithsonian Institution and has since been moved to several prominent museum sites in the United States. The exhibit turned out not to be as historical as the original Division 1 proposal, but it is a model of modern museology, with countless fascinating hands-on exhibits in which the viewer can relive psychology's past and can be a participant in many of psychology's classic experiments.

In 1973, the division's bylaws were revised once again; now the purpose of the division still stated that "The Division shall concern itself with the general problems of psychology considered both as a science and as a profession." But the public-interest emphasis disappeared, and a bridge-building focus was added:

> These include such problems as: (1) historical, systematic, and methodological aspects of psychology as a whole; (2) scientific and professional developments, especially as they cross specialty boundaries; (3) the relationships of psychology to other areas of human knowledge; and (4) relationships among specialties in psychology.

In 1977, the secretary–treasurer, Kenneth B. Little, reported to the executive committee that Division 1 was the fifth largest division in the APA, but it had only garnered enough votes to have a single representative on the APA Council of Representatives. Many APA members retained their membership in the division, but clearly their support tended to be lukewarm. Membership in the division was to rise further in the next decade, but during the past 20 years or so Division 1 has typically managed to have only one seat on the APA Council of Representatives, although it has occasionally filled two seats (and even three again in 1975 and 1979). The division usually had four APA Council seats in the first quarter century of its existence.

Issues facing the division grew in number and complexity over the years to such an extent that the annual 2- or 3-hour meeting of the division's executive committee during the summer APA convention was insufficient to deal with them thoroughly. Hence a midwinter meeting of the executive committee was instituted. During the 1980s and beyond, the meeting was regularly held for 2 days in January in the dining room of the La Jolla, California, hillside home of Helen Warren Ross and Kenneth B. Little, with out-of-town visitors staying in the nearby Andrea Villa Inn. Ross and Little became well known and much appreciated for their warm hospitality during those meetings, as well as for the efficient retreatlike atmosphere of those get-togethers that greatly facilitated a positive and productive approach to dealing with the committee's business.

The winter 1981/1982 issue, Number 31, of the newsletter was the first edited by C. Alan Boneau. He retained much of the general editorial policy and format that Virginia Voeks had established a decade and a half earlier. In that issue, President Gregory A. Kimble ended his message with the hope that "we may be able to do a little more than other divisions in helping our organization to carry on as a unified force promoting psychology as a science, as a profession, and as a means of promoting human welfare." Kimble thus restated the now venerable point that Division 1 should be a microcosm of the APA itself. The fall 1982 issue contained an editorial by the editor, Boneau, which commented that the title of Kimble's presidential address, "Is a General Psychology Possible?" is fitting enough; clearly, the identity crisis was once again unresolved. In a column next to this remark, George Mandler, president-elect, wrote the following:

> The Division of General Psychology is one of the largest, but also one of the most diffuse[,] of the divisions of APA. It should be larger, but no less diffuse. The Division has no commitments to particular intellectual or professional approaches to psychology. It is the Division for college teachers as well as private practitioners, for physiological as well as humanistic psychologists. . . . We represent psychology in general and . . . act as a counter force to some of the centrifugal forces in APA.

In the winter 1985/1986 issue, Number 44, the division announced the first annual competition for what it called the William James Award for "an integrative publication in psychology." The recipient of the award was to receive $1,000 and an invitation to present a William James Lecture at the following annual convention. The award was to recognize "a recent article or book best providing a conceptual framework that brings coherence among subfields and subspecialties of psychology." The award has been made annually since its inception; several scholars have commented, incidentally, that its being named the William James Award is somewhat paradoxical, because James himself was a champion of pluralism and diversity rather than of unity and integration.

The same issue of the newsletter provided a wealth of statistical information on the 5,049 then-members of Division 1. About one quarter were employed in a university setting and another quarter worked in a hospital or in independent practice; about 60% claimed that they were engaged in research, in educational activities, and in health and mental health services (clearly many checked several of these categories); about one half of all members were licensed or certified in their states. The division membership clearly was still de facto a microcosm of the APA as a whole.

The editor, Boneau, provided controversial, provocative, thoughtful editorials for most issues he produced. A recurrent theme is the fragmentation or fractionation of psychology; in the same issue that provided statistics on the division's members, Boneau asked explicitly for "comments about the whole issue of fractionation and the role of the Division in dealing with it."

During his years as editor of *The General Psychologist*, Boneau developed a hope that the newsletter might someday become a regular, full-fledged journal. That dream, largely through the efforts of Robert J. Sternberg, has come close to a reality as of the present writing; Sternberg shepherded the proposal through appropriate APA staff offices and the APA governance structure.

BOOKS BASED ON DIVISION PROGRAMS

In 1990, on the centennial of the publication of William James's *Principles of Psychology*, the division sponsored a number of program items with a Jamesian theme. Several of these items were collected into a volume that was subsequently published by the APA (Donnelly, 1992). The division also took seriously the theme of the APA's centennial celebrations by sponsoring a number of program items at the 1991 and 1992 APA conventions, such as a talk on which this chapter is based, helping at least indirectly to generate the present volume. It provided a subvention and sponsorship for a special centennial volume that was copublished in 1991 by Lawrence Erlbaum Associates and the APA, *Portraits of Pioneers in Psychology* (Kimble, Wertheimer, & White, 1991). That book was so successful that a second volume was issued in 1996 (Kimble, Boneau, & Wertheimer), and a third one is in the planning stage. Gregory A. Kimble served as the main editor for both volumes and is planning the third.

CONCLUSION

The Division of General Psychology has existed since the new APA was established in the mid-1940s. It continued as a voice within the APA while other organizations, such as the Psychonomic Society (Dewsbury & Bolles, 1995) and the American Psychological Society, which were devoted to a generalist perspective, were founded.

The division has been losing ground in terms of the proportion of APA members who choose to belong to it, but perhaps that is not surprising in view of the increasing emphasis on professional practitioner foci within the APA as a whole during the past few decades. At any rate, those identified with the division can point with pride to a number of accomplishments. The division spearheaded the program that eventuated in the rather large-scale APA visiting lecturer program, which later was supported for many years by the National Science Foundation. It also spawned the idea of a historical museum, which later turned into the massive APA Traveling Psychology Exhibit project. It initiated and continued to fund a prize for the best integrative publication in psychology, the William James Award, and sponsored programs at the centennial of the publication of James's *Principles of Psychology*, which in turn generated a book published by the APA. It has also sponsored two volumes, published jointly by Lawrence Erlbaum and by the APA, on significant figures in the history of the discipline, *Portraits of Pioneers in Psychology*. As of the writing of this book, the division is about to launch a full-fledged APA journal. These are concrete accomplishments; more abstract, perhaps, is that the sheer existence of the division has, for 50 years of increasing fractionation, specialization, and fragmentation, kept alive the idea of a "general psychology."

As long as prominent, competent, and dedicated APA members are willing to devote some of their energies to the cause of general psychology (whatever that might mean), the division may well continue its already respectably long, if modest, existence.

REFERENCES

Dashiell, J. F. (1967). John Frederick Dashiell. In E. G. Boring & G. Lindzey (Eds.), *A history of psychology in autobiography* (Vol. 5, pp. 95–124). New York: Appleton-Century-Crofts.

Dewsbury, D. A., & Bolles, R. C. (1995). The founding of the Psychonomic Society. *Psychonomic Bulletin & Review, 2,* 216–233.

Doll, E. A. (1946). The divisional structure of the APA. *American Psychologist, 1,* 336–345.

Donnelly, M. E. (Ed.). (1992). *Reinterpreting the legacy of William James.* Washington, DC: American Psychological Association.

Hilgard, E. R. (1945a). Psychologists' preferences for divisions under the proposed APA by-laws. *Psychological Bulletin, 42,* 20–26.

Hilgard, E. R. (1945b). Temporary chairmen and secretaries for proposed APA divisions. *Psychological Bulletin, 42,* 294–296.

Hilgard, E. R. (1974). Ernest Ropiequet Hilgard. In G. Lindzey (Ed.), *A history of psychology in autobiography* (Vol. 6, pp. 129–160). Englewood Cliffs, NJ: Prentice-Hall.

Hilgard, E. R. (1987). *Psychology in America: A historical survey.* San Diego, CA: Harcourt Brace Jovanovich.

Kimble, G. A., Boneau, C. A., & Wertheimer, M. (Eds.). (1996). *Portraits of pioneers in psychology* (Vol. 2). Washington, DC: American Psychological Association and Hillsdale, NJ: Erlbaum.

Kimble, G. A., Wertheimer, M., & White, C. L. (Eds.). (1991). *Portraits of pioneers in psychology.* Washington, DC: American Psychological Association and Hillsdale, NJ: Erlbaum.

Wertheimer, M., Barclay, A. G., Cook, S. W., Kiesler, C. A., Koch, S., Riegel, K. F., Rorer, L. G., Senders, V. L., Smith, M. B., & Sperling, S. E. (1978). Psychology and the future. *American Psychologist, 33,* 631–647.

Wolfle, D. (1946). The reorganized American Psychological Association. *American Psychologist, 1,* 3–6.

2

A HISTORY OF DIVISION 6 (BEHAVIORAL NEUROSCIENCE AND COMPARATIVE PSYCHOLOGY): NOW YOU SEE IT, NOW YOU DON'T, NOW YOU SEE IT

DONALD A. DEWSBURY

In 1995, Division 6 of the American Psychological Association (APA) adopted a new name: the Division of Behavioral Neuroscience and Comparative Psychology. Known by its original name, the Division of Physiological and Comparative Psychology, since its founding, Division 6 has been a focus for the interests of the comparative and physiological approaches in psychology since the inception of the division structure. It has been through Division 6 that physiological and comparative psychologists have found representation within the APA and have worked to ensure a place for their approaches within the rich fabric of U.S. psychology.

Although it was a charter division established during the 1940s, the history of Division 6 is discontinuous; it disappeared in 1948, only to reappear in 1963, and it may be in danger of disappearing once more. Division 6 can boast of outstanding accomplishments, but it has been beset by serious difficulties as well. Underlying some of the major shifts in the early history of the division is the question of the unity or diversity of experi-

There are many individuals who merit acknowledgment for providing various materials and information included in this history and for answering my various letters and pesterings. At the risk of neglecting some who have made major contributions, I will single out Herbert C. Lansdell, Donald B. Lindsley, and Sidney Weinstein for special thanks for their roles in gathering materials and responding to my requests. I thank Thomas Dalton, Herbert Lansdell, Donald Lindsley, Wade Pickren, James Todd, William Verplanck, and Randall Wight for comments on earlier drafts of this manuscript.

mental approaches to the study of behavior: The division changed as broader shifts occurred in the emphases and alliances among subdisciplines shifted.

THE INITIAL FOUNDING OF DIVISION 6

The unity of psychology and of the APA has repeatedly been threatened by splits between basic and applied interests throughout the twentieth century (see Evans, Sexton, & Cadwallader, 1992). The development of the American Association of Applied Psychology (AAAP) posed such a threat and was an important stimulus in the convening of a series of committee and subcommittee meetings concerning reorganization during the war years of 1942–1944 (Doll, 1946; D. Wolfle, 1946). A new set of APA bylaws was adopted, and the AAAP was merged into the APA. A prominent feature of the new APA was a divisional structure. It is worth noting that a psychobiologist was a prime mover in effecting the acceptance of the new APA: "The membership has Professor [Robert] Yerkes, more than any other one person, to thank for its new constitution" (D. Wolfle, 1946, p. 3). Although the new organization worked well for many years, the basic versus applied dichotomy was at the root of many divisional controversies.

An initial survey of interests in prospective divisions was mailed to psychologists early in 1944. Nineteen prospective divisions were listed alphabetically. A proposed Division of Animal Psychology was listed as Division 2 and that of Physiological Psychology as Division 13. In selections by 2,791 psychologists of the single, primary division in which they were most interested, Physiological Psychology ranked 8th with 125 votes (4.5%) and Animal Psychology was 18th with just 35 votes (1.3%) (Doll, 1946). Hilgard (1945a, p. 22) concluded "that psychologists do not think of themselves as animal psychologists or as comparative psychologists in any considerable numbers is shown by the rating of animal psychology."

The results of these rankings were used to propose a modified divisional structure, with a hierarchical arrangement led by Divisions 1 (General) and 2 (Teaching). When the new APA bylaws were adopted in 1944, they incorporated 19 charter divisions, including Division 6, the Division of Physiological and Comparative Psychology, which was formed by combining the originally proposed Divisions 2 and 13 (Olson, 1944).

From the beginning it was recognized that there would be flux in the divisional structure. New divisions could be formed on petition from 50 or more associates and fellows. Divisions could be dissolved when the number of members fell below 50 or if two thirds of the total membership of the division recommended dissolution (Olson, 1944).

The possibility of combining Divisions 3 and 6 was raised even before the initial divisional structure was adopted. Lindsley (1981) recalled that in one of those classic hotel room meetings at the 1944 joint meeting of the APA and the American Association for the Advancement of Science (AAAS), Edward Tolman was already lobbying to include physiological and comparative psychology within a broadened Division of Theoretical–Experimental Psychology, as Division 3 was then called, because he believed that the areas should be unified. Others, who disagreed, carried the day, and thus separate divisions were formed. That decision would soon be reversed.

The temporary chairman of Division 6 was Clifford T. Morgan of Harvard University; the temporary secretary was B. F. Skinner of the University of Minnesota (Hilgard, 1945b). In 1945, Donald G. Marquis was elected as the first *chairman*; the title was changed to *president* soon thereafter. Roger B. Loucks was elected secretary and Frank A. Beach and Donald B. Lindsley were the initial division tepresentatives to the APA Council. Marquis was succeeded as president by Donald B. Lindsley and Clifford T. Morgan.

The fledgling Division 6 was small but appeared strong. Helen Wolfle (1948) prepared "A Comparison of the Strength and Weakness of the APA Divisions," and reported data for eight parameters for the 18 existing divisions. By her criteria, only two divisions, Division 6 and Division 12 (Clinical), ranked in the upper half with regard to seven of the eight variables considered. She noted that "a division can be small and still show up well on all other counts, as does the Division of Physiological and Comparative Psychology" (p. 380). The lone measure on which Division 6 was found wanting was its size. Division 6 was cited as one of only six in which 2% or fewer of the members had resigned from the division. Division 6 easily led all of the divisions with regard to the number of programs presented at the annual meeting per 100 members. Division 6 presented 16.3 programs per 100 members; the next highest was Division 19 (Military) with 10.5. Together, these data reveal a picture of a small division, but one made up of members committed to the APA and their division and who supported both in their activities.

AMALGAMATION OF DIVISION 6 WITH DIVISION 3

Division 6 was short-lived in its initial incarnation, as the decision was soon made to amalgamate Divisions 6 and 3. The proceedings of the APA business meetings of September 1948 and 1949 show the following entry: "The Executive Secretary announced the merger of the Division of Theoretical–Experimental Psychology and the Division of Physiological and Comparative Psychology" (Peak, 1949, p. 462). The paper trail surrounding the events leading up to this decision is poor. However, it is clear that the amalgamation was the voluntary, joint decision of the two divisions, not something forced on the divisions by the APA.

There seem to have been several reasons for the amalgamation. First, this was a time of great concern over fractionation within the APA. There was a fear that the divisions in the new structure could proliferate excessively to the detriment of the association as a whole. Verplanck (1992) called it "a futile attempt to maintain APA as a scientific and academic society rather than a predominantly professional one." Physiological and comparative psychology were not clearly differentiated from experimental psychology at this time. As noted by Frank Finger (1992),

> Those who considered ourselves comparative and/or physiological were adamant in considering ourselves also experimental/theoretical, and there was no reason for fragmenting our programs or other interactions. . . . Maybe we also foresaw the threat of proliferation of divisions, and dreaded it. You must remember that 50 years ago a psychologist was a psychologist, and many of us to this day resist and even resent the subdivisions within our departments that virtually require us to choose to "belong" to one or another.

Related to this issue was a second one: political effectiveness. Verplanck (1992) pointed out that the amalgamation of the APA and the AAAP to form the new APA with its division structure was effected when most of the experimental psychologists were engaged in the war effort and not attending to APA activities. It was only after they returned to the academic environment that they could carefully examine the arrangements that had been made and the implications for experimental, comparative, and physiological psychology. Although some experimental psychologists, such as Edwin G. Boring and Robert M. Yerkes, who had engineered the formation of the new APA, believed that they had provided an organization that would ensure control by academic psychologists, clinical interests already were growing and there was a feeling that one strong division in the APA might be more effective for experimentalists than two weak ones.

Probably a third reason for the amalgamation was the slow growth of Division 6. One membership list in the APA archives dated 1946 shows just 72 members. A list dated October 20, 1947, shows 89 fellows, 17 associates, and 2 affiliates. The 1948 APA *Directory* shows just 88 fellows (members) and 15 associates. As noted earlier, a small division could be strong. However, a certain critical mass was necessary; there were grounds for questioning the need for a separate entity.

Verplanck (1992) recalled that the 1948 business meetings of Divisions 3 and 6 were held at the same time, after dinner, in two nearby rooms of Memorial Hall at Harvard University. Many of the participants belonged to both Divisions 3 and 6. There was a continual flow of senior members back and forth between the two meetings as negotiations progressed. Verplanck noted, "These were very exciting, noisy, 'fun' meetings, with lots of heat, excitement, and suspense, all hanging on the outcome of separate votes of the two Divisions." The resulting decision was for amalgamation.

Physiological and comparative psychology remained a part of the APA during the period from 1948 to 1963. However, their locus was generally within Division 3. Comparative and physiological psychologists held office in Division 3 and many programs in physiological and comparative psychology were sponsored under the aegis of Division 3. However, Division 6 as a separate unit died in 1948. There is no Division 6 listing in the 1949 APA *Directory*.

REESTABLISHMENT OF DIVISION 6

Historians of our era tend to attribute greater importance in the determination of historical events to the Zeitgeist rather than individual effort. Surely, the Zeitgeist was important in the rebirth of Division 6. By the 1960s, physiological psychology had become a viable entity and comparative psychology, benefiting from both internal strength and interactions with European ethologists, also showed appreciable development. The fields had changed much since the 1940s.

It is a mistake, however, to underestimate the role of individual effort, in this case that of Sidney Weinstein, then of the Albert Einstein College of Medicine in New York City. There was a feeling among some physiological and comparative psychologists that Division 3 was not fulfilling their needs adequately. Weinstein (1981) recalled that

> The idea to start a physiological division occurred when Herb Birch and I had papers (which we both thought were of excellent quality) rejected by Division 3! We felt, and obviously we were in good company, that Division 3 had left physiological to wither away.

On December 22, 1960, Weinstein sent a petition to various colleagues, noting that a total of about 200 signatures, or 1% of the APA membership, would be required for action to be taken. A notice of the effort was carried in the 1961 *American Psychologist* (Notes and News, 1961) with the note that some 130 APA members already had signed the petition. It was the APA administrative associate, Jane Hildreth (1960), who suggested to Weinstein that the effort might be tied to the old Division 6.

The replies were mixed. Some respondents, such as Irwin Bernstein, Gilbert Gottlieb, Frederick King, and Brenda Milner, supported the effort (according to letters in the Division 6 archives). Others continued to oppose a splintering of the amalgamated Division 3.

Weinstein persisted with his efforts and eventually presided at an organizational meeting of physiological and comparative psychologists that was held at the APA meeting in New York on September 5, 1961 (Wilson, 1961). After considerable discussion among different factions concerning the shape that the proposed division should take, a move for harmony of interests between physiological and comparative psychologists was led by Helen Mahut, Freda Rebelsky, and Jonathan Wegener, and it appears to have carried the day. John Lacey proposed the name of *The Division of Psychobiology* as a solution to the semantic differences, but Hans-Lukas Teuber pointed to Adolf Meyer's use of that term and felt that the name would be inappropriate (for a discussion of this and other uses of *psychobiology*, see Dewsbury, 1991). A straw vote was taken, and the decision was made to accept the name *The Division of Physiological and Comparative Psychology*. A committee, composed of Weinstein, Lacey, and Rebelsky, drew up bylaws, or more correctly, adopted the bylaws of Division 3 with minor modifications as appropriate.

All was in place to petition the APA for formal acceptance of the new division. This came in the form of a cover letter from Weinstein to APA President Paul Meehl (Weinstein, 1962). In arguing for the petition, Weinstein noted that (a) this was a major interest group in the APA and there had been a prior APA Division 6; (b) 339 members (1.9% of the APA membership), 51% of whom belonged to no other division, were petitioning, (c) officers had been elected; and (d) bylaws had been adopted.

APA Executive Officer John Darley (1962) reported on June 13 that the Board of Directors had reviewed the petition and transmitted it to the Council of Representatives for consideration with a favorable recommendation. The vote would take place at the council meeting of September 4 in St. Louis. It is difficult to piece together the exact events occurring at the council meeting. The proposal was controversial. A substantial portion of the APA membership opposed the proliferation of divisions and still saw no need to split off physiological and comparative psychology from experimental psychology. Donald Hebb delivered a heated presentation in opposition to the founding of a new Division 6. Neal Miller questioned whether the new division might weaken Division 3. Weinstein recalled having to wake up Harry Harlow to get him to come to the council meeting to vote for the division. As another instance of the applied versus basic science conflict, Robert Holt questioned whether the proposal for a new division might not be a ploy to weaken the clinical divisions. When he realized that the opposition was coming from other experimentalists rather than clinicians, he was satisfied with the sincerity of the petitioners and voted in their favor. The vote was favorable and the new division was established (Newman, 1962). Later, Weinstein (1990) reflected "it is interesting that we may owe our existence, despite the opposition of our current confederates (Division 3), to the consequent support by the clinicians!"

The division was reborn and was on its way. A new chair of the election committee was chosen, Harold Wilensky. A membership committee, composed of Weinstein, Harlow, J. McV. Hunt, Nathan Shock, and H.-L. Teuber, was established. The new program committee included Weinstein, David Raab, John Stamm, Walter Essman, and John Lacey. The march toward APA bureaucracy had begun.

MEMBERSHIP

Division 6 has always been among the smaller of the APA divisions; membership problems have often been focal. Recall that in the original 1946 poll on division structure, just 172 individuals indicated an interest in joining the division, making it the third smallest of the 19 proposed divisions. The 1948 APA *Directory* shows a total membership of just 108, including associates and affiliates. At the time of the petition to reestablish Division 6, there were 339 members.

By way of clarification, it should be noted that the 1945 APA bylaws included three membership categories: fellows, associates, and affiliates. There were no "regular" members between 1946 and 1957. Fellows were holders of the PhD with published research or acceptable experience. Associates generally had a minimum of 2 years of graduate work. Affiliates generally were either nonqualifying graduate or undergraduate students or members of the division who did not belong to the APA. Fellows and associates could serve on various committees and hold office.

The number of Division 6 members for 1948 to 1994 is shown in Table 2. The early pattern was generally one of gradual growth, with occasional plateaus and a slight dip in membership in the mid-1970s. Membership peaked at 821 in 1988 and has shown a disturbing decrease since that year.

Comparing Division 6 membership changes to those of the APA at large reveals an interesting perspective on membership. If one considers the Division 6 membership as a proportion of the total APA membership, the pattern is one of steady and inexorable decline (see Figure 2). The peak year for Division 6 membership as a percentage of the APA (1.98%) was in 1963, the year the division was reestablished. In 1991, this figure dipped below 1% (0.96%) for the first time. Although the cause of the dip during the 1970s is not immediately apparent, the recent decline in membership correlates with the APA membership's rejection of proposals for reorganization and the resulting formation of the American Psychological Society (APS) in 1988. The 1984 increase in membership resulted from

TABLE 2
Membership in Division 6 and the APA as a Whole

Year	Division 6 N	APA N	Division 6 as Percentage of APA
1948	103	5,047	2.04
1963	415	20,933	1.98
1964	415	22,119	1.88
1965	442	23,561	1.88
1966	466	24,473	1.90
1967	495	25,800	1.92
1968	519	27,250	1.90
1969	562	28,785	1.95
1970	583	30,839	1.89
1971	602	31,985	1.88
1972	623	33,629	1.85
1973	647	35,254	1.84
1974	645	37,000	1.74
1975	626	39,411	1.59
1976	641	42,028	1.53
1977	614	44,650	1.38
1978	621	46,891	1.32
1979	705	49,047	1.44
1980	751	50,933	1.47
1981	751	52,440	1.43
1982	747	54,282	1.38
1983	751	56,402	1.33
1984	791	58,222	1.36
1985	794	60,131	1.32
1986	806	63,146	1.28
1987	801	65,144	1.23
1988	821	66,996	1.23
1989	788	68,321	1.15
1990	757	70,266	1.08
1991	693	72,202	0.96
1992	678	72,644	0.93
1993	656	73,263	0.90
1994	632	76,008	0.83
1995	610	79,098	0.77

the effort of Herbert Lansdell and Allan Mirsky to recruit members from Division 40 (Clinical Neuropsychology). Perhaps the major problem for Division 6 is that most physiological and comparative psychologists now find their professional affiliations in organizations other than the APA, especially the Society for Neuroscience and the Animal Behavior Society.

The membership decline has many implications for the division. For example, in the annual voting for apportionment in the APA Council of Representatives, a division must receive a minimum of 0.5% of the votes cast to retain even one seat on council. For 1992, Division 6 received .56%, thus barely retaining its seat (Composition of the Council of Rep-

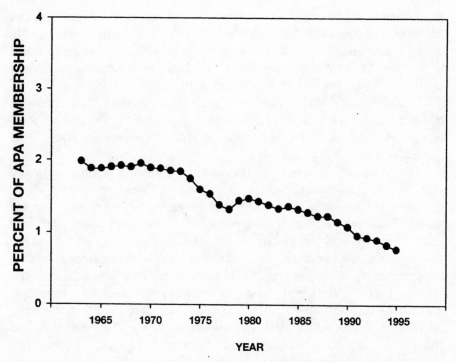

Figure 2. Division 6 Membership as a Percentage of APA Membership, 1963–1995.

resentatives, 1991). By 1995, Division 6 finally lost its seat on the council and was without representation for the first time in its history.

Various membership drives met with limited success. At the 1970 business meeting in Miami Beach, for example, John Stern, of Washington University, St. Louis, concluded that the gain in membership stemming from a recent drive did not justify the expense of the drive.

An unpublished 1985 study of division membership showed it to be 85% male and almost all White. The modal ages were from the 40 to 44 and 45 to 49 groups. In terms of geography, the Middle Atlantic region had the most members with 23%. In addition, 28% of the members reported research in physiological psychology as their current major field; 19% listed experimental psychology; 9% listed psychobiology/neuropsychology; just 4.4% listed comparative psychology. Finally, 10% of the membership was doing clinical work in the health service provider area.

BYLAWS

I have located no written record of bylaws for Division 6 in the 1940s. The original bylaws of the division when it was reactivated in 1963 were simply composed of the Division 3 bylaws with the term *physiological and comparative* substituted for *experimental* and a few other comparable changes. The original copy of Division 3 bylaws, with the changes penciled in, survives in the division archives. A certain conservatism in treatment of the bylaws is revealed by the fact that the 1962 and 1991 versions of the bylaws contain articles that are quite similar; also, both use the same major headings: name and purpose, membership, officers, executive committee, nominations and elections, meetings, committees, dues, and amendments.

Although the bylaws have been amended numerous times over the years, for the most part these relatively minor changes have been made to facilitate the day-to-day operations of the division. They typically involve modifications in the manner of appointment or terms of officers or committee members and the procedures for selecting members and fellows.

Perhaps the most sweeping changes are the most recent—those adopted in 1991. A new category of student affiliates was added to the article on membership and a new position was established for a historian/archivist. The positions of newsletter editor and historian/archivist were defined within the article dealing with officers (Article 3, Section 1), although they are not division officers. However, the executive committee was redefined to include "the Division President, Division Past-President, Division President-Elect, Secretary–Treasurer, Division Representative(s) to Council, Chairperson of the Program Committee, Chairperson of the Membership Committee, Newsletter Editor, Division Historian/Archivist, and additional Members-at-Large to make up twelve members of the Committee" (as explained in the 1991 bylaws). What is especially significant is that, for the first time, individuals were to be selected to serve as voting members of the executive committee who were not elected by the membership at large but rather were appointed by members of the committee on which they will serve. The philosophy was that those who are doing the work of the division should have the privilege of the vote in the division's executive committee meetings. This represents a reversal of the long-standing policy that voting members of the executive committee ought to be members elected by the general division membership.

FELLOWS

As previously noted, in its initial years Division 6 offered just two categories of membership: fellow and associate. The status of a fellow during those years was closer to that of a member in more recent years.

By the time Division 6 was reestablished, a fellow in the APA had become more of an honorary designation. The 1962 bylaws of new division specified that

Fellows of the Division shall be persons who have been elected Fellows by the American Psychological Association and who in addition satisfy the following requirements: (a) five years of experience in physiological or comparative psychology subsequent to the doctor's degree, (b) publication of significant contributions in the field of physiological or comparative psychology in addition to research carried out for the doctor's degree, and (c) actively engaged in research. The election of Fellows to the Division shall be upon nomination by the Executive Committee and by a majority vote of the Fellows attending the annual business meeting.

This basic statement has been retained for 30 years. However, procedures used in obtaining nominations and conducting elections have changed from time to time, as when the procedures were clarified and streamlined in 1987. It is difficult to obtain complete data regarding fellows. The division had 55 fellows in 1965. This number grew and peaked in 1989, when there were 237 active fellows.

In trying to reconstruct a complete list of all members elected as Division 6 fellows, I have located the names of the 318 individuals. As there were 230 fellows in 1991, this suggests that 88 fellows are no longer active in Division 6 because of either death or resignation.

OFFICERS

The elected officers of Division 6 include the president, representatives to the APA Council of Representatives when appropriate, and members-at-large of the Executive Committee. In practice, much of the day-to-day work of maintaining the division falls on the secretary–treasurer, an appointed office.

A list of the Division 6 presidents is presented in Table 3. By my calculations, the division has elected 34 presidents. Several cases are difficult to classify, however. Donald G. Marquis was a temporary chair, and Donald B. Lindsley and Clifford T. Morgan served as president prior to the merger with Division 3. It is my understanding that Frank A. Beach was elected president by Division 6, but served as copresident of Division 3 after the merger (as he was elected by Division 6). The portrait of Beach appearing in the 1949 *American Psychologist* (Beach, 1949) included the caption "President, Division of Physiological and Comparative Psychology"; I thus include him in the list. However, his presidential address was listed in the APA convention program as being under the auspices of Division 3, and as copresident he chaired the Division 3 business meeting. W. J. Brogden served as a copresident of Division 3 during 1949 to 1950 and may or may not have been elected through Division 6; I have not

TABLE 3
Presidents of Division 6

Year	President
1945–1946	Donald G. Marquis (chair)
1946–1947	Donald B. Lindsley
1947–1948	Clifford T. Morgan
1948–1949	Frank A. Beach
1949–1963	(Division inactive)
1963–1964	Sidney Weinstein
1964–1965	Harry F. Harlow
1965–1966	Hans-Lukas Teuber
1966–1967	Austin H. Riesen
1967–1968	Karl H. Pribram
1968–1969	Mortimer Mishkin
1969–1970	John I. Lacey
1970–1971	James Olds
1971–1972	Richard F. Thompson
1972–1973	Brenda A. Milner (Daniel S. Lehrman, deceased)
1974	Brenda A. Milner
1975	Donald R. Meyer
1976	Philip Teitelbaum
1977	Elliot S. Valenstein
1978	Richard M. Held
1979	Frances Graham
1980	Byron A. Campbell
1981	Richard L. Solomon
1982	William A. Mason
1983	Alan F. Mirsky
1984	Robert W. Doty
1985	Ethel Tobach
1986	George H. Collier
1987	Martha H. Wilson
1988	Duane M. Rumbaugh
1989	Linda Bartoshuk
1990	Frederick A. King
1991	J. Bruce Overmier
1992	Russell M. Church
1993	Donald A. Dewsbury
1994	Evelyn Satinoff
1995	Bertley G. Hoebel
1996	Stewart H. Hulse

included him. Daniel S. Lehrman died before assuming office and his term was filled by president-elect Brenda A. Milner.

I have analyzed characteristics of 36 Division 6 presidents (excluding Lehrman). Of the 36, 6 have been women, the first of whom was Brenda Milner. Six received their PhDs from Yale University. Four received their PhDs from Harvard; three received their PhDs (or MD for Karl Pribram) from the University of Chicago, the University of Pennsylvania, and Brown

University. Johns Hopkins, McGill, New York University, Stanford, and Wisconsin each produced two Division 6 presidents.

The places of employment at the time of assuming the presidency were more widely distributed. Two each were from Michigan, the Massachusetts Institute of Technology, and the National Institute of Mental Health, Princeton, Wisconsin, and Yale; 24 other institutions employed one Division 6 president each. The mean time from PhD to the presidency was 26 years, with a range of 9 to 39 years. Both Clifford Morgan and Frank Beach assumed the presidency 9 years after receiving their PhDs. The bumper crop for Division 6 presidents occurred in 1954, when five future presidents received their PhDs.

The 11 secretary–treasurers are listed in Table 4. Twenty-six individuals have served as council representatives. John Lacey, Robert Malmo, and Austin Riesen assumed office more than once. Prior to 1981, Division 6 had two representatives in every active year except 1978; it had just one representative between 1981 and 1994. A total of 59 individuals have served as members-at-large.

PROGRAM

The Division 6 program is but a small part of the overall program for the annual APA convention. The number of hours allocated by or negotiated with the APA and other divisions for the Division 6 program has varied over the years, with 52 hours in 1974 and 17 in 1986. The response to the limited number of hours has varied over time. In 1976 and 1977, for example, the decreasing number of program hours was causing strain

TABLE 4
Secretary–Treasurers of Division 6

Year	Secretary–Treasurer
1945–1946	R. B. Loucks
1946–1949	Harry F. Harlow
1963–1969	Frances K. Graham
1969–1971	Martha H. Wilson
1971–1974	Robert L. Isaacson
1975–1977	J. Michael Warren
1978–1980	Herbert C. Lansdell
1981–1983	Marlene Oscar-Berman
1984–1987	Mimi N. Halpern
1988–1990	William P. Smotherman
1991–1996	Karen L. Hollis

on the division's ability to accommodate members. By the late 1980s, by contrast, submissions were so few that program chairs experienced difficulty filling in even the minimal number of hours allotted. With these changes the character of the program changed, from a heavy emphasis on contributed papers to a heavier emphasis on longer, invited papers and symposia.

Early Years

The 1946 meeting was the first in which division sponsorships were noted. Division 6 sponsored sessions on sensory functions, general physiological psychology, and comparative psychology. Included as speakers in the latter session were P. T. Young, W. N. Kellogg, B. F. Skinner, W. R. Garner (on symbolic processes in rats), and D. O. Hebb.

The program for the 1948 meeting was listed by division. Divisions 3 and 6 were listed together; all other divisions had separate sections. A symposium titled "Cognitive Versus Stimulus-Response Learning" included participants Ernest R. Hilgard, David Krech, Kenneth W. Spence, and Edward C. Tolman. The 1949 program listed only Division 3, but included work formerly presented under the sponsorship of Division 6, such as a session on brain functions, chaired by Donald Lindsley, and one on physiological psychology, chaired by W. D. Neff. Frank Beach's famous "The Snark Was a Boojum" paper (Beach, 1950) was presented as an address by the copresident. This pattern of including material on physiological and comparative psychology on the Division 3 program continued during the division hiatus.

In 1963, the first year after the reestablishment of the division, some 21 hours of substantive programming were offered. This total included symposia with such titles as "Properties of the Memory Trace" and "Computer Analysis of Electrical Activity of the Brain and Behavior," two sessions (4 hours) of contributed papers in comparative psychology, eight sessions (11 hours) of contributed papers in physiological psychology, plus a social hour and business meeting.

Types of Presentations

The tradition of a presidential address was initiated with Donald Lindsley's talk at the 1947 meeting in Detroit. Often the speaker summarized the latest data collected in his or her laboratory.

In 1967, for the 75th anniversary of the APA, the decision was made to initiate a series of invited addresses. Initially these addresses were by individuals from outside of psychology but whose work had important implications for physiological or comparative psychology. Speakers invited by Division 6 in the early years of the program included David Hubel, Jerzy

Rose, Theodore Bullock, Vernon Mountcastle, Walle Nauta, Norman Geschwind, Edward Evarts, John Eccles, and Seymour Kety. Later, the number of invited addresses was expanded and Division 6 members, as well as nonmembers, were invited to present invited addresses, generally 50 minutes in duration. This may have peaked in 1983 when 10 invited addresses were given.

The Hebb–Olds Lecture speaker series, initiated in 1990, was an annual talk cosponsored by Divisions 6 and 2 (Teaching of Psychology). It was intended to help undergraduate instructors deal with the complexities of modern psychobiology. The first two speakers were Donald Dewsbury in 1990 and Neil Carlson in 1991.

In 1967, the division instituted the new policy of inviting newly elected fellows of the division to present invited talks; these have generally been of 20 to 35 minutes duration. In the inaugural year, Mark Rosenzweig, Roger Russell, Roger Sperry, William Grings, Conan Kornetsky, William Utall, John Flynn, Howard Moltz, and James Olds presented talks. In subsequent years a range of about 2 to 12 talks per year were presented as part of this program.

The traditional mode of presenting research results has been through contributed papers to be presented orally at the meeting. These have generally been refereed by a committee, with some papers rejected. This mode dominated the earlier Division 6 programs. For the 1968 meeting in San Francisco 100 such papers were submitted; 69 such papers were presented at the 1964 and 1976 meetings. However, interest in spoken papers has changed over the years. With the advent of poster sessions, oral papers became less important. For a while, they were completely eliminated from the program. They were reinstated in 1983 and have been on and off the program in subsequent years.

In 1978, following the successful use of poster sessions by other societies, the APA instituted a program of poster sessions. This became the major mode for contributed presentations to Division 6. There were 23 posters in 1983; in 1989, there were 8 posters and no oral presentations.

Many outstanding symposia have been presented over the years. Heinrich Klüver chaired a 1965 symposium titled "The Visual System of Nonmammalian Vertebrates" with William Hodos, David Ingle, Harvey Karten, and Nancy Mello. A 1967 symposium titled "Inferotemporal Cortex and Visual Discrimination" featured some of the regulars who kept Division 6 alive: Brenda Milner, Mortimer Mishkin, John Stamm, Karl Pribram, Charles Gross, Martha Wilson, and Charles Butter. A 1979 centennial symposium titled "Psychology and the Neurosciences" featured Donald Lindsley, John Lacey, and Karl Pribram. One titled "Development of Structural Sex Differences in the Brain" in 1981 included Masakazu Konishi, Roger Gorski, and Arthur Arnold.

Other Highlights

Various professional issues have been addressed. A 1975 historical panel, organized under the heading "Division 6 in Its Second Decade: Retrospective and Prospective Comments by Past Presidents," was held in 1975. Chaired by William Taylor, participants listed were Sidney Weinstein, Harry Harlow, Hans-Lukas Teuber, Austin Riesen, Karl Pribram, Mortimer Mishkin, John Lacey, James Olds, Richard Thompson, Brenda Milner, and Donald Meyer. A 1978 discussion hour was chaired by Frances Graham and addressed the "Place of Division 6 in APA." A discussion session in 1981 dealt with "The Role of the *Journal of Comparative and Physiological Psychology*." The status of comparative psychology has been analyzed and reanalyzed at Division 6 sessions. A 1972 symposium in Honolulu titled "Comparative Psychology at Issue" was cosponsored by the New York Academy of Sciences and featured Leonore Adler, Howard Moltz, Karl Pribram, H. P. Zeigler, Donald Dewsbury, Robert Lockard, Ethel Tobach, and Helmut Adler. The status and role of physiological psychology have been addressed on various occasions as well. In 1982, Philip Teitelbaum addressed the issue "Is Physiological Psychology Dying?" A symposium titled "Future of Physiological Psychology: Reasons for Optimism and Concern," held in 1986, included Mark Rosenzweig, Mortimer Mishkin, Hasker Davis, Richard Thompson, Neal Miller, Larry Squier, and George Collier (see Davis, Rosenzweig, Becker, & Sather, 1988).

Various sessions have addressed social issues. Perhaps a sign of the times was a set of three sessions labeled "Open Workshop on Peace Action" in 1971, which were chaired by B. G. Hoebel, C. Gross, and C. M. Butter. An open meeting of the Division 6 Committee on Social Responsibility, chaired by Charles M. Butter, was held in 1974. A 1984 symposium titled "The Comparative Psychology of Warfare" featured Ethel Tobach, John Paul Scott, Michael Hammond, and Metta Spencer.

Ethical issues were addressed on various occasions. The 1975 program included a session on "Ethical Issues in Neuroscience," with Charles Gross, Allan Mirsky, Edward Katkin, Elliot Valenstein, Judith Stern, and Stephen Chorover. A session on "Ethics and Animal Experimentation" appeared in 1978 with Austin Riesen, Robert Doty, Charles Gallistel, John Flowers, and Lester Aronson participating. In 1983, Division 6 sponsored a talk by Edward Taub titled "Tactics for Laboratory Attacks by Antivivisectionists: Can Anything Be Done?" Division 6 has cosponsored various other sessions on the ethics of animal research over the years.

THE D. O. HEBB AWARD

At its 1981 meeting, the Executive Committee decided to initiate an annual award to be named in honor of Donald O. Hebb. As originally conceived, the award was to be given for the best poster abstract submitted by someone who is within 5 years of receiving a doctorate. The award would be accompanied by a $100 check.

Donald Hebb made numerous seminal contributions to the fields of physiological and comparative psychology and was a mentor of many Division 6 members. It is fitting that the award was named in his honor. However, one cannot escape the irony that it was Hebb who fought the reestablishment of the division.

The older statement was later modified, perhaps informally, so that by 1990 the award could be earned for either a poster or a platform session. The award is not made every year but only when merited.

The committee declined to present an award in 1982, the first year of its operation. The first winner was Michael Fanselow in 1983. As best I can tell, there have been only three subsequent winners: Edward J. Holmes, Michael J. Renner, and April Ronca.

NEWSLETTERS

The members of Division 6 decided to start a small newsletter in 1979. Herbert C. Lansdell was chosen to be the founding editor. He was succeeded by James Kalat and Ernest Maples in 1985, Christina L. Williams and Warren H. Meck in 1991, Katarina Borer in 1994, and Herbert L. Roitblat in 1996.

In 1978 the membership was polled regarding the need for a newsletter and the vote was in the affirmative by a margin of 108 to 13. The first issue of the *Physiological & Comparative Newsletter* appeared in December 1979 and consisted of just two pages, including a brief summary of events leading up to its founding and a "President's Corner" column by Byron A. Campbell. There appear to have been 10 numbered issues published in this series, which ran from 1979 to 1984. The issues typically included a "President's Corner," information on the convention program, proposed bylaws amendments, and assorted announcements of interest to members.

In 1985, during the presidency of Ethel Tobach, the division members expanded the newsletter, with Kalat and Maples serving as coeditors. The numbering of the newsletter, now called *The Physiological and Comparative Psychologist*, was reinitialized, with the May 1985 issue bearing the designation of Volume 1, Number 1. That issue indicated that such items as job opportunities and available postdoctoral positions could be announced in the newsletter. The issue contained 31 pages, including the abstracts of papers to be presented at the 1985 APA convention. It appears that just two issues were published in 1985, and three issues per year were targeted beginning in 1986. Only two issues were published in 1988 and 1991, and one was published in 1989. This was a period of financial difficulty for the division.

CONTROVERSIES

As might be expected, various controversies have arisen in the division over the years of its existence. Most often these have centered around the rights of scientists to conduct and present research in controversial areas.

Wheeler on Parapsychology

A controversy within the Executive Committee began when John A. Wheeler of the University of Texas participated in a symposium at the 1979 AAAS meetings in Houston dealing primarily with parapsychology. He took a strong stand against parapsychology and advocated "that the AAAS disaffiliate the Parapsychological Association" (Wheeler, 1979). Division 6 Secretary–Treasurer Herbert Lansdell circulated a memorandum on January 10, 1979, requesting authorization to send a letter to *Science* magazine stating "The Executive Committee of the Division of Physiological and Comparative Psychology of the American Psychological Association wishes to express support for John Wheeler's position regarding parapsychology" (Lansdell, 1979).

Lansdell's proposal met with mixed responses. Several members supported the effort. Others advised caution. William Mason was particularly cautious and indicated that he would abstain from any vote. Although he shared Wheeler's reservations about the validity of the claims from parapsychologists, Mason (1979) indicated that his "chief concern is that Division 6 not adopt a position that could be viewed as an attempt to censure and control research which at the moment happens to be unpopular and outside its current Zeitgeist." As best I can determine, no letter was ever sent.

Thiessen on Rape

One of the most widely publicized controversies from Division 6 centered on an invited fellows address given by Delbert Thiessen at the 1983 meeting in Anaheim, California. A discussion of this controversy from the perspective of the critics can be found in the book edited by Sunday and Tobach (1985). In addition, some of the correspondence among Thiessen, Miller, and correspondents is reprinted there (Sunday & Tobach, 1985).

In response to an invitation from Program Chair David Miller, Thiessen submitted the title "Rape as a Reproductive Strategy: Our Evolutionary

Legacy." Thiessen interpreted the literature on forced copulations (rape) as being most common in nonhuman animal species with polygynous mating systems and in human societies with polygynous systems. He reflected that "it became apparent that at least some forms of rape could be viewed as alternative reproductive strategies among males who lacked the resources and potential to make themselves attractive to females" (Thiessen, 1990).

Publication of the title provoked a series of letters of protest from various people to Miller and Division 6 President Allan Mirsky. More controversy was apparent at the paper's presentation.

The issues are complicated and different critics focused on different aspects of the problem. Much of the criticism centered about Thiessen's title, which some felt was sensationalistic. Others were concerned that the proposition that there might be an evolutionary background to rape might imply a condoning of rape as an adaptive strategy with genetic routes (the so-called naturalistic fallacy). Accusations of genetic determinism were made.

Marlene Oscar-Berman chaired the session at which Thiessen's paper was given. In introducing Thiessen and his talk, she indicated that there would be a question-and-answer period after the talk, during which the Association of Women in Psychology would read a brief prepared statement. Linda Garnets, a Los Angeles therapist, made brief remarks supporting Thiessen's right to investigate the problem but condemning the alleged "inflammatory way he exploits women" (Cunningham, 1985). However one may feel about the controversy, it was extraordinary in that for the only time in the history of the fellows addresses, the session chair announced that there would be a rebuttal to a talk that had yet to be presented and that was available by title only.

Although other issues were intertwined, the clash seemed to be primarily between two sets of values. On the one hand, there was concern about the social implications of the talk and the appearance that the attribution of a genetic influence might imply a justification of rape. On the other hand, there was a belief that all aspects of human behavior should be open to investigation and that if there are, indeed, evolutionary foundations for such behavior, rape might be better understood and thereby decreased by understanding them than by suppressing relevant information.

Rushton on Race

In December 1989, J. Philippe Rushton of the University of Western Ontario submitted a paper for presentation at the 1990 meeting titled "Towards a Theory of Human Racial Group Differences." This submission presented some difficult problems for the program committee, whose members had serious reservations about Rushton's conclusions. At the same time, however, there was support for the right of a scientist to present the results of his or her research, no matter how controversial they might be. After an initial rejection, Rushton softened the title to "New Data on r/K Selection and Race" and changed some of the content. The revised paper was accepted for presentation, where it received a very negative reception. The principle of permitting a scientist to present controversial results, subject to critical examination, was affirmed.

Animal Research

It will come as no surprise that Division 6 has been involved in the controversies concerning animal research that have mushroomed during its existence. As might be expected, there has been relatively little disagreement within this division over the value of animal research. Because other units within the APA have been especially concerned with these issues, however, the involvement of Division 6 has been relatively minor. As noted earlier, various sessions on the program have addressed issues of the use of animals in research. Relevant issues have been raised in various executive committee and business meetings and in correspondence.

The most visible attack on a psychologist conducting animal research was that on Edward Taub; Taub's laboratory at the Institute for Behavioral Research was infiltrated by animal rights activist Alex Pacheco and in order to shut down Taub's research the police raided the laboratory on September 11, 1981. In 1984, Division 6 contributed $1,000, a considerable portion of its budget, to the Biomedical Research Defense Fund to help defray the legal costs that Taub had incurred in his defense.

A minor controversy arose in 1984 when Emmanuel Bernstein of the Psychologists for the Ethical Treatment of Animals submitted a proposal to Division 6 for a symposium titled "Ways to Minimize Pain and Suffering for Laboratory Animals." Program Chair James Kalat polled the officers and committee members of the division regarding the proposal. Only 1 of the 18 respondents flatly opposed sponsoring the proposal, but many others expressed reservations. APA President Janet Spence was able to secure program time from Divisions 1 (General) and 2 (Teaching), so the problem became moot, though Division 6 and others cosponsored the symposium.

Psychosurgery

The most acrimonious controversy to break out in Division 6 surrounded the issue of psychosurgery (see Pickren, 1992). In 1974, the division's Committee on Social Responsibility established a 17-member subcommittee to examine psychosurgery, chaired by Herbert Lansdell, with the goal of producing a position paper that would be approved by the Division 6 membership and forwarded to various other societies for consideration.

Lansdell circulated draft statements to the subcommittee and other scientists and produced a revised version in March 1975. In it the committee specified conditions under which psychosurgery might be appropriate and stressed the importance of psychological tests in assessing the outcomes of such treatments. Employment of contemporary assessment methods would be critical. They warned of the possible misuse of psychosurgical techniques and of the difficult ethical problems involved. In letters written to Division 6 Secretary–Treasurer J. M. Warren and President Donald R. Meyer dated January 1975, Suzanne H. Corkin of the Department of Psychology at MIT and a member of the subcommittee objected to the draft statement, arguing that it might be read as indicating that the APA supported psychosurgery. After various negotiations, the decision was made to circulate both versions of the draft statement to the membership.

Lansdell circulated draft statements to the subcommittee and other scientists and produced a revised version in March 1975 that provoked much controversy. This decision elicited several protests, including a letter from Stephen Chorover of MIT to President Donald Meyer, under whose signature the ballot was distributed. Chorover felt that the ballot was presented in a manner that was prejudicial in favor of the committee's draft version over the alternative. In a letter of April 23, 1975, Meyer wrote that he felt sufficiently disturbed by criticisms of his handling of the matter and the time he had to spend in dealing with it that he decided to resign as a Division 6 fellow and, as a consequence, as Division 6 president—the only such resignation in the division's history.

The results of the ballot were inconclusive and it was decided that no majority view could be presented as the view of the Division 6 membership. In addition, it was concluded that the committee and subcommittee were both constituted via procedures that violated the division bylaws and hence their deliberations were invalid. Although President Meyer was persuaded to present his presidential address as scheduled, President-Elect Philip Teitelbaum succeeded Meyer and presided at the 1975 meeting.

COMMITTEES

In addition to an executive committee, the division bylaws initially mandated a membership committee and a program committee. The former was generally responsible for the recruitment and selection of members and selection of fellows. These two functions were divorced in 1995 when a separate membership and growth committee and a fellows nomination committee were established. A program committee was responsible for assembling the program for the annual convention. A nominations committee, responsible for developing nominations for annual elections, was added in 1964.

Various special committees have been established as the needs have arisen. Among the special committees have been the Committee on Social Responsibility, the Committee on Psychosurgery, the Committee on the History of Division 6, the Committee on the Status of Physiological Psychology, and the Committee on Animal Research.

FINANCES

The Division 6 budget has always been small. Further, the accumulated sum in the treasury has either been small or has shown a deficit. Changes in dues and assessments must be approved by majority vote at the annual meeting (Article VIII, Section 1, of the bylaws). A special assessment of $2 per year was approved at the 1977 business meeting and was continued for some time. This was later raised to $5 per year. The assessment was raised to $9 per year at the 1989 business meeting in an effort to help the division out of a difficult budget situation.

ADDITIONAL HIGHLIGHTS OF EXECUTIVE COMMITTEE ACTIONS

The Executive Committee and business meeting act on many issues that do not fit neat categories. A few residual issues may be of interest. From time to time, division members considered broad social issues. For example, at the 1968 business meeting, the division approved a recommendation that the annual convention be moved from Chicago, in the wake of the Chicago Police Department's handling of protests at the Democratic National Convention. At the same meeting, Division 6 endorsed a principle calling for the division to become involved in social issues such as militarism, race, and poverty. The next year, the division approved a resolution that opposed the use of security clearance as a criterion for being awarded an appointment to study sections. In 1975, the Executive Committee voted to appoint a liaison to the Committee on Women in Psychology and to contribute $100 to the Association for the Advancement of Psychology, but it declined to support a suggestion from the Society for the Psychological Study of Social Issues favoring graduated dues.

CONCLUSION

Physiological and comparative psychologists should be proud of the history of their division. The heritage of Division 6 is laced with the efforts of some of the most important workers in these fields from the past half century. The programs sponsored by Division 6 have been exemplary. As with all such groups, one can find blemishes. However, Division 6 has generally been an effective and congenial academic group that has worked effectively to promote mutual interests.

That is the good news. The bad news concerns the current status of the division. The 1995 membership was 610 in a 79,000-member organization, and it is in a general declining pattern. Fewer than 1 in 100 APA members belongs to Division 6. According to APA bylaws, divisions can be dissolved when the membership reaches below 0.5% of APA membership. Although Division 6 has not yet reached that point, the APA is growing and Division 6 is shrinking, and it is not inconceivable that membership could drop below the minimum in a few years. Division 6 lost its council seat in 1995, a sign of the division's declining influence in the APA.

There are many reasons for this decline. In general, there is a perception among many that the APA is irrelevant to the concerns of physiological and comparative psychologists and to academic psychologists in general. The feeling is that the Society for Neuroscience, the Animal Behavior Society, the APS, the Psychonomic Society, or other organizations have usurped the position formerly held by the APA (e.g., Davis et al., 1988). This is unfortunate because there is much, such as effective lobbying and the publication of journals, that the APA does very well and that serves the constituency of Division 6 quite effectively.

In the 1990s, in an effort to make the division more appealing to its membership and others working in the field, Division 6 considered and debated a change of name. At the 1995 APA convention in New York, the name Division of Behavioral Neuroscience and Comparative Psychology was adopted. Whether the name change has any substantive effect on the course of the division's history remains to be seen.

The outlook for Division 6, and for a place for physiological and comparative psychology within American psychology, will not be bright if current trends continue. It is not inconceivable that another amalgamation of Division 6 into Division 3 or another unit may be in the offing. However, whereas the first amalgamation appears motivated by a perceived unity of effort, a second one would be the result of declining interest. Change more substantial than a renaming, perhaps a new organizational structure or the personal efforts of an exceptional leader, may be necessary lest history repeat itself and Division 6 once again disappears from the APA roster. If physiological and comparative psychology continue to decrease contact with psychology at large, and if psychology at large loses physiological and comparative psychology to other disciplines, both will suffer.

REFERENCES[1]

Beach, F. A. (1949). *American Psychologist, 4,* 115.

Beach, F. A. (1950). The snark was a boojum. *American Psychologist, 5,* 115–124.

Composition of the Council of Representatives. (1991). *American Psychologist, 46,* 746–749.

Cunningham, S. (1985). Rape speech angers women. *APA Monitor, 14*(10), 22.

Darley, J. G. (1962). Letter to Sidney Weinstein. Division 6 archives.

Davis, H. P., Rosenzweig, M. R., Becker, L. A., & Sather, K. J. (1988). Biological psychology's relationships to psychology and neuroscience. *American Psychologist, 43,* 359–371.

Dewsbury, D. A. (1991). "Psychobiology." *American Psychologist, 46,* 198–205.

Doll, E. A. (1946). The divisional structure of the APA. *American Psychologist, 1,* 336–345.

Evans, R. B., Sexton, V. S., & Cadwallader, T. C. (Eds.). (1992). *The American Psychological Association: A historical perspective.* Washington, DC: American Psychological Association.

Finger, F. W. (1992, March 4). Letter to Donald A. Dewsbury.

Hildreth, J. D. (1960, December 22). Letter to Sidney Weinstein. Division 6 archives.

Hilgard, E. R. (1945a). Psychologists' preferences for divisions under the proposed APA By-laws. *Psychological Bulletin, 42,* 20–26.

Hilgard, E. R. (1945b). Temporary chairmen and secretaries for proposed APA divisions. *Psychological Bulletin, 42,* 294–296.

Lansdell, H. (1979, January 10). Letter to members of the Division 6 executive committee. Division 6 archives.

Lindsley, D. B. (1981, January 20). Letter to Herbert Lansdell. Division 6 archives.

Mason, W. A. (1979, April 4). Letter to Herbert C. Lansdell. Division 6 archives.

Newman, E. B. (1962). Proceedings of the seventieth annual business meeting of the American Psychological Association, Incorporated, August 31 and September 4, 1962, St. Louis, Missouri. *American Psychologist, 17,* 843–864.

Notes and News. (1961). *American Psychologist, 16,* 211.

Olson, W. C. (1944). Proceedings of the fifty-second annual meeting of the American Psychological Association, Inc., Cleveland, Ohio, September 11 and 12, 1944. *Psychological Bulletin, 41,* 725–793.

---

[1]Some sources are listed as being from Division 6 archives. These materials were collected from various officers and currently are in the possession of the author. The intention is to deposit them in an appropriate archive, probably either the Archives of the History of American Psychology in Akron, Ohio, or the American Psychological Association Archives, currently at the Library of Congress in the James Madison Building in Washington, DC.

Peak, H. (1949). Proceedings of the fifty-seventh annual business meeting of the American Psychological Association, Inc., Denver, Colorado. *American Psychologist, 4,* 443–485. *American Psychologist, 3,* 470–502.

Pickren, W. E. (1992, August). Of committees and subcommittees: A note on a controversy concerning psychosurgery. Poster presented at the American Psychological Association meetings, Washington, DC.

Sunday, S. R., & Tobach, E. (Eds.). (1985). *Violence against women: A critique of the sociobiology of rape.* New York: Gordian Press.

Thiessen, D. D. (1990, March 20). Letter to Donald A. Dewsbury. Division 6 archives.

Verplanck, W. S. (1992, February 26). Letter to Donald A. Dewsbury.

Weinstein, S. (1962, March 14). Letter and petition to Paul E. Meehl. Papers of the American Psychological Association, Library of Congress, Washington, DC.

Weinstein, S. (1981, January 30). Letter to Herbert Lansdell. Division 6 archives.

Weinstein, S. (1990, October 31). Letter to Donald A. Dewsbury.

Wheeler, J. A. (1979). Parapsychology—A correction. *Science, 205,* 144.

Wilson, M. (1961, September 5). Minutes of the organizational meeting of physiological and comparative psychologists held as part of the American Psychological Association meeting, New York. Papers of the American Psychological Association, Library of Congress, Washington, DC.

Wolfle, D. (1946). The reorganized American Psychological Association. *American Psychologist, 1,* 3–6.

Wolfle, H. (1948). A comparison of the strength and weakness of APA divisions. *American Psychologist, 3,* 378–380.

3

A HISTORY OF DIVISION 7 (DEVELOPMENTAL PSYCHOLOGY)

THOMAS C. DALTON

The formation in 1946 of the Division on Childhood and Adolescence (now called Developmental Psychology) of the American Psychological Association (APA) reflected the need for research psychologists to have a forum to advance child development as an academic and scientific field of study. But the creation of Division 7 also reflected the sense of urgency among its members that high standards should guide the application of scientific knowledge to the practical problems of children and adolescents. The founding officers and members shared a common goal and expectation that scientific inquiry would naturally generate the knowledge and methods necessary to ameliorate the most pressing problems confronting childhood and family life.

The mid-1960s and early 1970s were watershed years for the division, as several members gained national prominence in the Head Start program

Reconstructing the history of a professional society is an arduous task. My job was made much easier, however, by several distinguished members of Division 7 who helped put events in perspective. I would like to express my special thanks to the following individuals for their generosity in sharing with me their recollections and observations and for offering key insights made possible by their extensive experiences: Urie Bronfenbrenner, Rodney Cocking, Dorothy Eichorn, Dale Harris, Jerome Kagan, William Kessen, Claire Kopp, Lewis Lipsitt, Herb Pick, Harriet Rheingold, Judy Rosenblith, and Harold Stevenson. I am particulary grateful to Alberta Siegel for giving the manuscript a close reading for accuracy and historical completeness. I would also like to thank Dale Boles of APA Library for his special assistance and Patricia Anderson for obtaining important records from the Library of Congress.

and through federal policies affecting children and families. However, as the division has grown to accommodate new members and interests, this unified vision has undergone considerable internal strain and contributed to significant policy conflicts between the division and the APA. Despite these struggles, Division 7 leaders have demonstrated resilience and a ceaseless capacity to adapt to the changing demands on their profession. They have done so by advancing knowledge in a way that encourages new applications and by taking initiatives to expand collegial contacts and collaboration beyond our national borders.

In writing this chapter, I have attempted to understand how the work of a community of scientists engaged in generating a unique body of knowledge relates to their efforts to acquire the authority to represent themselves as a profession. As a consequence, my account consists of more than just a chronology of the highlights of a professional society's organizational history. I trace how a group of scientists chose to get involved in policy-making processes and resulted in changing the cultural dimensions of the problems under inquiry. In seeking a professional identity as scientists, developmental psychologists have used science to ground their judgments about human behavior and have addressed issues involving considerable moral controversy and political conflict. But their engagement in public policy has generated new lines of inquiry, methods, and organizational strategies that continually replenish the professional capital needed to secure their own future.

FORMATIVE YEARS AND REORGANIZATION: 1945 TO 1960

In many ways, the history of Division 7 is intertwined with that of the Society for Research in Child Development (SRCD), which was organized in 1933. The SRCD was the product of initiatives taken by Robert Woodworth of the National Research Council (NRC) to fund research in child development in the 1920s. The NRC created a Committee on Child Development in 1925 and attracted substantial funding from the Laura Spelman Rockefeller Memorial. Lawrence K. Frank (a student and protégé of John Dewey) wisely invested the memorial's funds in a network of academic research institutes that included Columbia University, University of Iowa, University of Minnesota, University of California at Berkeley, and Yale University. (Dalton & Bergenn, 1995; Smuts, 1984). A significant proportion of the funds went to female psychologists who found it difficult to get academic positions (O'Connell & Russo, 1983, 1990). Many of the pioneers in the field were involved in these child study institutes and subsequently became Division 7 presidents, such as John Anderson, Florence Goodenough, Harold Jones, Robert Sears, and Nancy Bayley (see Table 5).

TABLE 5
Presidents of Division 7

1946–1947	John E. Anderson
1947–1948	Florence L. Goodenough
1948–1949	Harold E. Jones
1949–1950	Arthur T. Jersild
1950–1951	Robert R. Sears
1951–1952	Wayne Dennis
1952–1953	Roger G. Barker
1953–1954	Nancy Bayley
1954–1955	Boyd R. McCandless
1955–1956	Dale B. Harris
1956–1957	Irvin L. Child
1957–1958	Urie Bronfenbrenner
1958–1959	Alfred L. Baldwin
1959–1960	Pauline S. Sears
1960–1961	Dorothea McCarthy
1961–1962	Helen Koch
1962–1963	Marian Radke-Yarrow
1963–1964	Mary Cover Jones
1964–1965	Harold W. Stevenson
1965–1966	Sidney W. Bijou
1966–1967	William E. Martin
1967–1968	Jerome Kagan
1969–1970	Dorothy Eichorn
1970–1971	Irving Sigel
1971–1972	Eleanor Maccoby
1972–1973	Harriet L. Rheingold
1974	Alberta E. Siegel
1975	Edward Zigler
1976	Willard Hartup
1977	Paul Mussen
1978	Frances Degen Horowitz
1979	E. Mavis Hetherington
1980	William Kessen
1981	Lewis P. Lipsitt
1982	Jeanne H. Block
1983	Sandra W. Scarr
1984	Carolyn U. Shantz
1985	Sheldon H. White
1986	Rochel S. Gelman
1987	Urie Bronfenbrenner
1988	Herbert Pick
1989	Ann L. Brown
1990	Ross Parke
1991	Lois Wladis Hoffman
1992	Lois Bloom
1993	Anne C. Petersen
1994	Claire B. Kopp
1995	Aletha C. Huston
1996	Arnold J. Sameroff

The SRCD was founded to promote the interdisciplinary study of children and to publish research in the journal *Child Development*. Although many psychologists shared these aims, they looked to a reorganized and rejuvenated APA to provide a professional and organizational identity that was lacking in the SRCD (personal communications, 1995). The curtailment of SRCD meetings during World War II and severe financial difficulties later in the decade made a new forum all the more attractive (Rheingold, 1984).

During the early 1940s, Robert Yerkes deftly assembled a group of colleagues representative of diverse APA member interests to initiate the process of reorganization that included the drafting of a new constitution (Capshew & Hilgard, 1992). John E. Anderson, president of both the SRCD and the APA in 1943, chaired the committee for revision of the APA bylaws. The APA was reorganized to provide for a centralized but limited governance structure that served as an administrative umbrella for functionally autonomous divisions. Division 7 had the good fortune during its first decade of existence to have continuous representation on the APA Board of Directors, first by Robert Sears (1947–1950), who was president of the division in 1949, then by Jean MacFarlane (1950–1953) and Wayne Dennis (1953–1956).

As founding president, Anderson gathered together a core group of psychologists among the 330 members of Division 7 who had diverse interests in the fields of experimental, clinical, and educational psychology and mental testing. Their broad interests were reflected in the Division's purpose, which was "to promote high standards in the application of scientific knowledge to the practical problem of guiding children and adolescents" (By-Laws, 1954, p. 1). Infant experimentalists Wayne Dennis and Louise Ames were among the founding members. Infant experimentalist Myrtle McGraw withdrew from the APA in 1944 to attend to family domestic responsibilities, so she was unable to become a member-at-large during the early leadership of the division (Wolfe, 1947).

The founders also included Helen Thompson Woolley and Arthur Jersild of Columbia University and Teachers College who studied the clinical aspects of personality development pertinent to educators. The Iowa Child Welfare Research Station was represented by Beth Wellman and Howard Skeels who challenged the conventional wisdom that IQ predicted subsequent achievement. Iowan Boyd McCandless, a pioneer in diagnostic tools for the assessment of learning, was also involved at the beginning (Cravens, 1993; Dalton, 1995). Developmental biologist Leonard Carmichael, who was APA president in 1940, was a founding member, as were clinicians Charlotte Bühler and Grace Fernald and Berkeley experimentalists Harold Jones and Jean MacFarlane.

In 1949, Arthur Jersild appointed a policy and planning committee during his presidency to survey interest in sponsoring a scholarly journal to determine the quality and extent of research papers presented at annual meetings and to propose standards for clinicians dealing with children (*Division Activities*, 1949). These were significant initiatives, which shaped the policy agenda of the division through the next decade. In addition, 58% of the members saw no need to sponsor a new journal with only 29% supporting the proposition. (Gewirtz, 1951, p. 3). Many members felt that the SRCD journal, *Child Development*, provided an adequate forum. In 1969, the APA inaugurated the journal *Developmental Psychology* to publish research in infant and child development. Boyd McCandless was the journal's first editor.

With his election as division president in 1950, Robert Sears carried forward Jersild's concerns about certification by creating the Liaison Committee on APA certification and a Standing Committee on Ethics. The Liaison Committee, chaired by Helen Thompson, recommended that all clinical psychologists working with children should take courses covering a wide range of ages. The committee also urged that training programs be made available that included the study of children who did not have any diagnosed psychological abnormalities. Finally, the committee recommended that the Division of Clinical and Abnormal Psychology be invited to present these principles jointly to the APA Council of Representatives (hereafter referred to as the APA Council) (Cobb, 1951, p. 2).

Iowa researchers Ruth Updegraff and Harold E. Anderson set in motion a process for formulating a code of ethics for experimental research involving children. As Dale Harris, the founding secretary–treasurer of Division 7 and first editor of the division newsletter recalls (see Tables 6 and 7), experimentalists generally lacked sensitivity to the issue:

> I was beginning to pick up stories of indifference to child sensibilities, and parent concerns. It struck me as odd that the APA had for a number of years such a code for animal subjects but not for children! We got a committee working on it. (Harris, 1995)

Updegraff and Celia Stendler drafted a lengthy set of principles that required the informed consent of parents and teachers. The guidelines also barred the use of methods or techniques that were inconsistent with school rules, involved inappropriate incentives, aroused unhealthy emotional responses, or used deception. The members of the executive council of Division 7 recommended that this code of ethics be forwarded to the APA Committee on Ethics, headed by Nicholas Hobbs, for consideration and approval (Updegraff & Stendler, 1951, pp. 4–5).

Nancy Bayley (1953, p. 4) consolidated these policy initiatives during her presidential term (1953–1954) by charging the Policy and Planning Committee, composed of Alfred Baldwin, Urie Bronfenbrenner, Irvin Child, Dale Harris, Irving Stone, and Boyd McCandless, to draft a statement of the division's general objectives. They recommended that the com-

TABLE 6
Secretary–Treasurers of Division 7

1946–1949	T. W. Richards
1950–1952	Dale B. Harris
1953–1955	Elizabeth B. Hurlock
1956–1958	Dorthea McCarthy
1959–1961	Marian Radke-Yarrow
1962–1963	Frances K. Graham
1964–1967	Dorothy Eichorn
1968–1971	Irving Sigel
1972–1973	E. Mavis Hetherington
1974–1975	Lucy Ferguson
1976–1979	Jeanne Block
1980–1983	Carolyn U. Shantz
1984–1988	Tiffany Field
1989–1991	Ellen Scholnick
1992–1995	Lynn Liben
1996–	Leslie Cohen

mittee advise the Executive Committee as to issues affecting child psychology as a science and profession and to "disseminate to the public facts and theories regarding the psychological development of the individual in his or her social setting" (Bronfenbrenner, 1954, p. 5). The Policy and Planning Committee also proposed an interdisciplinary focus for annual meetings that would "implement a cycle of symposia" exploring the problems in developmental psychology that affected other fields in psychology (Bronfenbrenner, 1954, p. 6). The committee members recommended that panel discussions alternate between assessing methodological issues and presenting research with broad theoretical implications.

TABLE 7
Newsletter Editors for Division 7

1949–1953	Dale Harris
1953–1956	Elizabeth Hurlock
1957–1968	(not available)
1969–1971	Yvonne Brackbill
1972–1975	Sandra W. Scarr
1976–1979	Lee C. Lee
1980–1983	John C. Masters
1984–1985	K. Alison Clark-Stewart
1986–1988	Jay Belsky
1989–1991	Deborah Phillips
1992–1995	Suzanne M. Randolf
1996–	Robin Jacobvitz

During her term, Bayley also asked Dale Harris to chair a special committee that would revise the bylaws to reflect these organizational changes and to conform membership, nomination, and election processes with APA procedures. One issue that generated heated controversy was the criteria with which to define and select division fellows. The Policy and Planning Committee felt that APA criteria were too loose and that fellow status should be reserved for individuals "who contribute to the resolution of important issues in the field or who opened new areas of inquiry" (Bronfenbrenner, 1957, p. 2). An elaborate nomination process was proposed to ensure that the selection of fellows was not unduly influenced by division officers nor by those already possessing this member status.

There was considerable support in the late 1950s for changing the name of the division to better reflect research in the field. Bronfenbrenner reported that the Policy and Planning Committee felt that the name "childhood and adolescence" connoted "a special interest group concerned with applied problems and techniques rather than with broader considerations of general theory and research" (Bronfenbrenner, 1954, p. 2). There were other reasons for changing the division's name that seem significant and timely in retrospect. For example, the terms *genetic* or *developmental* would indicate that the field had import beyond childhood. Using these terms would help to attract members with research interests in learning and the effects of family, class, and community on developmental processes. The term *developmental* was eventually chosen, because it was less ambiguous than the term *genetic* and was less likely to be associated with particular journals (Bronfenbrenner, 1954, p. 3). The membership approved this and other changes in the Division 7 bylaws in 1959.

The division program throughout the 1950s reflected the waning interest in the debate about IQ, heredity, and environment and an emerging interest in the formation of identity, socialization, and growth processes. Much attention was devoted to aggression and other personality factors contributing to delinquency. But there was also research challenging conventional approaches. Roger Barker's ecological research revealed broad forces at work in the natural history of children's behavior. Dale Harris was ahead of his time in reporting experiments that challenged the conventional wisdom that rigid parental authority and discipline inculcated personal responsibility. Nancy Bayley anticipated research in the 1970s by finding that self-perceptions of masculinity and femininity vary within gender and by age.

WATERSHED IN PUBLIC POLICY ON CHILDREN AND FAMILIES: 1961 TO 1973

Developmentalists, as with most other psychologists of the era, became enthralled in the 1960s with the imposing tools that Robert Sears, Clark Hull, and B. F. Skinner offered to experimentalists. Research by Robert and Pauline Sears on nurturance, dependency, and aggression renewed a dormant fascination with Freudian concepts. Hull's drive theory inspired the experimental study of parent–child interactions and showed promise in revealing the mechanisms governing personality and identity, the formation of temperament, motivation, and achievement. Skinner's methods of operant conditioning were used to uncover new dimensions of discrimination in early learning processes.

Developmentalists were particularly interested in processes that influenced children's identification with their parents. Factors shaping personality traits, such as independence, consistency, role taking, and interpersonal relations were also of interest to researchers, the group of which included Jerome Kagan, Leon Yarrow, and Willard Hartup, among others. Eleanor Gibson's research on the interrelation of perception and exploratory behavior, which won her the APA's Distinguished Contribution to Science Award in 1968, constituted an important exception to stimulus-and-response studies. She charted new territory in showing how perception is enhanced by motor behaviors that make use of affordances of their environment—a theme that has been carried forward by Herbert Pick and Esther Thelen in their studies of infant locomotion and perception.

However, few developmental psychologists anticipated that the federal government would launch a major program, such as Head Start, during the 1960s involving early childhood education. Research centered on the debate on the effects of hereditary and environmental factors on educability had nearly disappeared in Division 7 programs. Nevertheless, the controversy about IQ was unexpectedly revived when several division leaders played significant roles in the invention and evaluation of Head Start. Some of the details of their involvement are worth describing because they illustrate how external political factors have shaped the division's agenda.

In his invaluable history of Head Start, Yale psychologist Edward Zigler, an administrator of the program from 1970–1972 (Zigler & Muenchow, 1992), recounts in an astonishing anecdote that Urie Bronfenbrenner may have been instrumental in gaining President Lyndon Johnson's commitment to Head Start. Bronfenbrenner served as a member of the National Advisory Council established by President Kennedy to oversee the programs of the National Institute of Child Health and Development. The Institute was created in 1963 to sponsor research in mental retardation and other problems afflicting early childhood. Bronfenbrenner, a Russian émigré, discovered in his cross-cultural studies of child rearing in the former

Soviet Union and the United States that Russian parents seemed to spend more time with their children and that this may have accounted for successful preschool experiences. After presenting his findings to a 1964 meeting of the National Institute for Child Health and Development, he was invited to the White House to give this same presentation to President Johnson and his family. Zigler reported that, according to Bronfenbrenner, "The Johnsons were impressed, especially by the pictures of Russian preschools. One of the Johnson daughters asked, 'why couldn't we do something like this'" (Zigler & Muenchow, 1992, p. 17). Bronfenbrenner and Zigler subsequently were appointed to the planning committee that drafted Head Start's legislation and oversaw its early implementation.

Other members of Division 7 at the time were making less dramatic but highly significant contributions to the conceptualization of Head Start. In the late 1950s, Bettye Caldwell and pediatrician Julius Richmond, the first director of Head Start, collaborated on longitudinal studies of infants conducted at Syracuse University to identify the origins of psychosomatic disorders in disadvantaged preschool children. To their surprise, periodic checkups revealed a startling pattern of developmental decline at the end of the first year that delayed language acquisition and cognitive achievement (Richmond, 1974, p. 19). A few years later, Boyd McCandless and his associates (see Spiker, Hodges, & McCandless, 1966) also reported that minority preschool children who showed poor motor development and weak verbal skills were likely to experience learning difficulties.

The politics involved in the early evaluations of Head Start illustrates the dilemmas that beset policy makers and scientists who try to make sound judgments in the absence of scientific consensus on what works and why. By conventional measures of IQ, policy makers were worried that the summer Head Start program was exhibiting signs that the initial positive effects in cognitive development were fading out. Head Start's political visibility and growing costs however, made its evaluation unavoidable—although premature—because it had not been in operation long enough to measure its long-term effects. The Head Start advisory committee rushed to furnish policy makers with noncognitive measures and instruments, such as Bettye Caldwell's Preschool Inventory, but these rejected in favor of evaluation designs that relied on conventional tests of IQ. It was as if a whole decade of advances in the science of child development was being written off in favor of tests whose validity was suspect.

When the Westinghouse–Ohio University study was commissioned in 1968, Zigler and Bronfenbrenner tried desperately to broaden and revise the proposed measures. They argued for an assessment of multiple impacts and a longitudinal rather than a retrospective study that used control groups based on random assignment. Sheldon White, a consultant on the project and subsequent president of the division in 1985 (Zigler & Muenchow, 1992, p. 68), tried to incorporate into the report different analyses of the data that would address some of Zigler's concerns, but the rush to judgment required a report that was unequivocal and authoritative.

The controversial Westinghouse report, which concluded that no "widespread cognitive and affective gains" could be demonstrated seemed to satisfy no one and simply increased the demand for more evaluations (Zigler & Muenchow, 1992, p. 70). Jule Sugarman, Head Start's administrator, expressed his frustration about getting reliable information about Head Start because of the "inability of researchers to agree with one another . . . that no expert will acknowledge that the studies of another expert are valid" (Sugarman, 1974, p. 14). Sugarman consequently observed that during the entire time he was with Head Start, he could never recall "an instance in which I was able to rely on any scientific study as a guide to policy" (p. 14–15). This quandary was well illustrated by the disappointment that Zigler expressed when, after conducting an exhaustive review of available longitudinal data on Head Start, Bronfenbrenner reported that short-term benefits were not sustained after 3 years (Zigler & Muenchow, 1992, pp. 168–169).

President Richard Nixon interpreted the early evaluation findings to "indicate that Head Start must begin earlier in life and last longer" and appointed Zigler to head a new Office of Child Development (OCD) in 1970 (Zigler & Muenchow, 1992, p. 74). Zigler thought this signaled strong support of Head Start, but he soon discovered otherwise. Nixon saw Head Start fitting into his 1970 Family Assistance Plan as a child day-care program. Senator Walter Mondale saw this as an opportunity to introduce the Comprehensive Child Development Act in 1971 that would make Head Start available to all children. Mondale's bill passed, earmarking substantial funds for research and training of professional and paraprofessional child-care specialists. However, Nixon vetoed the bill because child coalition advocates refused to lodge administrative authority in the states under revenue sharing, as Nixon preferred. Zigler resigned from the OCD in 1972, exclaiming that "parents are the most significant single determinant in the child's development" (Zigler, 1972, p. 8).

These events provoked an unprecedented attempt by Division 7 to influence subsequent federal programs involving child development. Division 7 activism called into question the APA's passive posture on federal policies affecting the profession and public welfare. Division 7 President Eleanor Maccoby appointed a new legislative committee to make members aware of significant developments in federal policy affecting children's interests. The executive committee of Division 7 met with Elliot Richardson to express their concerns (Maccoby, 1972, pp. 32–33). Maccoby responded that she was "not trying to politicize the Division" (p. 33). She contended instead that:

The people charged with the responsibility of directing the affairs of the Division feel that they must walk a fine line: they do not wish to be partisan nor to conduct propoganda compaigns; but at the same time they feel they would be neglecting their duty if they did not take action on behalf of the membership on certain public issues which are clearly of great professional concern to the majority of people in the Division. . . . There also seems to be wide agreement concerning basic issues, such as the importance of maintaining high scientific standards in evaluation research, and the desirability of "developmental" rather than "custodial" approaches in programs providing child care. (p. 33)

When she became president in 1973, Harriet Rheingold authorized members to create 11 state committees to monitor and report on the level of federal support, especially in the area of training sponsored by the National Institute of Mental Health. Division officers considered making a case to Secretary Caspar Weinberger for retaining funding in this area, but never followed through. Rheingold was also instrumental in persuading the APA Council to create a task force on child development to protect worthy federal programs, and she urged the task force to draw on the state groups of Division 7 to conduct program reviews. (See Table 8 for Division 7 Council of Representatives). Rheingold proposed that the APA Council adopt a strongly worded resolution supporting knowledge for the betterment of child welfare, which advocated the "amelioration of psychologically hazardous conditions which place children in developmental jeopardy" (Rheingold, 1973, p. 35).

Finally, Alberta Siegel, an acknowledged expert on the effects of television violence on children, served on the Surgeon General's Scientific Advisory Committee on Television and Social Behavior. In her testimony in 1972 before the Senate Subcommittee on Communications of the U.S. Senate Committee on Commerce headed by Senator Pastore, Siegel (1975) urged television producers to travel abroad and learn from the English, Dutch, and other nationalities about how to exercise restraint in depicting violence. The Surgeon General's report, "Television and Growing Up: The Impact of Televised Violence," (1972) was singled out by Ross Parke and Ronald Slaby (1983, p. 595) "as a major scientific achievement," because it was the first time that an executive department sponsored scientific research on this issue. The report instigated scores of subsequent studies, affirming a causal relationship between television violence and aggressive behavior among children (see Cater & Strickland, 1975). During her presidency in 1974, Siegel was actively involved in establishing federal guidelines for research with human participants. Siegel also helped increase federal funding for research in child development, and she served on several research and policy panels of the National Institute of Mental Health.

During the late 1960s and early 1970s, Division 7 launched a series of exciting awards and programs. The G. Stanley Hall Award was con-

TABLE 8
APA Council (Representative for Division 7)

1946	John E. Anderson
	Harold E. Jones
1947	Roger G. Barker
	Beth L. Wellman
1948	Nancy Bayley
	Robert R. Sears
1949–1950	Dorthea McCarthy
1949–1951	Willard C. Olson
1949–1952	Dale B. Harris
1950–1953	Nancy Bayley
	Pauline Sears
1951–1954	Helen L. Koch
	Beth Wellman
1952–1955	Boyd R. McCandless
	Elizabeth B. Hurlock
1953–1956	Ruth Updegraff
1954–1957	Herbert F. Wright
1955–1958	Dorthea McCarthy
1956–1959	William E. Martin
1957–1960	Alfred L. Baldwin
	Arthur T. Jersild
1958–1961	Marian Radke-Yarrow
1959–1962	Eleanor Maccoby
1960–1963	Sibylle Escalona
	Paul Mussen
1961–1964	Harold Stevenson
1963–1966	Roger Barker
	Sidney Bijou
	Dorothy Eichorn
1964–1967	Leon Yarrow
1966–1968	Richard Q. Bell
	Alberta E. Siegel
1966–1969	Harriet Rheingold
1969–1972	Alberta E. Siegel
1967–1970	Dorothy Eichorn
	Lewis P. Lipsitt
1968–1971	Willard Hartup
	Edward Zigler
1970–1973	Harriet Rheingold
1971–1974	Lewis P. Lipsitt
	Sidney Bijou
1974–1976	Ann D. Pick
1975–1977	David S. Palermo
1976–1978	John P. Hill
1978–1980	Jack Block
1979–1981	Rochel S. Gelman
1980–1983	Arnold J. Sameroff
1982–1985	John W. Hagan
1983–1986	Frances Horowitz
1985–1988	Sandra Scarr
1988	Nancy Eisenberg
1989–1992	Tiffany Field
	Lewis P. Lipsitt
1991–1994	Norma D. Feshback
1994–1997	Richard Lerner

ceived by Harold Stevenson and Willard Hartup in 1966 to be presented to individuals who made lasting conceptual and empirical contributions that link developmental psychology to issues confronting other disciplines and the larger society. [The award is presented each year at the annual business meeting begun with the strike of a gavel carved from a large piece of walnut picture framing found in Hall's home and donated to the division by Clark University] (Rowland, 1974, pp. 15–16). The honoree may be invited to address the annual meeting of the APA. The first people to win the Hall Award were Helen Koch for her studies of sibling relationships and Harold Skeels for his studies of IQ. (see Table 9). Nancy Bayley, who had been the first woman to win the APA Distinguished Contribution to Science Award in 1966 for her longitudinal research on infant growth in the 1950s, received the Hall Award in 1971 (see Table 9). Jean Piaget also received the Hall Award in 1971. Piaget was unable to attend. Nevertheless, Piaget's cognitive theories, first introduced to U.S. psychologists by Alfred Baldwin, dominated the research and program agenda throughout the 1970s and early 1980s. John Bowlby received the Hall Award in 1974 for his influential work on attachment. Perhaps one of the most significant contributions in social policy was made by Robert Sears' colleague and associate Eleanor Maccoby who won the Hall Award in 1982. Her presidential address, "Differential Socialization of Boys and Girls," has inspired an impressive body of gender-related research. Sandra Scarr introduced members to the newly emerging field of behavioral genetics for which she later received the APA award for a Distinguished Contribution to Research in Public Policy (see Table 10).

DEVELOPMENTAL PSYCHOLOGY AND CHILDREN'S ISSUES IN TRANSITION: 1974 TO 1980

There was a renewed sense of mission and hope following the defeat of the Comprehensive Child Development Act that vigilance and concerted effort would bring new legislation to fruition. Division leaders were encouraged by the APA Council's decision to support the incorporation of the Association for the Advancement of Psychology as a separate lobbying organization in 1974 (Pallak, 1992, pp. 248–250). Division 7 leaders sought the support of the APA in advancing their legislative agenda. But given the changing composition of the APA membership, which was dominated by clinicians, their primary concern was directed toward federal policies affecting mental health.

Indeed, federal priorities in the field of child development were clearly shifting. The National Institute of Mental Health (NIMH) designated dysfunctional children with behavior pathologies as a top research priority, with behavioral and applied research ranking next to last. Research in child

TABLE 9
Recipients of Division 7 G. Stanley Hall Award

1967	Helen L. Koch
	Harold M. Skeels
1968	Mary Cover Jones
	Lois Meek Stolz
1969	Roger Barker
	Robert R. Sears
1970	Eleanor J. Gibson
	Orvis C. Irwin
1971	Nancy Bayley
	Jean Piaget
1972	Margaret and Harry Harlow
	Jean W. MacFarlane
1973	Roger W. Brown
	John W. M. Whiting
1974	John Bowlby
1975	Jerome Bruner
1976	James McV. Hunt
1977	Harriet L. Rheingold
1978	Alfred Baldwin
1979	Edward Zigler
1980	Sidney Bijou
1981	Lois B. Murphy
	George Stoddard
1982	Frances Graham
	Eleanor Maccoby
1983	Majorie Honzik
	Donald O. Hebb
1984	Erik H. Erikson
	Mary D. S. Ainsworth
1985	Urie Bronfenbrenner
1986	John H. Flavell
	E. Mavis Hetherington
1987	Marian Radke-Yarrow
1988	Harold Stevenson
	Diana Baumrind
1989	Jacqueline J. Goodnow
1990	Jack Block
	Jeanne Humphrey Block
1991	Willard Hartup
1992	Norman Garmezy
1993	Robert A. Hinde
1994	Jerome Kagan
1995	Ross Parke

TABLE 10
Division 7 Recipients of APA Awards

Distinguished Contribution to Science Award	
1963	Roger Barker
1966	Nancy Bayley
1968	Eleanor Gibson
1971	Roger Brown
1975	Robert Sears
1987	Jerome Kagan
1988	Eleanor Maccoby
1990	Francis Graham

Distinguished Contribution to Psychology in the Public Interest Award	
1982	Edward Zigler
1987	Urie Bronfenbrenner

Distinguished Professional Contribution Award	
1986	Edward Zigler

Distinguished Contribution to Research in Public Policy Award	
1988	Sandra Scarr

Distinguished Scientific Award for an Early Career Contribution to Psychology	
1976	Rochel S. Gelman

Distinguished Scientist Lecture Series Award	
1990	Eleanor Maccoby
	Jerome Kagan

American Psychological Foundation Gold Medal Award	
1980	Robert and Pauline Sears
1982	Nancy Bayley

development reflected the increased influence of clinicians who were primarily interested in problems of child abuse and abnormal development. Sensing the need to reassert leadership in child advocacy, Division 1 President Paul Mussen requested a survey of interdivisional activities in 1977. The survey found a significant level of state involvement in children's rights and showed that five divisions of the APA were involved in child advocacy, which included Divisions 8, 9, 16, and 43 (Child Advocacy Survey, 1979, pp. 32–33). Division 7 members Patricia Keith-Spiegel and Louise Guerney set up an "advocacy clearinghouse" to coordinate information about interdivisional activities affecting children's rights (Keith-Spiegel, 1978, pp. 22–23).

These initiatives, however, did not forestall a significant challenge to the policy domain of Division 7 in the 1970s, when a group led by Milton Shore and Gertrude Williams petitioned the APA to create a new division on children and youth. The proponents argued that there was a need for a "visible and active organizational unit devoted to the substantive areas of child and youth" (Hartup, 1975, p. 3). This proposal was prompted, in part, by the creation in 1975 of a National Center for Child Abuse and Neglect, which sought expertise on these issues. Division President Willard Hartup and the Executive Council resoundingly rejected the proposal, saying that the division had "energetically and effectively promoted precisely these areas over a period of thirty years" (Hartup, 1975, p. 3). Hartup suggested instead that a coalition of Divisions 7, 8, and 9 would be a more appropriate mechanism for addressing the policy interests of those who wanted a new division. But the Division of Children, Youth, and Family Services was eventually accepted by an APA eager to increase its influence through its newly created Task Force on the Rights of Children.

During the late 1970s, the mood in the division was turning inward toward organizational and professional interests. The need to engage in the uncertain process of APA reorganization was also looming on the horizon. For the first time, Division 7 membership was leveling off after more than tripling since 1946. Under a system of proportionate representation, even a small decline in membership resulted in the loss of one of three seats on the APA Council in the 1970s. There was a concern within the division that graduate students and young scholars had not been given sufficient attention at the annual meeting to sustain their interest in division activities. Student conversation hours were introduced in 1974 to give students an opportunity to discuss research and policy with distinguished members.

Other initiatives were taken to analyze placement trends and bolster the recruitment and retention of new members by acknowledging the contributions of junior scholars and researchers. The division also made efforts to present to the public, the press, and potential students of psychology a clearer image of what developmental psychology is by featuring the work of its leading scientists and practitioners. However, division officers increasingly resorted to using special assessments to offset the annual budget deficits incurred by the mounting costs of these new program initiatives and awards.

The first signs that membership was leveling off appeared in the early 1970s (see Figure 3). Credentials Committee Chair Boyd McCandless (1975, pp. 39–40) alerted division officers about this trend, but the problem was not given serious attention until 1977, when the number of new applicants had noticeably declined and the division lost one of three representatives on the APA Council. Before then, the division had never really experienced much difficulty attracting a sufficient pool of applicants from which to accept new members. For example, in 1971, Division 7

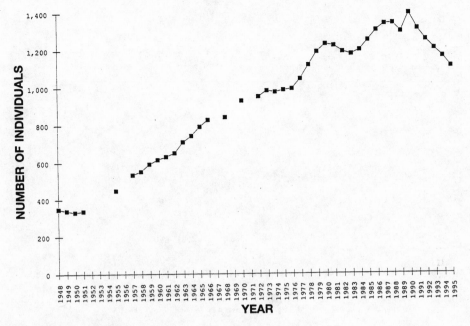

Figure 3. Membership in Division 7: 1948–1995.

received 313 inquiries from which 71 persons applied and 48 were accepted (Sigel, 1971, p. 24). In 1973, more than 400 inquiries were received generating 60 applicants, 59 of whom were accepted for membership (Hetherington, 1973, p. 22). But by 1977 only 19% of 105 new applicants were admitted as members (Block, 1977, p. 43).

Division 7 appeared to be attracting fewer applicants who were qualified for membership. Jeanne Block's (1978, p. 22) ideas to distribute an informational brochure to potential members and to simplify application requirements quickly rectified this situation with striking results. A membership drive in 1978 produced 109 new members. The following year, the division received 390 inquiries and 81 applicants became members (Block, 1979, p. 11). Despite these and other continuing efforts, Division 7 membership has been unable to keep pace with the growth of the APA (see Figure 4), and it lost a second council seat in 1991.

Since its inception in 1946, Division 7 members insisted that membership dues be affordable and that the budget be balanced each year. These principles were easily observed during years of steady growth through the 1960s. But rising costs and declining membership in the 1970s and early 1980s caused division officers to deviate from these principles. Shoestring budgets that rarely exceeded $1,000 in the first two decades increased sharply by the mid-1970s to more than $10,000, driven up largely by the costs of new awards, publication of the newsletter, and officer's travel ex-

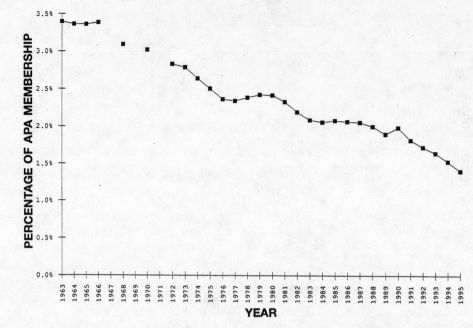

Figure 4. Division 7 as Percentage of APA Membership: 1963–1995.

penses. The practice of charging a special assessment commenced in 1975 with a $5 surcharge to make up anticipated budget shortfalls. This amount gradually increased to $9 by 1982. Funds raised through special assessments made up almost one half of the total income of the division throughout the late 1970s and the 1980s. Dues were eventually increased to $20 in the 1990s to better reflect the true costs of membership.

The infusion of a large grant in 1977 to conduct science writers' seminars (discussed later) doubled the Division 7 budget. However, unanticipated project costs contributed to a deficit that stubbornly persisted until it was finally erased in 1991. The most unfortunate casualty of deficit reduction was the *Division 7 Newsletter*, which was pared back drastically in length and coverage. This remarkably rich and informative source of news about Division 7 activities, sometimes ran more than over 100 pages and reached almost 1,800 readers in 1977 (Lee, 1977, p. 55). The *Division 7 Newsletter*, which once devoted 82% of its space to division news, feature articles, and continuing columns (Lee, 1977, p. 55), is now filled mostly with advertisements and occasional feature articles.

In the mid-1970s, the division surveyed the employment patterns of developmental psychologists in academic and other settings. Sandra Scarr reported that all but 4 of 179 PhD recipients representing 70 universities had obtained work. Of the total, 97 received academic appointments, 37 got jobs in either research or administration, and 16 pursued postdoctoral

84   *THOMAS C. DALTON*

fellowships (Scarr, 1975, pp. 6–7). The Division 7 executive committee also reacted favorably to the 1973 APA Boulder conference on training standards for clinical psychologists (see Fowler, 1992, pp. 274–275). Harold Grotevant, executive committee member, reported that the committee favored granting membership in the APA only to those who had fulfilled the requirements prescribed by the Boulder group, which was dominated by academic researchers (Grotevant, 1975, p. 6). However, clinicians later rejected the Boulder plan in favor of their own professional standards, thus ending a nearly 4-decade-long effort by Division 7 Members to ensure that clinicians possessed knowledge about normal development.

Under David Palermo's leadership, the Policy and Planning Committee took action to invigorate membership by creating a new award in 1978 to recognize the achievements of junior researchers. The committee finally settled on Lewis Lipsitt's idea to give the award in honor of Boyd McCandless, after considering Leonard Carmichael, among others. The Boyd McCandless Young Scientist Award is granted each year to nominees who, within 7 years of receiving their PhDs, have shown evidence of a distinguished theoretical contribution, programmatic research, or dissemination of scientific developmental knowledge within the profession and the public at large. One of the first recipients was Marc Bornstein of Princeton University, who has contributed important theoretical analyses of research in developmental biology and behavior. Lipsitt, recipient of the Mentor Award for Lifetime Achievement by the American Association for the Advancement of Science, has said he considers the McCandless Award of inestimable importance, "in honoring young developmentalists during a period of waning membership" (Lipsitt, 1995).

There was also a growing concern among members that a better job could be done informing the public and governmental organizations about the contribution developmental psychologists were making to the science of child development. Marian Radke-Yarrow consequently chaired an information committee in 1976, which was assigned to disseminate research findings that addressed significant public policies. Frances Horowitz, seminar developer, collaborated with Radke-Yarrow the following year to obtain $9,000 from the Foundation for Child Development to conduct a series of seminars attended by science writers from major newspapers and popular magazines. The Science Writers' seminars had three objectives: (a) to work with the Science Writers' Association to find interested journalists to attend the seminars; (b) to develop a roster of researchers (eventually including 107 developmental psychologists) willing to act as informed sources, who would be listed with the APA for referral; and (c) to develop background papers on specific issues such as gender differences and gender roles, which could be distributed as press releases (Radke-Yarrow, 1977, p. 48).

The first Child Research News Briefing was held in 1978 at the New York Academy of Sciences. It was attended by 40 representatives of the press and magazines. Among the presenters were Jerome Kagan on "The Emergence of the Mind," Marian Radke-Yarrow on "Altruism and Children," and Ross Parke on "Babies Have Fathers Too" (*Division 7 Newsletter*, 1978, p. 36). This innovative program proved to be too costly, so in the early 1980s it was scaled back and replaced with direct mailing through large organizations, such as Boys' Town. Division member Robert McCall, who was a senior scientist and science writer with the Boys Town Center for the Study of Youth Development, reported to have reached 23 million homes with press releases featuring developmental research (McCall, 1984, pp. 17–18).

Participation in annual meetings rose dramatically during the 1970s. Submissions for papers and symposia proposals combined averaged nearly 200, but only about 15% to 20% could be accepted given the division's limited allocation of 25 hours. Division 7 program chairs continually protested that this limit was unreasonable and inadequate, but they were able to almost double program hours through cosponsorship with other divisions. The 1977 annual program constituted a high watermark with more than 276 paper and symposia submissions. However, the number of proposals inexplicably declined 30% the following year. The decline continued throughout the 1980s, with submissions averaging about 150 or fewer each year. During this same period, the SRCD was attracting almost three times as many proposals for its biennial meeting. The International Society for Infant Studies, formed in 1976, was also attracting a significant number of participants.

The annual program from 1974 to 1980 reflected the rising interest in Piaget's cognitive theories and with Lawrence Kohlberg's complementary stage theories on moral development. Kohlberg's research spun off related themes, such as a concern for the law and children's rights, socialization and social cognition, and language acquisition and speech. The considerable attention that Kohlberg's research directed toward legal policy affecting children led to the formation in 1980 of Division 41, the Division of Law and Psychology. The dramatic change in program themes during the 1970s was best characterized by Robert McCall, program chair in 1977, when he proclaimed the following:

> There appear to be secular shifts in topical emphasis. No longer are conditioning, attention, Piaget tasks, and infancy in the general the most popular areas. Rather, social perception, children 2–12 years, peer-peer relations, memory in children, and the relationship between cognition, language and affect, and social behavior head the list. (McCall, 1977, p. 53)

Abstracts of the papers were published in the *Division 7 Newsletter* in 1975—an informative device that was discontinued in 1978 as a result of rising publication costs.

The programs in the middle and late 1970s were particularly noteworthy because they highlighted several seminal areas of research that have since defined the field of developmental psychology. Bronfenbrenner criticized the overreliance on laboratory techniques that focused on the ephemeral and unfamiliar. He challenged his colleagues to broaden the scope of their science to encompass the natural ecology shaping human development and behavior (Bronfenbrenner, 1974, p. 3). Bronfenbrenner's plea seemingly struck a responsive cord among colleagues seeking to broaden the boundaries of developmental phenomena. Parent–infant relationships were now being characterized as an "interactive network," peer relations and interpersonal competencies were being investigated, and attachment and empathy became the earmarks of prosocial behavior. The United Nations proclamation of 1979 as the International Year of the Child led to strengthening professional ties with psychologists in developing countries. Harold Stevenson and Urie Bronfenbrenner demonstrated how cross-cultural research could broaden the perspectives of psychologists grounded in Western conceptions of cognitive and moral development.

The Division 7 programs in the late 1970s also witnessed a resurgence of interest in studies of infancy and early development from the point of view of socialization processes. Factors influencing social competence, conceptions of gender, and mother–infant communication processes were given special emphases. Programs also devoted relatively more attention to the clinical dimensions of early development, such as the effects of prematurity, stress, and minor brain damage on learning and emotional development. In 1979, Claire Kopp made a notable contribution by identifying factors pertinent to the assessment of infants at risk in early development. In seminal research on empathy, Nancy Eisenberg challenged Kohlberg's premise that helping behavior in children is governed by whether there are inducements or penalties for failing to follow rules. Eisenberg and Fabes (1990) later found, contrary to James Q. Wilson (1993), that children do not react the same way to empathy-arousing situations involving distress. Children expressing sympathy are more assertive, less compliant, and less self-concerned than are those who avoid or withdraw from such situations.

The 1970s closed on a sour note for Division 7 when in 1980 conflict erupted over the APA's creation of a new lecture series in honor of G. Stanley Hall. Division officers were irked that the APA did not consult them before establishing the lecture series, and some expressed dismay at the APA's apparent indifference to considering acceptable alternatives (Masters, 1980; Pallak, 1980). Division President Lewis Lipsitt (1981) complained, to no avail, that using Hall's name for two different events was confusing and added that "the honor which we bestow is now diluted and misinterpreted by the recipients of the award."

THE POLITICS OF THE APA, APPLIED SCIENCE, AND INTERNATIONALISM: 1981 TO 1995·

As noted before, efforts were underway in the late 1970s to completely reorganize the APA. The APA was facing fiscal insolvency and was confronted with a crisis of confidence among members in its capacity to vigorously represent the profession and support the policy agendas of each division. New divisions continued to proliferate and the exponential increase in membership of clinicians posed an ominous threat to the effective representation of those involved in university-based scientific research. The division's stake in reorganization centered on how well the APA reorganization schemes represented the interests of academic researchers and how licensing would affect the emerging field of applied developmental psychology.

In 1978, the APA's Board of Directors appointed Dorothy Eichorn, president of Division 7 in 1969–1970, to cochair a special committee to report on issues pertaining to reorganization. At the time, some form of federated structure was preferred by most division members. This scheme entailed centralizing the staff and administration but permitted extensive autonomy and policy-making authority among the divisions. Another approach proposed splitting the APA into two sections—one professional and the other research–academic. This would give each existing division the opportunity to vote to affiliate with the section that most closely approximated its interests. Division 7 APA Council of Representatives did not find this idea appealing, according to Arnold Sameroff who said, "While we may have been founded with a primarily research and academic constituency, we have moved, as has APA itself, into more applied realms in both settings and practice" (Sameroff, 1981, p. 4). But the APA decided to squeeze reorganization discussions into this research–practice dichotomy by setting up two forums. This forced Division 7 council representatives to participate exclusively in Forum A to discuss their concerns about science issues, depriving them of an opportunity to address how clinical standards affected applied research.

The reorganization scheme that was eventually presented to the membership for a vote in 1988 reflected a tenuous compromise among contending interests. The plan, which failed by getting less than a two-thirds vote in favor, prompted several thousand academic researchers to form their own professional group, the American Psychological Society, in 1989. Sensing the need for reconciliation, the APA's Board of Directors author-

88   *THOMAS C. DALTON*

ized the chief executive officer to make several administrative and pro-grammatic changes to satisfy the diverse needs of its members. The creation of Directorates in Practice, Public Interest, Science and Other Areas was intended to provide a locus of representation for groups who shared common interests.

The appointment in 1990 of Lewis Lipsitt, who was president of Division 7 in 1981, as executive director of science was widely hailed by scientists and applied researchers. The respect Lipsitt commanded among scientists contributed to important achievements, which included the creation of a new interdisciplinary division in the National Science Foundation for the study of human behavior. Lipsitt's departure from the Science Directorate was untimely. Nevertheless, Lipsett generated significant support for his candidacy for president of the APA in 1994. Lipsitt promised to restore science as a constructive force, reduce divisiveness, and address the developmental problems associated with chronic poverty, such as homelessness, drug abuse, and school violence ("Division Fellow," 1993, p. 6). Lipsett came in second to Robert J. Resnick in the balloting in his first run for president in 1994. In his second attempt in 1995, Lipsitt lost to Dorothy Cantor after thwarting the APA's attempt to disqualify him from being placed on the ballot.

By the late 1970s, Division 7 leaders were feeling the pressure to clearly define and distinguish applied developmental research from clinical practice in order to prevent the imposition of inappropriate licensing guidelines that would unreasonably restrict research and the application of scientific knowledge. Frances Horowitz first broached this issue in 1977 when she created an ad hoc committee to investigate the need for a terminal master's degree in developmental assessment and intervention and an applied doctoral program. The following year, she cited the creation of a "developmental specialist" by the American Association of Psychiatric Services as a propitious time for Division 7 to do likewise because federal funds for training would be made available (Horowitz, May 1978, p. 15). Toward that end, Horowitz and William Kessen worked on criteria by which developmental psychologists could be included on the National Register of Health Providers (Hetherington, 1978, p. 9). The division leadership subsequently surveyed its members to determine how many members' institutions provided training for applied research. Of the 101 members responding, 46 indicated that such training was provided, but there was much variation in how the term *applied* was defined, with *child clinical psychology* listed most frequently (Shantz, 1980, p. 18).

The APA Council continued its rapid pace of accepting new divisions, despite the uncertainty as to how clinical and applied functions were to be differentiated for accreditation and licensing purposes. The APA Council approved the Division of Psychologists in Independent Practice in 1981, contending that the setting in which practice takes place should be given equal weight to that of substantive methods. Division 7 council member Arnold Sameroff expressed concern that the problematic issue of combining "a scientific discipline and a professional guild" should be "at the forefront of the reorganization program" (Sameroff, 1981, p. 3). Sameroff pointed out that two very different agendas had emerged in which clinicians sought increased leverage over services controlled by the medical profession, whereas researchers wanted to increase funding for the behavioral sciences. The APA leadership responded to these concerns the following year by creating the Research Support Network (a precursor to the Science Directorate) to provide researchers with a mechanism to increase awareness among congressional delegations about the need for federal support of behavioral research.

Division 7 also joined forces with Division 37 (Child, Youth, and Family Services) to formulate changes in the APA's code of ethics that would address issues of confidentiality and consent of children involved in research. This initiative was taken as an interim alternative to regulation through licensing. In addition, Gerald Koocher of Division 37 submitted a proposal that would give applied developmental psychologists access to training in medical and clinical settings (Shantz, 1982, p. 46). Although a consensus has yet to be reached on the issue of licensing and its impact on job placement, Division 7 leaders are seeking a rapprochement with Division 37 on this issue.

Irving Sigel and Rodney Cocking gave the fledgling field of applied developmental psychology greater professional visibility by founding an international journal in 1979 dedicated to multidisciplinary applied research across the life span. Cocking and Sigel assessed the state of the field through a review of journal articles as a part of a symposium on applied developmental psychology at the annual meeting in 1984. In 1991, a National Conference on Graduate Education in the Applications of Developmental Science Across the Life Span was organized to reach a consensus on the scope of the field, to devise curriculum including appropriate field experiences, and to develop models of graduate training (Fisher, et al., 1993). The conference was organized by a consortium of sponsors that included the APA Science Directorate; Division 7; SRCD; the Division of Adult, Development, and Aging; the Division of Child, Youth, and Family Services; the National Black Development Institute; the International Society of Infant Studies; and several other organizations. Frances Degen Horowitz and John W. Hagen gave keynote addresses putting the conference in historical perspective.

A significant consensus was achieved at this meeting to adopt resolutions embodying the principles, methods, and training of applied developmental scientists. The scope of the field is defined in terms that unmistakably reflected John Dewey's pragmatist ideals of connecting science and experience. The conferees agreed that applied developmental science views individual and family development as products of the interaction of biological, physical, and social environments that evolve over time through exposure to diverse cultural influences (Fisher, et al., 1993, p. 4). The goals of training would enable students to test and evaluate developmental theories and intervention strategies through field studies and experiences that use multiple levels of analysis to determine the factors promoting and impeding optimum human development in different institutional settings. Graduate education would draw on multiple disciplines such as pediatrics, gerontology, sociology, and other fields. These resolutions reflected the aims of the founders of Division 7 and the SRCD, who sought the widest possible application of developmental principles to problems and issues with significant societal consequences.

In recognition of the increased interest in cross-cultural psychology, Division 7 leadership authorized Bronfenbrenner to establish a new Committee on International Relations in Psychology in 1982. When he became division president in 1988, Herbert Pick further enhanced the work of this committee, now called the International Committee, by appointing members such as Barbara Rogoff, Lonnie Sherrod, and Richard Lerner who were well positioned to promote an international agenda. Patricia Greenfield, who chaired the International Committee in 1991, obtained support from the National Institute of Mental Health and William T. Grant Foundation to hold an international workshop, cosponsored by the International Society for the Study of Behavioral Development and headed by Harold Stevenson, to explore the differences in cognitive socialization of minority children. The workshop resulted in the publication of a special issue of the *International Journal of Behavioral Development* edited by Greenfield & Cocking, in 1993. Additional essays were collected in a book they titled *The Cross-Cultural Roots in Minority Child Development*, published in 1994.

The advent of poster sessions enabled the program chairs to accept a larger number of submitted proposals than before and cosponsorship expanded the number of total hours from 25 to 56. The division program through the 1980s and early 1990s continued to reflect the resurgence in research on infancy. Claire Kopp made conspicuous and thoughtful attempts to trace the path of self-regulation. Berry Brazelton presented a captivating assessment of early intervention strategies, and Philip R. Zelazo and Rochel Gelman offered incisive studies of infant cognition. Several addresses and symposia assessed federal programs: Zigler discussed Head Start and Lonnie Sherrod and Aletha Huston focused on Aid to Families with Dependent Children.

However, disappointingly meager attention has been paid in recent programs to the revolution in neuroscience and its contribution to understanding early development. Developmentalists cannot afford to neglect the relationship between brain and behavior without jeopardizing their status as scientists. Jerome Kagan's brilliant Division 7 G. Stanley Hall Award address at the 1995 APA meeting titled "Temperament and Development" suggests how personality and behavior are shaped in important ways by neurochemical processes. Moreover, Dutch developmental neurologist Bert Touwen for the first time to an American audience presented the results of years of research of prenatal and postnatal studies. The relative delay in such a presentation is indicative of the need for developmentalists to internationalize their contacts in this field. Touwen contended that it is the capacity to vary rather than the ability to approximate a norm, as Arnold Gesell proposed, that has primary diagnostic significance for development. Touwen indicated that the key to successful adaptation in infancy is the capacity to develop multiple motor strategies. This adaptive process commences prenatally and involves a series of neural and behavioral modifications that recalibrate motor and sensory capacities.

Advances in electroencephalography (i.e., study of brain waves), magnetic resonance imaging, and use of noninvasive ultrasound to study fetal growth also promise to revolutionize our understanding of the processes and patterns of early growth and development. Neurobehavioral research will also benefit from applying computer-assisted techniques to determine how transformations in neuroanatomical structures occur in ontogeny and to identify their effect on functional development. By employing these and other methods, developmental scientists will determine whether growth processes possess common attributes at the molecular, cellular, neural, and behavioral levels, and explain how they interact during development. Research of this kind will provide empirical concreteness now missing in theoretical debates about ontogeny.

Perhaps one of the most significant contributions to the history of developmental psychology was made by Ross Parke, president of Division 7 in 1990, who delivered a State of the Art Address in 1992, reviewing and synthesizing the work of the pioneers in the field. Parke and his collaborators, Peter Ornstein, John Reiser, and Carolyn Zahn-Waxler (1994), assembled a magnificent volume of essays that had been published under their editorship in *Developmental Psychology* in commemoration of the APA's centennial celebration in 1992. These remarkable essays, which documented the ideas and methods of pioneers such as G. Stanley Hall, James Mark Baldwin, John Dewey, Myrtle McGraw, Jean Piaget, Arnold Gesell, Nancy Bayley, and many others illuminated their profound and enduring impact on contemporary research. An invited symposium in 1995 titled "Myrtle McGraw and the Maturation Controversy Reconsidered" illustrated the importance of reexamining pioneering ideas long obscured by popular misconceptions in order to further elaborate their implications. Moreover, an invited address by Thomas Dalton, which reconstructed John Dewey's collaboration with Myrtle McGraw in the 1930s, showed how history can repay us by revealing unsuspected connections, which in

McGraw's case underscored the inseparable relationship between psychology and philosophy.

The division accumulated a distinguished list of award winners during the last decade and a half. Nancy Bayley was the first woman from the division to receive the American Psychological Foundation Gold Medal Award in 1982. Eleanor Maccoby and Jerome Kagan received the APA Distinguished Contribution to Science Award, and both gave inaugural lectures in the APA Distinguished Scientist Lecture Series in 1990. Sandra Scarr was recognized for her Distinguished Contribution for Research in Public Policy, and Urie Bronfenbrenner received the APA's Distinguished Contribution to Psychology in the Public Interest Award. In her 1993 presidential message, Anne Petersen (now deputy director of the National Science Foundation) said of Bronfenbrenner, "I believe that developmental science has advanced tremendously in the past decade since Urie Bronfenbrenner chastised us, appropriately, for being too narrow in scope" (Petersen, 1993, p. 1). Bronfenbrenner, who was the only member to serve twice as president of Division 7 (1957–1958 and 1987), received the G. Stanley Hall Award in 1985. Frances Graham was the first recipient of the American Psychological Society William James Fellowship in 1990 and was honored by the APA for her distinguished contribution to the science of infant development in the same year. Finally, Eleanor Gibson was awarded the prestigious National Medal of Science by President George Bush in 1992 for her research and theories about perceptual learning.

CONCLUSION

William Kessen (1979) stimulated considerable critical reflection among his Division 7 colleagues about the history and future of developmental psychology when he published his provocative essay, "The American Child and Other Cultural Inventions." His deceptively simple thesis is that our conceptions of childhood are shaped by unacknowledged assumptions deeply ingrained in our culture. Kessen singled out three preconceptions that include the notion that children are innocent and perfectible, that early childhood experiences carry lasting consequences, and that children can be isolated individually as scientific units of analysis. As Sheldon White aptly stated, developmental psychologists "have been living on borrowed history," using forms of knowledge that come from outside the field (Bronfenbrenner et al., 1986, p. 1220). Kessen and his colleagues Urie Bronfenbrenner, Frank Kessel, and Sheldon White had the occassion to revisit Kessen's thesis in a symposium in 1985 (see Bronfenbrenner et al., 1986). Their differing views about science and culture are pertinent in drawing some conclusions about the history of Division 7.

Kessen has contended that the progressive evolutionary presumption that children are perfectible no longer seems tenable in this era of deconstruction and moral relativism. Nevertheless, Kessen has argued that Dewey offers a viable alternative by positing growth as an open-ended potential rather than as an end-driven function of human development (Bronfenbrenner et al., 1986, p. 1223). Dewey and McGraw found that the relatively similar outward appearance of human anatomy and reflexes conceals a far greater potential for variation and psychological change through growth processes than is imagined possible by either genetic alteration or environmental influences (Dalton & Bergenn, 1996).

Bronfenbrenner concurred with Kessen but contended that developmentalists have generally failed to carry forward epigenetic biological analyses: "Once we get beyond early childhood, the notion of a complex integrated organism is forgotten" (Bronfenbrenner et al., 1986, p. 1219). Indeed, the first developmentalist, Wilhelm Preyer, was an embryologist, and Gesell and McGraw's work was enriched by that growth perspective. Yet Division 7 has given almost no attention to research in the field of developmental biology (see Dalton, 1995; Oppenheim, 1992). Leonard Carmichael and Donald Hebb (winner of the G. Stanley Hall Award in 1983) participated in a symposium on the ontogeny of learning in the early 1960s. Gilbert Gottlieb was the last major figure to present research on bonding in prenatal development in 1966 until Dutch neurologist Bert Touwen gave an invited address in 1995 (Touwen, 1995). The revolution in the neurosciences offers developmentalists more powerful tools, should they avail themselves of them, to understand the development and transformation of the brain and behavior throughout the life span.

Another issue that engaged Kessen and his colleagues in debate was how to explain the historically shifting priorities considered worthy of research by developmental psychologists. White argued that the waxing and waning of specific areas of research reflects changes in our cultural values, federal policies, and funding priorities, and that the "modularization" of knowledge is a necessary consequence of this policy–research cycle (Bronfenbrenner et al., 1986, pp. 1221–1222).

We certainly find examples in the foregoing history of how science and policy interact to alter cultural views about the forms of behavior that are considered normal and those that are problematic. Consider the shift in attention from personality factors contributing to delinquent behavior to the analysis of factors contributing to moral development. Science led us away from a preoccupation with aggression and conformity when Piaget, Kohlberg, and their followers demonstrated that children were capable of judgment and reasoning and that they preferred to govern their own behavior by rules rather than by capriciousness. Their theories became a part of our culture largely because they gained acceptance among a wide spectrum of scientists and educators. The replacement of the study of gender differences in role taking by analyzing gender as an instrument of cognitive differentiation and gender-role stereotyping offers another example. This shift occurred in part because science led parents, siblings, students, and teachers to question the desirability and fairness of treating differently individuals who possessed the same mental and physical capabilities and potential.

As Kessen astutely observed, what developmental psychologists choose to study ultimately entails moral judgments whose certainty depends on science. As Head Start illustrates, however, the scientific community cannot provide policy makers the consensus they seek to advance policies considered beneficial when they are divided over fundamental questions about human development. The premise that early childhood experiences are indelible remains an article of faith primarily because it furnishes justification for proponents of vastly different policies (i.e., learning readiness and child abuse prevention) to hold parents and other care givers responsible for the positive and negative consequences of their children's development. Developmental science can help mitigate this quandary by increasing our knowledge about how neurological, biological, and social factors interact to shape human experience.

The extraordinary involvement of Division 7 in federal policies reveals the limitations of science in politics. Politicians and their policy advisers ultimately control the agenda and process in which priorities are set. As Head Start vividly illustrates, public policies are subjected to incremental and ideologically unstable legislative processes that favor ambiguity rather than clarity and subordinate comprehensiveness to questions of cost and feasability. Developmental scientists seeking policy influence have been challenged to find new applications that require them to question and reassess the foundations of their knowledge on a continual basis. The rigorous scrutiny by developmentalists of the professional status of their discipline may prove beneficial, as long as basic research is not sacrificed because it lacks immediate applications. However, division leaders have also made a consistent and concerted effort to counter the centrifugal forces pulling researchers and clinicians apart by using science to define an agenda for organizational collaboration, reconciliation, and human advancement. Division members have also exercised their responsibility as scientists to disseminate the results of their research in a form that is accessible to the broadest possible popular audiences so the public can benefit from science, too.

Bronfenbrenner has argued that researchers today are finding "complementarities" among biological, cognitive, and social aspects of development, and they are finding commonalties among families, classrooms, and other social systems (Bronfenbrenner et al., 1986). Laboratory studies of infants and children increasingly rely on naturalistic experiments that give free play to individual capabilities. The members of Division 7 have definitely enlarged the boundaries of the individual, social, and national laboratories in which they practice their science. That trend shows promise, if nothing else, in revealing the potential of science to transform U.S. culture.

REFERENCES

Bayley, N. (1953, November 23). President's Report. *Division 7 Newsletter*, pp. 1–2.

Block, J. (1977, December). Report of the secretary. *Division 7 Newsletter*, pp. 42–45.

Block, J. (1978, December). Report of the treasurer. *Division 7 Newsletter*, pp. 22–24.

Block, J. (1979, Fall). Report of the secretary. *Division 7 Newsletter*, pp. 11–13.

Bronfenbrenner, U. (1954, May). Report of the policy and planning committee. *Division 7 Newsletter*, pp. 1–6.

Bronfenbrenner, U. (1957, Spring). Report of the policy and planning committee. *Division 7 Newsletter*, pp. 1–4.

Bronfenbrenner, U. (1974). Developmental research, public policy and the ecology of childhood. *Child Development, 45*, 1–5.

Bronfenbrenner, U., Kessel, F., Kessen, W., & White, S. (1986). Toward a critical social history of developmental psychology. *American Psychologist, 41*, 1218–1230.

By-laws for the Division of Developmental Psychology of the American Psychological Association. (1954, September).

Capshew, J. H., & Hilgard, E. R. (1992). The power of service: World War II and professional reform in the American Psychological Association. In R. B. Evans, V. S. Sexton, & T. C. Cadwallader (Eds.), *100 years. The American Psychological Association: A historical perspective* (pp. 149–176). Washington, DC: American Psychological Association.

Cater, D., & Strickland, S. (1975). *TV violence and the child: The evolution and fate of the Surgeon General's Report.* New York: Sage.

Child Advocacy Survey. (1979, Fall). *Division 7 Newsletter*, pp. 32–33.

Cobb, K. (1951, May 5). Report of the liason committee on problems concerning the certification of clinical child psychologists. *Division 7 Newsletter*, pp. 1–3.

Cravens, H. (1993). *Before Head Start: The Iowa station and America's children.* Chapel Hill: University of North Carolina Press.

Dalton, T. C. (1995a). Challenging the group bias of American culture. *Contemporary Psychology, 40*, 201–204.

Dalton, T. C. (1995b). McGraw's alternative to Gesell's maturationist theory. In T. C. Dalton & V. W. Bergenn (Eds.), *Beyond heredity and environment: Myrtle McGraw and the maturation controversy.* Boulder, CO: Westview Press.

Dalton, T. C., & Bergenn, V. W. (Eds.). (1995). *Beyond heredity and environment: Myrtle McGraw and the maturation controversy.* Boulder, CO: Westview Press.

Dalton, T. C., & Bergenn, V. W. (1996). John Dewey, Myrtle McGraw and *Logic:* An unusual collaboration in the 1930's. *Studies in History and the Philosophy of Science, 27,* 69–107.

Division Activities. (1949, December 1). *Division 7 Newsletter,* pp. 1–3.

Division fellow Lew Lipsitt makes run for the presidency. (1993, Spring–Summer). *Division 7 Newsletter,* p. 6

Eisenberg, N., & Fabes, R. A. (1990). Empathy: Conceptualization, measurement, and relation to pro-social behavior. *Motivation and Emotion, 14,* 131–149.

First science writer's news briefing held. (1978, December). *Division 7 Newsletter,* pp. 36–37.

Fisher, C., Murray, J. P., Dill, J. R., Hagan, J. W., Hogan, M. J. Lerner, R. M., Rebok, G. W., Sigel, I., Sostek, A. M., Smyer, M. A., Spencer, M. B., & Wilcox, B. (1993). Report of the national conference on graduate education in the applications of developmental science across the life span. *Journal of Applied Developmental Psychology, 14,* 1–7.

Fowler, R. D. (1992). The American Psychological Association: 1985–1992. In R. B. Evans, V. S. Sexton, & T. C. Cadwallader (Eds.), *100 years. The American Psychological Association: A historical perspective.* Washington DC: American Psychological Association.

Gewirtz, J. L. (1951, December 15). Report of committee on publications. *Division 7 Newsletter,* p. 3.

Greenfield, P. & Cocking, R. (Eds.). (1993). Special issue: International roots of minority child development. *International Journal of Behavioral Development, 16,* 385–506.

Greenfield, P., & Cocking, R. (Eds.). (1994). *The cross cultural roots of minority child development.* Hillsdale, NJ: Lawrence Erlbaum.

Grotevant, H. (1975, February). Division 7 touched by certification talks. *Division 7 Newsletter,* pp. 8–10.

Hartup, W. (1975, Winter). Text of executive committee letter. *Division 7 Newsletter,* pp. 3–5.

Hetherington, M. (1973, Winter). Secretary's report. *Division 7 Newsletter,* pp. 21–22.

Hetherington, M. (1978, December). Message from the president. *Division 7 Newsletter,* pp. 8–9.

Horowitz, F. D. (1978, May). President's message. *Division 7 Newsletter,* pp. 15–16.

Keith-Spiegel, P. (1978, May). On child advocacy: Projects within the Division. *Division 7 Newsletter,* pp. 20–23.

Kessen, W. (1979). The American child and other cultural inventions. *American Psychologist, 34,* 815–820.

Lee, L. C. (1977, December). Newsletter editor report. *Division 7 Newsletter,* p. 55.

Lipsitt, L. P. (1981, April 21). Letter to S. H. Osipow. Archives of the American Psychological Association, Manuscript Division, Library of Congress, Washington, D.C.

Maccoby, E. (1972, Winter). President's report. *Division 7 Newsletter*, pp. 31–34.

Masters, J. C. (1980, September 15). Memorandum to T. G. Burish. Archives of the American Psychological Association, Manuscript Division, Library of Congress, Washington, D.C.

McCall, R. (1977, Spring). Report of the program committee. *Division 7 Newsletter*, pp. 52–54.

McCall, R. (1984, Spring). Report of the public information committee. *Division 7 Newsletter*, pp. 17–18.

McCandless, B. (1975, November). Wanted: New members. *Division 7 Newsletter*, pp. 39–40.

O'Connell, A. N., & Russo, N. F. (Eds.). (1983). *Models of achievement: Reflections of eminent women in psychology*. New York: Columbia University Press.

O'Connell, A. N., & Russo, N. F. (Eds.). (1990). *Women in psychology: A biobibliographic sourcebook*. New York: Greenwood Press.

Oppenheim, R. W. (1992). Pathways in the emergence of developmental neuroethology: Antecendents to current views of neurobehavioral ontogeny. *Journal of Neurobiology, 23*, 1370–1403.

Pallak, M. S. (1980, November 28). Letter to J. C. Masters. Archives of the American Psychological Association, Manuscript Division, Library of Congress, Washington, D.C.

Pallak, M. S. (1992). Growth, conflict and public policy: The American Psychological Association from 1970 to 1985. In R. B. Evans, V. S. Sexton, & T. C. Cadwallader (Eds.), *100 years. The American Psychological Association: A historical perspective*. Washington, DC: American Psychological Association.

Parke, R. D., Ornstein, P., Reiser, J., & Zahn-Waxler, C. (Eds.). (1994). *A century of developmental psychology*. Washington, DC: American Psychological Association.

Parke, R., & Slaby, R. (1983). The development of aggression. In P. Mussen (Ed.), *Handbook of child psychology*, Vol. 4 (pp. 581–605). New York: Wiley.

Petersen, A. (1993, Fall–Winter). President's message. *Division 7 Newsletter*, pp. 1–2.

Radke-Yarrow, M. (1977, December). Report of the information committee. *Division 7 Newsletter*, p. 48.

Rheingold, H. L. (1973, Winter). Report from members of the Council of Representatives of the APA. *Division 7 Newsletter*, pp. 34–38.

Rheingold, H. L. (1984b). The first twenty-five years of the Society for Research in Child Development. *Monographs of the Society for Research in Child Development, 50*, (Serial No. 6).

Richmond, J. (1974). Interview with Milton Senn. Oral history of child development research. National Library of Medicine, Bethesda, MD.

Rowland, L. W. (1974, November). The story of Division 7's G. Stanley Hall Award. *Division 7 Newsletter*, pp. 15–16.

Sameroff, A. (1981, Spring). Report from the APA Council. *Division 7 Newsletter*, pp. 3–7.

Scarr, S. (1975, February). Results of the survey of job placements for new Ph.D.s in developmental psychology (1973–1974). *Division 7 Newsletter*, pp. 6–7.

Shantz, C. U. (1980, Fall). Report of meetings of the executive committee of Division 7. *Division 7 Newsletter*, pp. 15–20.

Shantz, C. U. (1982, Fall). Minutes of the meetings of the executive committee of Division 7. *Division 7 Newsletter*, pp. 45–48.

Siegal, A. (1975). The effects of television on children and adolescents. *Journal of Communications, 25,* 14–24.

Sigel, I. (1971, Winter). Report of the secretary. *Division 7 Newsletter*, p. 24.

Smuts, A. B. (1986). The National Research Council committee on child development and the founding of the Society for Research in Child Development, 1925–1933. *Monographs of the Society for Research in Child Development, 50* (Serial No. 6).

Spiker, H. H., Hodges, W., & McCandless, B. (1966). A diagnostically based curriculum for psycho-socially deprived, pre-school, mentally retarded children. *Exceptional Children, 33,* 215–220.

Sugarman, J. (1974). Interview with Milton Senn. Oral history of child development research. National Library of Medicine. Bethesda, MD.

Television and growing up: The impact of televised violence. (1972). Report to the Surgeon General, U.S. Public Health Service, from the Surgeon General's Scientific Advisory Committee on Television and Social Behavior. Washington DC: U.S. Government Printing Office.

Touwen, B. C. L. (1995, August 14). Variability as the norm of neurobehavioral development. Invited address for Division 7 of the American Psychological Association, New York.

Updegraff, R., & C. Stendler (1951, December 15). Report of committee on ethics with regard to children. *Division 7 Newsletter*, pp. 4–5.

Wilson, J. Q. (1993). *The Moral Sense.* New York: Basic Books.

Wolfe, D. (1947, April 24). Letter to T. W. Richards. Archives of the American Psychological Association, Manuscript Division, Library of Congress, Washington, D.C.

Zigler, E. (1972, Winter). Letter of resignation. *Division 7 Newsletter*, pp. 7–9.

Zigler, E., & Muenchow, S. (1992). *Head Start: The inside story of America's most successful educational experiment.* New York: Basic Books.

4

A HISTORY OF DIVISION 16
(SCHOOL PSYCHOLOGY):
RUNNING TWICE AS FAST

THOMAS K. FAGAN

The Division of School Psychologists (the name was changed to School Psychology in 1969) was founded as an official part of the proposed amendments to American Psychological Association (APA) bylaws at the 52nd APA Convention on September 12, 1944, in Cleveland, Ohio (Olson, 1944). These bylaws served during the transitional year 1944 to 1945 and were finalized at the 53rd Annual Convention, which took place September 6 to 8, 1945, at Northwestern University in Evanston, Illinois (Olson, 1945). It is difficult for contemporary school psychologists to comprehend the landscape of their field at the time Division 16 was founded, which accompanied the reorganization of the APA in 1944 to 1945. There

Portions of this chapter are reprinted from the *Journal of School Psychology*, 31(1), with kind permission from Elsevier Science Ltd., The Boulevard, Langford Land, Kidlington OX5 1GB UK. The title is taken in part from a division presidential address by Kathryn D'Evelyn (1961). D'Evelyn was quoting from *Through the Looking Glass* by Lewis Carroll (the pen name for Charles Dodgson) published in 1871. The author expresses appreciation for assistance from the Archives of the History of American Psychology, the Library of Congress, the Division Services Office of the APA, and the numerous correspondents over the years whose archival items and perceptions have been most helpful. Thanks also to Donald Dewsbury, Randy Kamphaus, Beeman Phillips, Carol Philpot, Donald Routh, and Ronda Talley for their comments on the manuscript. Portions of the manuscript are based on an unpublished paper on the early history of Division 16 (Fagan, 1990a) and a published paper on school psychology's organizational history with permission of the *Journal of School Psychology* (Fagan, 1993). Although the author serves as Division 16 historian, the opinions expressed herein are his own and do not necessarily reflect official positions of the division or its leadership.

were probably fewer than 1,000 practicing school psychologists in the United States at that time. Most of these were in urban locales in the East, Midwest, and West Coast; almost all were employed in school settings; and annual salaries were in the $1,000–$4,000 range, with a median salary below $3,000 (Cornell, 1942; Fagan, 1995a). Perhaps a dozen states offered certification for practice through their respective state departments of education, and no state had yet achieved licensure for the private practice of psychology. There were only one or two state associations of school psychologists, fewer than a half dozen graduate level training programs specifically for school psychologists, and only a few books written about the field. Having no journal specific to school psychological services, school psychology's professional and technical writings were scattered among education and psychology journals. The identity of school psychology itself was spread among those who viewed themselves as primarily clinical psychologists in school settings, educational psychologists, and consulting psychologists. In comparison to several groups of applied psychologists, the situation for school psychology was so tenuous at the time that it is surprising that divisional status was granted.

School psychologists, under various titles, had been practicing since the establishment of the first psychological clinic at the University of Pennsylvania in 1896. For several decades those seeking organizational representation joined the National Education Association (NEA), the APA, the short-lived American Association of Clinical Psychologists (1917–1919) and its offspring the APA Division of Clinical Psychologists (founded in 1919), the Association of Consulting Psychologists, and the American Association of Applied Psychologists (AAAP). Because a doctorate degree was often required for membership in these groups (except the NEA), and most people practicing school psychology did not hold a doctorate, in the first half of the twentieth century most school psychology practitioners were not affiliated with any national group. The development of these groups reflected the gradual emergence of broad specialties in applied psychology, the refinement of which would appear in the divisional structure of the APA. Historical information about these early groups of applied psychologists appears in Fagan (1990a; 1993), Fernberger (1943), Hilgard (1987), and Wallin (1938).

The Division of School Psychologists was 1 of 19 original APA divisions. Created amid controversy as to how much segmentation the field of psychology could withstand (see, e.g., Doll, 1946), the divisional structure represented the specializations that were already apparent to academics and practitioners and the applied groups within the AAAP; that is, the clinical, consulting, educational, industrial and business, and military sections of the AAAP were continued as divisions in the reorganized APA. The reorganization had simply allowed the APA to catch up with the emerging divisions within the field itself, especially within applied psychology.

For school psychologists, the creation of a separate division was a long-awaited recognition of the uniqueness of their services to school settings and children. Although school psychologists were previously represented within the AAAP's sections for clinical and educational psychology, they did not have the identity they preferred and were dissatisfied with having to share their representation with academics. Archival records indicate the lines of tension then extant and provide an explanation for the creation of Division 16, which in its first years limited membership to practitioners in school settings (Symonds & English, 1938). These records strongly suggest that an APA division for school psychologists evolved out of the AAAP, principally from the Educational Section (Fryer, 1937).

However, separate divisional status would not erase the decades of evolutionary influence on school psychology from both Witmerian clinical psychology and Hallian child study and educational psychology (Fagan, 1992). Although some division members viewed school psychology as clinical psychology applied to school settings, others viewed school psychology as more an applied educational psychology that emphasized academic development, curriculum, and program planning. Division membership varied along several lines: clinical versus educational applications; mental health versus academic problem orientations; preparation as psychologists versus preparation as educators; as well as those from public school, private school, and residential settings. Different training backgrounds in psychology and teacher education created confused identities and mixed loyalties for several decades (see, e.g., Darley & Berdie, 1940). The variations are still observable both in the division and the field at large. Even today division membership can be viewed along several axes in terms of the members' backgrounds, orientations, roles and functions, and settings, with modal groups gravitating toward clinical and educational psychology.

The perception that school psychology was (or should be) clinical psychology applied to educational settings derives historically from the fact that many school psychologists were trained as clinical psychologists and brought both psychometric and mental health orientations to the public and private schools. A contrasting perception of the field has been that school psychology was (or should be) applied educational psychology. In terms of the history of school psychologist training, it is clear that early programs drew on both clinical and educational psychology content (both fields emerged between 1890 and 1920), and many were housed in colleges of education; the first program specifically titled *school psychology* was in the School of Education at New York University (Fagan, 1995b). Among the current APA accredited doctoral programs in school psychology (which total 49, including 5 combined programs), at least two thirds continue to hold an affiliation with their institution's education college (APA-Accredited Doctoral Programs, 1995). The uniqueness of the school psychology specialty rests, in part, in its blend of both clinical and educational psychology contributions. The blend is observed in every statement of training and practice guidelines produced by Division 16 and those of its contemporary counterpart, the National Association of School Psychologists. The field, therefore, may be observed on a continuum, the extremes of which are reflected in predominantly clinical or educational orientations. Even though most members of the field are not at the extremes of this continuum, conflicts continue to arise from the dual orientations (e.g., the differences that exist between the advocates of traditional psychological assessment and the advocates of curriculum-based assessment). Such controversies can be observed throughout the history of the field, even in Witmer's clinical work. Thus, the uniqueness of school psychology is not just a matter of setting-specific applications, even though most practitioners continue to work in school settings. The dual contributions of psychology and education are central to understanding the history of school psychology and Division 16. This chapter discusses three periods of Division 16 history: the early years: 1944–1950; the middle years: 1950–1970; and recent history: 1970–present.

EARLY YEARS: 1944 TO 1950

In its first several years, the Division of School Psychologists struggled for survival and stability. Chief among these struggles were challenges from the large number of APA divisions. Had these challenges been successful, the division might have been forced to merge with Division 12 (Clinical) or Division 15 (Educational). Even though a few mergers did occur, they were voluntary and did not include Division 16. For example, in 1946, Division 12 (Clinical) was merged with Division 11 (Abnormal Psychology and Psychotherapy) to become the Division of Clinical and Abnormal Psychology, reverting back again to Clinical Psychology in 1954. Historical information on APA policies as related to divisions appears in Horai (1982).

The first threat occurred during 1944 to 1945 as the final draft of the APA constitution was being prepared. Suggestions to merge or reduce the 19 proposed divisions to as few as 10 divisions failed. A second threat emanated in 1946 from the Division Organization Committee, which recommended a smaller divisional structure based on a previous survey (Doll, 1946). This effort, spearheaded by Edgar Doll, failed for several reasons (see Fagan, 1990a; 1993). Instead of scaling back in its early years, the reorganized APA chose to add a division in 1945 (Psychology of Adulthood and Old Age, changed to Adult Development and Aging in 1970) and began adding divisions more regularly in 1956 and after (Hildreth, 1985). The threatened existence of Division 16 reemerged in 1949 as part of a 5-year review of APA organizational structure by its Policy and Planning Board. Despite several surveys on the issue, Division 16 survived perhaps as a result of Boring's (1949) explanation that divisions, even if weak, ought not to be eliminated when they are not causing the organization any harm. Wolfle's (1948) analysis suggested that the Division of School Psychologists was healthy in several respects, despite ranking 19th (out of 20) in division membership size and lagging in setting criteria for, and the electing of, fellows. For example, with only 88 members, the division had few resignations, few persons declining nomination to division offices, ranked second in percentage of members attending the 1947 business meeting, and ranked first in percentage of members voting in the 1948 election. Another analysis revealed rapid growth in the division's membership; its rank rose from 17th out of 18 divisions in 1948 to 11th out of 17 divisions in 1949 ("Our Division in Comparison With Others," 1949).

Organizational Structure and Development

Concurrent with these threats was the division's struggle to achieve organizational stability in elections, governance, membership, finances, and services. Few records of the division's activities between 1944 and 1947 exist. Archival records suggest that in its first few years Division 16 was loosely organized, kept few records, had difficulty conducting elections and business, and even appears to have had no letterhead or newsletter. The division's management, from elections to finances and committee appointments, was not stabilized until 1946 to 1947. The first officers of the division were temporary appointments made by the APA Division Organization Committee for 1944 to 1945, and their primary duties were to secure names and assist with the first elections in 1945 and to serve until the first elected officers were installed in 1945 to 1946. Warren W. Coxe served as temporary chair and Wilda Mae Rosebrook was temporary secretary (Hilgard, 1945). Subsequent division executive leadership appear in Tables 11 and 12. Although I occasionally mention names of specific individuals relevant to the history of Division 16, or they are listed in Tables 11 and 12, I have intentionally refrained from naming specific contributors to the division's history. Because of the numerous contributors to the success of Division 16, it would not be possible to do justice to them all in this chapter. Biographical sketches of several division leaders appear in Fagan and Warden (1996) and occasionally in the division's newsletter.

The earliest minutes appear to be from the meeting of September 6, 1946. The informality of operations is suggested by the statement, "After some discussion of means of activating the Division, it was moved, seconded, and passed that the twenty persons present constitute themselves

TABLE 11
Presidents of Division 16*

1944–1945	Warren W. Coxe (temporary)
1945–1946	Morris Krugman
1946–1947	Harry J. Baker
1947–1948	Margaret E. Hall-Powers
1948–1949	Ethel L. Cornell
1949–1950	Bertha M. Luckey
1950–1951	Wilda M. Rosebrook
1951–1952	George Meyer
1952–1953	Frances A. Mullen
1953–1954	Milton A. Saffir
1954–1955	Judith I. Krugman
1955–1956	James R. Hobson
1956–1957	Gertrude P. Driscoll
1957–1958	May V. Seagoe**
1958–1959	Frederick Barton Davis
1959–1960	Thelma G. Voorhis
1960–1961	Katherine E. D'Evelyn
1961–1962	Albert J. Harris
1962–1963	Keith J. Perkins
1963–1964	Ralph H. Tindall
1964–1965	Winifred S. Scott
1965–1966	Susan W. Gray
1966–1967	William Itkin
1967–1968	Boyd R. McCandless
1968–1969	Edward L. French
1969–1970	Jack I. Bardon
1970–1971	Mary Alice White
1971–1972	Rosa A. Hagin
1972–1973	James F. Magary
1973–1974	Julia R. Vane
1974–1975	Virginia D. C. Bennett
1975–1976	Mary Jo MacGregor
1976–1977	Joseph L. French
1977–1978	Irwin A. Hyman
1978–1979	Bartell W. Cardon
1979–1980	Merle L. Meacham
1980–1981	Calvin O. Dyer
1981–1982	Marcia B. Schaffer
1982–1983	Judith L. Alpert
1983–1984	Thomas D. Oakland
1984–1985	Joel Meyers
1985–1986	Beeman N. Phillips
1986–1987	Walter B. Pryzwansky
1987–1988	Barbara R. Slater
1988–1989	Jane Close Conoley
1989–1990	Sylvia Rosenfield
1990–1991	Roy P. Martin
1991–1992	Jonathan H. Sandoval
1992–1993	Stephen T. DeMers

1993–1994	Cindy I. Carlson
1994–1995	Randy W. Kamphaus
1995–1996	Jan N. Hughes
1996–1997	James Paavola

*The original name of Division 16 was the Division of School Psychologists. It was changed to School Psychology in 1969. Coxe was appointed to serve as temporary chair of the division during the first year of the APA reorganization. Others presided as the result of election.
**Eloise Cason had been elected for this term (1957–1958), but she resigned on doctor's orders during her president–elect term (1956–1957). Seagoe was subsequently elected by the Executive Committee (Minutes, 1957).

the Division of School Psychologists for the purpose of considering and passing the by-laws." (Minutes, September 6, 1946, p. 1). This small group apparently approved the first bylaws during the business meeting at the 1946 APA convention. The bylaws were amended the following year and revised in 1949 to contain nine articles covering the division's name and objectives, membership, officers, executive committee, procedures for the nomination and election of officers, meetings, committees, dues, and amendments. The purposes of the division were to (a) provide opportunities for professional fellowship and for the exchange of professional ideas among school psychologists, (b) advance the professional status of school psychologists, and (c) promote and maintain high standards of professional service among its members. The 1949 division bylaws defined a school psychologist as "a psychologist a major portion of whose work is the application of clinical psychological techniques to children and adolescents presenting problems in school, or the psychological supervision of psychologists doing such work" (By-Laws of the Division of School Psychologists, 1949, p. 1). The definition was still in effect in the bylaws of 1956. Further interpretation of the bylaws allowed for a school psychologist to "include those giving clinical service to college students" and those in a child guidance clinic or university clinic "only if a majority of cases are school problems and he makes recommendations to or consults with school officials in those cases" (Advisory Ballot, 1949, p. 2).

Consistent with APA policy, Division 16 had three classes of membership: associate, fellowship and life. Officers of the division included president, president-elect, and three members-at-large of the executive committee, all of whom held 1-year terms; secretary–treasurer, who held a 3-year term; and divisional representatives to the APA Council of Representatives, whose terms were determined by the APA. The officers and the immediate past-president constituted the Executive Committee, which could act by mail or physically but whose decisions "were subject to review by the annual meeting of the Division" (By-Laws of the Division of School Psychologists, 1949, p. 3). The only standing committees were the Executive Committee, the Membership Committee, the Program Committee, and the Nominating and Elections Committee. Other committees were established as needed by a vote of the division or the Executive Committee.

TABLE 12
Secretaries and Treasurers of Division 16*

Secretary

1944–1945	Wilda Mae Rosebrook (temporary)
1945–1946	Ethel L. Cornell
1946–1952	Milton A. Saffir
1952–1955	Frederick Barton Davis
1955–1958	Harriet E. O'Shea
1958–1961	Keith J. Perkins
1961–1962	Harry B. Gilbert
1962–1964	William Itkin
1964–1967	Edward L. French
1967–1970	Rosa A. Hagin
1970–1973	Bartell W. Cardon
1973–1976	Irwin A. Hyman
1976–1979	Calvin O. Dyer
1979–1982	Thomas D. Oakland
1982–1985	Walter B. Pryzwansky
1985–1988	Krista J. Stewart
1988–1991	James L. Carroll
1991–1994	Deborah J. Tharinger
1995–1997	Sandra L. Christensen

Treasurer

1944–1948	No position specified
1949–1952	Milton A. Saffir
1952–1954	James R. Hobson
1954–1957	Harold A. Delp
1957–1960	George A. Stouffer
1960–1963	Warren A. Ketcham
1963–1966	James M. Dunlap
1966–1969	William H. Ashbaugh
1969–1972	Henry Platt
1972–1974	Ann E. Boehm
1974–1978	Carol P. Hunter
1978–1981	Judith L. Alpert
1981–1984	Beeman N. Phillips
1984–1987	Sylvia A. Rosenfield
1987–1988	Jean Ramage
1988–1989	Susan G. Foreman**
1989–1992	Randy W. Kamphaus
1993–1995	Stephen F. Poland
1996–1998	Ena Vazquez Nuttal

* It appears these offices were combined from 1946 to 1952. There does not appear to have been a separate treasurer position before 1946. The first official listing in the *American Psychologist* of the division having a combined secretary–treasurer is for 1949 to 1950. The offices were split starting in 1952 to 1953.
** Susan Foreman lost the 1987 election for treasurer to Jean Ramage. Ramage served 2 years until her appointment in the APA Practice Directorate, at which time Foreman was asked to fill the unexpired term.

All committee members were appointed by the president with executive committee approval and served only for the term of the president (Fagan, 1993).

Information regarding early elections and their implications appears in Fagan (1990a). Despite inconsistent practices and some remaining mysteries, the election process stabilized by 1948. The 1946 to 1947 election was the first in which a president-elect and a combined secretary–treasurer position were elected. Of anecdotal interest is the 1949 to 1950 election for president-elect, which ended in a tie between Wilda Rosebrook and Elizabeth Woods. Woods won the election by a drawing of straws but was unable to serve because she was appointed educational consultant to the U.S. military authorities in Japan. The division's executive committee then elected Rosebrook as president for 1950 to 1951. Thus, the division's first secretary became the first person to serve as president by choice of the executive committee. Tables 11 and 12 reveal the frequency of such ascendancy and suggest a strong process of grooming division leadership over time.

Finance and Membership

The division was financially weak at this time. With a 1946 to 1947 allocation of $180 from the APA for "postage, correspondence, divisional letterheads, distribution of by-laws, circulation of a nominating ballot," the division lacked resources for anything but the basics (Baker, 1946, p. 1). Table 13 reflects the fragile nature of its finances; deficits were common in the early years, though the division achieved a small but balanced budget by 1950. The cost for division affiliation was $1 a year and no division assessment fee was charged until 1948 ($2 a year). Thus, by 1950 the division's revenue came almost completely from APA division dues and division assessment (or $3 a year per division member). The current revenues per member are more than 12 times as much. Finances were managed on a calendar-year basis whereas leadership served on a September-to-September basis. The practice of holding outgoing and incoming executive committee meetings and a business meeting during the annual convention continued until about 1990 when the leadership cycle was changed to conform to that of the APA. With the exception of midyear council meetings, early division leaders were seldom able to meet together between conventions. Table 14 reveals the relatively small membership during this period, and though it grew steadily, Division 16 membership remained small compared to most other divisions. Further, in 1948 many division members belonged to other divisions; with only 88 members, 38.6% also belonged to Division 12 (Clinical and Abnormal) and 30.7% to Division 15 (Educational) ("Our Division in Comparison With Others," 1949). In

TABLE 13
Division 16 Financial Data*

Source Date	Financial/Item or Data
August 1948	$ 28.90 (deficit paid by APA)
August 1949	$ 372.80 (deficit)
End of 1949	$ 187.81 (deficit)
December 1950	$ 845 (first balanced budget)
May 1952	$ 910 (surplus)
January, 1953	$ 1,035 Budget
1955–1956	$ 1,370 Budget
1960–1961	$ 2,850 Budget
1963–1964	$ 3,650 Budget
1966–1967	$ 4,840 Budget
1968–1969	$ 5,415 Budget
Division and Institute Accounts Merged in 1970–1971	
1971–1972	$20,977 Budget
1975–1976	$21,950 Budget
1977–1978	$23,400 Budget
1980–1981	$27,755 Budget
1982–1983	$29,100 Budget
1983–1984	$30,325 Budget
1984–1985	$37,075 Budget
1985–1986	$47,885 Budget
1986–1987	$52,600 Proposed budget
1988–1989	$61,396 Budget
1990–1991	$60,025 Budget
1992–1993	$66,348 Budget
1993–1994	$67,915 Budget
1994–1995	$77,546 Budget
1995	$79,896 Budget
1996	$52,892 Budget request

* The financial data are based on information in newsletters, minutes, and miscellaneous reports.

recent years, at least half of the division's membership belong to one or more other divisions (Fagan, 1993).

In sharp contrast to contemporary division leadership, those serving in the early years were usually practitioners. This reflects the division's intent to represent practicing psychologists in school settings and the fact that few training programs were available in school psychology (Fagan, 1986a). It was also common for the mixed loyalties of school psychologists to be expressed in service to other divisions, especially those of clinical, consulting, and educational psychology, which may explain why some people held positions in two divisions concurrently.

Division Activities

The services of Division 16 were limited to a few active committees, convention programs, and a newsletter whose publication schedule seemed erratic.

TABLE 14
Division Membership Data*

Source Date	Number of Members
1947	72
April 1948	88
August 1948	184
February 1949	229
August 1950	276
May 1954	300
January 1957	600
October 1959	735
November 1961	900
January 1968	1,228
January 1969	1,363
January 1970	1,793
October 1971	2,600
October 1975	2,858
October 1977	2,747
1979	2,543
1980	2,477
1981	2,422
1985	2,261
August 1988	2,268
1989	2,248
1993	2,102
Fall 1995**	2,171

* The membership data are based on reports in newsletters, minutes, and miscellaneous reports. A separate listing that corresponds closely to this table appears in *Leaders in School Psychology 1995* produced by APA and is based on APA official records. Numbers may vary as a function of time of year data are reported.
** The 1995 number includes fellows and members, but it does not include student and professional affiliates (*N* = 680).

A newsletter appears to have begun in 1946–1947 and was simply titled "Newsletter" throughout this period. Newsletters were of varying length ranging from 6–20 pages, published in mimeographed form one to three times per year, and dedicated largely to Division business, presidential addresses, membership rosters, by-laws, and committee reports. (Fagan, 1993, p. 27)

The division's programs during the APA annual convention were originally only business meetings but soon exanded to include topical sessions. The September 1947 convention included only two symposia—"Binet Testing Material as a Diagnostic Instrument for Personality Studies" and "Relationship Between Research and Service Functions of the School Psychologist"—and what may be the first presidential address (Harry J. Baker, "Current Trends in School Psychology") followed by an annual business meeting. Margaret Hall's presidential address in 1948, "Current Employment Requirements for School Psychologists," was the first to be published (Hall, 1949). The major issues in this period appear to have been role and function; employment; credentialing; test standards;

training; relationships with other groups at the national, state, and local levels; exceptional children; translating research into practice; and new practices in testing and intervention. (For a discussion of these, see Fagan, 1993, pp. 28–29.) Unlike its professional colleagues in clinical and counseling psychology, Division 16 was not formally included in the major postwar accomplishments of the APA in accreditation, the American Board of Examiners in Professional Psychology (ABEPP, now American Board of Professional Psychology; ABPP), or the Veterans Administration internship programs. School psychology was not yet perceived as a national specialty of professional psychology. Whereas many of the symbols of professionalization had been achieved by 1950 in clinical psychology, they were considerably distant for Division 16. Despite its struggles, the division survived its first several years and was becoming a national voice in the expansion of school psychology that would follow.

MIDDLE YEARS: 1950 TO 1970

Several accomplishments characterized the history of Division 16 during 1950 to 1970. The more prominent were the Thayer Conference, the development of credentialing and training standards, and the approval of school psychology within the APA programs of accreditation and the ABEPP.

Thayer Conference

Once its survival was secured, the division set out to better define itself and the field of school psychology by conducting a national conference. Following on the success of the Boulder Conference (attended by several Division 16 members), the Thayer Conference sought to apply the scientist–practitioner model to school psychology. Unlike the divisions for clinical and counseling psychology, Division 16 chose to embrace two levels of training, credentialing, and practice, recognizing that the vast majority of school psychologists were prepared at the nondoctoral level, worked in school settings, and were certified by a state board of education (Cutts, 1955). Although the conference recommendations have never achieved widespread application in school settings, they have been applied in most nonschool credentialing and practice agencies. The recommendations also served to blaze a trail on which the division could traverse the increasingly doctoral-only policies of its parent the APA, as well as the realities of training, credentialing, and practice. The Thayer recommendations continue to be relevant and the proceedings are considered to be among the best available descriptions of the field at that time. (The proceedings were so popular that a second printing was required to meet demand.) For the historical record, the Thayer Conference was named for the Hotel Thayer in West Point, New York, where it was held August 22 to 31, 1954. The hotel was named after Sylvanus Thayer, the superintendent of West Point from 1817 to 1833. (Cremin, 1988). T. E. Newland was involved in planning the Thayer Conference. It is possible that he knew of the hotel as a conference site because he had served as a psychologist at West Point (1946–1948).

Accreditation and Credentialing

With at least a skeletal outline of its future from the 1954 Thayer Conference, Division 16 membership moved to establish guidelines for training and credentialing in the hope that the division would eventually be allowed to participate in accreditation and the ABEPP. The division also published a widely disseminated brochure, *The Psychologist on the School Staff* (Committee on Reconsideration of the Functions of the School Psychologist, 1958), which appears to have been the first descriptive account of school psychologist duties ever distributed nationally. Several thousand copies were printed and disseminated to division members, state departments of education, and school superintendents. Its 11 vignettes about the practice of school psychology recognized the potential scope of the specialty in urban, suburban, and rural school settings, including part-time and subspecialized services. The publication's success no doubt stimulated interest in publishing a brochure for wider distribution in fall of 1967. A revised division brochure (*The School Psychologist*) was available for several years.

The 1958 publication was followed by recommendations for the credentialing of school psychologists prepared in 1962 and published in the *American Psychologist* in 1963 (APA, Division 16, Committee on Training Standards and Certification, 1963). The proposals were directed to state departments of education, which were the primary regulators of school psychologist credentials, and to school districts, which were the primary employers of school psychologists. The recommendations reflected the two levels of training, credentialing, and practice derived from the Thayer Conference. The two levels were not likely to be widely accepted in the public schools, especially at a time when demand for school psychologists was outstripping supply and when doctoral-level school psychologists were few in number. Though not widely adopted, some states did use the guidelines to shape their certification requirements. Nevertheless, the proposals represented the division's allegiance to the APA ideology and no doubt provided the base from which training standards could be developed that ultimately would open doors to the accreditation process.

Efforts toward achieving accreditation in school psychology were initiated around 1963 with the APA Education and Training Board. During the process of achieving accreditation, Division 16 representatives made pilot visits in 1967 to 1968 to Rutgers University, the University of Minnesota, and San Jose State College. The latter, a nondoctoral program, was visited as part of a plan to consider accrediting both doctoral and nondoctoral programs in school psychology (see Fagan, 1991). However, only doctoral programs were later recognized. After overcoming obstacles related to program training levels and challenges to the APA's authority for accreditation vis-à-vis the authority of the National Council for Accreditation of Teacher Education (NCATE), Division 16 achieved accreditation status for school psychology and the first program was accredited at the University of Texas at Austin on February 1, 1971. The proposals also opened doors for the acceptance of school psychology in the ABEPP process. This was achieved following a trial examination period in 1967 to 1968, and 14 people were awarded the diplomate in 1968 to 1969.

Professional Institutes

Another major accomplishment of the period occurred in 1956 when Division 16 founded a professional institute to be held annually in conjunction with the APA convention. The institutes appear to have been an outgrowth of cosponsored programs during earlier APA conventions. The institutes were separate from the APA convention, were sometimes held in campus facilities, and maintained accounting records that were separate from the division's budget and financing. In addition to their obvious contributions to continuing education, the institutes may have been seen as a means of obtaining additional revenue—in these early years a division's funds could only be used for operating expenses and its end-of-year surplus funds reverted to the APA. It is unclear when this accounting practice ended, but later the institute account was merged with the main division account, substantially increasing the division's annual budget allotments (see Table 13). The annual institutes were successful until the late 1970s and the last (26th) was held at the 1981 APA convention in Los Angeles. The 26th Professional Institute included a choice of four workshops conducted over 2 days (learning disability, behavioral ecology, neuropsychological strategies, or working with families). It is likely as well that the expense and planning of the Spring Hill and Olympia conferences in 1980 and 1981, respectively, also influenced the division leadership's decision to shift to occasional preconvention workshops at future conventions. For information regarding the final institute and probable reasons for their discontinuance see *The School Psychologist* (June 1981 and October, 1981). With the 1972 APA convention in Hawaii, the division membership decided to hold four regional institutes instead of the professional institute at the convention.

Practitioner Growth and Problems of Representation

The accomplishments of 1950 to 1970 were orchestrated to create a greater visibility and identity for school psychology and Division 16 within both the APA and the larger field of practice. Although it was highly successful within the APA, the division encountered problems in relating to the rapidly growing numbers of practicing school psychologists.

Practitioners, who continued to be prepared and credentialed in large numbers at the nondoctoral level, perceived many of the accomplishments of Division 16 as having greater benefits for the doctoral members than for the nondoctoral members of the field. Specific numbers are lacking, but nondoctoral school psychologists must have accounted for at least 90% of the field (Farling & Hoedt, 1971). Despite several well-intended efforts, the division simply failed to respond to the Zeitgeist in school psychology of the 1960s in a manner that would have captured the membership of the field. For a complex set of circumstances and reasons, this failure influenced the founding of the National Association of School Psychologists (NASP) in 1969. For historical analyses of these events and the founding of the NASP, see Fagan (1979, 1993, 1994a), Fagan and colleagues (1989), Farling and Agner (1979).

Membership and Finances

From 1950 to 1970, Division 16 continued to grow in membership, financial stability, publications, and programs. Membership grew to almost 1,800, a noteworthy accomplishment considering estimates that the field was about 5,000 strong at the time. Although still far from a majority representation, this was a vast improvement over what was probably less than 25% representation in 1950. The rapid success of NASP in attracting members would influence the division's membership representation henceforth (see Table 14). The division's current total market representation is probably around 10%, though its doctoral-level representation is about one third of the doctoral school psychologist market.

Division 16 was in good stead financially throughout the period. As a result of rising membership, an increase in the divisional assessment from $2 to $3 per year, and the success of its institutes, the division's financial condition was strong by the end of the period. Even without the merged institute account, the division's 1968 to 1969 budget was more than six times its budget for 1950 (see Table 13).

Organization Developments

The Division 16 newsletter grew in length and diversity and was published on a more regular basis three or four times per volume year. It gained an official editor in 1955 to 1956, a job that had previously been the responsibility of the secretary. The newsletter was renamed *The School Psychologist* in 1965 (Vol. 19, No. 3). Volumes often carried an "institute issue," which covered the annual convention professional institute. A more journal-like format was published in the late 1960s, but this reverted to a shorter newsletter format in the early 1970s. In the late 1950s, the division executive committee explored the possibility of establishing a journal but decided not to do so. It also chose not to take over the *Journal of School Psychology*, which encountered financial difficulties in its early years; it was founded in 1963. Division convention programs grew in time allotted, and the number of paper proposals exceeded the available space. In addition to executive council meetings and annual business meetings, there were invited presentations, research and symposia sessions, and roundtable discussions. Often convention time would be given to committee reports. The division's committees were active in this period and during some years from 50 to 100 people served on committees or in elected and appointed division positions.

The governance of Division 16 underwent only modest changes. Membership categories were changed in 1958 to associate, member, and fellow, the latter having more stringent requirements (Seagoe & O'Shea, 1958). The 2-year experience requirement continued to be controversial throughout this period, especially as it applied to college faculty training school psychologists, as did the issue of distinguishing between a school psychologist and others such as guidance counselors or remedial teachers (Minutes, 1957). In 1966, the division replaced its experience requirements for membership with the statement that the applicant "has expressed a major interest in the field of school psychology." Its definition of a school psychologist was also changed:

> A. A psychologist, a substantial proportion of whose professional knowledge, competencies and time are spent: (1) in collaboration, consultation, or conference with school personnel on: (a) enhancing the learning potential of school-age pupils; (b) advancing their socio-emotional development; or (2) in clinical work, including psychodiagnostics, with children who present problems in school; or (3) training and instruction of school psychologists as defined in (1) and (2) above; and/or
> B. A psychologist, who through teaching, professional, or research activity, has made significant contributions to the training of school psychologists or the field of school psychology. (Results of the Balloting on By-Laws Amendment and Definition, 1966, p. 21)

These changes extended membership to a broader base of the field and attracted academics from the rapidly growing number of training programs specific to school psychology. By the late 1960s, the division's leadership was not only primarily made up of doctorate holders, but it also included many academics. The shift brought prestige to the division, enhanced the research characteristics of its convention programs, and initiated a trend for leadership to be drawn from among trainers rather than practitioners. This trend characterized Division 16 and the NASP for many years (Fagan, 1993). Perhaps to placate the growing concerns of nondoctoral school psychologists, in 1969 the division leadership extended voting privileges to associate members. Even though students could presumably join, the division had not as yet developed a formal vehicle for their affiliation.

Summary of the Middle Years

As the previous discussion demonstrates, Division 16 made considerable progress on several fronts in 1950 through 1970. It finally began to catch up with clinical and counseling psychology's success in developing standards, it established accreditation, and it participated in the ABEPP. These gains encouraged Boyd McCandless (1967–1968) to comment that "as a profession within our parent organization, APA, we are *in*" (p. 3). The division's leaders also made gains in identifying state and local groups of school psychologists and bringing them together to discuss issues. Their attempts at building relationships with school administrators are still observed in efforts associated with the current APA Practice and Education Directorates. The division was also represented at meetings of the Council for Exceptional Children, American Association of School Administrators, National Education Association-Department of Elementary Principals, Association for Supervision and Curriculum Development, and at the 1960 White House Conference on Children and Youth (Drews, 1960a, 1960b).

Finally, the Executive Committee, at its meeting of February 3–4, 1968, changed the division's name from the Division of School Psychologists to School Psychology. The change was made "in order to conform to the nomenclature used by other Divisions of the Association" (Minutes, 1968, p. 1).

> APA identifies the change as having officially occurred in 1969, presumably acknowledging that year as when it received official notice of the change. The change occurred when the Division was on the brink of achieving the ABEPP and accreditation. No doubt, the decision was made to reflect the Division's interest in representing the field of school psychology and not just school psychologists; that is both the science and practice of the profession. (Fagan, 1993, p. 42)

The period was one of rapid growth in the field of school psychology in general. By 1970 there were about 100 training programs; about 40 states had established education agency credentialing of school psychology practitioners, and as many states had psychology credentials for nonschool practice; and there may have been as many as 5,000 school psychologists in the field. A literature also began to develop; numerous books were published in the 1960s and the first two journals were established: *Journal of School Psychology* (est. 1963) and *Psychology in the Schools* (est. 1964). Trends in the publication of books about school psychology appear in French (1986) and Whelan and Carlson (1986) and professional literature generally in Fagan (1986c). At least 17 state associations of school psychologists were established, practitioner-to-child ratios improved to around 1:5,000, and median salaries in 1971 were in the $12,000 to $15,000 range (Fagan, 1995a; Fagan & Wise, 1994). Despite a general sense of optimism about the future of school psychology, no one could have predicted at the time that the growth of the field in the past 20 years would be exceeded in the next 20 years.

RECENT HISTORY: 1970 TO PRESENT

The entire field of school psychology has experienced unprecedented change since 1970. Beyond the categories discussed earlier, the 1970s was an era of intense litigation and regulation. Several major court decisions, the *Larry P. v. Riles* (1972) case being among the better known, changed the way that school psychological services were delivered. Related to these decisions, three major congressional acts in the mid-1970s—Family Educational Rights and Privacy Act of 1974, Section 504 of the Rehabilitation Act (1973) and Education for All Handicapped Children Act of 1975—helped to redefine the context of the school psychologist's work. With signals from the early 1960s (e.g., D'Evelyn, 1961), The Family Education Rights and Privacy Act made public many of the records routinely gathered, maintained, and disseminated by school psychologists. The Education for All Handicapped Children Act affected issues of nondiscriminatory assessment, reevaluation, due process, treatment and placement practices, and the general operation of special education. The legal and ethical aspects of the field became intense areas of interest as reflected in frequent publications and convention programs (e.g., Jacob-Timm & Hartshorne, 1994). Because psychological services were now required for the conduct of special education in all public school settings, the demand for practitioners fueled a growth in training programs. The growing number of graduates increased the development of state associations and expanded national organization memberships. At the same time, the organizations representing school psychologists rushed to be part of the growing governmental effort to reshape standards of practice.

Regulation was rapidly developing externally, mainly from the state and federal governments. Organizations could no longer survive by attending only to membership perks such as publications and conventions. They were also forced to attend to the reciprocal influences of the organizations on government agencies. Reactive and especially proactive involvement became commonplace. With limited resources, members of Division 16 were forced to become more actively involved in APA affairs, which was also making proactive efforts in national issues of practice vis-à-vis mental health programs, third-party reimbursements, and managed care. In a distinct shift from the 1960s, members of the APA and Division 16 moved doggedly to gather strength through a Washington office presence.

Assessment roles of school psychologists took on a greater burden, perhaps at the expense of intervention and consultation roles that were emerging in the early 1970s. As service demands expanded to children considered to be at risk but not categorically qualified for special education, the full impact of Section 504 of the Rehabilitation Act (1973) delayed until the late 1980s, amplified the need for a continuum of educational and psychological services to replace the dual system of regular and special education. New versions of earlier noncategorical schemes emerged couched in terms like *seamless services* and the *regular education initiative*. The functions of the practitioner's assessment role came under attack, rekindling earlier versions of criterion-referenced assessment but now called *nontraditional, authentic, functional,* and *curriculum-based assessment*. By the mid-1990s, many in school psychology were pressing for standards that viewed the school psychologist's primary roles and functions within a problem-solving model that linked assessment to intervention. The efforts represented another in a long history of attempts to broaden the role of the school psychologist. Caught up in broader movements of educational and health care reform, how much this persistent change will affect education or school psychology remains to be seen.

Connections to Professional Education

In addition to litigation and legislation, the recent period has been characterized by greater public scrutiny and criticism of the nation's public schools. Public education, still the constitutional responsibility of the individual states, has acquired a strong national and political presence. Many of society's problems (race, ethnicity, and multiculturalism; poverty; crime; teenage pregnancy and illegitimacy; physical and sexual abuse; and corporal punishment) have been debated in the context of the nations' public schools. There has been widespread and intense focus on education as the single most important factor in children's lives. With so much apparently at stake in the schools, both association services and research shifted to school settings. The former methodologies of campus-based research and laboratory school study of children were yielding to real-life in situ study of child behavior. Education, long the largest industry in the United States, had finally become a major focus of the APA.

In recent years, the APA has established several organizational agencies related to education. In 1988 the APA leadership formed its Practice Directorate and hired Jean Ramage (then Division 16 treasurer) to serve as its director for Policy and Advocacy in the Schools; Ronda Talley assumed this post in 1990 and directed the Practice Directorate's Psychology in the Schools Program. The APA Education Directorate was founded in 1990 and the Task Force on Psychology in Education was formed in 1991. Within the APA Education Directorate, the APA Center for Psychology in the Schools and Education was formed in 1994, and Ronda Talley was promoted to center director. At the same time, Rick Short, who had been with the APA Education Directorate since 1993, became director of the Center for Training and Education in Psychology, which enhanced the link between school psychology to accreditation ("School Psychology Staff Moving Up, 1994). These collective efforts have brought school psychology and the division into closer proximity to APA policy and planning and have spurred successful efforts at communicating school psychology more effectively to the schools. The efforts with administrators of school psychological services are particularly visible, and the publications *Delivery of Comprehensive School Psychological Services: An Educators Guide* (Task Force on Psychology in the Schools, 1993) and *Comprehensive & Coordinated Psychological Services for Children: A Call for Service Integration* (Task Force on Comprehensive and Coordinated Psychological Services for Children: Ages 0–10, 1994) are reminiscent of the division's earlier *The Psychologist on the School Staff* (Committee on the Reconsideration of the Functions of the School Psychologist, 1958). The APA involvement with education and the input of Division 16 were far more favorable than in 1958 when the division members protested their lack of involvement on the APA Committee on Relations Between Psychology and Education (Minutes, Annual Business Meeting, 1958, p. 3).

Relationships With NASP and Other Groups

Entering the 1970s with a semblance of parity between the division of school psychology and other divisions on accreditation and the ABEPP, the division encountered new challenges. The rapid membership growth of the National Association of School Psychologists (NASP) forced the division leadership to accept a future in which Division 16 would struggle to maintain its former prominence as the primary national representative for school psychology. The division leadership could have chosen to ignore the NASP and its largely nondoctoral ideology and strike out in the direction of the rest of professional psychology at the doctoral level. The division's legacy, however, had been to attempt to represent all of school psychology, doctoral and nondoctoral, in school and nonschool settings. At least in matters related to threats from the APA, the division did effectively represent all of school psychology (e.g., obtaining an exemption to the APA Council's resolution defining the professional psychologist at the doctoral level in 1977). It would have been difficult to abandon the fast-growing nondoctoral school psychology pool. From its origin in the 1940s, Division 16 had sought to represent doctoral practitioners and to broaden its membership base over time. The division still struggles with this dilemma today.

The doctoral–nondoctoral conflict in school psychology is a complex array of issues related to training, credentialing, titles, and levels of practice. The overall issue has haunted the field since its inception. As the doctoral–nondoctoral issue waxed and waned (especially between the division and the NASP), and as the members considered revisions to the divisions' specialty guidelines, serious discussions have taken place as to just whom and what Division 16 could and should represent. The divisive viewpoints were sharply contrasted in a debate held at the 1978 NASP convention (see Bardon, Brown, & Hyman, 1979) and in positions taken by Bardon, Goldwasser, Kratochwill, Reschly, Slater, and Winikur (1982). (See "The Future of School Psychology." For a review of the major issues involved in this conflict, also refer to Engin and Johnson (1983), Fagan (1986b, 1994b), Fagan and Wise (1994), Phillips (1990), and Pryzwansky (1982).)

A related shift in perspective is represented by the division's "Draft Definition of the Specialty of School Psychology" (Division 16 Task Force on Specialty Definition, 1995). The draft was the centerpiece of a 1995 preconvention institute for trainers, "Redefining the Doctoral Specialty of School Psychology for the 21st Century," and for administrators and practitioners, "Creating a New Vision of School Psychology." Perhaps the division will shift to a position of primarily representing doctoral-level school psychology, working in closer harmony with the NASP's efforts in representing both doctoral and nondoctoral persons. With a membership that is highly representative of academics and doctoral practitioners, Division 16 can best represent their needs to the APA.

Despite policy differences and varying periods of discord and harmony (Bardon, 1989), members of Division 16 and the NASP managed to work effectively on several projects of mutual interest. From a 1969 joint resolution on organizational cooperation, joint efforts have included responses to federal legislation and local and state matters related to credentialing and practice, position statements, school district service delivery awards, and accreditation. Among the most visible joint efforts has been the work of the APA–NASP Interorganizational Committee (IOC, formerly the APA–NASP Task Force) created in 1978 in response to differences related to accreditation matters of the APA and the National Council for Accreditation of Teacher Education. The IOC facilitated the planning of the Spring Hill and Olympia Conferences, conducted a successful joint accreation effort, and served as a bridge in sharing information and policy positions such as the 1994 statement on appropriate supervisors (Talley, 1995). Though the APA and the NASP have not resolved their major policy differences, they have achieved a level of mutual understanding.

Another organizational development of the past two decades has been the emergence of smaller groups appended to Division 16 or the NASP. Although Division 16 and the NASP had been the primary voices in school psychology for many years, there now exist the American Academy of School Psychology (established in 1993), linked to the American Board of Professional Psychology; the Society for the Study of School Psychology (established in 1994), linked to the *Journal of School Psychology*; the Council of Directors of School Psychology Programs (CDSPP), linked to the APA; the Trainers of School Psychologists, the National Association of State Consultants for School Psychological Services, and the International School Psychology Association, linked to both Division 16 and to the NASP; and the APA–NASP Interorganizational Committee. Historical information about these groups may be found in Fagan (1993), Oakland (1993), and Phillips (1993). One example of collaborative efforts is the annual *Directory of Internships for Doctoral Students in School Psychology* (Joint Committee on Internships for the CDSPP, Division 16, and the NASP, 1995). The directory not only serves division members but also nonmember doctoral students and practitioners nationwide. However, in the absence of an overarching authoritative body to regulate the efforts of these groups, the future of school psychology and the division's participation in it will be determined by the alignments and coalitions that develop among them on the primary issues of training, credentialing, and practice. Less clear influences exist among other external groups and coalitions such as the National Alliance of Pupil Services Organizations.

Membership and Finances

The growth of Division 16 membership and finances during the period 1950 to 1970 was not as expansive after 1970. Membership peaked at about 2,700 in 1977 and declined to a fairly stable range of 2,100 to 2,200. The decline in members and their annual voting patterns have influenced the number of division representatives to the council. The division had two representatives (the legislated minimum) in 1946, three in 1949, four in 1957, and a high of six in 1974. In 1960 the APA adopted the policy of establishing council representation through member allocations of ten votes each (Horai, 1982). The division's council representation was reduced to four in 1981, three in 1982, and two by 1991; it currently remains at two.

Budgets continued to increase, though not at the pace of the 1950 to 1970 period (see Table 13). Expensive projects included the division's

School Psychology Monograph series, cosponsorship of the Spring Hill conference in 1980 and the Olympia conference in 1981, and the operation of a journal first published in 1986 (*Professional School Psychology*, which changed to *School Psychology Quarterly* in Volume 5, 1990). The decision to found a journal was made in January 1983 and grew out of deliberations about the division's former monograph series, which appeared five times between 1973 and 1980. For correct monograph citations and topics, see Fagan, Delugach, Mellon, and Schlitt (1986). The rising cost of these projects was reflected in increasing divisional assessments from $9 in 1979 to $30 in 1991 to 1992.

Organizational Developments

Despite problems with finances and membership, Division 16 matured as an organizational entity. A major success has been achieved in program accreditation. The number of programs accredited increased gradually in the 1970s and accelerated in the 1980s (there were 3 such programs in 1973, 10 in 1977, 19 in 1980, 34 in 1985, and 41 in 1990). With 49 APA-approved doctoral programs in 1995, about 60% of the recognized doctoral programs in school psychology are now APA accredited. The division has also been successful in promoting the accreditation of doctoral internships.

The maturity of Division 16 was also evident in its establishment of several national awards. (See Table 15). These included the granting of a Distinguished Service Award since 1970 and a Lightner Witmer Award (for early career achievements) since 1973. Since 1993 the division has also awarded a Senior Scientist Award, an Outstanding Dissertation in School Psychology Award, and the journal's School Psychology Quarterly Division 16 Fellows Award for the outstanding article published during the previous year. Brief descriptions of division awards appear in *The School Psychologist* (1992). The Distinguished Service Award, not granted in 1992 or 1993, was renamed the Jack Bardon Distinguished Service Award beginning in 1994. The idea of having awards to recognize a distinguished worker or outstanding school psychological work earlier appeared in the Minutes of the Executive Committee (Minutes, 1955). During the late 1970s, Witmer Award recipients were also granted $100 from the *Journal of School Psychology*. Updated lists of award recipients appear annually in *Leaders in School Psychology* (APA, 1996) with the assistance of Ronda Talley and Tom Kubiszyn of the APA.

Another area of success was in creating a stronger presence on APA boards and committees. With a clear strategy in mind, the division achieved representation on nine APA committees or boards in the early 1980s, including the APA's Policy and Planning Board and its Education and Training Board. Recognition of school psychology in the APA also came in the form of the personal accomplishments of a few of its members.

For example, the APA granted Jack Bardon a Distinguished Contributions to Applied Psychology as a Professional Practice Award in 1981. Since 1984 Jack Bardon, Nadine Lambert, and Frank Farley—all Division 16 members—have been nominated for the presidency of the APA; Farley was elected to serve in 1993. Dorothy Cantor had been a member of the division earlier in her career.

The division newsletter retained the name *The School Psychologist*, and its format remained similar for most of the period, switching from six issues per volume to a quarterly publication in 1990 (Volume 44). As budgets tightened, the newsletter was unable to maintain the colorful format and photo layouts that were published until 1977; however, the quality of content continued. In 1992 (Volume 46) the newsletter began publishing a more comprehensive format including feature articles as well as division and APA business, announcements, convention programs, and advertising. It has continued to serve as the most available source of division information. Another source of continuing education is the division's Conversation Series videotapes. Appearing annually since 1991 the tapes include

TABLE 15
Division 16 Award Recipients

Distinguished Service Award Recipients	
1970	Edward French
1971	Frances Mullen
1972	Marie Skodak Crissey
1973	Boyd V. McCandless
	David Wechsler (special award)
1974	Mary Alice White
1975	T. Ernest Newland
1976	Jack I. Bardon
1977	Virginia Bennett
1978	Beeman Phillips
1979	Rosa A. Hagin
1980	Nadine Lambert
1981	Gilbert O. Trachtman
1982	C. Edward Meyer
1983	Susan Gray
1984	Seymour Sarason
1985	Joseph L. French
1986	John H. Jackson
1987	Calvin O. Dyer
1988	Irwin Hyman
1989	Judith L. Alpert
1990	Thomas Oakland
1991	Thomas K. Fagan
1992	No award granted
1993	No award granted
1994	Sylvia Rosenfield
	Walter Pryzwansky
1995	Jane Close Conoley

Lightner Witmer Award Recipients

1973	James Ysseldyke
1974	Ellen C. Bien
1975	No award granted
1976	Judith L. Alpert
1977	Thomas R. Kratochwill
1978	Emanuel J. Mason
1979	Raymond S. Dean
1980	Cecil R. Reynolds
1981	Terry B. Gutkin
	Frederic J. Medway
1982	Frank W. Gresham
1983	George W. Hynd
1984	Stephen Elliott
1985	Cathy F. Telzrow
1986	Joe Witt
1987	Edward Shapiro
	Jack Kramer
1988	Timothy Keith
	Maribeth Gettinger
1989	Janet Graden
	Howard Knoff
1990	Brian Martens
	Kevin Stark
1991	William Erchul
1992	Sandra Christenson
1993	Susan Sheridan
1994	Gregg Macmann
1995	Christopher Skinner

Senior Scientist Award Recipients

1993	Richard Woodcock
1994	Barry J. Zimmerman
1995	Thomas R. Kratochwill

Outstanding Dissertation Award Recipients

1993	Daniel E. Olympia, University of Utah
	Honorable mention: Ruth Kaminski, University of Oregon
1994	Jacqueline Lemme Cunningham, University of Texas
	Honorable mentions: Pamela Burri Grossman, Texas A&M University; William David Carlyon, University of South Florida

School Psychology Quarterly Division 16 Fellows Award Recipients

1993	Maurice J. Elias and George J. Allen
1994	Steven Forness and Kimberly Hoagwood
	Cindy Carlson

several short interviews with people in the field of school psychology and related areas such as consultation, assessment, and intervention.

Finally, the division has taken important steps to broaden representation of the field by restructuring its overall governance. In 1977 the division membership began electing monitors to its Executive Council instead of members-at-large. The monitors were for the committee and activity areas of collaboration and cooperation, scholarly knowledge, professional standards, school practice, and professional fellowship. In 1985 to 1986 this scheme was changed to electing four vice presidents, one each to cover professional affairs; education, training, and scientific affairs; social and ethical responsibility and ethnic minority affairs; and publications, communications, and convention affairs; a vice president for membership was approved in 1995 to 1996. The areas were linked to the division's objectives in the revised bylaws of August 1985, when specific committees were required to report to each vice president. This structure is still in place.

Another change was the founding of a fourth class of membership in 1981 to 1982, student affiliates in school psychology, with charter chapters on at least 16 campuses. The idea appears to be related to an effort at Indiana University in 1978 (Talley, 1978). A fifth class, professional psychologist affiliates, was added in 1994. These areas opened up membership to a broader base of the field and even provided an opportunity for NASP members to affiliate with the division without becoming APA members.

CONCLUSION

Fifty years after Division 16 was founded, the landscape of school psychology has changed dramatically. With more than 22,000 persons in the field, separate associations and credentialing in every state, more than 200 training program institutions, and strong external and internal regulatory mechanisms, school psychology is now a large, well-organized specialty in U.S. psychology. The ratio of practitioners to schoolchildren has improved to approximately 1:2,000 nationwide. No longer restricted to certain geographic regions, school psychology services are available in almost every local school district and have expanded into the nonschool sector. Salaries, now averaging more than $43,000, are among the best for a largely nondoctoral psychology field. The field continues to be among the more representative of women in school psychology, currently around 70%, up from perhaps 40% to 50% at the time the division was founded (Fagan, 1995a; Fagan & Wise, 1994). In 1992, 47% of the division's membership was made up of women, ranking it fifth among the available 49 divisions in its representation of women.

Division 16 has played a vital role in several aspects of the field's development. Continuing educational efforts have progressed from convention programs and institutes to participation in several national conferences, including those of Spring Hill and Olympia, and a training conference sponsored by the APA. The division's newsletter has been a vehicle for national communication for almost 50 years. Its monograph series, journal, and conversation series videos have also facilitated the continuing education of school psychologists. The division membership's ongoing efforts to upgrade training and credentialing guidelines—which can be traced to activities that took place more than 40 years ago—initiated doctoral school psychology program accreditation and brought it to its current level of success.

Some have concluded that since the founding of the NASP, Division 16 has failed to keep pace with the field of school psychology and has lost its influence and prestige. That is too simple a conclusion to a complex process of developments in recent decades. There is no doubt that the presence and strength of the NASP have forced the Division 16 members to reconsider the division's mission both in conjunction with the APA and in the field in general. The division is no longer the only game in town, and the officers took steps to keep peace within the policy constraints of the APA and to compete with NASP for membership representation of the field. Although it has kept peace, its membership representation waned after the 1970s and lags far behind the NASP. There is no disputing that NASP more broadly represents the field, especially at the nondoctoral and school district levels. Even though Division 16 has not yet chosen to do so, the presence of NASP allows the division to pursue advocacy for doctoral-school psychology with less worry of alienating a potential membership base of nondoctoral-school psychologists.

Perhaps the future direction of Division 16 will be to concentrate more on representing its doctoral constituency (see, e.g., Illback, 1996). Although considerable difference of opinion has been expressed about its redefining of the doctoral specialty of school psychology, the positions are reminiscent of the 1960s when the division leadership sought to better establish an identity for the doctoral school psychologist and solidify the division's power base within the APA. With a gradually increasing proportion of the field acquiring doctoral degrees and seeking practice in the nonschool sector, the division's current efforts could provide a stronger base of influence for the future. As I have discussed earlier (Fagan, 1993), the division's existence depends more on the survival of the concept of psychological services in the schools and to problems of schooling than to the survival of a specific group of practitioners in school settings. This viewpoint is consistent with the division's title change in 1969 from School Psychologists to School Psychology. So long as the division maintains credibility and visibility within the arena of psychology, its future is generally optimistic. The division has served as the primary national representative of school psychology to the most important arena in the United States for psychology—the APA. Even if the division's service has been more successful in representing the interests of doctoral personnel, its success in such representation cannot be ignored.

Running twice as fast in order to catch up is a pervasive theme in the history of Division 16. This is true today, as the division seeks to catch up to the level of professionalization observed in other psychology groups and yet maintain its identity within the broader field of school psychology, which continues to be perceived as a mix of psychology and education. Although it has played this game of catch up since it was founded, neither the division nor the field of school psychology has run fast enough to catch up with other professional psychology fields in the nonschool sector, especially clinical psychology. Nevertheless, the field of school psychology strongly controls the school sector, and because of this strength there is a strong future for the field. However, with managed care pressuring practitioners in nonschool settings, other psychologists are seeking to invade the school setting. Even some of the leaders in the field are reconceptualizing school psychology in health care provider terminology in which school-based and school-linked service schemes are connected to comprehensive school health education and services (Talley & Short, 1996).

Times have changed considerably from the days when a school psychologist was often a clinical or educational psychologist practicing in a school setting. Today such practitioners are not school psychologists unless they have met specific requirements and expectations established by the field, including organizational affiliation with the Division of School Psychology or the NASP. Despite the desirability of having qualified psychologists of various specialties available to serve schoolchildren, the school psychologist has a specific and protected training, credentialing, and role in American psychology, and the division has a proud history of involvement in this professionalization.

Division 16 membership has also tried to catch up with the broader field of school psychology, which has seldom been in close alignment with the APA's policies. The policies of the APA and the realities of a largely nondoctoral field are such that the division may never catch up with both professional psychology and the broader nondoctoral field of school psychologists to each party's satisfaction. Reflecting on this issue in 1961, then Division 16 president, Katherine D'Evelyn, stated,

> Some of us in Division 16 feel we have been running very fast, like Alice and the Red Queen in *Through the Looking Glass*. As Alice said, "You'd generally get to somewhere else, if you ran very fast for a long time. . . .

Perhaps we have gotten somewhere. I know we have, but we still have a long way to go. I think we will have to do as the Red Queen advised Alice when she said, ". . . it takes all the running you can do to keep in the same place. If you want to get somewhere else, you must run at least twice as fast as that!" (D'Evelyn, 1961, p. 19)

The future of Division 16 may be determined by how it defines *somewhere else* and how fast and how long it can continue to run. Redefining its goals and expectations for representation could set the division on a course that will not only catch up to the goals it has sought but even move ahead, setting a pace for others in professional psychology.

For those interested in further study, several resources exist that are especially relevant to Division 16 (School Psychology). The more important archival sources are the Archives of the History of American Psychology (e.g., the papers of Marie Skodak Crissey) at the University of Akron (Ohio) and the APA papers in the Library of Congress and at the APA. The Arnold Gesell papers in the Library of Congress are useful for studying early practice in school psychology and organizations such as the AACP. The APA papers in the Library of Congress provide information on the early years of the APA divisions and related organizations (e.g., AAAP). Some papers and items relevant to more recent Division 16 history are maintained by the division's historian in the Department of Psychology at the University of Memphis (Tennessee). The author maintains a Center for the History of School Psychology, which includes an extensive literary collection with most issues of the division's newsletter, all issues of the division's former monograph series, and its journal. The center also includes correspondence with several members of the division's former leadership (e.g., Jack Bardon, Norma Cutts, Marie Skodak Crissey, Frances Mullen, T. Ernest Newland, and Keith Perkins). The Division Services Office in the APA headquarters is another source of information about the division. APA membership directories are also excellent sources for listings of leadership as well as division members and fellows.

Literary works with specific relevance to Division 16 include Cutts (1955), Fagan (1990a, 1990b, 1993), Fagan, Hensley, and Delugach (1986), and Fagan and Wise (1994), Fagan and Warden (1996), Fagan, Delugach, Mellon, and Schlitt (1986), French (1984, 1988, 1990), Hagin (1993), Lambert (1993), Phillips (1990, 1993) and Pryzwansky (1993). The 1995 Conversation Series videotapes edited by Alex Thomas, provide an oral history of perceptions from leaders whose experiences span 30 years of division history. The videotapes are available from Division 16. The division historian also maintains archival copies. An audiotape was also made of a roundtable discussion of the division's history at the 1995 APA convention (Fagan, et al., 1995). In conjunction with the present chapter, these resources provide a fairly complete history of Division 16 for interested researchers.

REFERENCES

Advisory ballot, August, 1948. (1949, February). *Newsletter*, 1–2.

American Psychological Association, Center for Psychology in the Schools and Education (Education Directorate), and Policy and Advocacy in the Schools Program (Practice Directorate). (1996). *Leaders in school psychology, 1996*. Washington, DC: Author.

American Psychological Association, Division 16, Committee on Training Standards and Certification. (1963). Proposals for state department of education certification of school psychologists. *American Psychologist, 28*, 711–714.

APA-accredited doctoral programs in professional psychology: 1995. (1995). *American Psychologist, 50*, 1069–1080.

Baker, H. (1946, October 8). Correspondence between D. Wolfle and H. Baker. Library of Congress, APA Archives, File F-7, Washington, DC.

Bardon, J. I. (1989). NASP as perceived by the Division of School Psychology, American Psychological Association: Past and future interactions. *School Psychology Review, 18*, 209–214.

Bardon, J. I., Brown, D. T., & Hyman, I. A. (1979). Debate: Will the real school psychologist please stand up? *School Psychology Digest, 8*, 162–186.

Bardon, J. I., Goldwasser, E. B., Kratochwill, T. R., Reschly, D. J., Slater, B. R., & Winikur, D. W. (1982). The future of school psychology. *Professional Psychology, 13*, 954–1018.

Boring, E. G. (1949). Policy and plans of the APA: Part V. Basic principles. *American Psychologist, 4*, 531–532.

By-Laws of the Division of School Psychologists of the American Psychological Association, Amended as of March 21, 1949. (1949, March). *Newsletter*, 2.

By-Laws of the Division of School Psychologists of the American Psychological Association, As Amended thru March 1, 1956. (1956, June). *Newsletter, 10*(4), attachment.

Committee on Reconsideration of the Functions of the School Psychologist, Division of School Psychologists—APA. (1958). *The psychologist on the school staff*. Washington, DC: Author.

Cornell, E. L. (1942). *The work of the school psychologist*. Albany: Division of Research, New York State Education Department.

Cremin, L. A. (1988). *American education: The metropolitan experience 1876–1980*. New York: Harper & Row.

Cutts, N. E. (Ed.). (1955). *School psychologists at mid-century*. Washington, DC: American Psychological Association.

Darley, J. G., & Berdie, R. (1940). The fields of applied psychology. *Journal of Consulting Psychology, 4*(2), 41–52.

D'Evelyn, K. E. (1961). Running twice as fast. *Division 16 Newsletter, 16*(1), 13–19.

Division 16 Task Force on Specialty Definition. (1995, September 1). *Draft definition of the specialty of school psychology*. Washington, DC: Author. (See also *The School Psychologist, 49*(4), 95, 98–104.)

Doll, E. A. (1946). The divisional structure of the APA. *American Psychologist, 1*, 336–345.

Drews, E. (1960a). Report: 1960 Convention of the Council For Exceptional Children, Los Angeles, April 18–23. *Newsletter, 14*(4), 5–6.

Drews, E. (1960b). Report: Golden Anniversary White House Conference on Children and Youth, March 27–April 2, 1960. *Newsletter, 14*(4), 6–7.

Education for All Handicapped Children Act of 1975. (1975). Pub. L. No. 94–142, 20 U.S.C., 34 C.F.R.

Engin, A. W., & Johnson, R. (1983). School psychology training and practice: The NASP perspective. In T. R. Kratochwill (Ed.), *Advances in school psychology* (Vol. III, pp. 21–44). Hillsdale, NJ: Lawrence Erlbaum.

Fagan, T. K. (1979). Professional pulse: Tenth anniversary NASP historical trivia salute. *School Psychology Digest, 8*, 224–231.

Fagan, T. K. (1986a). The historical origins and growth of programs to prepare school psychologists in the United States. *Journal of School Psychology, 24*, 9–22.

Fagan, T. K. (1986b). School psychology's dilemma: Reappraising solutions and directing attention to the future. *American Psychologist, 41*, 851–861.

Fagan, T. K. (1986c). The evolving literature of school psychology. *School Psychology Review, 15*, 430–440.

Fagan, T. K. (1990a). *Mixed loyalties, tentative existence, and survival: Origins of the Division of School Psychologists in the American Psychological Association*. Unpublished manuscript.

Fagan, T. K. (1990b). Research on the history of school psychology: Recent developments, significance, resources, and future directions. In T. R. Kratochwill (Ed.), *Advances in school psychology* (Vol. VII, pp. 151–182). Hillsdale, NJ: Lawrence Erlbaum.

Fagan, T. (1991, August). *Historian's report, Division 16 Executive Committee*. Available from author.

Fagan, T. K. (1992). Compulsory schooling, child study, clinical psychology, and special education: Origins of school psychology. *American Psychologist, 47*, 236–243.

Fagan, T. K. (1993). Separate but equal: School psychology's search for organizational identity. *Journal of School Psychology, 31*, 3–90.

Fagan, T. K. (1994a). A critical appraisal of the NASP's first 25 years. *School Psychology Review, 23*, 604–618.

Fagan, T. K. (Ed.). (1994b). Miniseries: Will the real school psychologist please stand up: Is the past a prologue for the future of school psychology? *School Psychology Review, 23*, 560–603.

Fagan, T. K. (1995a). Trends in the history of school psychology in the United States. In A. Thomas & J. Grimes (Eds.), *Best practices in school psychology–III* (pp. 59–67). Washington, DC: National Association of School Psychologists.

Fagan, T. K. (1995b). Training school psychologists before there were school psychologist training programs: A history 1890–1930. In T. B. Gutkin & C. R. Reynolds (Eds.), *Handbook of school psychology* (3rd ed.). New York: Wiley.

Fagan, T. K., Block, N., Dwyer, K., Petty, S., St. Cyr, M., & Telzrow, C. (1989). Historical summary and analysis of the first 20 years of the National Association of School Psychologists. *School Psychology Review, 18,* 151–173.

Fagan, T. K., Delugach, F. J., Mellon, M., & Schlitt, P. (1986). *A bibliographic guide to the literature of professional school psychology 1890–1985.* Washington, DC: National Association of School Psychologists.

Fagan, T. K. (Cochair), French, J. (Cochair), Hagin, R., Phillips, B., Rosenfield, S., & Lambert, N. (Discussant). (1995, August 13). *Perspectives on the history of the Division of School Psychology.* Annual Convention of the American Psychological Association, New York.

Fagan, T. K., Hensley, L. T., & Delugach, F. J. (1986). The evolution of organizations for school psychologists in the United States. *School Psychology Review, 15,* 127–135.

Fagan, T. K., & Warden P. (Eds.). (1996). *Historical encyclopedia of school psychology.* Westport, CT: Greenwood.

Fagan, T. K., & Wise, P. S. (1994). *School psychology: Past, present, and future.* White Plains, NY: Longman.

Family Educational Rights and Privacy Act of 1974 (1974). Pub. L. No. 93–380, 20 U.S.C., 34 C.F.R.

Farling, W. H., & Agner, J. (1979). History of the National Association of School Psychologists: The first decade. *School Psychology Digest, 8,* 140–152.

Farling, W. H., & Hoedt, K. C. (1971). *National survey of school psychologists.* Washington, DC: National Association of School Psychologists.

Fernberger, S. W. (1943). The American Psychological Association: 1892–1942. *Psychological Review, 50,* 33–60.

French, J. L. (1984). On the conception, birth, and early development of school psychology: With special reference to Pennsylvania. *American Psychologist, 39,* 976–987.

French, J. L. (1986). Books in school psychology: The first forty years. *Professional School Psychology, 1,* 267–277.

French, J. L. (1988). Grandmothers I wish I knew: Contributions of women to the history of school psychology. *Professional School Psychology, 3,* 51–68.

French, J. L. (1990). History of school psychology. In T. B. Gutkin & C. R. Reynolds (Eds.), *Handbook of school psychology* (pp. 3–20). New York: Wiley.

Fryer, D. (1937). The proposed American Association for Applied and Professional Psychologists. *Journal of Consulting Psychology, 1,* 14–16.

Hagin, R. A. (1993). Contributions of women in school psychology: The Thayer report and thereafter. *Journal of School Psychology, 31*, 123–141.

Hall, M. E. (1949). Current employment requirements of school psychologists. *American Psychologist, 4*, 519–525.

Hildreth, J. D. (1985, January). Memorandum: "History" of Divisions (mimeo., 2 pp). Washington, DC: American Psychological Association.

Hilgard, E. R. (1945). Temporary chairmen and secretaries for proposed APA divisions. *Psychological Bulletin, 42*, 294–296.

Hilgard, E. R. (1987). *Psychology in America: A historical survey*. San Diego: Harcourt Brace Jovanovich.

Horai, J. (1982, May). *The American Psychological Association and its divisions* (mimeo., 12 pp.). Washington, DC: American Psychological Association.

Illback, R. (1996). Doctoral school psychology and the mission of Division 16. In Division of School Psychology, American Psychological Association, *Agenda book for midwinter meeting of the Division of School Psychology of the APA, February 2–4, 1996, Guadalupe Ranch, Boerne, Texas* (pp. 171–174). Washington, DC: American Psychological Association.

Jacob-Timm, S., & Hartshorne, T. (1994). *Ethics and law for school psychologists*. Brandon, VT: Clinical Psychology Publishing.

Joint Committee on Internships for the Council of Directors of School Psychology Programs; Division of School Psychology, APA; & National Association of School Psychologists. (1995). *Directory of internships for doctoral students in school psychology*. University Park: School Psychology Clinic, Pennsylvania State University.

Lambert, N. M. (1993). Historical perspective on school psychology as a scientist–practitioner specialization in school psychology. *Journal of School Psychology, 31*, 163–193.

Larry P. v. Riles (1972). 343 F. Supp. 1306 (N.D. Cal. 1972).

McCandless, B. (1967–1968). President's message: Some comments of the incoming president to the membership of Division 16. *The School Psychologist, 22*(1), 1–3.

Minutes, Annual Business Meeting, Division of School Psychologists. (1958, August). Available from author or from Archives of the History of American Psychology, Box #22, APA Div. 16 Folder.

Minutes, Division of School Psychologists Executive Council Meeting. (1957, August 29). Available from author or from Archives of the History of American Psychology, Box #22, APA Div. 16 Folder.

Minutes of the Executive Committee of the Division of School Psychologists, APA. (1955, September 2). Washington, DC: Author.

Minutes of the midyear meeting of the Executive Committee of Division 16. (1968, February 3–4). Washington, DC: Division of School Psychology, American Psychological Association.

Oakland, T. (1993). A brief history of international school psychology. *Journal of School Psychology, 31,* 109–122.

Olson, W. C. (1944). Proceedings of the fifty-second annual meeting of the American Psychological Association, Inc., Cleveland, Ohio, September 11 and 12, 1944: Report of the secretary. *Psychological Bulletin, 41,* 725–793.

Olson, W. C. (1945). Proceedings of the fifty-third meeting of the American Psychological Association, Inc., Evanston, Illinois, September 6, 7, 8, 1945. Report of the retiring secretary. *Psychological Bulletin, 42,* 695–697.

Our Division in Comparison With Others. (1949, August). *Division 16 Newsletter,* p. 4.

Phillips, B. N. (1990). *School psychology at a turning point: Ensuring a bright future for the profession.* San Francisco: Jossey–Bass.

Phillips, B. N. (1993). Trainers of School Psychologists and Council of Directors of School Psychology Programs: A new chapter in the history of school psychology. *Journal of School Psychology, 31,* 91–108.

Pryzwansky, W. B. (1982). School psychology training and practice: The APA perspective. In T. R. Kratochwill (Ed.), *Advances in school psychology* (Vol. II, pp. 19–39). Hillsdale, NJ: Lawrence Erlbaum.

Pryzwansky, W. B. (1993). The regulation of school psychology: A historical perspective on certification, licensure, and accreditation. *Journal of School Psychology, 31,* 219–235.

Rehabilitation Act of 1973 (1973). Pub. L. No. 93–112; 29 U.S.C., 34 C.F.R. Pt. 105.

Results of the Balloting on By-Laws Amendments and Definition. (1966). *The School Psychologist, 21*(1), 21-22.

School Psychologist, The. (1981) *35*(5) (June).

School Psychologist, The. (1981). *36*(1) (October).

School Psychologist, The. (1992). *46*(4).

School psychology staff moving up at APA. (1994). *The School Psychologist, 48*(4), 12.

Seagoe, M. V., & O'Shea, H. E. (1958). Fellow status, new APA requirements. *The School Psychologist, 12*(3), 1–2.

Symonds, P. M., & English, H. B. (1938, April–June). Correspondence between P. M. Symonds and H. B. English during April–June 1938, Library of Congress, APA Archives, File K-3, Washington, DC.

Talley, R. (1978, January). Intervention for the sake of our futures: The organization of a school psychology students' association. *The School Psychologist, 32*(2), 4.

Talley, R. C. (1995). APA approves guidelines for identifying appropriate supervisors for psychological services in schools. *The School Psychologist, 49*(3), 69.

Talley, R. C., & Short, R. J. (Eds.). (1996). Special section: Future of psychological practice in the schools. *Professional Psychology: Research and Practice, 27,* 5–40.

Task Force on Comprehensive and Coordinated Psychological Services for Children: Ages 0–10. (1994). *Comprehensive & coordinated psychological services for children: A call for service integration.* Washington, DC: American Psychological Association.

Task Force on Psychology in the Schools. (1993). *Delivery of comprehensive school psychological services: An educator's guide.* Washington, DC: American Psychological Association.

Wallin, J. E. W. (1938). The establishment of the Clinical Section of the American Psychological Association. *School and Society, 48,* 114–115.

Whelan, T., & Carlson, C. (1986). Books in school psychology: 1970 to the present. *Professional School Psychology, 1,* 279–289.

Wolfle, H. (1948). A comparison of the strength and weakness of APA divisions. *American Psychologist, 3,* 378–380.

5

A HISTORY OF DIVISION 18 (PSYCHOLOGISTS IN PUBLIC SERVICE)

RODNEY R. BAKER

The Division of Psychologists in Public Service emerged as 1 of 19 charter divisions established in the 1945 reorganization of the American Psychological Association (APA) in which the American Association of Applied Psychologists (AAAP) merged with the APA. The division was formed to give recognition and a focus to psychologists serving in government. In its bylaws, Division 18 developed goals to improve the quality and adequacy of existing psychological services in public agencies, to encourage additional needed psychological services in those agencies, and to contribute psychological assistance to the management of government organizations. The division members further resolved to acquaint the psychology profession, particularly in universities, with the needs and opportunities for psychological work in public service.

Parts of this chapter were taken from a brief history of Division 18 by the author (Baker, 1992). Other information was taken from Division 18 newsletters and other archival material. Appreciation is due to Harold M. Hildreth awardees Cecil Peck and Lee Gurel, Presidents of the division in 1960 and 1972, respectively, for reviewing a draft of this chapter. Thanks are also due to Sidney Cleveland and Harold Dickman, Presidents of the division in 1981 and 1982 for their review.

EARLY DIVISION HISTORY: 1946 TO 1966

In a summary of his 1967 division presidential address, which focused on the history of Division 18, Harry McNeill noted that the early prime movers in the division included a number of personnel psychologists who had worked in government before and during the World War II years (McNeill, 1976). The first division president, Marion Richardson, had been employed by the U.S. Civil Service Commission before the war and served as chief of personnel research for the U.S. Army from 1942 to 1946. The division's first secretary–treasurer was Beatrice Dvorak, who began working for the U.S. Employment Service in 1939. The division's first APA Council representative in 1946 was Max Hutt, who was chief of the clinical psychology division of the Army. The division's first newsletter editor in 1949 was Ernest Primoff, director of research at the Civil Service Commission. The second president of the division, Roger M. Bellows, worked in personnel research for the adjutant general's office during the war. The next two presidents, Kenneth Ashcraft and Herbert Conrad, also had government personnel experience—Ashcraft with the Army and Conrad with the Civil Service Commission.

In 1954 the leadership of Division 18 passed to Quinter Holsopple of the Veterans Administration (VA) Central Office in Washington, D.C. This inaugurated a period in which the division's officers shifted from personnel psychology to that of clinical psychology, many coming from the VA or the National Institute of Mental Health (NIMH). Table 16 identifies the presidents and secretary–treasurers of the division from 1946 through 1996, and Table 17 lists the division's APA Council representatives for the same period.

Margaret Ives, the Division 18 historian and president in 1971, reported initial opposition to the founding of the division in an article recounting the role of psychologists in public service over the years (Ives, 1981). With the reorganization of the APA in 1945, she noted that other APA leaders observed that most psychologists were employed in public service settings and that nearly everyone would be eligible to join the division. The concern expressed by others was that Division 18 would become the largest APA division. The first Division 18 president found it necessary to pledge that the division would not have a newsletter or a program at the APA annual convention in order to obtain support for the division formation. Although Division 18 did start a newsletter in 1949 and began sponsoring convention symposia shortly thereafter, it was not until 1970 that the APA granted Division 18 convention program hours commensurate with the size of its membership.

In a discussion of the division's history by its officers (Minutes of the Executive Committee Meeting, 1975), Lee Gurel, council representative and former division president, pointed out that Division 18 started as a

TABLE 16
Presidents and Secretary–Treasurers of Division 18

Year	President	Secretary–Treasurer
1946	Marion W. Richardson	Beatrice J. Dvorak
1947	Marion W. Richardson	Beatrice J. Dvorak
1948	Marion W. Richardson	Beatrice J. Dvorak
1949	Roger M. Bellows	Beatrice J. Dvorak
1950	Roger M. Bellows	Beatrice J. Dvorak
1951	Kenneth B. Ashcraft	Beatrice J. Dvorak
1952	Herbert S. Conrad	Beatrice J. Dvorak
1953	Herbert S. Conrad	Beatrice J. Dvorak
1954	J. Quinter Holsopple	Beatrice J. Dvorak
1955	Lawrence S. Rogers	Elaine F. Kinder
1956	Robert S. Waldrop	Elaine F. Kinder
1957	Albert P. Maslow	Elaine F. Kinder
1958	Harold M. Hildreth	Frances O. Triggs
1959	Carl L. Anderson	Frances O. Triggs
1960	Cecil Peck	Frances O. Triggs
1961	Lawrence S. Rogers	Luigi Petrullo
1962	Herbert S. Conrad	Luigi Petrullo
1963	William M. Hales	Luigi Petrullo
1964	Wendell R. Carlson	Luigi Petrullo
1965	Jerome Levy	Frank H. Boring
1966	Henry P. David	Frank H. Boring
1967	Henry V. McNeill	Frank H. Boring
1968	Edwin S. Schneidman	Lee Gurel
1969	Lewis B. Klebanoff	Lee Gurel
1970	John E. Bell	Lee Gurel
1971	Margaret Ives	Mortimer Brown
1972	Lee Gurel	Mortimer Brown
1973	Frank H. Boring	Anne P. Cunningham
1974	Fred E. Spaner	Anne P. Cunningham
1975	Norman L. Farberow	Joel Cantor
1976	Asher R. Pacht	Stanley L. Brodsky
1977	Bernard Saper	Stanley L. Brodsky
1978	Brenda Gurel	Stanley L. Brodsky
1979	James G. Kelly	Evelyn Perloff
1980	Miriam F. Kelty	Evelyn Perloff
1981	Sidney Cleveland	Evelyn Perloff
1982	Harold R. Dickman	Vincent Wallen
1983	Durand F. Jacobs	Vincent Wallen
1984	Stanley L. Brodsky	Vincent Wallen
1985	Jonathan W. Cummings	Lars Peterson
1986	Harold H. Dawley, Jr.	Lars Peterson
1987	Kenneth A. Klauck	Lars Peterson
1988	Orville J. Lips	Ellen Scrivner
1989	Patrick A. Boudewyns	Ellen Scrivner
1990	Rodney R. Baker	Ellen Scrivner
1991	Karen E. Kirkhart	Edmund J. Nightingale
1992	Ellen M. Scrivner	Edmund J. Nightingale
1993	Thomas W. Miller	Robert Gresen
1994	Mark Cohen	Robert Gresen
1995	Bernhard E. Blom	Robert Gresen
1996	Scotty Hargrove	Robert Gresen

TABLE 17
APA Council Representatives for Division 18

Year(s)	Representative
1946	Max L. Hutt
1947	Marion W. Richardson
1948	Harold M. Skeels
1949–1950	Helen G. Price
	John T. Dailey
1950–1954	Beatrice J. Dvorak
1951–1953	Roger M. Bellows
1953–1956	Harold M. Hildreth
1954–1957	Elaine F. Kinder
1956–1959	Lawrence S. Rogers
1957–1960	Frances O. Triggs
1959–1962	Wendell R. Carlson
1960–1963	Luigi Petrullo
1962–1965	Harold M. Hildreth
1963–1966	M. W. McCullough
1963–1966	Edwin Shneidman
1965–1968	J. Wilbert Edgerton
1966–1967	Cecil P. Peck
1966–1969	James G. Kelly
1967–1970	Henry R. David
1968–1971	Lawrence S. Rogers
1969–1972	Cecil P. Peck
1971–1974	Harry V. McNeill
1975–1977	Lee Gurel
1978–1980	William Schofield
1981–1983	Suzanne B. Sobel
1984–1987	Durand F. Jacobs
1987–1990	Dana L. Moore
1990–1993	Kenneth Klauck
1993–1996	Rodney R. Baker

union organization concerned with bread-and-butter issues such as establishing psychology in the Civil Service. Early presidential addresses expressed these concerns. The title of Roger Bellows' address in 1949 was "Selling Psychological Services to Administrators." Quinter Holsopple's topic in 1954 was "Toward a Fair and Realistic Research Salary Scale in Government."

Before World War II, almost all psychologists were employed by universities. With the increased interest in applied aspects of psychology, by the mid-1950s, one third of the APA's membership was employed by a government agency. In a review of the APA directory, Lawrence Rogers reported that the federal government employed 14.5% of the APA's membership, 11.4% were employed by cities and counties, and 7.4% were employed by state governments (Rogers, 1956). Adding psychologists employed in public universities and colleges brought the total of psychologists paid a public salary to 48% of the APA's membership.

Rogers attributed the increased employment of psychologists in government to the profession's ability to demonstrate the effectiveness of its services. The public had begun to recognize the need for research in understanding and modifying human behavior. The important role of psychology in providing mental health treatment was also recognized, especially in the VA. Following World War II, the VA employed hundreds of clinical and counseling psychologists to provide treatment services for returning veterans.

Rogers further identified a number of problems for psychologists working in government. As Civil Service employees, Rogers reported in his 1956 article that psychologists had to work in settings with a considerable amount of administrative control and were restricted to working only with a certain category of client. Psychologists were also limited in their work by not having outside resources available to their clients, such as programs for retraining people for new careers. Nonpsychologist Civil Service employees were not always clear about what psychologists did, and psychologists who worked in higher education tended to believe that the only proper setting for a psychologist was a university. Both had difficulty accepting the practicing psychologist who provided professional services or did research in governmental agencies.

Rogers' article was written during his first term as president of Division 18, and he went on to describe what he believed were important responsibilities of psychologists in public service. He observed that the education, training, and experience of the psychologist were well suited to understanding many of the needs of the community. He suggested that psychologists were not only more aware of these needs than the average person but would also be familiar with some ways to meet these needs.

Rogers commented also on the responsibility and collective potential of professional groups like the APA and Division 18 in responding to societal needs. As citizen–members of such groups, these psychologists in public service were challenged to mobilize local, state, and national organizations to accomplish societal goals, to take the time and energy to attend professional meetings, to see that ideas are thrashed out, to do the work, and to accept the responsibility of putting policy into action. He argued that, although it was the responsibility of all psychologists to improve society, it was the special responsibility of those who directly served the public in government agencies.

The earliest copy of the minutes for a Division 18 business meeting available to the author was that of September 1964 (Minutes of Business Meeting, 1964). Those minutes reflected the relaxed nature of the division's affairs. Twenty-five members attended the meeting, during which it was announced that the division had sponsored four symposia and one paper during the convention. The officers approved the Membership Committee's recommendation to accept 104 new members and 36 associates. It was also announced that the past secretary's honorarium was being held in the division treasury pending acceptance as a contribution to the APA Committee on National and International Affairs. The Awards Committee reported that Harold Hildreth was the recipient of the 1964 Award for Distinguished Public Service by a psychologist. A letter was read from the APA Committee on Appointments requesting a check for $150 for assistance in finishing the new APA home, and the division's three APA Council members were instructed to use their own judgment regarding the request for the APA Council's approval for a new division to cover the experimental analysis of behavior.

In the mid-1960s, the division's members and the APA became more involved in policy decisions in state and federal governments. The Civil Service Commission had started looking into new regulations affecting the employment of psychologists. In the summer of 1966, the APA membership asked Division 18 for assistance in responding to the Civil Service Commission's request for help in studying pay comparability of psychologists in the Civil Service. In responding to that request, Division 18 began working with the APA on a number of Civil Service employment issues of interest to psychologists. Although VA officials had decided in 1946 that the doctoral degree and internship were to be required of clinical psychologists working in VA hospitals, great variability in other public service programs regarding education and training requirements for employment as a psychologist still existed in the 1960s. VA officials had asked the APA to develop a list of universities that prepared psychologists with a strong clinical and research background to assist them in recruiting psychologists for VA hospitals. This request eventually led to the APA's accreditation program. The division's members became interested along with other APA members and divisions in issues of credentialing for licensure and accreditation of training programs.

In 1948 the division's membership totaled 93. By 1966 membership had steadily grown to 615. In 1966 42% of the division's members worked in state and local mental health or correctional facilities, 20% worked in universities and colleges, 19% worked for the VA, and 19% worked for other federal agencies. That year, 2.5% of the APA's members belonged to Division 18, hardly justifying early concerns that the division would become the largest in the APA. In 1966, 13 APA divisions were larger than Division 18 and 12 were smaller.

THE GROWTH AND MATURATION YEARS: 1966 TO 1986

During the third and fourth decades of its history, the membership of Division 18 continued to grow. Member interests expanded from the guild issues of the first 20 years to more academic and professional content interests and increased professional concerns with the broad notion of public interest and well-being. It was during this period that the division established its most distinguished award, the Harold M. Hildreth Award. Membership in the division reached 795 in 1976 and rose to 1,461 in 1979. The membership growth resulted in large part from the establishment of sections within the division in the 1970s. Division dues had remained at $1 per year since the division began. Dues were increased to $5 per year in 1980 and to $10 per year in 1982.

Harold M. Hildreth Award

Harold Hildreth was a longtime friend to Division 18. A division president in 1958 and an APA Council member for the division from 1953 to 1956, Hildreth seemed to be naturally inclined toward public service and devoted much of his life to the application of psychology to wide areas of endeavor. He described himself as having special research interests in socially sensitive areas. His diverse clinical activities ranged from helping to develop police training films to interests in emergency mental health services. He was the second person to serve as the chief clinical psychologist in the VA (1948–1956), helping to establish psychology as an important clinical service in that agency, and he followed that appointment with a distinguished career in the Community Research and Service Branch of the NIMH. He served as a model of dedication and achievement in serving the public. Hildreth's activities were performed with an enthusiasm, pleasantness, and interest in people that still make those who knew him talk about him in glowing terms.

In an interview with the author in 1992, Lee Gurel described Hildreth as an extraordinary leader who made you believe in the importance of psychology and whose fantastic memory for personal events endeared him to others. Beyond personal qualities and interpersonal skills, Gurel suggested that it was Hildreth's role as a visionary that constituted his major contribution and set him apart from his contemporaries. He sketched a glorious, eminently believable, future for psychology. Responding to his charisma and infectious enthusiasm, his more practical-minded associates eagerly enlisted in the effort to apply psychology to bettering the human condition.

It was singularly appropriate that on his death in 1965 the division established an award for outstanding public service in his memory. The

Harold M. Hildreth Award for Distinguished Public Service has remained the highest award that the division can bestow.

The first Hildreth Award was presented to Edwin S. Schneidman in 1966. Each succeeding year, with few exceptions, the division recognized individuals who had devoted their careers to public service and who had demonstrated exemplary contributions and highest professional standards in serving the public. Table 18 lists the recipients of the Division's Hildreth Award from 1966 through 1995.

Division 18 Sections

In the 1970s, changes occurred in Division 18 that paralleled changes in the APA. The division's members still held a common bond in serving the public by working in public institutions, but specialized professional

TABLE 18
Recipients of the Division 18 Harold M. Hildreth Award for Distinguished Public Service

Year	Recipient
1966	Edwin S. Schneidman
1967	Joseph M. Bobbitt
1968	John C. Eberhart
1969	Maurice G. Kott
1970	Jerry W. Carter
1971	Henry W. Riecken
1972	Norman L. Farberow
1973	Margaret Ives
1974	Henry P. David
1975	Milton W. McCullough
1976	Lee Gurel
1977	Herman Feifel
1979	Betty H. Pickett
1981	Stanley Schneider
1982	Cecil P. Peck
1983	Charles A. Stenger
1985	Patrick DeLeon
1986	James Grier Miller
1987	Durand F. Jacobs
1988	Asher R. Pacht
1989	Alfred M. Wellner
1990	Charles Windle
1991	John E. Davis, Jr.
	Robert L. Custer
1992	Gary B. Melton
1993	Patricia F. Waller
1994	Lee Sechrest
1995	Bruce Sales

interests began emerging in the membership. The development of sections within the division arose out of this growth of substantive content and professional interest areas among its members, and members approved a bylaws change in 1974 to establish sections within the division. In 1975 the Criminal Justice Section became the first section to be organized in the division. Carl Clements was the primary individual involved in organizing the new section and became its first chair with 72 members enrolled in the fall of 1975.

At that time, 87 APA members were elected to Division 18 with an expressed interest in forming the Health Research Section. This new proposed section planned to work with the Task Force on Health Research, which had been formed by the APA's Board of Scientific Affairs in 1973. The task force was headed by Division 18 member William Schofield who was the prime organizer for the Health Research Section. The Division approved this section in 1976, and Lee Sechrest was elected as the first section chair with William Schofield as chair-elect.

The impetus for VA psychologists to join Division 18 and form a section came at a conference of VA chiefs of psychology held in Washington, D.C., in November 1976. A work group chaired by Jacob Levine identified a need for some organization to express the views and interests of the 1,250 psychologists in the VA. That work group decided that Division 18 could best serve that need. The division's officers welcomed this interest in forming a section as well as the increased input from VA psychologists in APA affairs. The VA Section was approved in 1977 with Ralph Fingar as its first chair. More than 300 new applications for Division 18 membership were received and accepted in 1977 from VA psychologists interested in the new section.

During the years following the approval of the VA Section, VA psychologists assumed an increasing number of leadership roles in the division. When Sidney Cleveland was elected division president in the fall of 1980, he commented on concerns expressed by some members that Division 18 would be dominated by the VA or that the division might even become a VA division. He assured readers of the fall 1980 division newsletter that he and President-Elect Harold Dickman (both chiefs of psychology services in VA hospitals) were psychologists in public service first and VA psychologists second (Cleveland, 1980).

Members of the Health Research Section voted to dissolve that section in 1980 with many of the members helping to create the new Health Psychology Division of the APA. A number of members of the Criminal Justice Section had also left that section to join the new Psychology and Law Division of the APA in 1981, but remaining members voted to continue the section.

A call for division members interested in forming a section on public accountability was published in the fall 1979 newsletter with Charles Windle promoting this new interest group. An organizational meeting was held at the 1980 APA convention, and the division voted to approve the new section in 1981 with Windle serving as interim chair. The official name of the new section was the Accountability, Program Evaluation, and Information Use Section.

In 1981 division members were asked to respond to interest in forming a police psychology section by writing to Harvey Goldstein. The division's Criminal Justice Section voted in 1982 to reconstitute itself as the Section on Police and Correctional Psychology. Later that year, however, Goldstein presented a proposal to the Executive Committee of Division 18 to form an independent section on police psychology. Division members approved this proposal in 1983, and Goldstein was elected chair of the new section with about 80 members enrolled.

In 1981 the Ohio-based State Association of Psychologists and Psychological Associates began conversations with Division 18 over common interests and the possibility of forming a new section within the division for psychologists working in state government. Division members were asked to communicate their interest in the proposed section to Mark Colman who agreed to collect this data. It was not until 1985, however, that Fred Frese submitted a proposal and bylaws for this section to the Executive Committee. The Community and State Hospital Psychologists Section was approved that year with Frese elected as its first chair.

In 1984 the Accountability, Program Evaluation, and Information Use Section shortened its name to the Program Evaluation Section. The Police Section expanded its name and constituency to Police and Public Safety Psychologists in 1988, and the Veterans Administration Section became the Veterans Affairs Section in 1989 to reflect that agency's name change and new cabinet-level status. Members of the Criminal Justice Section voted to change its name to the Corrections Psychology Section in 1985 and started using that name in its reports. However, a section bylaws change was never adopted and submitted to Division 18's Executive Committee, and the Criminal Justice Section retained its original name.

Other Division Issues and Activities

In 1968 an APA task force chaired by George Albee submitted a plan to the APA to elect division and state representatives to the APA Council based on an apportionment ballot. Under this plan, each APA member would have the opportunity to designate which states or divisions would represent the member on the council by distributing ten votes to any combination of states or divisions. Divisions and states receiving at least 0.5% of the apportionment ballot would receive one seat on the APA Council and an additional seat for every additional 1% of the vote received. The Albee plan, as it came to be known, was eventually adopted, although numerous proposals were presented and rejected for modifying the plan. One rejected proposal directly affecting Division 18 was a proposal to grandfather existing divisions and states on the APA Council so that they would always have one seat. With the adoption of the Albee plan and following the first apportionment ballot, Division 18 was given one seat on the council. The division has continued to receive one council seat in all subsequent apportionment ballots.

The 1970s were marked by indecision on the part of APA members about whether the organization should become more politically active. The independent clinical practice of psychology was becoming more of an issue for the profession, with many APA members opposed in principle to the concept of psychologists in independent private practice. Because of the APA members' reluctance to become involved in litigation, in part due to their fear that the organization would lose its tax-exempt status, the Council for the Advancement of the Psychological Professions and Sciences (CAPPS) was established in the early 1970s outside of the APA's formal organization. CAPPS was organized to bring suit against the U.S. Civil Service Commission and Blue Cross and Blue Shield for their refusal to recognize the independence of psychologists as providers of health services in the Federal Employees Health Benefits Plan. Division 18 contributed funds for CAPPS to use in its suit for 2 years but declined an invitation to participate as coplaintiff. Interested in increasing its involvement in advocacy, Division 18 subsequently joined the Association for the Advancement of Psychology (AAP) as a corporate member following the merger of AAP and CAPPS in 1975—a merger designed to unify APA's advocacy efforts.

New health care delivery systems were also emerging in the 1970s. In a presentation at the 1972 APA convention, Division 18 Council representative Cecil Peck, chief psychologist in the VA and 1960 Division 18 president, commented on the existing and emerging varieties of health care delivery systems in the United States and some implications for the effective participation of professional psychology in the health field (Peck, 1973). He first noted that the health care field was the third largest industry in terms of employment in the early 1970s. The federal government had entered the picture in Medicare and Medicaid programs for the general public to ensure that no individual would be denied health benefits. The Civilian Health and Medical Program of the Uniformed Services (CHAMPUS) had been developed as a health insurance system for dependents of military personnel, and the VA was firmly established as an important federal health program for veterans. The Civil Service Commission, providing health care benefits for 8 million federal employees, had oversight for the largest insurance program in the nation. In addition to a large number of traditional private insurance programs, health maintenance organizations (HMOs) were also emerging.

Peck predicted that the demand for health services would continue to overwhelm workforce production and resources available for the delivery of services. He argued that professional psychologists had to respond to increased needs for accountability in the health care field. Licensing was needed to define the function and responsibility of health care professionals. He furthered described the trend for service delivery systems to establish a fee structure for services and review mechanisms that would require adequate information systems, blind analysis of work samples, and peer review teams.

Until 1975 the only standing committee in the division other than housekeeping committees for membership, fellowship, elections, and the convention program was the Committee on Civil Service Standards. In 1975 Division 18 President Asher Pacht appointed the Ad Hoc Professional Affairs Committee to work in liaison with the APA's Board of Professional Affairs and its Professional Affairs Office. This committee replaced the Committee on Civil Service Standards as a standing committee of the division in 1976. The new committee was chaired by Alfred Wellner who had chaired the Civil Service Standards Committee and was also serving as executive officer of the National Register of Health Service Providers in Psychology. The following year, Pacht established a special Committee on the Structure and Function of Division 18 to look at the future functioning of the division. John Stern who served on the APA's Committee on the Structure and Function of Council and was chair of the APA Policy and Planning Board agreed to chair that committee. Pacht also appointed a liaison to the APA's Committee on Women in Psychology. The division members gave strong support for establishing an APA division that would focus on children and youth.

During this time, the division officers were raising questions about efforts to increase the membership recruitment of other APA members. Because two thirds of all of the APA's membership was employed full time or part time in government agencies, the potential existed for increased membership. However, Division 18 differed from most other divisions in that the membership was based on place of employment rather than on particular professional or scientific interests (Rogers, 1975.) Some debated further whether the current member's diversity of professional interests hindered the division from establishing goals that would satisfy even a majority of its members. Although the establishment of sections within the division gave more focus to professional interests, other divisions addressed professional content interests more directly.

The 1970s also marked a time when psychology needed to look at its relations with the public. In 1973, the Hildreth Award address by Henry Riecken was titled "Psychological Communication with the Public" (Riecken, 1973). He described the problems the profession had with the public's difficulty in understanding psychology and psychologists. He blamed this in part on the profession's proclivity toward "psychologizing" and "jargonizing," which he described as the embellishment or concealment of a perfectly good idea by needless psychological terms and the disguise of thought in concepts that an ordinary citizen or bureaucrat could not understand.

Division President Bernard Saper also reflected on the public conscience in his presidential column in the division's newsletter (Saper, 1977). He reported that a federally funded research program with which he had been associated had eliminated cigarettes from the reinforcement items used in a study of incontinent individuals on a geriatrics ward. Reviewers of the study indicated that they could not in good conscience approve a program that offered subjects reinforcers that were dangerous to their health. Saper further noted the public's concern for accountability. He added that accountability was a concept that had been demanding recognition and professional acceptance for almost as long as public service had been rendered. He called for psychologists in public service to welcome the trend for accountability in peer review and program evaluation and to continue developing it as a major specialty area and as a natural outgrowth of professional contributions to tests and measurements, psychological statistics, and research methodology. As noted earlier, Charles Windle of NIMH took up this challenge in his successful efforts to establish the Accountability, Program Evaluation, and Information Use Section of the division.

DIVISION 18 FROM 1986 TO 1996

During the mid-1980s, APA leadership dealt more directly with concerns over whether the APA should be a learned society or a trade association or, if both, in what proportions. Heated arguments on this issue between clinical practitioners and scientist–academicians led to fears that if the APA was not restructured, the organization would lose the science base of its membership. The APA formed the Task Force on the Structure of the APA Council to look at different ways to organize in order to best meet member needs.

At its March 1987 midwinter meeting, Division 18 officers met with representatives of the APA's Governance Affairs Services to discuss concerns for representation of divisions in the APA's reorganization plans. The membership of Division 18 had always had strong interests in both clinical practice and research areas as well as in public interest and education, especially in its members' involvement in academic and internship training. Proposals being considered appeared to ask division members to select from these four areas the one that would best address their primary professional interests. Division members generally saw this as unnecessary, unproductive, and, in fact, destructive to the APA's mission. Durand Jacobs, former Division 18 president and current Division 18 Council representative was appointed as liaison to the APA's group on restructuring to represent the division's concerns in the planning discussions of that group.

In 1988 the restructuring proposal went to the membership. That proposal provided for the establishment of two to five "societies." Members could join more than one society but could vote in only one. Divisions could be conveners of the founding societies along with other nondivision assemblies or coalitions. The concern of Division 18 members that they would need to declare their allegiance to a segment of the profession became a reality. Many saw this proposal as an end to the strengths in diversity of the APA and an artificial separation of the membership. Division 18 membership opposed the restructuring proposal, and it was defeated by the APA membership in a 57% to 43% vote.

Division Advocacy Activities

The public service client advocacy which had formed in the 1970s, took on the responsibility of helping move the APA in critical directions through advocacy in APA Council resolutions in the 1990s. Communication and working relationships with the APA's directorates also increased, especially with the Practice and Public Interest Directorates. In 1986 the division began working with the Public Interest Directorate to prepare a resolution requesting the APA to promote a White House conference on the needs of homeless individuals who were seriously mentally ill. A division task force was appointed in 1987 to formulate a position statement for the APA on this issue.

In 1990, Division 18 published its first public interest platform to guide the leaders and members of the Division in addressing concerns and promoting action steps to meet the needs of a diverse client population. That platform identified concerns regarding the lack of access to quality mental health services for several underserved populations, the need to train psychologists to meet the needs of these populations, the need to conduct meaningful research and evaluation activities in human services, the promotion of consultation and other interventions to prevent physical and mental illness, and the importance of public policy advocacy in addressing these concerns. The platform guided the division membership in preparing its resolutions promoting the need for adequate and permanent shelter for homeless people and for addressing the needs of persons with serious and persistent mental illness. The APA Council of Representatives passed both of these resolutions in 1991.

Working with the Practice Directorate and the Board of Professional Affairs, the division membership prepared a resolution to work toward removing state licensure exemptions for psychologists in public health care programs in order to provide the same standards of care as existed in the private sector. The APA Council of Representatives approved this resolution in 1992. In 1994 the APA Council of Representatives approved a Division 18 resolution to fund a task force that would make recommendations to APA on professional practice, research, and training issues in the treatment of serious mental illness and serious emotional disturbance. The task group would also develop coalitions with consumer groups, state mental health program directors, and others to recommend further collective action in support of the needs of that patient population and their families. Other resolutions pending before the council developed by Division 18 and submitted in 1994 and 1995 included (a) recommendations for the identification, treatment, research, prevention, and reporting of domestic violence; (b) recommendations for the identification, training, and organizational responses to workplace violence; and (c) recommendations to address the needs of persons with mental disorders in the nation's jails and prisons.

The division's 1995–1996 public service agenda was constructed around a goal of developing APA, state association, and public support for both a public institution and private-sector health care system as national and state leaders examined health care reform. The agenda also called for continued public funding for the training of future psychologists. Through its agenda, Division 18 membership finally urged that patients and family members be included in the planning for health care services and programs.

Internal Division Activities

The division membership increased dues to $15 per year in 1987 and to $20 per year in 1992. Throughout most years of the division's existence, the largest division expense was the newsletter, which had been published and distributed to members two or three times a year since the early 1970s. In 1987 the division established its Distinguished Service Awards to recognize special contributions of its members. It was also in 1987 that a Division 18 suite was established at the APA convention to serve as a formal and informal meeting place for the division's members. Starting with the 1988 convention and continuing through the 1995 convention, Division 18 membership reduced expenses by sharing a suite during the convention with the Association of VA Chief Psychologists.

Starting with the 1989 convention, a division symposium was established titled "Critical Issues in Public Service Psychology." For these annual symposia, each section of the division selected a representative to discuss a topic of current importance for their section. Each year's symposium provided a forum for a division-wide discussion of important topics and for learning about issues that confronted each section.

In 1991 the division's executive committee began holding its midwinter meeting in conjunction with the APA Division Leadership Conference. This scheduling permitted Executive Committee members to meet with other division officers and APA staff members and to learn about issues facing the APA and their impact on divisions. It also provided an opportunity for members of Division 18 to express their concerns and help shape the APA's agenda for its divisions. The division became a founding member of the Executive Roundtable of Practice Divisions, which was established to look at ways the practice divisions could increase their input into APA governance and policy. In preparation for the APA centennial in 1992 and in recognition of its charter status as one of the original divisions formed in the APA, the division membership voted to donate $1,000 to the APA Centennial Fund and became a member of APA's Gold Circle Club.

Section Activities

The division currently has five sections: Criminal Justice, Evaluation, VA, Police and Public Safety, and Community and State Hospital Psychologists. These sections continue their important role in division activities. The sections serve as a common professional interest focus for its members and additionally provide subject matter expertise for the APA and division projects that promote public interest agendas.

The Criminal Justice Section, the division's oldest section, had 295 members and affiliates in 1995. Over the past decade this section had developed a membership directory to increase and enhance communication among its members. The members of the section also contributed to section networking by developing a list of members interested in special section activities such as employment issues in correctional institutions, mental health services to prison inmates, and work with sex offenders. Members of the section had also begun work on developing an annotated bibliography of articles on the delivery of psychological services in criminal justice settings. The members also worked with the American Association of Correctional Psychologists to develop standards of care, and they increased section and division membership by working with psychologists in the Federal Bureau of Prisons. In 1994 the section developed its first miniconvention for its members. In 1995, the section's leaders completed work on the division's APA resolution on workplace violence and submitted it to the APA Council.

The Evaluation Section had 238 members and affiliates in 1995. In addition to developing a membership directory, section members have been active over the past 10 years promoting program evaluation, including the development of a program evaluation statement for the division's 1990 Public Interest Platform. Section members were generally concerned with the lack of program evaluation and needs assessment activities that were expected of programs in the 1960s and 1970s. In 1994, the section members developed a task force to examine the needed role of evaluation in government-sponsored programs. Members of the section also worked toward increasing liaison with the American Evaluation Association. In a response to a 1989 NIMH request for proposals to study alcohol, drug, and mental health treatment services for individuals with multiple diagnoses, Evaluation Section members distinguished themselves by receiving three of the five awarded grants.

Shortly after its formation, the VA Section quickly became the largest section in Division 18 and has retained that distinction through its 1995 membership of 433 members and affiliates. Over the past decade, the VA Section has worked with the Association of VA Chief Psychologists and the National Organization of VA Psychologists on such issues as bonus pay for board-certified VA psychologists and the promotion of Title 38 employment for psychologists in the VA. The latter would set pay based on qualifications of the individual psychologist instead of basing it only on requirements for the position. Although Title 38 employment was not approved, authority to provide bonus pay for board certification was approved; however, it has not yet been implemented. Section members similarly assisted the VA Mental Health and Behavioral Sciences Service in Washington in studying recruitment and retention issues for psychologists, support for VA internship programs, and support for VA research funding for psychology and other VA mental health investigators. In 1988, members of the section helped reject a proposal to establish alternative management styles in VA mental health programs, proposals which challenged the status of psychology as an independent service. The same issue arose in 1995 with section members working with other VA groups and APA leadership to develop position papers used when APA officers were asked to testify before Congress which was looking at a VA reorganization plan. The objective of this testimony was to maintain psychology as a separate discipline with direct lines of authority to the medical center chief of staff.

The Police and Public Safety Section, with 396 members and affiliates in 1995, is the second largest section in Division 18. In addition to developing a membership directory for its own members, the section members successfully marketed and sold the directory to others interested in identifying psychologists with expertise in police and public safety psychology. During its history in the division, the section members developed recommended practices for the preemployment screening of police officer applicants. The section membership also concerned itself with issues ranging from demands on police psychologists to release confidential information from critical incident debriefings to problems created by the Americans with Disabilities Act of 1990 that resulted in regulations adverse to the appropriateness of the preemployment screening of police applicants. The section leaders also developed a series of specialized seminars or miniconventions immediately preceding the APA convention, which provided the opportunity for members to interact with each other and with a wide range of law enforcement personnel in the city of the convention. The miniconventions were so successful that they were offered for APA continuing education credits starting with the 1993 convention.

The newest section in the division, the Community and State Hospital Psychologists Section with 303 members and affiliates in 1995, took the lead in developing division policies and APA resolutions for homeless people and people with serious mental illnesses. The section also promoted and helped develop the division's policy on licensure for psychologists in public service as well as the resolution that established and funded a task force on the seriously mentally ill. The section membership developed liaisons with consumer groups, especially the National Alliance for the Mentally Ill, and established contact with the National Association of State Mental Health Program Directors. The section has addressed concerns ranging from mental health services provided in rural areas to the need for a more appropriate and relevant graduate school curriculum addressing the needs of seriously mentally ill individuals. Its members represented Division 18 in the APA and NIMH policy meetings on national conferences for this training topic and similarly represented the division on the APA Task Force on Rural Psychology and the APA Task Force on the Seriously Mentally Ill. The section also provided leadership in the division's partnership with the Public Interest Division of the California Psychological Association in establishing the first public interest luncheon at the 1994 APA convention to bring together public service psychologists, members of state associations, and representatives of state departments of mental health to provide a forum for discussing important public mental health issues.

CONCLUSION

With 1,348 members and affiliates in 1995, including 137 graduate student members, Division 18 has retained its relative membership strength among APA divisions over the past 30 years. Within the APA, 24 divisions have fewer members and 26 have more. Today's members of Division 18 work in diverse locations, including community mental health centers, state hospitals, VA medical centers, criminal justice systems, police and public safety settings, and academic institutions. About 38% of all APA approved internship sites and 36% of all APA approved full-time internship slots for the 1994 to 1995 training year are located in VA medical centers, state hospitals, or community mental health centers. Public service psychologists manage and implement mental health treatment programs for millions of patients treated in inpatient and outpatient settings and in community support systems. Members are also involved in varied basic and applied research programs throughout the country. In 1995, the division had 114 fellows, placing it in the top third of all APA divisions in the proportion of its members that have been recognized with this status for their contributions to the profession.

As the APA enters its second century, Division 18 continues its 50-year history of providing a forum for its members to discuss common professional interests. The division also continues its advocacy in helping the profession serve the diverse mental health needs of the public.

REFERENCES

Baker, R. R. (1992, Fall). Division 18: 1945 to 1992. *Newsletter for the Division of Psychologists in Public Service*, pp. 5, 11.

Cleveland, S. (1980, Fall). Division 18 will not become VA division. *Newsletter for the Division of Psychologists in Public Service*, pp. 1, 7.

Ives, M. (1981, Fall). Public service in psychology. *Newsletter for the Division of Psychologists in Public Service*, pp. 2–4, 7, 8, 11, 13.

McNeill, H. V. (1976, Winter–Spring). Reflections on the history of the Division of Psychologists in Public Service. *Newsletter for the Division of Psychologists in Public Service*, pp. 5–7.

Minutes of the Business Meeting of the Division of Psychologists in Public Service. (1964, September 4). Available from author.

Minutes of the Executive Committee Meeting. (1975, August 30). *Newsletter for the Division of Psychologists in Public Service*, pp. 3–5.

Peck, C. P. (1973, Summer). Varieties of health care delivery systems. *Newsletter for the Division of Psychologists in Public Service*, pp. 12–17.

Riecken, H. W. (1973, Summer). Psychological communication with the public. *Newsletter for the Division of Psychologists in Public Service*, pp. 3–11.

Rogers, L. S. (1956). Psychologists in public service and the public. *American Psychologist, 7,* 307–313.

Rogers, L. S. (1975, Fall). Whither Division 18: A point of view. *Newsletter for the Division of Psychologists in Public Service*, pp. 19–20.

Saper, B. (1977, Winter–Spring). Left over notions about public service. *Newsletter for the Division of Psychologists in Public Service*, pp. 1–2.

6

A HISTORY OF DIVISION 25 (EXPERIMENTAL ANALYSIS OF BEHAVIOR)

JAMES T. TODD

On September 8, 1964, the Council of Representatives of the American Psychological Association (APA) approved the formation of the Division for the Experimental Analysis of Behavior. The divisions of the APA are numbered consecutively, so the new division was formally designated Division 25. It followed the formation of the Division of Theoretical and Philosophical Psychology in 1962 and preceded the founding of the Division of the History of Psychology in 1965 (Hilgard, 1987). Division 25 is devoted to the promotion of behavior analysis—a comprehensive natural science approach to psychology that emphasizes the discovery of principles by which the behavior of individual organisms may be described, predicted, and controlled without reference to hypothetical mediating or initiating mechanisms or processes. The predominant, but not exclusive, philosophical perspective represented by Division 25 is radical behaviorism (Skinner,

Preparation of this chapter was supported by the Division 25 Executive Committee and by a Faculty Travel Award from Eastern Michigan University. The author expresses gratitude to Herbert Barry III, Joseph V. Brady, A. Charles Catania, Anthony Cuvo, Thomas C. Dalton, Donald A. Dewsbury, James Dinsmoor, Ronald Drabman, Israel Goldiamond, Steven C. Hayes, Karen A. Lambert, Victor G. Laties, Edward K. Morris, Ellen P. Reese, Beth Sulzer-Azaroff, Jane A. Summers, Priscilla Taylor, and Gina E. Truesdell-Todd. Some archival information was obtained from the Archives of the History of American Psychology, University of Akron, John Popplestone, director. All archival sources cited in this manuscript are in the possession of the author in preparation for transfer to the Archives of the History of American Psychology.

1974). Radical behaviorism combined some aspects of the classical behaviorism of John B. Watson (e.g., 1913, 1919)—especially its emphasis on pragmatism, direct application, and the analysis of the behavior of the whole organism (Todd & Morris, 1994)—with a type of descriptive positivism derived from Francis Bacon and Ernst Mach (Smith, 1992, 1995). Thus, most Division 25 members espouse and practice a highly descriptive, empirical, and technological approach to basic research and application, which has been considered by many to be out of the mainstream of psychology even though it does, in some ways, represent one of its most precise instantiations (see, e.g., Barash, 1977, pp. 1–8).

As this chapter shows, Division 25, like the *Journal of the Experimental Analysis of Behavior (JEAB)*, was founded in response to behavior analysts' dissatisfaction with the reception of their work by traditional psychologists during the 1950s and early 1960s (Laties, 1987). In particular, some behavior analysts believed that their work was unwelcome in the experimental divisions of the APA. Division 25 was created to solve those problems by giving behavior analysis its own forum within organized psychology. For many years, in fact, the primary function of the division was to have a program at APA conventions. In the mid-1970s, however, the division membership began to broaden the scope of its activities. Division members became active in supporting behavior analysis on a national level by sponsoring awards and participating directly and proactively in APA affairs.

This chapter describes some selected aspects of the development of Division 25 including its founding, membership trends, programs, newsletter, awards, and role in the the APA reorganization efforts. It features, in addition, tables and graphs of Division 25 officers, newsletter editors, award recipients, and membership. This chapter is not, however, a complete accounting of every aspect of the division's history. It does not cover, for instance, most of the minutiae of Division 25 Executive Committee deliberations or minor adjustments in division operation. Rather, it is intended as an overview of the important activities of the division from 1964 to 1994. As such, its intended audience is the Division 25 membership, especially newcomers, and all others within and outside the APA who are interested in learning more about how Division 25 evolved and its role within organized psychology in North America.

FOUNDING OF DIVISION 25

Although Division 25 was founded in 1964, its roots can be traced back almost two decades earlier to the first Conferences on the Experimental Analysis of Behavior (see Dinsmoor, 1987). The Conferences on the Experimental Analysis of Behavior began in 1947 as a means of exchanging and disseminating behavior analytic research. At that time, Clark

Hull's (1943) mediational neobehaviorism was the dominant viewpoint in the conditioning and learning field (Knapp, 1995). Radical behaviorists had no journals or major organizations of their own. The conferences and the mimeographed notes that they produced (see Dinsmoor, 1987) were the only formal means the behaviorists had to communicate among themselves. For the first few years, the conferences were conducted at universities or during regional psychological conventions. But as the number of behavior analysts grew, something more regular and convenient was needed. In 1956, therefore, the Conferences began to be conducted as part of the annual convention of the APA.

As B. F. Skinner (1983) recalled, even holding the Conferences at the APA convention was not an ideal arrangement, especially as the number of behavior analysts increased:

> More and more people were attending, and we had trouble finding space. By 1960 we needed three or four half-day sessions, but we were dependent upon the largesse of the Division of Experimental Psychology and often found ourselves crowded into small, poorly ventilated—and in those days smoke-filled—rooms. We often looked for larger, unscheduled rooms and moved our meetings, but that was inconvenient and wasted time. (Skinner, 1983, p. 262)

According to Skinner, to remedy the space problem, the Board of the Society for the Experimental Analysis of Behavior (SEAB (pronounced say-ab); SEAB was formed to publish JEAB; see Laties, 1987) appointed a committee to look into starting a new division. This "committee" was actually Skinner himself, as SEAB board minutes reveal:

> The new division of A.P.A was discussed as a means of providing better programs during the A.P.A. convention and other advantages of division status. Skinner was appointed a committee of one to look into the formation of the new division. (SEAB Minutes, September 3, 1963)

In any case, the requirements for starting a new division were simple, as specified in the APA bylaws:

> A Division shall be established whenever one percent or more of the Members of the Association petition for it and the Council of Representatives approves. A two-thirds vote of those present at any Annual Meeting of the Council of Representatives is required for the establishment of a new division. (Reed, 1963, p. xiv; see Hilgard, 1945a, 1945b, 1987 for information on the history of the APA divisional structure.)

The membership of the APA at the time was approximately 23,000 (Hilgard, 1987), so a petition of 230 signatures was required. The signatures for the most part were obtained by means of a petition in the form of a memorandum to the Council of Representatives of the APA that *JEAB*'s business manager Kay Dinsmoor sent to the approximately 400 personal subscribers to *JEAB* (Brady, 1965; Skinner, 1983). The text of the memorandum described how the space offered by Division 3 had become "less and less adequate" and used the success of *JEAB* as evidence for interest in a new division. This mailing garnered, according to Skinner, "over two hundred and eighty replies—a very handsome return." After researcher Stanley Pliskoff conducted some negotiations with the APA, the motion to install the division easily passed. According to APA records, the division had 254 founding members, 41 of whom were APA fellows.

The formation of the new division was announced in the February 1965 *American Psychologist*:

> The purposes of the Division are stated in its Bylaws: (a) to promote basic research both animal and human, in the experimental analysis of behavior, (b) to stimulate the exchange of information concerning such research, (c) to encourage the application of the results of such research to human affairs, (d) to promote the teaching of basic analysis and its technological extensions, (e) to cooperate with scientific, technological, and humanistic disciplines whose interests overlap those of the Division. (p. 170)

In reality, however, the primary purpose of Division 25 was to ensure that behavior analysts had sufficient time on the APA program to meet their growing needs. The division's first president, Joseph V. Brady, described this focus in the first issue of the division's newsletter, the *Division 25 Recorder* published in July 1965.[1]

> The APA convention will provide the forum for this communication exchange and our formal status as a division of the national organization assures us equal time and meeting space with respect to other special interest groups within the profession. Beyond that this formal affiliation with APA may contribute to our ability to make ourselves heard as a group on certain policy issues involving the national organization and professional matters. As a rule, however, the group concerned with the experimental analysis of behavior had not distinguished itself in the political area and it is unlikely that our reinforcements as members of Division 25 will extend much beyond the advantages offered in arranging the annual meeting. (Brady, 1965, p. 1)

---

[1]An unpublished report on the history of the divisional newsletter, the *Division 25 Recorder* (Todd, 1992) is available from the author and includes a bibliography of all articles and substantive pieces published in the *Recorder* from 1965 to 1995.

In a similar vein, SEAB President Victor Laties recalled,

> The whole point of the Division really was to have a program at APA. I don't think it had any activity past that. . . . it was not about to start a journal or go out in any direction. (Laties, personal communication, May 1992)

As mentioned earlier, the formation of the new division was not based solely on the desire to avoid inconvenience and crowding at conventions. Underlying the "high-sounding language" (Brady, personal communication, April 1992) of the division's bylaws was a significant level of dissatisfaction among behavior analysts concerning their treatment by traditional psychologists. That is, some behavior analysts felt that the lack of program time was not simply the result of the increasing demands of all experimentalists on the limited amount of time available. Behavior analysts perceived a backlash against their work from the traditional animal learning community represented primarily by the Division of Experimental Psychology (Division 3). The discussions that led to the founding of *JEAB* were also based on a similar dissatisfaction, particularly with policies (formal and informal) of the *Journal of Comparative and Physiological Psychology* (see, e.g., Brady, 1987; Dews, 1987; Herrnstein, 1987; Laties, 1987). Those policies, which reportedly required arbitrarily large groups of animal subjects and the use of statistical tests, meant that behavior analytic research was becoming unwelcome in the traditional animal learning journals. A similar situation, it appeared, was occurring at the APA. In this regard, Skinner (1983) complained of the "pitifully small space" (p. 263) assigned to the behavior analysts by Division 3 in 1963 and worried that if he had been called to explain the need for a new division, he might have raised resentment against the petition by revealing the "real reasons" (p. 263) behind it. Brady has concurred with this assessment:

> The rationale was very much the same as the rationale for starting the journal [*JEAB*]. We weren't getting no respect, as Rodney Dangerfield would say. And that was reflected in the fact that program time at the annual meetings was always rationed. (Brady, personal communication, April 1992)

It should not be surprising, therefore, that the SEAB board, which founded Division 25, was composed of virtually the same people involved in the founding of *JEAB* (see Hineline & Laties, 1987), for descriptions of the founding of *JEAB*). As the leaders of a rapidly growing field, *JEAB*'s founders had already experienced difficulty having their findings published and were sensitive to the possibility that the same processes could occur in another context.

DIVISION GOVERNANCE

One important practical concern facing the founders of Division 25 was the structure of its governance. APA bylaws required each division to have its own set of bylaws specifying an executive committee consisting of at least a president and a secretary. Thus, SEAB board members faced two questions: (a) How should the Division 25 executive committee be structured, and (b) who should serve as the first president of the division?

With respect to the latter question, the sentiment of the SEAB board members was that Skinner was the obvious choice to serve as president. There was no one more closely identified with behavior analysis and no one more prominent in the field. The name of the division, like the title of *JEAB*, was taken directly from the title of Skinner's *The Behavior of Organisms: An Experimental Analysis* (1938). In fact, because Skinner was so active in the formation of Division 25, he is widely considered its founder (Dinsmoor, personal communication, September 13, 1992; Laties, personal communication, May 1992).

Skinner, for his part, was not eager to serve as president of the division—although, according to Brady, "We did everything we could to twist his arm" (personal communication, April 1992). A primary reason for Skinner's reticence was his concern that the division not be viewed as a personality cult consisting of his followers or disciples. Rather, he believed that the division should be aimed at promoting and disseminating behavior analysis as a discipline and behaviorism as a philosophy of science. In a letter to Brady, Skinner wrote,

> I am very anxious that this organization not be dubbed Skinnerian. You have all suffered from that, and you have my sympathy. I think it would be best for everyone if the new Division were drawn up and set on the road without my being involved in it. There are a great many reasons why [the president] ought to be you. You have done a lot of work and supported a lot more, and you are not a student of either Keller or Skinner. Moreover, you are an amiable chap who can spread good will as needed. The President would, of course, be serving on the Council during his term of office. I don't know of anyone who would be a better liaison man. (Skinner, 1983, p. 263)

The division followed Skinner's advice and Brady served as its first president. Even so, the perception that Division 25 consisted largely of Skinner's followers could not be prevented. This view has, in fact, become part of the standard history of psychology. According to Hilgard (1987) in *Psychology in America: A Historical Survey*:

> The Division for the Experimental Analysis of Behavior showed that a single leader with a coherent viewpoint and methodology could still attract a following. In 1980 there were more members in this division

committed to B. F. Skinner's variety of behaviorism than there were in the Division of Experimental Psychology. (pp. 759–760)

Another reason why Skinner might have declined to serve as the first president of the division lies in the structure of its executive committee. Unlike any other division at the time, the president of Division 25 served a 3-year term. Brady explained the reason for the extended term in the first issue of the *Division 25 Recorder*:

> One of the unique features of the Division 25 organization ... is the duration of the terms of its officers. Unlike other APA divisions which limit tenure to one year, Division 25 officers serve for three years in an effort to encourage more effective participation in the affairs of the organization and minimize the solely "honorific" character which such roles frequently tend to assume. (Brady, 1965, p. 2)

Given this, Brady has suggested that Skinner was not willing to assume the presidency because the post was unlikely to further his own interests in any substantive way (Brady, personal communication, April 1992). Skinner, Brady said, had a "long-standing aversion" to activities that consumed his time but did not produce lasting products. Skinner did agree to serve as the division's first vice president. However, the bylaws of the division did not specify duties for this office. (See Tables 19 and 20 for lists of Division 25 officers and APA Council representatives.)

PROGRAM YEARS, 1965 TO 1971

After its founding, the division membership immediately began to perform the division's primary mission: to organize a program at the annual APA convention. For its first formal program, Division 25 was allocated eight 1- or 2-hour blocks over 4 days for a total of 11 hours. The first division-sponsored event was a joint symposium with the Division of Clinical Psychology (Division 12) on "Therapeutic Ideologies and Practices—Psychoanalysis and Operant Behavior," which was scheduled from noon to 1:50 P.M. on Saturday, September 4, 1965, in Illinois Room 57 at the LaSalle Hotel in Chicago. The symposium was chaired by Robert A. Harper; Israel Goldiamond represented behavior analysis and Bertram Pollens represented psychoanalysis. The program also included a symposium titled "Teaching the Experimental Analysis of Behavior," and paper sessions with such titles as "Operant Behavior," "Aversive Control," and "Operant Behavior in Humans." The most important session, held in the grand ballroom of the Palmer House Hotel, was a symposium chaired by Joseph Brady titled "The Problem of Consciousness," featuring B. F. Skinner and Yale philosopher Brand Blanshard (see Skinner & Blanshard,

TABLE 19
Division 25 Officers

Term	President	Vice President	Secretary–Treasurer
1964–1966	Joseph V. Brady	B. F. Skinner	Stanley S. Pliskoff
1967–1969	Nathan H. Azrin	Israel Goldiamond	Roger Ulrich
1970–1972	Charles B. Ferster	Donald M. Baer	Norman W. Weissman
1973–1975	William N. Schoenfeld	Roger Ulrich	Leila Cohen
1976–1978	A. Charles Catania	James A. Dinsmoor	Elkan Gamzu
1979–1981	Victor G. Laties	Rosemery O. Nelson	Jon Krapfl
1982	Rosemery O. Nelson		Jon Krapfl
1983	Jack Michael		Barbara Wasik
1984	Jack Michael (term extended through 1984)		Barbara Wasik
1985	Beth Sulzer-Azaroff		Barbara Wasik
1986	Stephanie B. Stolz		Ronald Drabman
1987	Steven C. Hayes		Ronald Drabman
1988	Kurt Salzinger		Ronald Drabman
1989	Todd R. Risley		Ronald Drabman
1990	James G. Holland		Bruce A. Thyer
1991	Ellen P. Reese		Bruce A. Thyer
1992	James A. Dinsmoor		Bruce A. Thyer
1993	Barbara C. Etzel		Bruce A. Thyer
1994	Kennon A. Lattal		Clair Poulson
1995	Philip N. Hineline		Clair Poulson
1996	Edward K. Morris		Clair Poulson

Note. Division presidents served 3-year terms until 1982, when a three-tiered system was adopted. After 1982, individuals were elected to serve 1 year each as president-elect, president, and past-president. In 1983, terms of office were extended from August to the end of the year in order to make terms of office correspond to the calendar year. Thus, Jack Michael's term as president extended from mid-1983 to the end of 1984.

1967). The relative informality of the division was suggested by the allocation of more time to the first division social hour than to the business meeting. (Division 25 hospitality suites have been described as "legendary" by some attendees.)

For the next several years, until about 1972, the primary functions and foci of the division continued to be planning and running the annual program at the APA convention. Papers and symposia on aversive control were common in the late 1960s. The proportion of papers on applied topics increased each year. Some were dissatisfied with the relatively small number of papers in the first few years. The program committee corrected this situation by streamlining the submission process and adding a category for informal presentations, with a deadline just a few weeks before the convention. Division membership was growing rapidly; more than a hundred new members annually were added for several years (see Figure 5). By 1973,

TABLE 20
Division 25 Representatives to the APA Council of Representatives

1964–1966	Israel Goldiamond, Joseph V. Brady
1967–1969	Nathan Azrin, James A. Dinsmoor, Charles B. Ferster, and Fred S. Keller
1970	Charles B. Ferster, William N. Schoenfeld, and Herbert S. Terrace
1971	James A. Dinsmoor, Charles B. Ferster, William N. Schoenfeld, and Herbert S. Terrace
1972	James A. Dinsmoor, Charles B. Ferster, and Jack Michael
1973	James A. Dinsmoor, Jack Michael, and William N. Schoenfeld
1974	Jack Michael and William N. Schoenfeld
1975	William N. Schoenfeld and Beth Sulzer-Azaroff
1976–1977	A. Charles Catania and Beth Sulzer-Azaroff
1978	Nathan H. Azrin and A. Charles Catania
1979–1981	Nathan H. Azrin and Victor G. Laties
1982	Victor G. Laties and Todd R. Risley
1983–1984	Todd R. Risley and Stephanie B. Stolz
1985	Todd R. Risley and Evalyn F. Segal
1986	Rosemery O. Nelson and Evalyn F. Segal
1987	Evalyn F. Segal
1988	Nathan H. Azrin and Steven C. Hayes
1989–1991	Nathan H. Azrin
1992	Kurt Salzinger
1993	Bruce Thyer
1994–1995	Barbara Wasik

Note. From 1967 to 1973, Division 25 had three representatives on the APA Council of Representatives. Because individuals took turns on the APA Council, some years have more representatives listed than the division had council seats. From 1974 to 1986 and from 1988 to 1991 the division had two representatives. In 1986 to 1987, the number dropped temporarily to one. From 1991 to the present, the division has had one representative.

as Hilgard (1987) noted, Division 25 was larger than Division 3 (1,241 versus 1,158 members respectively).[2]

Nonprogram issues did arise in the early years. Some minor problems arising from the original structure of the Division 25 executive committee were corrected when the membership revised its bylaws to coordinate the terms of the executive committee with the 3-year term of the president. The three Division 25 representatives to the APA Council of Representatives provided input on a wide variety of matters, including ethical standards for psychologists. Brady (1966) reported on early plans toward APA reorganization. The Division 25 executive committee also decided to support the proposed cancellation of the 1969 APA convention planned for Chicago. (Chicago's civil rights record and practices were the basis of the

[2]This report uses APA records of division membership. Because membership is posted at different times at the divisional and APA levels, some discrepancies exist between official APA records and Division 25 membership records. The missing figures in the tables and graphs represent categories for which membership figures are not available or appear to be in error.

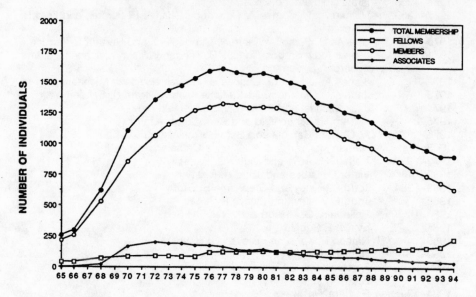

MEMBERSHIP IN DIVISION 25 BY CATEGORY (1965-1994)

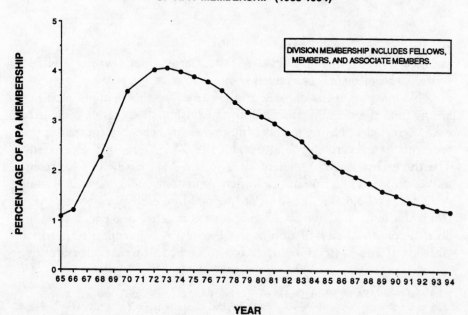

**DIVISION 25 MEMBERSHIP AS PERCENTAGE
OF APA MEMBERSHIP (1965-1994)**

Figure 5. Top: Division membership by category, 1965–1994. Bottom: Division
Membership as a percentage of total APA membership.

cancellation; televised accounts of police excesses in controlling protests outside the 1968 Democratic National Convention had spurred national outrage.)

GROWING PAINS, 1972 TO 1979

From 1972 to 1979, Division 25 responded to the changing nature of psychology and the growth of the field of behavior analysis by expanding its focus beyond running a program at the annual APA convention. As one of the largest divisions, Division 25 was able to support a number of initiatives and deal directly with issues such as the professionalization of behavior analysis, the role of women in psychology, and APA reorganization.

Early 1970s

By 1972, the issues facing the division had become more complex. The APA was growing rapidly and Division 25 had become one of the largest (Hilgard, 1987). A new publication, the *APA Monitor*, appeared and took over some of the functions of the *Division 25 Recorder*—APA news and job postings in particular. A reorganization plan that would change the APA from a divisional system to one made up of federated societies was an important concern. Indeed, the only item in the May (Spring) 1972 issue of the *Recorder* was an informational message from President Charles Ferster concerning the federated societies plan (Ferster, 1972). A poll of division members found strong support for reorganization, with most of the respondents favoring federation with Divisions 3 and 6 (Weissman, 1972, p. 1). Despite such support, however, the members of the division did not seem overwhelmingly interested in the details of APA politics. In 1972, the division lost one of its three seats on the 1973 APA Executive Council because fewer than one quarter of the possible votes by division members (ten each) were allocated to the division (*Recorder*, March 1972, p. 3).

The growth of behavior analysis meant a growth in the number of students of behavior analysis. Thus, in 1973 and 1974, under the leadership of Ellen P. Reese, Division 25 began to take an active role in promoting student activities and involvement in the division. The Division 25 executive committee initially voted to sponsor student participation at regional meetings (Reese, 1974). Later, student activities would become a priority of the division. In 1974, the *Recorder* began to include a "Student Recorder" section. The first editor of the "Student Recorder" was Steven C. Hayes, who was a graduate student at West Virginia University and would later become a Division 25 president and one of the founders of the

American Psychological Society (APS; see Tables 21 and 22 for lists of *Division 25 Recorder* and "Student Recorder" editors). By 1977, the Division 25 student organization reported more than 400 members[3] and it had its own governance, convention dinner, and business meetings (see the "Student Recorder" section of the Winter and Summer 1977 *Recorders*).

Mid-1970s

Behavior analysis was changing from a discipline devoted primarily to basic research to one devoted primarily to application. Even the mastheads of the *Recorder* and "Student Recorder" gave evidence of that change. Since its inception, the cover of the *Recorder* featured a cumulative record derived from basic research. The "Student Recorder" logo, in contrast, featured a stylized graph of the reversal design commonly used in applied behavior analysis research (see Figure 6). The increasing numbers of members working in applied behavior analysis meant that legal and ethical issues became an important concern for the division in the mid-1970s. Applied behavior analysis was nontraditional in its approach to understanding and treating problem behaviors. Few people outside the field actually witnessed applied programs in operation. However, conceptual works such as Skinner's *Walden Two* (1948), *Beyond Freedom and Dignity* (1971), and *About Behaviorism* (1974)—or, more likely, inaccurate accounts of those works—had sensitized the public to the fact that the seemingly

---

[3]The deriviation of this figure is uncertain; no list of student members could be located. However, the division had established a category of "affiliate" membership for students and others who were not APA members. These members are not recognized or counted in any official APA category.

TABLE 21
Editors of the *Division 25 Recorder* and *Behavior Analysis*

1965–1966	Israel Goldiamond
Summer 1967–1970	Roger Ulrich
Fall 1970–1973	Norman W. Weissman
1974–1976	Todd R. Risley
1977–1978	Michael F. Cataldo
1979–1981	John R. Lutzger
1982–Spring 1984	Judith E. Favell
Summer 1984–1985	Peter Harzem
1986–1987*	William Buskist
1988–1989*	Linda J. Hayes
1990–1992	Edward K. Morris
1993–1995	James Mulick
1995–	Timothy J. Hackenberg

Note. Unless otherwise indicated, editors served full-year terms. From 1986 to 1988, the *Recorder* temporarily become the journal *Behavior Analysis*.

TABLE 22
Editors of the "Student Recorder" Section

Fall 1974–Spring 1975	Steven C. Hayes
Summer 1975	William Myerson
Winter 1975–Summer 1976	Donald Prue
Winter–Fall 1977	Eva Feindler
Winter–Summer 1978	Gillian Kupfer
Winter–Fall 1979	James W. Partington
Spring–Fall 1980	George G. R. Kunz
Summer 1981	Irwin Rosenfarb
Summer 1986	Donald A. Burge
Fall 1986–Fall 1987	Timothy J. Freeman
Fall 1987–Winter 1988	Barbara J. Kaminski
Summer—Fall 1988	Barbara S. Kohlenberg

Note. There was no "Student Recorder" prior to Fall 1974, between Summer 1981 and Summer 1986, and after 1989. Freeman and Kaminski served as coeditors of the Fall 1987 issue.

antidemocratic notion of "control" was fundamental to behavioral interventions (Dinsmoor, 1992; Todd & Morris, 1983, 1992). As a result, the fundamental ethics of behavioral treatments were questioned in the media and popular press (see, e.g., Hilts, 1974). Division members responded to instances of misrepresentation through the *Recorder* (e.g., Bernstein, 1976; Goldiamond, 1975). The division membership also created a committee to "deal with . . . distorted and unfairly behavior mod type of publicity" (Hol-

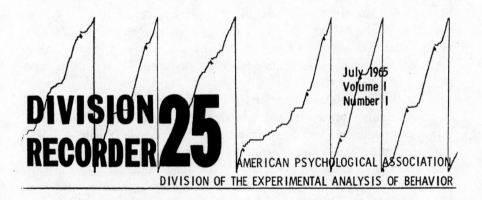

Figure 6. Top: Masthead from the first issue of the *Division 25 Recorder* (July 1965) showing cumulative record. Bottom: Masthead from the first installment of the "Student Recorder" section (Fall 1974) with reversal design logo.

land, 1975, p. 12) and initiated a *Recorder* column on "Legal Developments Related to Behavior Modification" (Schwitzgebel, 1974, 1975a, 1975b).

Their nontraditional approach to psychology also put behavior analysts outside the mainstream of training and certification. In many cases, the procedures being implemented by behavior analysts in applied settings were not covered by existing rules or laws. In addition, some behavioral academic programs did not conform to the APA's proposed accreditation guidelines. These issues were to become an ongoing concern for Division 25 members beginning in the mid-1970s because the APA was the single most important body promoting the certification and licensing standards of psychologists. At that time, psychologists were pushing for equal status with psychiatrists as providers of psychological treatments, and if regulations were to be created governing licensure and other matters, legislative bodies were going to need to know what a psychologist was and could do. Unless the APA officially acknowledged the existence and effectiveness of behavioral techniques, students in behavioral programs and individuals already in the field might find themselves professionally unrecognized. That is, they might not have the professional credentials necessary for employment, therapeutic autonomy, and third-party reimbursements.

Although the division began to deal with ethics and certification within the APA, the appearance and growth of behaviorally oriented organizations outside APA in the mid-1970s began to undermine the membership of Division 25. The Association for the Advancement of Behavior Therapy (AABT) was already having yearly conventions and was of interest to those employing Pavlovian-based behavior therapy and cognitive-behavioral treatment approaches. More important for the operant core of the division, the Midwestern Association for Behavior Analysis (MABA; pronounced mah-bah) was founded in 1974 and in 1979 became the Association for Behavior Analysis (ABA; pronounced Ah-bah); see Dinsmoor, 1979; Peterson, 1978, 1979). Because ABA was small and independent, it was not in a position to influence decisions with respect to behavior analysis on a national level as was Division 25. In the 1970s, however, the division was not very active in this regard, so many behavior analysts found ABA a more comfortable home. Its regional origins put it near several important behavior analytic centers, including the University of Kansas, Indiana University, Western Michigan University, and West Virginia University. MABA and ABA conventions (held primarily in Chicago and Milwaukee during the first decade) were smaller, less expensive, and more open to significant student participation than APA conventions. (ABA made no distinction between submissions by students and full members and did not include degree or membership designations on its name badges or in its convention program.) Perhaps most important, the social atmosphere of ABA was more comfortable than that of APA conferences;

behavior analysts were not a minority in an organization that was increasingly clinically oriented, as was the case at APA conventions.

The growth of ABA did not have a large effect on Division 25 membership for a few years. The division continued to grow, and by 1976 its program spanned almost 40 hours—approximately four times the amount allocated a decade earlier. Students continued to be active and had their own program time at the APA and the regional conferences. The "Student Recorder" section had become longer than the entire *Recorder* had been just a few years earlier. Applied presentations now outnumbered basic presentations. The division membership continued to be concerned with misrepresentation of behavior analysis.

Late 1970s

Certification began to take center stage in the late 1970s. The APA held its first meeting on education and credentialing in June 1976. Future Division 25 President Rosemery O. Nelson represented Division 25 at the second meeting in June 1977 and wrote a detailed report on certification for the *Recorder* (Nelson, 1977). Without question the APA would promote uniform and traditional definitions of a professional psychologist and psychological training. At issue for behavior analysts was how their nontraditional, research-oriented applied training programs would fit into the APA proposals. A related issue that would draw the attention of the division's members was the possible recognition of behavior analysis as a specialty area. The APA accredited programs in three specialty areas: clinical, counseling, and school psychology. According to Nelson, behavior analysts would have to decide to push for the creation and recognition of a new specialty area or take the easier route and label behavior analysis a subspecialty of one of the existing areas (Nelson, 1977).

The late 1970s were also a time of increasing attention to women's rights. At its August 1977 meeting, for example, the APA Council of Representatives voted to inform some of its scheduled convention cities that the convention would be moved unless that city's state legislature ratified the Equal Rights Amendment. The *Recorder*, for its part, reported on the Feminist Behaviorists Workshop held earlier at the meeting of the Association of Women Psychologists and division members solicited nominations for a liaison to the newly formed APA Committee on Equality of Opportunity in Psychology (*Recorder*, Fall, 1977). Moreover, a *Recorder* article titled "The Female Behaviorist: Professional Inequalities" (Bernstein, 1977) argued that women were underrepresented in professional roles in behavior analysis. The division's origins in male-dominated basic research was undoubtedly the major contributing factor. In 1977, only 13% of the division members were women.

Despite a small flurry of responses to Bernstein's article in a subsequent *Recorder* (see Bernstein, 1978a, 1978b; Laties, 1978; Peyser, 1978; Shepard, 1978; Stolz, 1978), women's participation in the division did not become the subject of ongoing official concern. The Midwestern Association for Behavior Analysis, by contrast, had already established a Committee on the Professional Development of Women in Behavior Analysis. Because MABA was drawing many of its new members from applied programs, which had higher ratios of women to men than basic research programs, by 1992 43% of the members of the Association for Behavior Analysis were women (ABA, personal communication, August 1992). Membership by women in Division 25, by contrast, does not yet exceed 20%. Of course, many of the concerns about the professional development of women in psychology were handled by the APA at the national level, thus relieving the division of the necessity to take some specific actions. Even so, many women served in Division 25 leadership posts, with representation on the Executive Committee and other leadership roles equaling or exceeding the proportion of women in the division at large (Dinsmoor, personal communication, September 13, 1992).

The important issue of 1978, one that would eventually consume much of the division's attention and energy, was APA reorganization. Academic and research-oriented psychologists (this included most of the division's membership) had complained that the APA was neglecting their interests in favor of those of the clinical divisions. (The APA's increasing attention to accreditation and related issues, described earlier, were seen as symptoms of this trend.) The academics and researchers feared the APA would become a guild, with its primary focus being to protect the fees and professional status of clinicians in private practice. As a result, academics and researchers were leaving or simply not joining the APA.

A new reorganization plan summarized by Beth Sulzer-Azaroff and A. Charles Catania (1978) in the *Recorder* was supposed to remedy some of these problems by establishing four semiautonomous assemblies that would recognize the "major functions" of psychologists: Assembly A would include clinical service providers, Assembly B would encompass basic and applied researchers (and presumably Division 25), Assembly C would correspond roughly to industrial–organizational psychology, and Assembly D would include those psychologists whose major function was teaching. The leadership for each assembly would run its own affairs and speak officially on matters of concern to it. The APA would then represent psychology as a whole and coordinate the activities of the assemblies. In essence, the applied and basic researchers would have their own organization, money, and forum. They would not have the funds the clinicians brought to the APA (although they believed they were not getting their share anyway), but they could at least control what funds were theirs.

The division membership still put on a program, of course. In 1978, for the first time, all data-based research reports were scheduled as posters. This was called an "experiment" by program chairs Paul Touchette and Barbara Ray (1978, p. 1). Division representatives solicited written reaction to the new format from attendees. That year, 43 posters were scheduled with applied and basic researchers about equally represented. The Division 25 hospitality suite continued to be an important feature of the APA meeting (Lutzger, 1978). The success of the hospitality suites was a result, in part, of the availability of a detailed instruction manual, *How to Run a Hospitality Suite*, prepared by Jon S. Bailey and Darrell Bostow in 1975. The manual proved so useful, in fact, that Hayes' (1985) revision of it was adopted as official policy of the division in 1985 (*Recorder*, Spring 1986, p. 10).

As 1980 approached, the field of behavior analysis as a whole was growing and applied behavior analysis becoming its dominant component. The division would soon have to face the consequences of that growth. The model accreditation standards reported by Nelson in 1977 had been dropped for legal and technical reasons. But, as President Catania stated in his outgoing message (1979), the problems created by the standards were not thereby solved. They were merely deferred: Sooner or later the place of behavior analysis within the profession of clinical psychology would have to be dealt with and settled. The relevance of the APA (and traditional psychology) to behavior analysis was increasingly questioned. The growth of the division had stopped as behavior analysts opted for membership in ABA and AABT. Catania argued that the ultimate survival of behavior analysis would be compromised by abandoning organized psychology—departments of psychology were the training grounds and academic homes for most behavior analysts. That is, he argued, the discipline could not afford to become too isolated and parochial.

THE ACTIVIST DIVISION: 1980 TO 1989

During the 1980s a new activism emerged in Division 25. Issues of major concern to the division were arising frequently at the national level and the new circumstances caused a corresponding change in the composition of the membership and executive committee "from free-spirited rather casual pioneers to people who take political activities very seriously" (Dinsmoor, personal communication, September 13, 1992). Division representatives became active in promoting the interests of behavior analysts through the Council of Representatives, and the division membership continued to be concerned with the changing nature of the field, particularly the "professionalization" of applied behavior analysis. The division members also made several efforts to expand the division's scope beyond the APA, especially through journal acquisition and publication efforts. Reorganization of the APA became a central issue. The repeated defeat of successive reorganization plans would lead Division 25 membership to consider leaving the APA.

The Seeds of Activism: Professionalization and Reorganization

The seeds of the new activism can be seen in the publication in the *Recorder* of "The Professionalization of Division 25" by Nelson and Hayes (1980). The impact of the article may have been small in itself, but its publication marked the point at which Nelson, Hayes, and a few others would begin to provide the energy and direction for many of the division's activities through the 1980s. For their part, Nelson and Hayes' efforts to focus the attention of the division were clear from the beginning. The central question of their article was, "What is the mission of Division 25?" Their answer was, "The advancement of the experimental analysis of behavior" (Nelson & Hayes, 1980, p. 7) as a discipline rather than applied behavior analysis as a profession. They argued that devoting too much attention to professional issues (see, e.g., Born, 1979; Wood, 1980) would divert needed resources from developing and promoting behavior analysis per se. A few years later, Hayes' "Long Term Plan" for the Division would expand on these ideas (see Hayes, 1983a, 1983b, 1984).

Still, professionalization was an important issue. A segment of the behavior analytic community was becoming professionalized because of the growing demand for master's-level behavior analysts in human service agencies. PhD-level skills were simply not needed to design and conduct most interventions in these settings (Wood, 1980). The APA leadership, however, wanted to discourage terminal master's programs because it considered the PhD the minimal requirement for one to be a psychologist or provide services. (Guilds tend to stiffen entrance requirements to control the number of providers. This restricts supply and enables guild members to command higher fees.) The division membership attempted to counteract such moves. For example, division representatives objected to an APA Council motion specifically designed to discourage master's programs, and the motion was dropped (Azrin, 1980).

The guild trend would not be halted. In 1984, APA council representative Todd Risley reported on the problems that the APA's approach to accreditation would create for behavior analysis (Risley, 1984). The APA leadership was in the process of designating "true" psychology programs and accrediting those that prepared students to become "health service providers" (i.e., eligible for third-party reimbursements.) The system the APA was developing emphasized traditional, eclectic training and thereby ensured that some established applied behavior analysis programs could not be accredited. Students of those programs would not be automatically eligible for licenses and might not be employable in many settings regardless of their skills. Moreover, APA council representative Stephanie Stolz complained that "many psychologists active in the governance of APA do not know anything about the analysis of behavior" (1984c, p. 57). Risley and Stolz pointed out that the division was the only means by which the APA could be made to recognize these problems in its proposals and called on increased active support from division members.

As stated earlier, reorganization was also a major concern within the APA. A new plan called for a bicameral APA with the academics and practitioners in separate "forums" (see Azrin, 1980). The forums would meet separately, then together, to decide on APA matters. The division membership endorsed this plan, but it realized that the proposal put Division 25 into a unique position because of its mix of members with basic and applied interests. If the APA split into two forums, the division leadership would have to place one representative in each. Thus, the possibility that the division might lose a representative in 1981 was a cause for action. As had happened in 1972, too few votes were being allocated to the division and a downward trend suggested that the division would soon lose a seat on the APA Council of Representatives. Front page appeals in the *Recorder* (e.g., Fall 1980) prevented the loss of representation—but only temporarily.

Division 25 "Self-Examination" and the "Long-Term Plan"

Within the division itself, Victor G. Laties became the final president to serve a 3-year term. A new system had been ratified in 1981 that established a three-tiered presidency. The winning candidate would serve for a year each as president-elect, president, and past-president. This preserved the continuity of the previous 3-year system but eliminated the awkward transition that occurred when each 3-year term ended abruptly. The first president (pro tem) under the new system was Rosemery Nelson. The first president-elect was Jack Michael.

Among Nelson's goals as president in 1982 was a "critical self-examination of the goals and activities of Division 25" (Nelson, 1982, p. 5). This self-examination was to be accomplished by an ad hoc long-term planning committee chaired by Hayes. In an effort to construct a plan of action for the division, Hayes solicited comments concerning the division's purpose and goals through the *Recorder* and by making direct inquiries of divisional fellows and the Executive Committee members. Hayes (1983a, 1983b) summarized the results of his inquiries in the *Recorder*, but he continued to solicit input.

The division was active in the Council of Representatives. Reorganization, as previously mentioned, was a major topic, but other issues of concern to behavior analysis were also being dealt with. Work on accreditation was ongoing. Animal rights groups were becoming more active and made a special target of psychological research. A series of *Recorder* and "Student Recorder" articles and announcements called attention to the need for division members to address the APA council and various committees concerning the importance of research with animals (see, e.g., Stolz, 1984b, 1984c). An ad hoc committee was created to explore means by which applied behavior analysis might be added to the existing four specialty areas. In addition, opposition to the use of aversive control with children was growing. In 1982, for example, the Division of School Psychology (Division 16) introduced a resolution asking that the APA take a stand condemning aversive control. In 1983 the issue was still under study with Division 25 representatives taking the position that the existing APA Code of Ethics provided sufficient safeguards. Throughout a series of meetings and conference calls, Division 25 was allied with the Divisions of Mental Retardation (Division 33) and Health Psychology (Division 38), in opposing the resolution, but Division 16 and the Division of Child, Youth, and Family Services (Division 37) favored it. Through the efforts of division members Stolz, Risley, Michael Cataldo, and Bruce Sales, the opposing factions finally reached a compromise in 1984, which called for an examination of all types of physical interventions used with children (see Stolz, 1984a).

In 1984 a report by Hayes, "Long Term Plan: Focus on Our Special Role" was published in the *Recorder*. Hayes described the major factors that guided the plan: (a) The division was no longer the only voice in behavior analysis; other groups, especially the ABA, were more attractive to many behavior analysts. (b) Applied behavior analysis was no longer as closely tied to and dependent on basic research. (c) Applied behavior analysis faced a unique set of problems related to increasing professionalism. These factors would be addressed by several actions: (a) The division would take as its major focus the promotion of the interrelationship between applied and basic behavior analysis. (b) The division would recognize basic and applied behavior analysis as having unique concerns and address those concerns "in a way that does not lead to strains between them, or too much deflection of the attention of the Division away from its more general mission" (p. 17). (c) The division would take a more activist stance to promote behavior analysis within organized psychology. (d) The division established a midyear meeting.

All of these recommendations were adopted. The first midyear meeting was scheduled for November 18, 1984, in Greensboro, North Carolina (then Hayes' affiliation.) The Division 25 executive committee moved to appoint liaisons to other organizations such as ABA, AABT, and SEAB. Most visible to the general membership, however, was the establishment of the Donald F. Hake Award. Hake had been an influential and well-respected researcher at West Virginia University before his untimely death at age 45 in 1982. The awards committee members felt his work exemplified the kind of productive interaction between applied and basic behavior analysis that they wished to promote. A memorial fund for the Hake Award was established and supplemented by $1,000 from SEAB (see *Recorder*, Spring 1986, p. 10). The award itself consisted of a plaque and an honorarium. The recipient is expected to give an address, and the honorarium is given, in part, to help defray the recipient's travel expenses. In 1986 the first recipient of the Hake award was Murray Sidman, whose *Tactics of Scientific Research* (1960) introduced single-subject methodology to an entire generation of behavior analysts. (See Table 23 for lists of awards recipients.)

In 1986 the *Division 25 Recorder* temporarily became a journal with the title *Behavior Analysis*. (see Todd, 1992, for a history of the *Recorder*). This change was made to provide a more formalized means of apprising members of developments of interest to them within the APA. President Stolz ran the division from Japan. Her "Message from the President" (Stolz, 1986a, 1986b, 1986c) columns in the first issues of the new journal clearly showed that the division had succeeded in implementing the long-term

TABLE 23
Division 25 Awards Recipients

	Donald F. Hake Basic/Applied Research Award
1986	Murray Sidman
1987	Donald M. Baer
1988	Barbara C. Etzel
1989	Nathan H. Azrin
1990	Travis Thompson
1991	Fred S. Keller
1992	Sidney W. Bijou
1993	Joseph V. Brady
1994	Israel Goldiamond
1995	F. Charles Mace
	B. F. Skinner New Research Award
1994	Craig H. Kennedy
1995	Linda Cooper
	Fred S. Keller Behavioral Education Award
1994	Patricia J. Krantz and Lynn E. McClannahan
1995	Siegfried Englemann
	Outstanding Dissertation Award for Basic Learning Processes
1993	Derek Davis
1994	Armando Machado and Lynn Aronson
1995	Linda Van Hamme

plan. New committees, liaisons, and task forces were at work on a wide variety of projects. Old issues such as specialty status for behavior analysis continued to receive attention. New issues, such as teaching the experimental analysis of behavior in high schools and an effort to require practitioners to be aware of scientific developments in psychology and employ them in practice, were the focus of special committees. Relative successes, such as changes to the APA's revision of the 1967 model guidelines to explicitly recognize "behavior analysis and therapy" and to liberalize slightly the accreditation standards (to the possible benefit of behavior analysis) were credited to the division's efforts (Hayes, 1986).

Not all was well, however. Division membership was declining rapidly and steadily through the 1980s, although the APA itself was growing (see Figure 5). As a consequence, the division lost one seat on the APA Council of Representatives for the 1987 to 1988 year. A letter signed by Skinner and Fred Keller to all division members would help achieve the allocation necessary to temporarily reinstate the representative a year later, but the division would lose the seat again in 1992. *Behavior Analysis* ceased publication in 1988 because of budgetary and organizational problems. The *Recorder* would reappear in 1990 under the editorship of Edward K. Morris.

Plan to Merge With SEAB

Some notable division initiatives failed. A proposal by Stolz in 1985 to merge the SEAB and Division 25 proved unsuccessful. Stolz saw the opportunity to acquire and publish two successful, well-respected journals (*JEAB* and *The Journal of Applied Behavior Analysis*) and thereby increase the division's visibility and ability to promote issues of concern to behavior analysis on a national level (Stolz to Executive Committee, undated 1986 memo). The SEAB board, in contrast, did not have much to gain by a merger and was particularly concerned about losing its independence. Victor Laties, executive editor of *JEAB*, led the opposition to the merger. In a memo to the SEAB board of directors (August 18, 1986), Laties identified a number of problems inherent in Stolz's suggestion that "SEAB would become a standing committee of Division 25" (Stolz's memo to SEAB board, July 15, 1986). Chief among them was the issue of control over the decisions of the SEAB board. That is, as a committee of the division, any decision by SEAB would be tentative, requiring the ultimate approval of the division's executive committee. A critical concern was over who would control SEAB's assets. Although Stolz's plan called for SEAB to become one component of Division 25, SEAB's yearly budget (in 1986) was actually more than 30 times that of the division ($300,000 a year for SEAB versus $9,000 for the division). Given that such large sums were involved, the division could not be expected to allow SEAB to act entirely independently. Based on such considerations, Laties wrote, "SEAB appears to be working well; it seems a shame to disturb the status quo." (Laties to the

SEAB board, August 18, 1986). The issue was discussed a final time at the executive committee meeting on August 21, 1986, but no decision was made. The issue became moot when the SEAB board voted on August 24 not to pursue the merger with Division 25.

Division Name Change

An effort by Hayes (1987b) to have the word *experimental* removed from the name of the division (see also Minutes, August 1987 Executive Board Meeting) was similarly unsuccessful. According to its bylaws (Article I, Section 1), the official name of the division was the Division for the Experimental Analysis of Behavior, a Division of the American Psychological Association. This name was selected because division leaders believed it accurately described the interests and composition of the members at the time the division was founded. Over time, however, the characteristics of behavior analysis as a discipline changed. By the mid-1970s, the number of applied behavior analysts began to exceed the number of basic researchers. When the division took on its increasingly activist posture, the apparent discrepancy between its experimentally oriented designation and increasingly applied character became an issue. President-elect Hayes argued that the Association for Behavior Analysis used a similar shorter term successfully:

> "Behavior analysis" is a wonderfully straightforward term, if a rather bold one. Because of its very simplicity, it has a good chance of withstanding the test of time. (Hayes, 1987b, p. 45)

Even so, in 1986, the Division 25 executive committee felt that changing the name of the division might be a mistake considering the other ongoing initiatives (see Hayes, 1987c). Hayes did, however, solicit input on the matter from the fellows of the division in 1987 (see Hayes, 1987c) and reported that the overwhelming sentiment of those who responded to his query was to drop the word *experimental*. Of the 49 fellows who responded (35% of the total), 80% favored changing the name of the division to "Behavior Analysis," 8% favored a change but were undecided about the term *behavior analysis*, and another 12% were opposed either in principle or because the plan was ill timed. Among those reportedly favoring a name change were Skinner, Reese, Sidney W. Bijou, and Donald M. Baer. Among those opposed were Laties, Stolz, Larry Byrd (who was concerned that basic researchers might view the change as a threat from the applied side), and James Dinsmoor (who argued that deleting the term would deemphasize the core feature of the discipline, namely that its principles are based on "experimental analyses"; Dinsmoor undated 1987 memo).

Despite the apparent support for the idea of dropping the term *experimental*, no official proposal for changing the name of the division was ever considered. That is, the issue was neither won nor lost, it was simply dropped. Issues of greater immediate importance arose. Paramount among them was the failure of the APA reorganization plan, the subsequent appearance of the American Psychological Society (APS), and the division's responses to both events.

Reorganization Takes Center Stage

Another new APA reorganization plan was unveiled in 1986. (The plan to establish forums had not been adopted.) Called the Bardon plan, it was similar to the plan reported by Sulzer-Azaroff and Catania in 1978 in many respects except that it called for two to five assemblies, each to represent a major division within psychology. Like the earlier reorganization efforts, the Bardon plan was designed to reverse the exodus of scientists and academics from the APA by giving them a large degree of autonomy while maintaining a strong central voice for psychology. The plan did weaken the hand of the clinicians, however, and failed to pass in February 1987 by a narrow margin despite the strong support of the scientific and academic divisions, including both Division 25 representatives (see Hayes, 1987a).

The reasons for the defeat of the Bardon plan were controversial (see Hayes, 1987a; Nelson, 1987). When the plan came to the floor of the Council of Representatives meeting, it was met by two alternative reorganization proposals. One alternative was authored by an ad hoc coalition called The Constituencies Working Group and the other reportedly came from the APA Board of Directors itself. According to Hayes, the controversy arose from the fact that the clinicians (fearing a loss of power) had seemingly forced the APA to create a last-minute alternative to the plan it had itself commissioned. The existence of three proposals divided support and none received a majority. Following the loss, the Council of Representatives formed the Group on Restructuring APA (GORAPA) from members of various groups involved in restructuring.

Two days following the loss of the Bardon plan, 36 representatives of the scientific divisions, one member of the board of directors, and Beth Sulzer-Azaroff of the Board of Scientific Affairs (and Division 25) endorsed a letter written by Hayes (see Hayes, 1987a) that announced the formation of the Assembly for Scientific Psychology (ASP). ASP members would fight for the interests of academics and scientists within the APA and, if necessary, leave the APA. Two days later, Division 25 was the first Division to support the ASP formally and financially with a contribution of $100.

The Assembly for Scientific Psychology was quickly renamed the Assembly for Scientific and Applied Psychology (ASAP), bylaws were written, and elections held. Division 25 President Hayes became the first secretary–treasurer of the ASAP (see Hayes, 1987b). ASAP members continued to have the support of Division 25 and continued to threaten to leave the APA, taking with it entire divisions and their journals. A process by which divisions might leave the APA and reaffiliate with an independent ASAP was never developed, but the ASAP gained strength nevertheless.

In 1988 Kurt Salzinger became division president. Salzinger was well respected for his balanced, thoughtful approach to issues. He had served as president of the New York Academy of Sciences as well as on a number of APA posts such as the Board of Scientific Affairs and the Council of Representatives. In his presidential column, "Living in Interesting Times," in *Behavior Analysis*, Salzinger strongly encouraged members to support both the division and the ASAP (see Salzinger, 1988b, 1988c, 1988d). Salzinger suggested that such support was one way to counteract the guild interests within the APA. Salzinger was also supportive of the new GOR-APA reorganization plan, which he described in his first column. He also headed the Committee on the Reorganization Effort (CORE) with Hayes and Division 25 member Ronald Drabman. CORE encouraged members to support the new reorganization efforts and raised approximately $2,000 to campaign for the passage of the new plan.

Reorganization became a top priority of the division. The Division 25 executive committee meeting minutes for 1987 and 1988 show considerable attention and debate about actions the division might take with respect to the APA, the ASAP, and the soon-to-be-formed APS. Even so, the division had time to address other concerns. An important anniversary year for behavior analysis occurred in 1988: John B. Watson's (1913) "Psychology as the Behaviorist Views It" had been published 75 years earlier; Skinner's *The Behavior of Organisms* (1938) was 50 years old; *JEAB* had appeared 30 years before in 1958; *The Journal of Applied Behavior Analysis* was 20 years old; and *The Behavior Analyst* was 10. Special invited addresses commemorated these events (Buckley, 1988; Burnham, 1988; Hineline, 1988; Morris, 1988a; Salzinger, 1988a; Samelson, 1988; Skinner, 1988a, 1988b; Timberlake, 1988). *Behavior Analysis* published a special section on the psychology of interbehaviorist J. R. Kantor (L. Hayes, 1988; Lundin, 1988; Lyons & Williamson, 1988; Morris, 1988c; Ribes, 1988; Roca, 1988). Specialty status for behavior analysis continued to be explored and Reese's Committee on Behavior Analysis in high schools was active. Edward K. Morris, who had been appointed the division's first public information officer in 1982, continued his work and placed a detailed report in *Behavior Analysis* (Morris, 1988b). New committees to address diverse issues such as the history of behavior analysis, public information, and adherence to scientific findings by clinicians had been formed.

By the opening of the 1988 APA Convention in Atlanta, the GOR-APA plan had lost. Political pressure from the guild interests was blamed. This pressure had reportedly turned GORAPA member and APA presidential candidate Stanley Graham from a supporter of reorganization to an opponent. Graham subsequently won the election, thereby raising suspicion of a sweetheart deal. The defeat of the GORAPA plan galvanized the ASAP forces. The ASAP's name was changed to the American Psychological Society (APS) and its leaders announced that the society would become an independent organization devoted to the needs and interests of scientific psychology. Scientists and academics at the 1988 APA convention could be easily identified by their new APS buttons, and the Division 25 hospitality suite was a center of APS activity. Factions even formed within Division 25. Some members, such as Past-President Hayes (also secretary–treasurer of the APS), supported moving the scientific divisions, including Division 25, to the APS. Others, such as Salzinger (1988b, 1988c), opposed moving the division. (There was no mechanism for such a move in any case.) However, Salzinger did support some form of affiliation between Division 25 and the APS to "put the APA on notice" (Salzinger, 1988c, p. 119).

THE PRESENT: 1990 TO 1994

After the APA reorganization debates of the 1980s, the membership of Division 25 began a period of relative calm. Reorganization and related issues no longer consumed large amounts of members' time and energy. Instead, the membership was able to attend its mission of promoting behavior analysis as well as to pressing issues in the field of psychology such as the rise of facilitated communication and proposals to extend drug prescription privileges to psychologists.

The Passing of B. F. Skinner

The 1990s began on a sad note for Division 25 members. On August 18, 1990, the division lost its founder, B. F. Skinner. Skinner had been suffering from leukemia and died just 8 days after receiving the APA Lifetime Scientific Contribution Award on August 10, 1990 (Keller, 1990a; Vargas, 1990). Skinner's (1990) keynote address on that occasion was defiant. After beginning with a bit of dry humor concerning the requirement that he give a paper in exchange for the award, Skinner forcefully attacked traditional and cognitive psychologists for squandering the potential of the discipline by retaining the prescientific assumptions they had inherited from religion and everyday language. Drawing a parallel to fundamentalist religious objections to the materialism inherent in Charles Darwin's concept of natural selection, Skinner accused cognitive psychology of being the "creationism" of psychology because of its tendency to attribute behavior to hypothetical, unobservable creative and initiating processes rather than to objectively verifiable causal mechanisms. In the place of cognitive and traditional psychology, Skinner called for a true science of behavior based on the analysis of the interaction of behavior and the environment.

Behavior analysts had known of Skinner's illness for several months. Even so, his death so soon after his virtuoso performance at the APA ceremony came as a shock to many. A special issue of the Fall 1990 *Recorder* was devoted to memorials for Skinner by all of the former presidents of the division (with Marilyn Gilbert writing for her late husband, Charles Ferster). The memorials described a dedicated scientist and engaging person. In his contribution, Skinner's lifelong friend Fred Keller (1990b) effectively summarized the social and empirical goals of Skinner's life's work:

> He is still alive for those who value the unity in multiplicity of a scientific system. He is still alive for those who would apply behavior's laws to the solution of society's problems, large or small, in whatever nation of the world, now or in the future. He is still alive, especially, for those who would build a non-punitive, non-competitive, non-discriminatory system of education, mutually reinforcing for everyone involved, and applying to all ages and every kind of skill. (p. 21)

Old Debates and New Awards

Skinner's passing did not mean the end of Division 25. Division 25 was, as Skinner hoped it would be, devoted to the promotion of ideas, not to the promotion of an individual, and it continued its work. The division would be the site of a few final shots in the reorganization controversy, but even those battles eventually subsided. The APS grew and, in 1992, claimed about 14,000 members (Bower, 1992). The division did not try to move to the APS and the APS made no place for it. A form of APA reorganization occurred in the form of the new directorate system. (The division's interests were represented primarily by the Science Directorate.) Division membership continued to shrink (although the Association for Behavior Analysis and most state behavior analysis organizations grew in size). As a result, the division again lost one seat on the Council of Representatives in 1992. Still, the high level of involvement in APA affairs that the division membership initiated in the early 1980s continued. This included efforts to establish applied behavior analysis as a specialty area, concern and debate over the use of aversive treatments, input into a new APA code of ethics with changes favorable to the concerns of behavior analysts, and a call by Salzinger during an APA council meeting for full disclosure of the salaries of APA officials (see 1990 and 1991 *Recorders*).

Within the Division itself, the Hake Award had become an annual tradition and three new awards were announced: (a) the B. F. Skinner

Young Researcher Award (for "innovative and important research in the broad field of behavior analysis within the first five years after receiving a doctorate"); (b) the Fred S. Keller Behavioral Education Award (to go to "a distinguished long-term member of the behavioral community whose research and/or teaching had led to a broad appreciation of behavior analysis"); and (c) the Division 25 Award for Outstanding Dissertations on Basic Learning Processes (see Table 23). The division programs included numerous papers on diverse topics and, in 1991, the division initiated an annual dinner to replace the hospitality suite.

Some fallout from the reorganization debacles continued in 1991. In an article called, "Why APA Does Not Deserve Our Support," Hayes (1991) recapped events surrounding the defeats of the Bardon and GOR-APA plans and questioned both the integrity of the APA as an organization and APA President Graham. Interest in old battles had apparently waned. The subsequent *Recorder* published a strongly worded response from Graham (1991) and letters from several division members and officers who argued in favor of remaining in the APA (Catania, 1991; Paniagua, 1991; Salzinger, 1991; Stolz, 1991). The final volley in this debate was a letter to the editor by Hayes in the Summer 1992 *Recorder* in which he reiterated his claims about Graham, described his dissatisfaction with the APA and the APS, and outlined the reasons he helped found yet another new organization: the American Association of Applied and Preventative Psychology (AAAPP).

Division members were doing well outside the division. In 1990 future division president Kennon A. Lattal was appointed guest editor for a special issue of the *American Psychologist* to be devoted to the work of B. F. Skinner. Of the 86 articles submitted, 23 were accepted (*American Psychologist*, 1992). The contents of the special issue, titled "Reflections on B. F. Skinner and Psychology," were announced in the Summer 1992 *Recorder* and the issue was published in November 1992. Lattal became president-elect of the division in 1993. In 1993 Charles R. Schuster, a Division 25 fellow, received the 1992 Distinguished Scientific Award for the applications of psychology from the APA ("Schuster Honored," 1993). The 1990s were also good for Kurt Salzinger. Salzinger was selected to deliver one of the five prestigious Centennial Master Lectures. His 1992 paper, "The Experimental Approach to Psychopathology," showed the power and subtlety of the principles of behavior analysis when applied to the problems associated with mental illness. Two years later in 1994, Salzinger used the support and stature he had earned for his work on a variety of APA posts to garner a nomination for the presidency of the APA. Salzinger had good support from the scientific and academic divisions, but he eventually lost the election to Norman Abeles, Director of the Psychology Clinic at Michigan State University.

The division's main function continued. The 1994 APA convention featured more than 40 Division 25 papers, symposia, and awards presentations in 19 1- and 2-hour blocks over the course of 4 days. As in 1965, the time allocated to division social functions exceeded the time allocated to business—7 hours for business versus two 2-hour events and one indefinitely long dinner party. The Summer 1993 issue of the *Recorder* informed division members of the results of a poll on the desirability of a dues increase to support the initiation of a digest journal, *Psychscan: Behavior Analysis and Therapy*. Out of approximately 900 members, 183 supported the initiation of the journal, 50 opposed, and 7 abstained (Etzel, 1993). Bruce Thyer, the Division 25 secretary–treasurer, coordinated the *Psychscan* effort and the new journal appeared in early 1995. Under the leadership of Celia W. Gershenson, Division 25, along with the ABA, the SEAB, the Cambridge Center for Behavioral Studies, and the Society for the Advancement of Behavior Analysis (SABA, the publisher of *The Behavior Analyst*), participated in the APS's Human Capital Initiative (Gershenson, 1993). The Human Capital Initiative is an effort to develop research objectives and initiatives in six areas of broad national concern including productivity in the workplace, drug and alcohol abuse, and the aging society.

The division weighed in on controversial issues. Foremost among them during this period was *facilitated communication* (FC). FC is a technique by which persons with communication disabilities are assisted by a "facilitator" who guides the disabled person's arm or hand during typing. Empirical research had demonstrated unequivocally that FC could not be shown to produce literacy above pretreatment levels and, worse, single- and double-blind studies had demonstrated that the words supposedly typed by the disabled individual were actually authored by the facilitator (Jacobson, Mulick, & Schwartz, 1995). On August 14, 1994, a resolution critical of FC, proposed by Division 33 council representative and Division 25 fellow Richard M. Foxx, was cosponsored by Division 25 and adopted by the APA council (see Mulick, 1994). A major review article critical of FC, coauthored by *Recorder* editor James Mulick, appeared in the September, 1995 *American Psychologist* (Jacobson, Mulick, & Schwartz, 1995).

Finally, to ensure that the division would continue to be an important voice in organized psychology in North America, 1994 President Lattal reported on a six-part strategic plan. Lattal had expressed concern over the implications of the division's declining membership and complained of a disproportionately low allocation of funds from the APA. He argued, nevertheless, that behavior analysts must continue to work within the APA to promote its social and scientific goals (Lattal, 1994b). The six objectives of the plan were: (a) to represent behavioral psychology within the larger and more diverse community of American psychology, (b) to advance the science and practice of behavioral psychology, (c) to communicate effectively and in a timely manner with members about issues of importance, (d) to recognize the achievements of behavioral psychologists, (e) to develop the membership of the division, and (f) to provide sound governance for the division (Lattal, 1994a). The implementation of this plan was ongoing (e.g., awards) and to be developed. However, some positive signs were on the horizon. In 1994, for the first time since 1975, division membership apparently would not decrease and, for the first time ever, the term *behavior analysis* would be included as a subject index term in the APA Convention program.

CONCLUSION

Division 25 was founded by free-spirited pioneers at a time when it was possible for a relatively small group of highly productive psychologists to have the force of a major movement (Todd & Morris, 1992). Despite the energy and goals of its founders, however, the formation of Division 25 was not based on lofty aspirations. Division 25 was founded in order to secure program time for behavior analysis at APA conventions. Nevertheless, as psychology grew and became more complex, the division membership responded by expanding the division's scope as issues arose. When it became clear that the APA's course was not likely to be diverted from the promotion of guild issues, the division membership began to take measures to protect its own interests by being proactive in APA affairs—that is, it became an activist division.

Division 25 has had a degree of success in its activist role. It has been at the head of several important issues and initiatives and, with the adoption of Lattal's strategic plan, promises to continue to be an active force. However, the influence of Division 25 within the APA, even in concert with other scientifically oriented divisions, is tempered by the combined power of the clinical divisions, the pressure of the guild interests, and the proliferation of speciality divisions. Division 25 membership, like the memberships of other scientific divisions, is shrinking—both in actual numbers and in its proportion to total APA membership. It is possible, therefore, that Division 25 may soon be unable to maintain the allocation of votes required to keep its one remaining seat on the Council of Representatives. The members of the division, if they are to protect their interests, might find it necessary to affiliate more closely with one of the specialty divisions, such as Division 33 (Mental Retardation), or abandon the APA altogether for organizations such as the Association for Behavior Analysis (which is itself becoming increasingly active in promoting professionally related issues). Thus, given the internal dynamics of the APA and other events, it remains to be seen how effective the leaders of the division will continue to be in promoting the division's interests through the APA. Moreover, new issues—such as the growth of the profession of psychology, especially as a result of the large output of "professional schools" of psychology outside the academic mainstream, and prescription privileges for clinical psychologists—suggests that members of the APA may be forced to pay increasingly serious attention to scientific standards in clinical practice. Otherwise, the APA may be unable to counter the criticism that clinical psychologists are no different or more effective than clinical social workers, marriage therapists, freelance counselors, or any of the other types of "therapeutic professionals" available to the public (Dawes, 1994) or prevent the indiscriminant prescription and overuse of psychotropic medications by poorly trained clinical psychologists (Hayes & Heiby, 1996). Thus, maintaining a strong, active Division 25 would seem to be in the interest of the APA—if only to show that the APA supports the view that psychology can be an uncompromisingly rigorous natural science from which effective, behaviorally based therapeutic strategies can be derived.

REFERENCES

American Psychologist (Special Issue). (1992, Summer). *Division 25 Recorder, 27*(2), 21, 25.

Azrin, N. H. (1980). APA Council Representative report. *Division 25 Recorder, 15*(3), 2.

Barash, D. P. (1977). *Sociobiology and behavior*. New York: Elsvier-North Holland.

Bernstein, G. S. (1976). A reply to critics of behavior mod. *Division 25 Recorder, 11*(2), 15.

Bernstein, G. S. (1977). The female behaviorist: Professional inequalities. *Division 25 Recorder, 12*(3), 13–16.

Bernstein, G. S. (1978a). [Response to Peyser.] *Division 25 Recorder, 13*(2), 15.

Bernstein, G. S. (1978b). [Response to Shepard.] *Division 25 Recorder, 13*(1), 2.

Born, D. G. (1979). Where will they all get good jobs? *Division 25 Recorder, 14*(2), 1–7.

Bower, G. H. (1992). A perfect wave. *APS Observer, 5*(4), 2.

Brady, J. V. (1965). A message from the president. *Division 25 Recorder, 1*(1), 1–2.

Brady, J. V. (1966). APA Reorganization [Report]. *Division 25 Recorder, 1*(2), 3–5.

Brady, J. V. (1987). Back to baseline. *Journal of the Experimental Analysis of Behavior, 48*, 458–459.

Buckley, K. W. (1988, August). The brave new world of John B. Watson. In J. T. Todd (Chair), *Psychology as the behaviorist views it at 75*. Symposium conducted at the convention of the American Psychological Association, Atlanta, GA.

Burnham, J. C. (1988, August). John B. Watson: Interviewee, professional figure, symbol. In J. T. Todd (Chair), *Psychology as the behaviorist views it at 75*.

Symposium conducted at the convention of the American Psychological Association, Atlanta, GA.

Catania, A. C. (1979). An outgoing presidential message. *Division 25 Recorder*, *14*(4), 2–3.

Catania, A. C. (1991). Politics is the art of the possible. *Division 25 Recorder*, *26*(3), 30.

Dawes, R. M. (1994). *House of cards: Psychology and psychotherapy built on myth*. New York: Macmillan.

Dews, P. B. (1987). An outsider on the inside. *Journal of the Experimental Analysis of Behavior*, *48*, 459–462.

Dinsmoor, J. A. (1979). A note on the historical record: MPA and MABA. *Behavior Analyst*, *2*, 22–24.

Dinsmoor, J. A. (1987). A visit to Bloomington: The first Conference on the Experimental Analysis of Behavior. *Journal of the Experimental Analysis of Behavior*, *48*, 441–445.

Dinsmoor, J. A. (1992). Setting the record straight: The social views of B. F. Skinner. *American Psychologist*, *47*, 1454–1463.

Etzel, B. C. (1993). President's column. *Division 25 Recorder*, *28*(1, 2), 1, 3.

Ferster, C. B. (1972). Message from the president [Concerning reorganization]. *Division 25 Recorder*, *7*(2), 1–2.

Gershenson, C. W. (1993). The APS human capital initiative. *Division 25 Recorder*, *28*(1, 2), 19.

Goldiamond, I. (1975). On fair and unfair assessments of our behavior. *Division 25 Recorder*, *10*(3), 6–10.

Graham, S. R. (1991). Stanley Graham replies to Steve Hayes. *Division 25 Recorder*, *26*(3), 29.

Hayes, L. J. (1988). The psychology of J. R. Kantor. *Behavior Analysis*, *23*(3), 93.

Hayes, S. C. (1983a). Long term plan beginning to take shape. *Division 25 Recorder*, *18*(2), 17.

Hayes, S. C. (1983b). What is Division 25 about?: Developing the long term plan. *Division 25 Recorder*, *18*(1), 20–23.

Hayes, S. C. (1984). The long term plan: Focus on our special role. *Division 25 Recorder*, *19*(1), 16–18.

Hayes, S. C. (1985). *The Division 25 hospitality suite manual*. Unpublished report to the Division 25 Executive Committee.

Hayes, S. C. (1986). Guidance by scientific data: Requiring it of service providers. *Division 25 Recorder*, *21*(1), 4–6.

Hayes, S. C. (1987a). Bracing for change [President's Column II]. *Behavior Analysis*, *22*(1), 7–10.

Hayes, S. C. (1987b). The gathering storm. *Behavior Analysis*, *22*(2), 41–47.

Hayes, S. C. (1987c). Moving ahead. *Behavior Analysis*, *22*(3), 85–90.

Hayes, S. C. (1991). Why APA does not deserve our support. *Division 25 Recorder*, 26(2), 19–21.

Hayes, S. C. (1992). Facing the values conflict: A challenge [Letter to the Editor]. *Division 25 Recorder*, 27(1), 24–25.

Hayes, S. C., & Heiby, E. (1996). Psychology's drug problem: Do we need a fix or should we just say so. *American Psychologist*, 51, 198–206.

Herrnstein, R. J. (1987). Reminiscences already? *Journal of the Experimental Analysis of Behavior*, 48, 448–453.

Hilgard, E. R. (1945a). Psychologists' preferences for division under the proposed APA by-laws. *Psychological Bulletin*, 42, 20–26.

Hilgard, E. R. (1945b). Temporary chairmen and secretaries for proposed APA divisions. *Psychological Bulletin*, 42, 294–296.

Hilgard, E. R. (1987). *Psychology in America: A Historical Survey*. San Diego: Harcourt Brace Jovanovich.

Hilts, P. J. (1974). *Behavior Mod*. New York: Harper's Magazine Press.

Hineline, P. N. (1988, August). Origins of environment-based psychological theory. In E. F. Segal (Chair), *The Behavior of Organisms at Fifty*. Symposium conducted at the convention of the American Psychological Association, Atlanta, GA.

Hineline, P. N., & Laties, V. G. (Eds.). (1987). Anniversaries in behavior analysis [Special Section]. *Journal of the Experimental Analysis of Behavior*, 48, 439–514.

Holland, J. G. (1975). Letter of protest. *Division 25 Recorder*, 10(2), 12–15.

Hull, C. L. (1943). *Principles of behavior*. New York: Appleton-Century-Crofts.

Jacobson, J. W., Mulick, J. A., & Schwartz, A. A. (1995). A history of facilitated communication: Science, pseudoscience, and antiscience. *American Psychologist*, 50, 750–765.

Keller, F. S. (1990a). Burrhus Frederic Skinner (1904–1990) (a thank you). *Journal of the Experimental Analysis of Behavior*, 54, 155–158.

Keller, F. S. (1990b) In memoriam? *Division 25 Recorder*, 24/25(3), 21.

Knapp, T. J. (1995). A natural history of the *Behavior of Organisms*. In J. T. Todd & E. K. Morris (Eds.), *Modern Perspectives on B. F. Skinner and Contemporary Behaviorism* (pp. 7–23). Westport, CT: Greenwood Press.

Laties, V. G. (1978). [Letter to the editor in response to Bernstein's, "The female behaviorist."] *Division 25 Recorder*, 13(2), 16.

Laties, V. G. (1987). Society for the Experimental Analysis of Behavior: The first 30 years (1957–1987). *Journal of the Experimental Analysis of Behavior*, 48, 495–512.

Lattal, K. A. (1994a). President's column: Plans and functions of Division 25. *Division 25 Recorder*, 29(1), 1, 3.

Lattal, K. A. (1994b). President's column. *Division 25 Recorder*, 29(3), 1–2.

Lundin, R. W. (1988). An interbehavioral approach to the psychology of music. *Behavior Analysis*, 23(3), 106–109.

Lutzger, J. (1978). Hospitality suite. *Division 25 Recorder, 13*(3), 2.

Lyons, C. A., & Williamson, P. N. (1988). Contributions of Kantor's "psychological linguistics" to understanding psychotic speech. *Behavior Analysis, 23*(3), 110–113.

Morris, E. K. (1988a). The behavior of organisms: A context theory of meaning. In E. F. Segal (Chair), *The behavior of organisms at fifty*. Symposium conducted at the convention of the American Psychological Association, Atlanta, GA.

Morris, E. K. (1988b). Report of Division 25 Public Information Office. *Division 25 Recorder, 23*(1), 40–44.

Morris, E. K. (1988c). Twice a heretic? *Behavior Analysis, 23*(3), 114–117.

Mulick, J. A. (1994). For the record. *Division 25 Recorder, 29*(3), 3–4.

Nelson, R. O. (1977). Notes on the APA education and credentialing meeting of June 4–5, 1977. *Division 25 Recorder, 12*(3), 7–12.

Nelson, R. O. (1982). Comments from the president. *Division 25 Recorder, 17*(3), 5–6.

Nelson, R. O. (1987). Council of Representatives Report. *Division 25 Recorder, 22*(1), 32–33.

Nelson, R. O., & Hayes, S. C. (1980). The professionalization of Division 25. *Division 25 Recorder, 15*(3), 5–7.

Paniagua, F. A. (1991). Why APA does deserve our support. *Division 25 Recorder, 26*(3), 30–31.

Peterson, M. E. (1978). The Midwestern Association for Behavior Analysis. *The Behavior Analyst, 1*, 3–15.

Peterson, M. E. (1979). A reply to Dinsmoor. *The Behavior Analyst, 2*(1), 25.

Peyser, C. S. (1978). [Letter to the editor in response to Bernstein's, "The female behaviorist."] *Division 25 Recorder, 13*(2), 14.

Reed, E. (Ed.). (1963). *APA 1963 directory*. Washington, DC: American Psychological Association.

Reese, E. P. (1974). Report from membership chairman. *Division 25 Recorder, 8*(3), 2–4.

Ribes, E. (1988). Kantor's contribution to psychology, or what is behavior? *Behavior Analysis, 23*(3), 94–100.

Risley, T. R. (1984). APA Council. *Division 25 Recorder, 19*(1), 4–6.

Roca, J. (1988). On the organism and the environment. *Behavior Analysis, 23*(3), 101–105.

Salzinger, K. (1998a, August). Discussant comments. In J. T. Todd (Chair), *Psychology as the behaviorist views it at 75*. Symposium conducted at the convention of the American Psychological Association, Atlanta, GA.

Salzinger, K. (1988b). Live in interesting times. *Behavior Analysis, 23*(1), 35–37.

Salzinger, K. (1988c). Living in interesting times: A serial. *Behavior Analysis, 23*(3), 118–120.

Salzinger, K. (1988d). Living in interesting times (continued). *Behavior Analysis*, 23(2), 73–75.

Salzinger, K. (1991). The American Psychological Association has its place. *Division 25 Recorder*, 26(3), 29–30.

Salzinger, K. (1992, August). The experimental approach to psychopathology. In APA Master Lecture Series, *A centennial celebration—From then to now: Psychology applied*. Series conducted at the convention of the American Psychological Association, Washington, DC.

Samelson, F. (1988, August). John B. Watson in 1913: Rhetoric and practice. In J. T. Todd (Chair), *Psychology as the behaviorist views it at 75*. Symposium conducted at the convention of the American Psychological Association, Atlanta, GA.

Schuster honored by APA. (1993, Summer). *Division 25 Recorder*, 28(1, 2), 18.

Schwitzgebel, R. K. (1974). Legal developments related to behavior modification I: Research. *Division 25 Recorder*, 9(3), 7–8.

Schwitzgebel, R. K. (1975a). Legal developments related to behavior modification II. Treatment and contracts. *Division 25 Recorder*, 10(1), 7–8.

Schwitzgebel, R. K. (1975b). Legal developments related to behavior modification III. Behavioral devices. *Division 25 Recorder*, 10(2), 15–16.

Shepard, R. H. (1978). [Letter to the editor in response to Bernstein's, "The female behaviorist."] *Division 25 Recorder*, 13(1), 2.

Sidman, M. (1960). *Tactics of scientific research*. Boston: Authors' Cooperative.

Skinner, B. F. (1938). *The behavior of organisms: An experimental analysis*. New York: Appleton-Century-Crofts.

Skinner, B. F. (1948). *Walden Two*. New York: Macmillan

Skinner, B. F. (1971). *Beyond freedom and dignity*. New York: Knopf.

Skinner, B. F. (1974). *About behaviorism*. New York: Knopf.

Skinner, B. F. (1983). *A matter of consequences*. New York: Knopf.

Skinner, B. F. (1988a, August). Discussant comments. In E. F. Segal (Chair), *The behavior of organisms at fifty*. Symposium conducted at the convention of the American Psychological Association, Atlanta, GA.

Skinner, B. F. (1988b, August). *The behavior of organisms at fifty*. Invited address presented at the convention of the American Psychological Association, Atlanta, GA.

Skinner, B. F. (1990, August). Keynote address presented at the convention of the American Psychological Association, Boston.

Skinner, B. F., & Blanshard, B. (1967). The problem of consciousness—A debate. *Philosophy and Phenomenological Research*, 27, 317–337.

Smith, L. D. (1992). On prediction and control: B. F. Skinner and the technological ideal of science. *American Psychologist*, 47, 216–223.

Smith, L. D. (1995). Inquiry nearer the source: Bacon, Mach, and the behavior of organisms. In J. T. Todd & E. K. Morris (Eds.), *Modern Perspectives on B. F.*

Skinner and Contemporary Behaviorism (pp. 39–50). Westport, CT: Greenwood Press.

Stolz, S. (1978). Memorandum: Information on sex of editorial boards and reviewers. *Division 25 Recorder, 13*(2), 16–17.

Stolz, S. B. (1984a). Division 25 in APA: A case example. *Division 25 Recorder, 19*(1), 11–13.

Stolz, S. B. (1984b). Report on January 1984 APA Council of Representatives meeting. *Division 25 Recorder, 19*(1), 7–10.

Stolz, S. B. (1984c). August 1984 meeting of the APA Council of Representatives. *Division 25 Recorder, 19*(3), 55–57.

Stolz, S. B. (1986a). Message from the president: A message from the present. *Division 25 Recorder, 21*(2), 27–28.

Stolz, S. B. (1986b). Message from the president: A look into the future. *Division 25 Recorder, 21*(3), 53–54.

Stolz, S. B. (1986c). Message from the president: Where are we, and are you with us? *Division 25 Recorder, 21*(1), 3–4.

Stolz, S. B. (1991). Why stay in APA? An open letter to Steve Hayes. *Division 25 Recorder, 26*(3), 31–32.

Sulzer-Azaroff, B., & Catania, A. C. (1978). Report of the ad hoc committee on the organization of APA. *Division 25 Recorder, 13*(2), 2–5.

Timberlake, W. D. (1988, August). Is contingency defined behavior enough? In E. F. Segal (Chair), *The behavior of organisms at fifty.* Symposium conducted at the convention of the American Psychological Association, Atlanta, GA.

Todd, J. T. (1992). The Division 25 Recorder: A *selected history of the first three decades, 1965–1992.* Unpublished report to Division 25 Executive Committee.

Todd, J. T., & Morris, E. K. (1983). Misconception and miseducation: Presentations of radical behaviorism in introductory psychology textbooks. *The Behavior Analyst, 6,* 153–160.

Todd, J. T., & Morris, E. K. (1992). Case histories in the great power of steady misrepresentation. *American Psychologist, 47,* 1441–1453.

Todd, J. T., & Morris, E. K. (Eds.). (1994) *Modern perspectives on John B. Watson and classical behaviorism.* Westport, CT: Greenwood Press.

Touchette, P., & Ray, B. (1978). Division 25 activities. *Division 25 Recorder, 13*(3), 1.

Vargas, J. S. (1990). B. F. Skinner—the last few days. *Journal of Applied Behavior Analysis, 23,* 409–410.

Watson, J. B. (1913). Psychology as the behaviorist views it. *Psychological Record, 20,* 158–177.

Watson, J. B. (1919). *Psychology from the standpoint of a behaviorist*. Philadelphia: Lippincott.

Weissman, N. W. (1972). [Message on Federation questionnaire.] *Division 25 Recorder, 7*(3), 1.

Wood, W. S. (1980). The future of the masters degree in applied behavior analysis. *Division 25 Recorder, 15*(1), 1–4.

7

A HISTORY OF
DIVISION 37 (CHILD, YOUTH,
AND FAMILY SERVICES)

DONALD K. ROUTH and JAN L. CULBERTSON

This chapter begins with an account of the founding of Division 37 (Child, Youth, and Family Services) by Gertrude J. Williams, Milton F. Shore, and others. The division is placed into a broader context by a description of the early history of child advocacy in relation to psychology. Some of the leaders of this division are described. The growth of the Division's membership, the nature of its convention programs, and the development of its periodical are outlined. The division's new section on maltreatment is described, and then the interactions of Division 37 with other divisions. Among the most important activities of the division have been its awards for child advocacy and its task forces and the monographs they have produced. We will begin with a general review of the early history of Division 37.

We thank Maureen Black, Barbara Bonner, Donald Dewsbury, Dennis Drotar, Thomas K. Fagan, Jane Knitzer, Gary Melton, Judith Meyers, Marion W. Routh, Suzanne Sobel, Milton F. Shore, Lois A. Weithorn, and Diane J. Willis for their comments on an early draft of the manuscript. The chapter is dedicated to the memory of Rebecca Routh Coon (1964–1988). As an obstetrical nurse, she cared deeply for mothers and children. Her untimely death in an automobile accident is all the argument one needs for the importance of research and policy analysis on injury prevention, one component of this division's advocacy.

FOUNDING OF THE DIVISION

Division 37, despite the prominence of the word *services* in its name, has always been primarily concerned with advocacy and social policy issues related to children, youth, and families. Gertrude J. ("Trudie") Williams (1927–1986) originally conceived the idea of forming a division within the American Psychological Association (APA) that would be devoted to promoting child advocacy, which eventually became Division 37. She discussed these ideas as early as 1973 (Marsden, 1974). Williams thought of it as an umbrella for what she referred to as "child people," focusing on such advocacy and policy issues and including developmental psychologists, clinicians, school psychologists, and affiliates outside psychology (social workers, physicians, lawyers, and others) who placed a high value on the well-being of children (e.g., Williams, 1975, 1976). It was decided, by Milton F. Shore and Williams that Shore would chair the committee to get the division accepted by the APA Council of Representatives (personal communication from Milton F. Shore, December 6, 1995). As this chapter will explain, it was no accident that all of the members of Shore's organizing committee (see Table 24) were at one time or another officers of the Section on Clinical Child Psychology (Section 1 of the Division of Clinical Psychology, Division 12 of the APA).

In 1971 Williams had begun editing a new journal for Section 1 called the *Journal of Clinical Child Psychology*, devoted to child advocacy. It in-

TABLE 24
Chronology of Significant Events in the History of Division 37

1975	Organizing Committee formed: Loretta Cass, Erwin Friedman, Sol Gordon, Adah Maurer, Milton F. Shore (acting chair), Gertrude J. Williams, Paul Wohlford
	Petition for new division of Children and Youth ("to provide a mechanism for child and youth advocacy") turned down by APA Council (it received a majority vote but was 7 votes short of the necessary 2/3)
1977	Petition for new division of Child and Youth Services approved by APA Council
	First issue of newsletter (Milton Shore and Suzanne Sobel, Editors)
1978	Official beginning of Division of Child and Youth Services
1981	Name of division changed to Child, Youth, and Family Services
1990	Newsletter name changed to *Child, Youth, and Family Services Quarterly*
1991	Mission statement revised: "The Division of Child, Youth and Family Services is committed to the application of psychological knowledge to advocacy, service delivery, and public policies affecting children, youth, and families."
1994	Section on Child Maltreatment founded

cluded photographs and artwork; articles by consumers; and the writings, drawings, and poems of children and young people themselves (Routh, 1994; Willis, 1987a, 1987b). Among the causes that Williams championed were abolishing corporal punishment, combating violence against children, finding new ways to deal with the problems of adolescent sexuality, and deinstitutionalizing people with mental retardation. Over time, the journal became a more conventional (scholarly, peer reviewed) clinical and scientific journal (Routh, Patton, & Sanfilippo, 1991). Williams became the president of Section 1 and later received its Distinguished Contribution Award. However, such honors did not satisfy her wish to found an organization devoted to child advocacy, so she began the effort to establish such a division within the APA.

The first aspect of the battle to establish this division was with Section 1 members (for example, Herbert Rie, a clinical child psychologist who was chair of the Psychology Department at Case Western Reserve University in Cleveland) who did not want to see the section's focus on professional clinical child psychology dissolved in a more generic APA division (Cass, 1975; Rie, 1975). Other Section 1 members, such as Theodore Blau, thought the new division should be the occasion for abolishing the section (as it turned out, Section 1 of Division 12 survived as a separate entity). Within the APA, the battle against the new division was waged mostly by existing divisions. Like Rie, some members of Division 12 opposed the new division out of a fear that it would dilute the section's focus on clinical child psychology. Willard Hartup, the president of Division 7, Developmental Psychology, objected to the original name proposed for the new division (Division of Children and Youth) as overlapping too much on the territory covered at the time by Division 7. Some Division 7 members also thought their group was already serving as a staunch child advocate. In response, some of those in favor of the new division felt excluded from Division 7 because of its research-oriented membership criteria. In any case, Williams found that her passionate style of argument was not winning supporters for this cause. An example of her debating style is provided by the following quotation:

> We have an unwavering conviction that the irrational, divisive, zero-sum-game frenzy will be defeated by reason, evidence and democratic principles—the ties that bind us all—and that a Division on Children and Youth will, at long last, be established within the APA. (Williams, 1976, p. 9)

Thus Milton F. Shore, who was more politically experienced and thus better at negotiating with opponents of the petition for a division, assumed the leadership role. As might be expected, Shore also had an established record as a child advocate. He had been involved in innovative longitudinal research on the effects of comprehensive, vocationally oriented counseling for delinquent boys (e.g., Massimo & Shore, 1963; Shore & Massimo, 1979) and had previously published an influential book on the psychological effects of medical hospitalization of children, *Red Is the Color of Hurting* (Shore, 1965). (Later, in 1980 to 1981, he served as the president of the American Orthopsychiatric Association and from 1989 through 1993 was the editor of its journal.)

As Table 24 shows, the APA Council of Representatives turned down the petition for a new division in 1975 (Conger, 1976). The petition for a Division of Child and Youth Services was again turned down in 1976. In 1977 the APA council finally approved the establishment of Division 37 only after its proposed name was changed (Conger, 1977) and all language relating to child advocacy was removed from the petition. "Child and Youth Services" was actually the name suggested by Willard W. Hartup of Division 7, with the following rationale:

> One issue remains: the name of the new division. It is my strong belief that the name of any new division should not imply that it is *the* APA division devoted to child and youth activities. The proposed name would represent a mislabeling that would have negative implications for the work of Divisions 12 and 16 (and perhaps others) as well as for Division 7. A simple solution would be to name the new division the Division on Child and Youth Services. (Hartup, 1976)

Shore (1976) quickly accepted this suggestion, with a minor change in the name from "on" to "of." In the new petition, the division was described as being concerned with professional and scientific issues related to services and "service structures" for children and youth. This compromise permitted the division to begin and ultimately it did not prevent the division from emphasizing exactly the kinds of issues Williams had in mind at the outset. The division began officially on January 1, 1978, and temporary officers were appointed. Milton F. Shore was appointed acting chair of the division and then served as its first elected president (as shown in Table 25). The other interim officers were Herbert Freudenberger (vice chair), Suzanne B. Sobel (treasurer), Carolyn Schroeder (secretary), Patricia Keith-Spiegel (program chair), and Carole A. Rayburn (membership chair) (*Division of Child and Youth Services Newsletter*, 1977).

PHILOSOPHY AND APPROACH OF THE DIVISION

According to a relatively current version of its bylaws (Directory of the American Psychological Association, 1993), "The objects of the American Psychological Association shall be to advance psychology as a science and profession and as a means of promoting human welfare" (p. xxii). Division 37, in terms of its first official name, the Division of Child and

TABLE 25
Presidents of Division 37

1978–1979	Milton F. Shore
1979–1980	Lee Salk
1980–1981	Suzanne B. Sobel
1982	Carolyn Schroeder
1983	Gerald P. Koocher
1984	Donald K. Routh
1985	Diane J. Willis
1986	Gary B. Melton
1987	Benjamin Pasamanick
1988	James Garbarino
1989	Thomas J. Kenny
1990	John P. Murray
1991	Judith C. Meyers
1992	Gail S. Goodman
1993	Maureen M. Black
1994	Jan L. Culbertson
1995	Dennis Drotar
1996	Jane Knitzer
1997	David Wolfe

Youth Services, appeared to be focused on the goal of advancing psychology as a way of providing services—that is, it seemed to be a division that emphasized practice. As has already been made clear, the founders of Division 37 (as well as its current leaders) were actually more interested in promoting human welfare than advancing psychology as a profession, and the former objective is consistent with their subsequent actions. In terms of the APA's present directorate structure, Division 37 is usually regarded as a public interest division (rather than as a science or a practice division). Section 1 of Division 12, which spawned Division 37, has continued its focus on the scientific and professional aspects of clinical child psychology. Culbertson (1991) discussed the child advocacy activities of Section 1 in relation to its role as a forerunner of Division 37. As a public interest division, Division 37 has frequently collaborated with others with the same focus, including Divisions 9 (Society for the Psychological Study of Social Issues), 27 (Community Psychology), and 41 (Psychology and Law).

The name change to the Division of Child, Youth, and Family Services made it clear that Division 37 membership was devoted to advancing the welfare of families as well as that of children and youth. The name change was originally proposed by Gerald Koocher, passed unanimously by the APA Executive Committee, and sent out for a vote of the membership in 1981 (Bachman, 1981). Thus Division 37 was perhaps the first division to suggest openly that psychologists ought to concern themselves with families as well as individuals. Before this time, many psychologists relegated scientific concern with the family to sociology and relegated practical service delivery for families to the field of social work. Division 43 subsequently developed as the Division of Family Psychology, benefiting from the pioneering work that Division 37 had done to include families. A relatively straightforward division of labor has resulted between the two, as Division 37 is more concerned with family advocacy and social policy and Division 43 concentrates more on family therapy (and, to a lesser extent, on psychological research on the family).

A 1991 change in the division's official mission statement, as indicated in Table 24, stated, "The Division of Child, Youth, and Family Services is committed to the application of psychological knowledge to advocacy, service delivery, and public policies affecting children, youth, and families." The alert reader will note that *advocacy* comes before *service delivery* in this statement.

Over the course of the division's history, its leaders and members have clarified how Division 37 could actually have an effect on policy regarding children, youth, and families. At a practical level the organization's members have had to learn how to influence legislative, administrative, and judicial actions. This means forming task forces to produce articles and monographs that sway policy makers. It means working with APA lobbyists to provide materials to congressional staff members or testifying at congressional hearings. Advocacy also may involve preparing *amicus curiae* (friend of the court) briefs or testifying in court. Finally, effective advocacy means providing continuing education and mentoring for colleagues who may be excellent scientists or practitioners but who are inexperienced in the arenas of policy.

EARLY HISTORY OF CHILD ADVOCACY IN RELATION TO PSYCHOLOGY

Child advocacy is an old topic and has many roots outside of psychology (e.g., Takanishi, 1978). Downs, Costin, and McFadden (1996) noted some of the prominent origins of child advocacy in the United States as follows: A social worker, Julia Lathrop, was appointed by the president as the chief of the newly established Children's Bureau in 1913. Congress had established this bureau in response to the concerns that Progressive Era reformers had about issues such as the high infant mortality rate. The Sheppard–Towner Act was enacted in 1921 to promote the health of mothers and babies by providing federal matching grants to the states for maternal and child health services. The Social Security Act of 1935 included not only maternal and child health provisions but a more comprehensive program of child welfare, including income support for dependent children.

A number of relevant early developments also took place within the psychology community, according to Hilgard (1987). The Society for the Psychological Study of Social Issues (SPSSI) was formed independently of the APA in 1936 by a group of psychologists led by David Krech. The subsequent leaders of SPSSI included Kurt Lewin and Gardner Murphy. These psychologists were concerned about the effects of the economic depression of that era and about racial and ethnic prejudice. They were generally sympathetic to the New Deal policies of Franklin Roosevelt. The SPSSI yearbooks published before and during World War II were devoted to such topics as the conflict between unions and management, civilian morale, and world peace. When the reorganized APA was formed after World War II, SPSSI participated in the planning stages and eventually became Division 9. The reorganized APA added to its bylaws the phrase about using psychological knowledge to promote human welfare, thus developing at least a conceptual link between Division 37 and the objectives of this older organization. It is not clear, unfortunately, that illustrious figures such as Krech, Lewin, or Murphy were specifically interested in advocacy on behalf of children, youth, and families or that they directly influenced the subsequent development of Division 37 or its activities. Division 37 grew out of the work of clinicians, not of social psychologists. SPSSI did begin in 1992 to offer an annual award for research in child abuse ("The Child Abuse Research Award," 1994), a topic of great continuing interest to Division 37.

The APA Division of Community Psychology (Division 27; also known as the Society for Community Research and Action) was established by the APA Council of Representatives in 1967, almost a decade before the idea of Division 37 emerged. One of the heroes of Division 27, Seymour Sarason (for whom its highest award is named) seems like someone who could have been lionized by Division 37 under a different set of historical circumstances. Sarason coauthored an influential book on the psychosocial aspects of mental retardation before that topic became nationally popular under the Kennedy administration. Sarason was also a founder of the Yale Psychoeducational Clinic, an organization featuring outreach to disadvantaged inner-city minority children (Sarason, 1988). Divisions 27 and 37 have cooperated in certain ways over time (as will be discussed later in this chapter).

ADMINISTRATION

Tables 25 and 26 list the individuals who served as either president, secretary, or treasurer of Division 37 over the approximately 20 years of its existence. Table 27 lists the members-at-large. It may be appropriate to go

TABLE 26
Secretaries and Treasurers of Division 37

Year	Secretary	Treasurer
1978–1979	Carolyn Schroeder	Suzanne B. Sobel
1979–1980	Carolyn Schroeder	Gerald P. Koocher
1980–1981	Suzanne Bachman	Gerald P. Koocher
1982	Suzanne Bachman	Gary Melton
1983	Suzanne Bachman	Gary Melton
1984	Lois A. Weithorn	Gary Melton
1985	Lois A. Weithorn	Thomas J. Kenny
1986	Sophie Lovinger	Thomas J. Kenny
1987	Kay Kline Hodges	Thomas J. Kenny
1988	Kay Kline Hodges	Louise Guerney
1989	Kay Kline Hodges	Louise Guerney
1990	Ellen Greenberg Garrison	Louise Guerney
1991	Ellen Greenberg Garrison	Ross Thompson/Glen P. Aylward
1992	Ellen Greenberg Garrison	Glen P. Aylward
1993	Sheila Eyberg	Glen P. Aylward
1994	Sheila Eyberg	Barbara Bonner
1995	Sheila Eyberg	Barbara Bonner
1996	Susan Rosenthal	Barbara Bonner

down the list of presiding officers. Gertrude Williams died in 1986, and though she was in a sense the godmother of the division, she never served as one of its officers. She did, however, give one of the first invited addresses to the division, "Traumatic Abuse and Neglect of Children at Home: Overview and Critical Issues" (Keith-Spiegel, 1978). Milton F. Shore, the first president, has already been mentioned.

Lee Salk (1926–1992) was perhaps better known as a pediatric psychologist than specifically as a child advocate. He was one of the founders of the Society of Pediatric Psychology (Section 5 of Division 12 of the APA) and twice served as its president. Its Distinguished Service Award is named after him (Routh, 1994). Salk also authored several popular books for parents, often appeared on national television, and wrote a column for parents called, "You and Your Family," which appeared in *McCall's* magazine for 19 years. According to Milton F. Shore (personal communication, December 6, 1995), Salk played an important role in the founding of Division 37 by speaking on behalf of its petition to the APA Council of Representatives. Another part of Salk's legacy to Division 37 consists of the famous 1975 divorce case of *Salk v. Salk*. Lee Salk's attorneys argued successfully that in a child custody case, the gender of the parent should not be in itself a determining factor, and he was thus awarded custody of his children. Salk's (1992) final popular book, *Familyhood*, had a theme of high relevance to members of Division 37.

Suzanne B. Sobel, who served as the Division's first treasurer before being elected president, at one time was employed by the Mental Health Study Center of the National Institute of Mental Health. According to Milton Shore (personal communication, December 7, 1995), Sobel did a lot of the detailed, day-to-day work necessary to get the division going, for which he felt she had never received sufficient credit. She was later a professor and associate dean in the School of Professional Psychology at Florida Institute of Technology. She subsequently went into private practice in Florida. Like Gertrude Williams, Sobel could be highly intense in the role of advocate. Her energy both fostered the development of Division 37 and alienated some who might otherwise have been more supportive of its purposes. In 1981, during Sobel's term as president, Division 37 began recognizing some of its more prominent individuals with fellow status, beginning with ones who were already fellows in other APA divisions.

Like Lee Salk, Carolyn Schroeder is also probably best known as a pediatric psychologist. She established a collaborative practice with a group of pediatricians in Chapel Hill, North Carolina (e.g., Schroeder, 1979), which has become the model for a number of other pediatric psychologists around the country. She has managed to incorporate into her practice research on the efficacy and consumer acceptance of some of the psychosocial interventions used, as well as on child maltreatment. She served as the first secretary of Division 37 before being elected its president, and she later served as a representative to the APA council ("Candidates for Division 37 Offices," 1993).

Gerald P. Koocher, also a pediatric psychologist, serves as the chief psychologist of the Judge Baker Children's Center and the Boston Children's Hospital and executive director of the Linda Pollin Institute of Harvard Medical School. He is well known for his research on the psychosocial aspects of children's cancer (e.g., Koocher, 1980). He also has published extensively on the subject of ethics and is the editor of a behavioral science journal devoted to the study of ethical issues. Koocher has more recently served as president of both Division 29 (Psychotherapy) and Division 12 (Clinical Psychology) of the APA as well as the APA treasurer. In 1992 he received an APA Professional Contribution Award for his work on children's legal rights, services to families of children with life-threatening illnesses, and the protection of consumers of mental health services ("Gerald P. Koocher," 1993). Koocher also served as a mentor for Gary Melton, an important figure in the subsequent history of Division 37 (discussed later in this section). During Koocher's term as Division 37 president in 1983, the division began its annual award to a nonpsychologist for child advocacy. Koocher himself received the division's Nicholas Hobbs Award (given to a psychologist who has made distinguished contributions to child advocacy) in 1988 ("Nicholas Hobbs Award Presented," 1988). An interesting historical sidelight is that well before becoming involved with Division 37, Gerald Koocher helped to found a children's rights committee in the Society for the Psychological Study of Social Issues (Division 9).

Donald K. Routh, the first author of this chapter, was a charter member of Division 37 and first became involved in its activities when he was appointed program chair by Lee Salk in 1980 and was eventually elected division president for 1984. Routh is also a pediatric psychologist, a journal editor (*Journal of Pediatric Psychology, Journal of Clinical Child Psychology, Journal of Abnormal Child Psychology*) and served as a mentor to Dennis Drotar, who subsequently served as president of Division 37. It was during Routh's term as president that the first of the division's Nicholas Hobbs Awards was given to a psychologist for contributions to child advocacy (see the section on awards for more information on Nicholas Hobbs and the rationale for this award). In line with his commitment to pediatric psychology as a form of child advocacy, Routh was one of the people responsible for the fact that Division 37 later had a physician (Benjamin Pasamanick) as its president and for giving the division's Child Advocacy Award to a pediatrician (Robert Haggerty). Thus, it was not surprising that Routh's Division 37 presidential address on recurrent abdominal pain in children was subsequently republished as a chapter in the *Handbook of Pediatric Psychology* (Routh, 1988). Routh also received the Nicholas Hobbs Award in 1996.

Continuing the established pattern of several previous Division 37 leaders, Diane J. Willis is a pediatric psychologist and had been a journal editor (she was the founding editor of the *Journal of Pediatric Psychology* and was Gertrude Williams' choice as second editor of the *Journal of Clinical Child Psychology*). In addition to her interest in children and families, Willis has an interest in ethnic minority issues. Willis has a family heritage of political advocacy (her father was speaker of the Oklahoma House of Representives). Subsequent to being president of Division 37, she chaired the Association for the Advancement of Psychology. Long an advocate on behalf of maltreated children and youth, Willis served as chair of the APA Coordinating Committee on Child Abuse and Neglect (1991–1996) and later was appointed chair of the steering committee to form a new section on child maltreatment within Division 37 (discussed later in this chapter). It is probably not a coincidence that in February 1985, during the year Willis was president of Division 37, the APA established its own permanent Committee on Children, Youth, and Families. While president of Division 37, Willis focused on prevention of child maltreatment, and the accomplishments made by her task force on this topic are reported in a book (Willis, Holden, & Rosenberg, 1992). Willis also received the Nicholas Hobbs Award in 1993 ("Diane Willis: 1993 Nicholas Hobbs Award Recipient," 1993).

Gary Melton received his doctoral training in psychology at Boston University. His training there included not only a focus on clinical child psychology, but it also emphasized legal and ethical issues and advocacy. In 1979, a year after completing his PhD, Melton become a faculty member at the University of Virginia's Institute of Law, Psychiatry, and Public Policy. While at the University of Virginia, he began work as the editor of Division 37's newsletter. In 1981, he moved to the University of Nebraska, Lincoln, where within a year he became director of the Law and Psychology Program. Several years later he was appointed the Carl A. Happold Professor at the University of Nebraska. Subsequent to his term as newsletter editor, Melton served as treasurer, and then as president of Division 37. Melton (1983) wrote a well-received book on child advocacy and psychology. In 1985 Melton received the APA Award for Distinguished Contribution to the Public Interest ("Gary B. Melton," 1986) for his work on rural community psychology and the needs of Appalachian children, child maltreatment, sexual abuse, sterilization of persons with mental retardation, ethical issues in research, the effects of legislation on voluntary school prayer, and the rights of psychologically impaired defendants. It is fair to say that Melton, more than any other individual, moved the division in the direction of more intense scholarly involvement in legal, ethical, and policy issues relating to children, youth, and families. He was instrumental in creating a book series, *Children and the Law*, with the University of Nebraska Press in 1986 that served as a publication outlet for several of the Division 37 task force reports. For example, in 1986 the University of Nebraska began publishing a series of related books (see Table 31 later in this chapter). Recently, Melton has become the director of the Institute for Families in Society at the University of South Carolina (Melton, 1994). Melton also spearheaded the development of a Congressional Briefing Series that has sponsored several briefings each year since 1989 for congressional staff members and legislators. The purpose of this series is to heighten the awareness of congressional staff members on issues affecting the well-being of children and families and to provide them with information about relevant psychological research. This forum has been one effective method of "bringing psychology to Capitol Hill" (Melton, 1995, p. 770). Division 37 has been one of several cosponsors of this series since its inception.

Benjamin Pasamanick (1914–1996) has so far been the only physician to serve as president of Division 37 (though several physicians have received the division's awards for child advocacy). He is also the first division president who could not be characterized as a clinical child psychologist and thus helped Division 37 break free of that stereotype. Pasamanick and his colleagues became well known for epidemiological research on the effects of low birthweight on children's subsequent psychosocial development (e.g., Knobloch & Pasamanick, 1966). In 1949 he had already received the Hofheimer Prize of the American Psychiatric Association for his research on the development of African American children; he received numerous other awards. His concept of a "continuum of reproductive casualty" was one with definite public health implications. One focal point of Pasamanick's child advocacy was the view that low birthweight is a preventable disorder and therefore so are many of its sequelae, such as cerebral palsy, epilepsy, mental retardation, and various behavioral and learning disabilities ("Introducing the President," 1987). At the time he served as president of Division 37, Pasamanick was experiencing such poor health that he had difficulty chairing a meeting of the board and was unable to deliver a presidential address.

James Garbarino was the first developmental psychologist to serve as president of Division 37 and has continued to be one of its most active leaders. He received his PhD at Cornell University under Urie Bronfenbrenner in 1973. By the time he became an officer of Division 37, Garbarino was president of the Erikson Institute for the Advanced Study in Child Development in Chicago ("Introducing the President," 1988). Garbarino received the first C. Henry Kempe Award from the National Conference on Child Abuse and Neglect for his work in that area, and he also received the 1989 APA Award for Distinguished Professional Contributions ("James Garbarino," 1990). The theme of child maltreatment, in which Garbarino did such important work, has continued to be a key focus for Division 37.

With Thomas J. Kenny, Division 37 returned to its pattern of electing pediatric psychologists as leaders ("Introducing the President," 1989). Kenny was a faculty member in the Department of Pediatrics at the University of Maryland Medical School and was responsible for setting up one of the first pediatric psychology internships there to be funded by the National Institute of Mental Health (NIMH).

John P. Murray was trained in counseling psychology but his academic position at Kansas State University was in the area of Human Development and Family Studies. Murray brought the division the benefit of his international contacts (he formerly taught in a university in Australia) and his well-known research on the psychological effects of television on children ("Introducing the President," 1990). During Murray's term as president in 1990, Division 37 gave its first Student Award (see the awards section for more information on the rationale for this award).

Judith C. Meyers, a clinical and community psychologist by training, was an official in state government (she was the director of the Division of Adult, Children, and Family Services for the state of Iowa) at the time she served as president of Division 37 ("Introducing the President," 1991). As a former congressional fellow, she played an influential role in the development of the Child and Adolescent Service System Program (CASSP) at NIMH. She had previously served in the governor's Office of Human Resources in Massachusetts ("Division 37 Candidates," 1989). Subsequent to serving as president of Division 37, Meyers was a senior associate at the Annie E. Casey Foundation, which is concerned with service reform and advocacy for children, youth, and families. At present she is an independent consultant on the organization, finance, and delivery of services to children and families.

Gail S. Goodman, a developmental psychologist trained at the University of California, Los Angeles, is presently a professor at the University of California, Davis. Goodman is known for her research on factors influencing children's testimony in relation to child abuse, a key research topic for child advocates interested in child maltreatment. Her research was cited by the U.S. Supreme Court in the case of *Maryland v. Craig* (1990). In a former position at the University of Denver, she directed a dual degree program in Law and Psychology ("Introducing the President," 1992).

Maureen M. Black, trained as a developmental psychologist, earlier in her career had studied nutrition in Bangladesh and in Peru. She is a long-time associate of Thomas J. Kenny at the Department of Pediatrics of the University of Maryland Medical School. There she directs the multidisciplinary Growth and Nutrition Clinic for children who fail to thrive and conducts intervention research among children and families living in low-income, urban communities ("Introducing the President," 1993).

Jan L. Culbertson, the second author of the present chapter, served as the next president of Division 37. She was the first president of the division who was trained in school psychology (though her present work is better characterized as pediatric neuropsychology). She received her PhD in 1978 from the University of Tennessee ("Division 37 Candidates," 1989). Culbertson began serving as the division's newsletter editor in 1986, and she transformed the publication into a forum for scholarly debate of topical issues related to policy affecting children, youth, and families. The success of this format led to changing the name of the newsletter in 1990 from *Division of Child, Youth, and Family Services Newsletter* to the *Child, Youth, and Family Services Quarterly*, a name thought to be more representative of the content and purpose of the division's publication. In a sort of historic reversal, Culbertson then went on to become the editor of the *Journal of Clinical Child Psychology* (for Section 1 of Division 12), in part bringing a focus on child advocacy back to the organization that originally spawned Division 37. During Culbertson's presidency, Division 37 established a Lifetime Advocacy Award to honor those individuals whose efforts made a major contribution to child advocacy. This award, first bestowed in 1995, brought full circle the division's awards for distinguished contributions to child advocacy, from the student to the senior levels of a professional career. The division's first section, the Section on Child Maltreatment, was established in 1994 during Culbertson's presidency in order to fill an existing void within the APA for those psychologists interested in research, training, advocacy, and professional practice in the area of child maltreatment and to bring needed recognition to an important topic area (Culbertson, 1995).

Dennis Drotar, the president of Division 37 in 1995, is also a pediatric psychologist. He is a professor at Case Western Reserve University and is an advocate for children and families within the medical hospital setting (Drotar, 1995a). Drotar is a prolific researcher on such topics as the psychological aspects of chronic illness in children and more specifically on the childhood problem of nonorganic failure to thrive ("Candidates for Division 37 Offices," 1993). His most recent book is *Consulting With Pediatricians* (Drotar, 1995b).

Jane Knitzer, the president of Division 37 in 1996, was the first recipient of the Division's Nicholas Hobbs Award in 1984. Originally trained at Harvard as a school psychologist, receiving an EdD there in 1968, she has worked for such organizations as the Children's Defense Fund, the Bank Street College of Education, and the National Center for Children in Poverty at Columbia University. She is especially known for policy research. Her book, *Unclaimed Children: The Failure of Public Responsibility to Children and Adolescents in Need of Mental Health Services* (Knitzer, 1982) has already become a classic in its impact on social policy.

Finally, David Wolfe, who will be Division 37's president in 1997, was trained in the United States as a clinical psychologist but is currently a professor of psychology at the University of Western Ontario in Canada and a senior fellow at the Institute for the Prevention of Child Abuse there ("Division 37 Announces," 1995). He is a prominent researcher on child abuse, thus continuing the emphasis Division 37 has maintained throughout its 2-decade history.

Table 26 lists individuals who served the division in the roles of secretary or treasurer. Table 27 lists the individuals who served as elected members-at-large of the division.

MEMBERSHIP CHANGES OVER TIME

The original 1975 petition to the APA Council of Representatives for the formation of Division 37 was required to have 400 names of APA members. The petition that was approved in 1977 was required to have 500 names and barely attained that number. Table 28 provides official figures from various APA directories and membership registers since that time. By 1978, its first official year, Division 37 had slipped below the 500 mark in members but began to climb. Within its first decade the division reached a plateau of between 1,300 and 1,600 members, which it has maintained ever since. Among the nearly 50 APA divisions, Division 37 is

TABLE 27
Members-at-Large of Division 37

1978	Herbert J. Freudenberger (3-year term)
	Carole A. Rayburn (2-year term)
	Barbara J. Silver (1-year term)
1979	Diane J. Willis
1980	Barbara J. Silver
1981	Sandra R. Leichtman
1983	Joann H. Grayson
1984	Norman Mitroff
1985	Sophie Lovinger (served only 1 year)
1986	Lenore Behar
	Lois A. Weithorn (served Lovinger's unexpired term)
1987	Judith Meyers
1988	Marsha B. Liss
1989	Kathy Katz
1990	Jan L. Culbertson
1991	Louise F. Guerney
1992	Cynthia Schellenbach
1993	Brian Wilcox
1994	Karen Saywitz
1995	Cynthia Schellenbach
1996	Barbara Boat

Note. Much of this information was obtained from Division 37 "Members-at-Large" (1990).

neither the largest nor the smallest. As the table shows, the division is slowly decreasing as a percentage of the overall APA membership, which is dominated by the practice sector more than the public interest sector. Among the child-oriented divisions, Division 37 is larger than Division 7 (Developmental Psychology) but smaller than Division 16 (School Psychology). Table 28 shows that Division 37 members began with approximately a 6:4 ratio of male to female members but has moved steadily toward a 5:5 ratio.

TABLE 28
Membership Changes Over Time

Year	Number of Members and Fellows	Percentage Male	Percentage of APA Total Membership
1978	491	64.0	1.0
1981	865	61.6	1.6
1985	1,465	59.4	2.4
1989	1,397	57.1	2.0
1993	1,464	53.8	2.0
1995	1,314	53.9	1.7

Note. These official APA figures are underestimates of the number of people who participated in Division 37, because they do not include affiliate members who do not belong to the APA.
Source. APA Directories and Membership Registers.

According to the *1995 APA Membership Register* (APA, 1995), Division 37 had 142 fellows. When this entry was examined to determine if these individuals held membership in other divisions, 79 of these fellows (56%) were also found to belong to Division 12 (Clinical Psychology). This was not unexpected, nor was it surprising that 45 of the fellows belonged to Division 7 (Developmental Psychology); 30 of the fellows (21%) belonged to Division 38 (Health Psychology), and probably in most cases were pediatric psychologists; 24 fellows (17%) belonged to Division 16 (School Psychology), and an equal number belonged to Division 29 (Psychotherapy). In addition, 23 fellows (16%) belonged to Division 33 (Mental Retardation and Developmental Disabilities), and 21 (15%) belonged to Division 27 (the Society for Community Research and Action).

PROGRAM PRESENTATIONS AT ANNUAL CONVENTIONS

Like most other APA divisions, Division 37 features a number of different formats for its APA programs, including posters, papers, symposia, conversation hours, invited addresses by distinguished speakers, plus a business meeting and a division social hour. It also sponsors continuing education workshops. In 1979, for the first time, the division membership invited a nonpsychologist, Marian Wright Edelman (attorney and founder of the Children's Defense Fund), to give an invited address (Koocher, 1979). The invited addresses typically include a presidential address and talks given by the recipients of the various Division 37 awards. A program chair is appointed each year and is assisted by many members in reviewing submissions. The 1995 program proposal guidelines, published in the division's *Child, Youth, and Family Services Quarterly*, provide a recent statement of the kinds of APA convention program materials the division prefers. The APA program activities of Division 37 often involve interdivisional collaboration, with many sessions being cosponsored. Social hours are often cosponsored also to bring Division 37 members into informal contact with colleagues in related groups.

THE DIVISION PERIODICAL

Table 29 lists the names of the editors of the Division 37 newsletter and its successor in 1990, the *Child, Youth, and Family Services Quarterly*. The first issue of the newsletter was published in October 1977 by Milton F. Shore and Suzanne Sobel, even before the official beginning date of the division (*Division of Child and Youth Services Newsletter*, 1977). Beginning with Gary B. Melton, most editors have served 3-year terms. The exception was Jan L. Culbertson, who served for 5 years. The publication eventually evolved toward a pattern of issues devoted to a single theme, consisting mainly of articles that ran about three printed pages in length, often invited by a guest editor. This format allowed the newsletter to present debate on current policy issues that often were the focus of congressional action. At times division task forces have organized thematic issues to share information. On occasion, members of Congress or other high ranking public officials have written short articles for the newsletter/quarterly (e.g., Rep. Patricia Schroeder; Sen. Daniel K. Inouye; Sen. Daniel P. Moynihan; Donna E. Shalala, the secretary of Health and Human Services; and Rep. Louis Stokes). In addition to invited articles, the publication contains book reviews and information about the organization, such as messages from the president, the minutes of board meetings, and updates on the progress of task forces and other divisional activities.

SECTION ON CHILD MALTREATMENT

Over the years of the division's existence, psychologists have become more involved professionally in dealing with child maltreatment. According to Downs and colleagues (1996), a survey taken in 1983 and 1984

TABLE 29
Editors of the Newsletter/Quarterly

Year	Volume	Editors
1977–1978	1	Milton F. Shore, Suzanne B. Sobel
1978–1979	2	Milton F. Shore, Suzanne B. Sobel
1979–1980	3	Gary B. Melton
1980–1981	4	Gary B. Melton
1982	5	Gary B. Melton
1983	6	Donald Wertlieb
1984	7	Donald Wertlieb
1985	8	Donald Wertlieb
1986	9	Jan L. Culbertson
1987	10	Jan L. Culbertson
1988	11	Jan L. Culbertson
1989	12	Jan L. Culbertson
1990	13*	Jan L. Culbertson
1991	14	E. Wayne Holden
1992	15	E. Wayne Holden
1993	16	E. Wayne Holden
1994	17	Seth Kalichman
1995	18	Seth Kalichman
1996	19	Seth Kalichman

*The name of the publication changed from Newsletter to Quarterly in 1990, Volume 13.

found that every state had at least one multidisciplinary child protection team, and more than 900 such teams existed across the nation. By the date of the survey, at least half these teams included psychologists as members.

In 1994 the division created a new section on Child Maltreatment. This was the culmination of many years of interest and leadership in this area. The new section was established to provide a home within the APA for psychologists interested in research, training, practice, and advocacy in the area of child maltreatment. Diane J. Willis was appointed to head a steering committee for the new section. The established prominence of Division 37 in the area of child maltreatment is perhaps indicated by the fact that in 1989 two of its past leaders, Gary B. Melton and Diane J. Willis, were among the 13 appointed members of the U.S. Advisory Board on Child Abuse and Neglect. The first president of the Section on Child Maltreatment (and the new coeditor of the division's book series) is Jeffrey J. Haugaard of the Department of Human Development, Cornell University. The other interim officers (who serve until the first election is held in 1996) include Barbara Bonner, Joel Dvoskin, N. Dickon Repucci, Penelope Trickett, and Sandy Wurtele. As a sign of its serious support of the new section, the division membership granted it $5,000 to support a face-to-face meeting of its executive committee.

The bylaws of the Section on Maltreatment require that at least 50% of its members be members of Division 37 and provide that section members will appoint a person to act as a liaison to the division. To quote the section bylaws directly, its purposes include the following:

> to support and to encourage the development of the area of child maltreatment in both its scientific and professional aspects; to provide up-to-date information about maltreatment, to encourage networking across Divisions/Sections in the area of maltreatment, and to advance scientific inquiry, training, and professional practice in child maltreatment as a means of promoting the well-being, health, and mental health of children, youth, and families.

INTERACTIONS WITH OTHER DIVISIONS AND WITH THE APA

In its early days, Division 37 leaders coordinated their advocacy activities with those of other organizations within the APA such as Division 7 (Developmental Psychology), Division 12 (Clinical Psychology) and its sections (Clinical Child Psychology and Pediatric Psychology), Division 16 (School Psychology), Division 33 (Mental Retardation and Developmental Disabilities), and others. The initial mechanism for doing this was to set up an interdivisional committee. The group first met in 1982 and ultimately led to communication with the creation of the APA Committee on Children, Youth, and Families (CYF), which was established in 1985 and first scheduled to meet in 1986 ("Committee on Children, Youth and Families Selected," 1985). The CYF committee currently reports to the Board for the Advancement of Psychology in the Public Interest (BAPPI). The CYF committee (elected by the APA council) has nearly always included psychologists from Division 37. For example, the CYF committee chairs have included Gerald Koocher and Donald K. Routh. Jane Knitzer, Judith Meyers, Michael C. Roberts, and Edward Zigler have served as members. The APA staff member responsible for the CYF committee in recent times, Mary Campbell, also often comes to Division 37 board meetings to report on CYF activities and get input from the division. Many other APA divisions with an interest in this area also have developed liaisons with the CYF committee.

Division 37 has long cosponsored—along with Divisions 27 and 41 (Psychology–Law) and the Consortium on Children, Families, and the Law—a briefing series for congressional staff. This series was described in a special section of the *American Psychologist* in September 1995.

So far Division 37 has always had a single representative on the APA council. Its first representative was Theodore Blau, who served from 1979 to 1981. As a former APA president, Blau knew his way around the council. Next, Milton F. Shore served as the division's APA council representative (1982–1985). As the founding president of the Division, he was among the best qualified to articulate its views. Next came Ira Iscoe (1985–1988), a person long identified with both developmental and community psychology. As Division 37 representative, Iscoe supported the creation of a new Division of Family Psychology (Division 43). He tried to align Division 37 more with developmental psychology and social policy interests than with the practitioner divisions (personal communication from Ira Iscoe, February 13, 1996). Gary Melton, who was the division's representative from 1988 to 1991, has already been mentioned. According to Melton (personal communication, February 8, 1996), during his time of active involvement the division tended to remain neutral in the battle between the APA practice and science factions. As its APA council representative he belonged to the Public Interest Coalition. At one point the practitioner forces within the council (opposed by the representative for Division 37) were nevertheless successful in repealing the designation of the CYF committee as the coordinating body for child maltreatment issues. Carolyn Schroeder served as the division's APA council representative from 1991 to 1994 and was responsible for council legislation that increased the visibility of the APA's commitment to children, youth, and families. A regular column titled "Kids' Corner" will now appear in each issue of the *APA Monitor*, thanks in part to Schroeder's influence. W. Rodney Hammond (who is the associate dean at Wright State University's School of Professional Psychology) served as the division's APA council representative in 1995. Brian Wilcox began his term as representative in 1996. Wilcox received his PhD in 1979 in community psychology from the University of Texas, Austin. He was a faculty member in the Psychology Department at the University of Virginia, served as a Society for Research in Child Development Congressional Science Fellow, and then seved as the director of the APA's Public Policy Office ("Candidates for Division 37 Offices," 1992). Most recently he moved to the University of Nebraska as professor and director of its Law and Psychology Program. He authored many columns on events in Washington for the division's publications.

The APA also employs its own lobbyists (as it did Brian Wilcox), who deal with members of Congress and their staff members and with the officials of various federal agencies. Often these APA staff members have previously served as congressional fellows. It so happens that a number of these individuals have also been active in Division 37. Ellen Greenberg Garrison, who served as the secretary of Division 37 from 1990 to 1992, had previously been a congressional fellow and then an APA staff member. Other APA national policy staff member who have had close ties to Division 37 have included Ruby Takanishi and Brian Wilcox. It is typical for national policy staff members to make regular reports to the boards of APA divisions (such as Division 37) which are interested in their work. The APA Committee on Children, Youth, and Families also serves as a venue where some Division 37 members and APA national policy staff members often meet.

But influencing the APA council and talking to APA lobbyists proved to be only a beginning. As Division 37 matured, its leaders discovered that one of the most effective forms of advocacy available to them was the appointment of task forces to produce monographs on policy issues (see section on task forces later in this chapter). Such task forces have often involved cooperation and cosponsorship with other divisions such as the Psychology–Law Society (Division 41).

FINANCES

The initial income of the division in 1978 was determined by the $2 per year fee that the APA collected from the members of any division. It was immediately obvious that the approximately $1,000 produced in this way (plus voluntary contributions; see *Division of Child and Youth Services Newsletter*, 1977) would be insufficient even to support a midyear board meeting (estimated cost $2,000), so a $5 per year assessment was submitted to a vote of the membership (Sobel, 1978) for the next year, making the total dues $7. The biggest expenses for the division during its early years were for its winter board meetings (transportation, lodging, and meals). In

1984 the division raised its dues to $8 per year. For 1985, income was about $14,000 and the actual expenditures about $10,000. During this year for the first time, the newsletter expense of $4,006 slightly surpassed the cost of the midwinter meeting ($3,782), setting a pattern that would continue. By 1987 the expense of the newsletter ($8,222) far surpassed that of the midwinter meeting ($2,995). The newsletter was then changed to a quarterly in 1990 and expanded somewhat, making it even more expensive to publish. By 1991 the dues were $17 per year. In 1992 dues were increased to $25 per year, with the *Child, Youth, and Family Services Quarterly* continuing as the major expense of the division.

In 1994 Division 37 computerized its financial records. In 1995 it moved its financial record keeping to APA Financial Services, although the division treasurer oversees all transactions. Finally, in recent years, the division has accumulated ample reserve funds and these have been invested.

SPECIAL ACTIVITIES

There were two types of special activities, namely awards and task forces.

Awards

As Table 30 shows, Division 37 began to give its annual Child Advocacy Award in 1983, always to a nonpsychologist, thus expressing its wish to turn outward to influence the world of policy rather than simply facilitating its members' conversations with one another. The first annual award was officially called by the somewhat cumbersome name, "Award for Distinguished Contribution to Public Policy in the Interest of Children, Youth, and Families." The recipients of this award are an exceptional group of humanitarians, as the following brief description of some of their accomplishments reveals.

The first such award was to Robert H. Mnookin, a professor of law at Stanford University (Pellegrini, 1984). In the field of family law, Mnookin is known as an expert on such topics as teenage abortion and child custody and has made major contributions to policy analysis in these areas (e.g., Mnookin, 1975, 1978).

Michael Wald, the 1984 award winner, is also an attorney and a professor of law at Stanford University. Wald has a strong interest in findings from the behavioral and social sciences (e.g., Wald, 1976). He had been a major figure in proposals for reform of child protection policy. For example, he was the reporter for the volume on child maltreatment of the Juvenile Justice Standards, and he recently served as deputy general counsel in the U.S. Department of Health and Human Services. In the latter position, Wald was a member of the U.S. Advisory Board on Child Abuse and Neglect, and he worked on welfare reform.

The next recipient was Robert Haggerty, a pediatrician and the head of the W. T. Grant Foundation. Haggerty is known for his contributions to community pediatrics dating from his time at the University of Rochester. More recently, Haggerty and his associates have made continued strides toward reconceptualizing stress and resilience in children and adolescents (Haggerty, Sherrod, Garmezy, & Rutter, 1994).

In 1986 the Child Advocacy Award was given to Kenneth Wooden, an investigative reporter and author of several books on injustices suffered by children, including *Weeping in the Playtime of Others* and *The Children of Jonestown* (Wooden, 1976, 1981).

In 1987 the recipient was Mark Soler, an attorney associated with the Youth Law Center in San Francisco. Soler majored in psychology as an undergraduate at Yale before attending law school there. At the Youth Law Center, his focus has been on issues such as juvenile incarceration and foster care. The case of *Milonas v. Williams* (1982), in which Soler participated, led to a federal circuit court decision recognizing the constitutional rights of youth in private treatment facilities. In recent years, Soler's work has focused on the development of legal structures to support coordinated systems of services for children, youth, and families ("Soler Recipient of 'Distinguished Contribution Award,' " 1987).

Two people received the Child Advocacy Award in 1988: Robert Clampitt and Robert Keeshan ("Division 37 Distinguished Contribution to Child Advocacy," 1988). Clampitt is a journalist who in 1975 founded the Children's Express, a news service run by children under age 13 with teenage assistant editors ("Children's Express," 1988). The service has published its columns in more than 100 newspapers including the *New York Times*. Keeshan, a television actor, played the well-known Captain Kangaroo and delivered positive messages to children and families in this role. He has long been an advocate for quality children's programming on television.

William W. Harris, the recipient of the award in 1989, was the founder of the Children's Research and Education Institute and of KIDSPAC, a political action committee supporting members of Congress who had shown commitment to child and family issues. He was among those who spearheaded the passage of Senator Kennedy's Comprehensive Child Development Act of 1988 (Wertlieb, 1989).

Ira M. Schwartz, the 1990 recipient of the Child Advocacy Award, is dean of social work and director of the Center for Youth Policy at the University of Michigan. Schwartz is a researcher and a thoughtful critic of the "lock 'em up" approach of the present juvenile justice system (e.g., Schwartz, 1989). Schwartz served as director of the U.S. Office of Juvenile

Justice and Delinquency Prevention during the Carter administration ("Ira M. Schwartz: Advocate for Children, Youth and Families," 1990).

Jule M. Sugarman, the 1991 recipient of the award is a public administrator who directed Head Start from 1965 to 1969 and has served subsequently as the executive director of the Special Olympics, the sports program for youngsters with intellectual and other disabilities. He once served as president of an organization known as the Children's Lobby ("Sugarman to Receive Distinguished Contribution Award," 1991).

Irving Harris, the 1992 recipient, is a Chicago philanthropist (he is chair of the Irving Harris Foundation, which funds programs to prevent family dysfunction, teenage pregnancy, and infant mortality, and programs to promote infant mental health, early childhood development, and educational television). He was the founder and first president of the Erikson Institute and subsequently cofounded the Ounce of Prevention Fund ("Harris to Receive Distinguished Contribution Award," 1992).

Richard Krugman, the recipient of the 1993 award, is a pediatrician who is the director of the Henry Kempe Center, editor of the international journal *Child Abuse and Neglect*, and dean of the Medical School at the University of Colorado School of Medicine. He was the first chair of the U.S. Advisory Board on Child Abuse and Neglect and, in that capacity, announced the board's declaration of a national emergency in its first report in 1990 ("Krugman to Receive Distinguished Contribution Award," 1993).

Lenore Terr, the 1994 recipient, is a child psychiatrist and an expert on the effects of trauma on children (e.g., see Terr, 1990). Among other distinctions, she was the recipient of a career teacher award from the National Institute of Mental Health. Although there is no evidence that the division intended any gender discrimination, it is interesting that Terr was the first woman to win its Child Advocacy Award.

Jack Shonkoff, the 1995 recipient, is a pediatrician and social policy expert and was formerly a professor of Pediatrics and chief of the Division of Developmental and Behavioral Pediatrics at the University of Massachusetts Medical School. He is now dean of the Florence Heller Graduate School for Advanced Studies in Social Welfare at Brandeis University. Shonkoff was honored for his contributions to the research and evaluation of early intervention programs for children with developmental disabilities; he examined these programs from a broad ecological perspective. Working within a multidisciplinary context, he has conducted longitudinal research on the development of biologically vulnerable infants and their families. He also has played a leadership role in establishing research and policy agendas for maternal and child health funding for the coming decade.

Howard Davidson, an attorney who is executive director of the American Bar Association Center on Children and the Law, was the 1996 recipient of the Child Advocacy Award. Davidson has long been an advocate in such areas as child custody, children and HIV/AIDS, child abuse and neglect, and children's legal rights. His work bridges the research and policy areas, and he has contributed to both the legal and social science knowledge base (personal communication from Marsha B. Liss, September 11, 1994).

The second column of Table 30 lists the recipients of the division's annual Nicholas Hobbs Award, presented beginning in 1984 (the year after Hobbs' death). In contrast to the Child Advocy Award, this award is always given to a psychologist (who need not be a member of the division). Nicholas Hobbs (1915–1983) was a charter member of Division 37 whose life represented the values for which the division stands (Wright, 1983). Hobbs studied under Sidney Pressey and Carl Rogers at Ohio State University and spent most of his career at George Peabody College and Vanderbilt University, where he was provost at the time of his death. Hobbs developed and carried out controlled research on a model known as Project Re-Ed for delivering services to children with emotional and behavioral problems, a program subsequently adopted in several states. Even before the Kennedy era, Hobbs helped Peabody College develop its innovative research and training program in mental retardation (Peabody–Vanderbilt is still a leading center for research and training, especially on the psychosocial aspects of intellectual disability.) In addition, Hobbs chaired the committee that developed the APA's official Ethical Principles and took the lead in training psychologists for service in the Peace Corps. In 1975 (about the time Division 37 was being conceived) Hobbs established an Institute of Public Policy Studies, including a Center for the Study of Families and Children, at Vanderbilt. There is now a Nicholas Hobbs Laboratory of Human Development on the Peabody–Vanderbilt campus (Smith, 1985). Hobbs' work also helped foster the study of policy issues related to chronic illness in children (e.g., Hobbs, Perrin, & Ireys, 1985).

Jane Knitzer, the first recipient of the Hobbs Award in 1984 (Routh, 1984), was honored for her research and writings on policy regarding the mental health needs of seriously emotionally disturbed children.

Edward Zigler, the Hobbs recipient in 1985, is a developmental psychologist who left his laboratory to serve as the national director of Head Start, a federal program designed to intervene with young children from disadvantaged backgrounds. Zigler has continued to guide and defend Head Start and related programs ever since the 1970s. He also developed the Bush Foundation Program in Child Development and Social Policy at Yale, which trains scholars to combine science and policy roles. Zigler is the Sterling Professor of Psychology at Yale.

Milton F. Shore, discussed earlier in the chapter, was the 1986 recipient of the award (" 'Gentle advocate' to receive Nicholas Hobbs Award," 1986).

Urie Bronfenbrenner, a clinical child and developmental psychologist and a professor at Cornell University, is responsible for influential conceptualizations of the social ecology of children and families and was the 1987 award recipient ("Bronfenbrenner to receive 'Nicholas Hobbs Award,' " 1987). Among other accomplishments, Bronfenbrenner was a mentor to James Garbarino (discussed previously). Readers of this volume of APA division histories may wish to note the coverage of Bronfenbrenner in chapter 3 on Division 7 (Developmental Psychology).

Gerald P. Koocher, discussed earlier in the chapter, received the Hobbs Award for 1988.

Carolyn Schroeder and Stephen Schroeder received the Hobbs Award in 1989 for their joint work (Hodges, 1989). Carolyn Schroeder has already been discussed. Stephen Schroeder, trained as an experimental psychologist, is well known as a researcher in mental retardation (on topics such as self-injurious behavior and behavioral toxicology and teratology). He is the current editor of the leading journal in that area, the *American Journal on Mental Retardation*. The project the Schroeders developed together is Annie Sullivan Enterprises, a nonprofit center in Chapel Hill, North Carolina, that cares for disturbed or handicapped children that no other agency will handle (Culbertson & Willis, 1989).

Lewis Lipsitt, the 1990 recipient of the award, is a developmental psychologist and professor at Brown University; he carried out outstanding research on infancy, which laid some of the groundwork for the growing field of infant mental health. He was honored by Division 37 for his work in bringing knowledge about child development to the general public, practitioners, and policy makers and for supporting the growth of policy-relevant applied developmental research ("Lipsitt to Receive Nicholas Hobbs Award," 1990).

David Elkind, the 1991 award recipient, is a clinical child and developmental psychologist who went beyond his research activities to communicate effectively with the public in books such as *The Hurried Child* (Elkind, 1988), *All Grown Up and No Place to Go* (Elkind, 1984), *Miseducation* (Elkind, 1987), and *Grandparenting: Understanding Today's Children* (Elkind, 1990); ("Elkind to Receive Nicholas Hobbs Award," 1991).

Gary B. Melton, 1992 recipient, has already been discussed, as have Diane J. Willis, 1993 recipient, and James Garbarino, 1994 recipient, as they were all previous presidents of Division 37.

Lenore Behar, the 1995 recipient of the Hobbs Award, is a clinical child psychologist who is employed by the North Carolina Department of Mental Health. She played an important role in the class action suit known as *Willie M.*, which led to the development of a court-ordered, $26 million per year mental health service delivery system in North Carolina designed to aid violent youth (*Willie M. et al. v. James B. Hunt et al.*, originally filed in 1980; see Behar, 1985). Behar's work in North Carolina provided the foundation for the federal Child and Adolescent Service System Program (CASSP).

Donald K. Routh, the 1996 award recipient, was honored for his contributions to advocacy through his roles as professor, researcher, and editor in such areas as injury prevention and the effects of poverty on children, youth, and families. He was instrumental in keeping child advocacy issues in the forefront of such organizations as Division 12 (Clinical Psychology) (Sections 1 and 5, Clinical Child Psychology and Pediatric Psychology respectively) and Division 33 (Mental Retardation and Developmental Disabilities). Many of his students have gone on to become leaders in the field of child, youth, and family services and have contributed to advocacy in their own right.

In 1995, a Lifetime Advocacy Award was established. The first one was given to Adah Maurer. Maurer, a school psychologist (and a classic Berkeley social activist), had spent literally decades of dedicated work as the executive director of the Committee to End Violence Against the Next Generation (EVAN-G). Her goal and that of the organization was to end the use of corporal punishment on children in public schools. Twenty years previously, she had been one of the original petitioners for the establishment of Division 37.

The 1996 Lifetime Advocacy Award was presented to Kenneth B. Clark and (posthumously) to Mamie Phipps Clark to honor their influential research on the development of self-esteem among minority children. Their research had a profound effect on the legal basis for dismantling school segregation in the United States (Clark & Clark, 1939a, 1939b, 1940). Kenneth Clark, the 79th president of the APA, was a leader who urged the APA to speak out against social injustice and who founded the APA Board of Social and Ethical Responsibility in Psychology (BSERP; the predecessor to the present Board for the Advancement of Psychology in the Public Interest, BAPPI). Together, Kenneth and Mamie Clark founded the Harlem Youth Opportunities Unlimited as a prototype community development program intended to increase the participation of low-income individuals in decisions on education, housing, employment and training, and economic development (Clark, 1964). They also founded the interracial North Side Center for Child Development to treat children with emotional and learning problems (Clark, 1988). They are being honored for their pioneering, lifetime efforts in defending the civil rights and promoting the welfare of minority children and youth.

A student award was created in 1988 ("New student," 1988). As Table 30 shows, Division 37 actually began to give this annual student award in 1990. This award is for a specific project but recognizes that advocacy and attention to social policy issues should also have a role in training psychologists and can influence research topics chosen by students. The student award includes a check for $500. This sum may at least defray some of the student's expenses in attending the APA convention at which the award presentation is made. The first to receive the student award was

Suniya Luthar, a native of New Delhi, India ("Dr. Suniya Luthar to Receive Division 37 Student Award," 1990). She was a graduate student in clinical and developmental psychology at Yale and a student of Edward Zigler. At present, she is a faculty member at the Yale Child Study Center and is becoming well known for her research on high risk inner-city teenagers (e.g., Luthar, 1991, 1995). The second recipient, Mark Weist, was a student at Virginia Polytechnic Institute and State University, whose winning paper was titled "Toward the Empirical Validation of Treatment Targets in Children" ("Mark Weist to Receive Division 37 Student Award," 1991). The 1992 award winner, Peter K. Isquith, studied at the State University of New York, Buffalo, where his dissertation was supervised by Murray Levine. Isquith's research was titled, "Attribution of Responsibility to Child Sex Abuse Victims: The Impact of Jury Instructions" (Schellenbach, 1992). Subsequent winners included Mary Anne Yanulis, a graduate student at Fordham; Gwynne Kohl, a Yale undergraduate; and Eric Bruns, a graduate student at the University of Vermont. (Information on the three most recent student award winners was provided in a personal communication from Brian Wilcox, December 5, 1995.)

Task Forces

As Table 31 shows, in 1980 Division 37 began a pattern of appointing task forces on various policy issues related to children, youth, and families.

TABLE 30
Recipients of Division 37 Awards

Year	Child Advocacy Award	Nicholas Hobbs Award	Student Award
1983	Robert H. Mnookin		
1984	Michael Wald	Jane Knitzer	
1985	Robert Haggerty	Edward Zigler	
1986	Kenneth Wooden	Milton F. Shore	
1987	Mark Soler	Urie Bronfenbrenner	
1988	Robert Clampitt Robert Keeshan	Gerald P. Koocher	
1989	William W. Harris	Carolyn Schroeder Stephen R. Schroeder	
1990	Ira M. Schwartz	Lewis Lipsitt	Suniya Luthar
1991	Jule M. Sugarman	David Elkind	Mark Weist
1992	Irving Harris	Gary B. Melton	Peter K. Isquith
1993	Richard Krugman	Diane J. Willis	Mary Anne Yanulis
1994	Lenore Terr	James Garbarino	Gwynne Kohl
1995*	Jack Shonkoff	Lenore Behar	Eric Bruns
1996*	Howard Davidson	Donald K. Routh	

*In 1995, a Lifetime Advocacy Award was also established. In that year the award was given to Adah Maurer. In 1996 it was given to Kenneth B. Clark and (posthumously) to Mamie Phipps Clark.

TABLE 31
Task Forces and Some of Their Publications

Year	Chair	Task Force (Publications)
1980	William Rae	Children, Youth, and Health Services
1980	Norman Mitroff	Children, Youth, and the Law
1980	Alan Krichev	Children, Youth, and Education
1981	James Reisinger and S. Leichtman	Funding of Services for Children
1982	Marilyn Erickson	Training Issues in Child, Youth, and Family Services (Roberts, Erickson, & Tuma, 1985)
1982	Gary B. Melton	Adolescent Abortion (Interdivisional Committee, 1987; Melton, 1986, 1987; Melton & Russo, 1987)
1982	Gary B. Melton	Civil Commitment of Minors (Melton, Lyons, & Spaulding, in press)
1982	Gerald P. Koocher and P. C. Keith-Spiegel	Informed Consent for Treatment and Research Involving Children (Koocher & Keith-Spiegel, 1990)
1982	Lois A. Weithorn	Psychologists' Involvement in Child Custody Determinations (Weithorn, 1987)
1984	Diane J. Willis and M. Rosenberg	Prevention of Child Maltreatment (Rosenberg, 1987; Willis, Holden, & Rosenberg, 1992)
1985	Kathleen Wells	Residential Treatment
1985	Gerald P. Koocher	State-Level Legislative Consultation
1986	Gary B. Melton	Economics and Regulation of Children's Services (Melton & Small, in press)
1986	Jeffrey Seibert	Pediatric AIDS (Seibert & Olson, 1989; Task Force, 1989)
1986	T. Sonderegger	Behavioral Toxicology: Maternal and Fetal Toxins
1986	S. R. Schroeder	Behavioral Toxicology: Environmental, Developmental and Behavioral Neurotoxicology (Schroeder, 1987)
1987	James Garbarino	Child Abuse Training
1992	Murray Straus	Effects of Physical Punishment on Children
1992	Michael C. Roberts	Model Programs for Service Delivery in Clinical Child Psychology
1993	Diane Scott-Jones Amada Padilla and Diane Willis	Parenting Styles and Normative Development among Families from Ethnic Minorities
1993	Scott Henggeler	Innovative Models for Service Delivery (Henggeler, 1994)
1993	Geraldine Brookins and Brian Wilcox	Poverty, Family Processes, and Child Development: Recommendations for Intervention

Note. The source of much of this information was Melton, 1990, p. 5.

As the procedure has evolved, the process now involves several steps. First a member of the division prepares a proposal for the task force and presents it to the board. The proposal outlines the subject matter of the task force, states what kind of product it is intended to produce (a book, a journal article, a white paper for the board to review, etc.), indicates the funds required, and specifies the expected time line of the task force's activities. The board members consider the proposal, and if they approve it the board members appoint someone to chair the task force (usually, but not necessarily, the person who initiated the proposal). Members of the task force may meet at an APA convention (at no expense to the division), or they may meet at some other time and place (in which case they might require funds for transportation, meals, and lodging). In addition, much of the task force business is conducted via telephone (including conference calls), mail, fax, or (increasingly) e-mail. Often task forces are appointed jointly by Division 37 and other APA divisions and by outside organizations as well.

The earliest Division 37 task forces produced results in the form of items in the minutes of board meetings, symposia at conventions, or articles in the newsletter. Then, beginning in 1982, the task force idea began to show greater potential. The task force on adolescent abortion, headed by Gary Melton, lead to a 1986 edited book, published by the University of Nebraska Press in its series on children and the law (Melton, 1986). In a sense, this book was the first to put Division 37 on the national advocacy map. A steady stream of other books and articles followed. Many of the books were published by the University of Nebraska Press as part of the same series on children and the law, but other task force books were produced by various commercial publishers. The division recently adopted the Series on Child, Youth, and Family Services of the University of Nebraska Press as its own book series (coedited by Jeffrey Haugaard and Gary Melton). The editors of several of the Division 37 books (Koocher, Melton, Willis, S. Schroeder) are already well known to readers of this chapter. One who has not yet been mentioned is Lois A. Weithorn, the editor of the task force book on psychologists' involvement in child custody determinations (Weithorn, 1987), clearly the most influential volume extant on this topic. Weithorn obtained a PhD in clinical psychology from the University of Pittsburgh. She subsequently earned a law degree from Stanford, headed the law review, and clerked for a federal judge. According to Gary Melton (personal communication, January 7, 1996), a policy statement that Weithorn drafted to Koocher and Keith-Spiegel before she relinquished the chair of the ethics task force was influential in the most recent revision of the APA code of ethics.

Jeffrey Seibert, chair of the Task Force on Pediatric AIDS and coeditor of the resulting book (Seibert & Olson, 1989), is a developmental psychologist and a former research associate at the University of Miami's Mailman Center for Child Development. Miami is a center of active behavioral science research on AIDS, including its effects on children and families.

LOGO

In 1981, after an official contest, Division 37 membership adopted a logo designed by Susan Frank of Brooklyn (Bachman, 1982). The winning design was the figure of a woman with upraised hands, resembling a Greek letter psi, surrounded by two concentric rounded rectangles. This logo immediately began to be used on the newsletter and on division stationery.

The division's present logo, designed by John Murray, is a circle enclosing silhouettes of two larger figures in the back row, three smaller figures in the middle row, and one more distinctive smaller figure in the front row. The logo thus suggests a child in a family.

CONTROVERSIES

The main controversy involving Division 37 was the 1975 debate, described earlier, over whether such a division should exist at all, and whether it would be allowed to do what it wanted to do from the beginning: encouraging child advocacy and attempting to influence social policy. Developmental, clinical, and school psychologists could all argue, with some justification, that they were already involved in such advocacy and child and family policy issues. But these other divisions each had some other priority, be it research or the advancement of professional practice. Their child advocacy and policy work had to share time with research or practice agendas, whereas for Division 37 advocacy and influencing social policy had top priority. The authors realize that advocacy comes in many forms. When developmental psychologists support government funding of health-related research, clinical psychologists argue for legislation promoting third-party reimbursement, or school psychologists do the same for special education for children with disabilities, the results benefit children and families. Thus, once Division 37 began, the most remarkable fact was the lack of any controversies among people coming from different divisions. The history of the Division has been a highly cooperative venture.

CONCLUSION

As this chapter has made clear, Division 37 has already made significant contributions in advocating for the welfare of children and families, both within and beyond the APA. As one index of the impact of the division's work outside the field of psychology, an influential contemporary textbook in social work (Downs et al., 1996) chose to define the meaning of child advocacy largely in terms taken from the writings of the division's own Jane Knitzer (1976). This book lists the assumptions of child advocacy as follows:

1. Advocacy assumes that people have, or ought to have certain basic rights. . . .
2. Advocacy assumes that rights are enforceable by statutes, administration, or judicial procedures. . . .
3. Advocacy efforts are focused on institutional failures that produce or aggravate individual problems. . . .
4. Advocacy is inherently political. . . .
5. Advocacy is most effective when it is focused on specific issues. . . .
6. Advocacy is different from the provision of direct services. (Downs et al., 1996, pp 445–446)

Again following Knitzer (1976), Downs and colleagues (1996) list the tasks, strategies, and techniques of advocacy in the following way:

- fact finding. . .
- the development of strategies and remedies . . .
- maintenance of coalitions . . .
- reach[ing] out to and co-opt[ing] groups of volunteers . . .
- articulating findings in appropriate forums . . .
- lobbying. (Downs et al., 1996, pp. 456–458)

It would be difficult to produce a better blueprint for the kinds of activities Division 37 plans to carry out in the future.

REFERENCES

American Psychological Association. (1995). *1995 APA membership register*. Washington, DC: Author.

Bachman, S. (1981, Summer). Executive Committee meeting minutes, New York, March 28, 1981. *Division of Child and Youth Services Newsletter, 4*, 5–6.

Bachman, S. (1982, Winter–Spring). Executive Committee minutes, August 25, 1981. *Division of Child, Youth, and Family Services Newsletter, 5*, 5–6.

Behar, L. (1985). Changing patterns of state responsibility: A case study of North Carolina. *Journal of Clinical Child Psychology, 14*, 188–195.

Bronfenbrenner to receive 'Nicholas Hobbs Award.' (1987, Summer). *Division of Child, Youth, and Family Services Newsletter, 10*, 6–7.

Candidates for Division 37 offices. (1992, Spring). *Child, Youth, and Family Services Quarterly, 15*, 23–24.

Candidates for Division 37 offices. (1993, Spring). *Child, Youth, and Family Services Quarterly, 16*, 18–19.

The child abuse research award for 1994. (1994). *Child, Youth, and Family Services Quarterly, 17*(2), 9.

Cass, L. (1975). Minutes: Annual Business Meeting Section on Clinical Child Psychology, American Psychological Association, New Orleans, August 30, 1974. *Journal of Clinical Child Psychology, 1975, 4,* 59.

Children's Express. (1988, Summer). *Division of Child, Youth, and Family Services Newsletter, 11,* 14.

Clark, K. B. (1964). *Youth in the ghetto: A study of the consequences of powerlessness and a blueprint for change.* New York: HARYOU.

Clark, K. B. (1988). Contribution by a Psychologist in the Public Interest Gold Medal Award. *American Psychologist, 43,* 263–264.

Clark, K. B., & Clark, M. P. (1939a). Segregation as a factor in racial identification in Negro preschool children: A preliminary report. *Journal of Experimental Education, 8,* 161–163.

Clark, K. B., & Clark, M. P. (1939b). The development of consciousness of self and the emergence of racial identification in Negro preschool children. *Journal of Social Psychology, 10,* 591–599.

Clark, K. B., & Clark, M. P. (1940). Skin color as a factor in racial identification in Negro preschool children. *Journal of Social Psychology, 11,* 159–160.

Committee on Children, Youth and Families selected. (1985, Winter). *Division of Child, Youth, and Family Services Newsletter, 9,* 5.

Conger, J. J. (1976). Proceedings of the American Psychological Association, Incorporated for the year 1975: Minutes of the annual meeting of the Council of Representatives. *American Psychologist, 31,* 406–434.

Conger, J. J. (1977). Proceedings of the American Psychological Association, Incorporated for the Year 1976: Minutes of the Annual Meeting of the Council of Representatives. *American Psychologist, 32,* 408–438.

Culbertson, J. L. (1991). Child advocacy and clinical child psychology. *Journal of Clinical Child Psychology, 20,* 7–10.

Culbertson, J. L. (1995). 1994 in review: Division focuses on long range planning and creates new Section on Child Maltreatment. *Child, Youth, and Family Services Quarterly, 18,* 16–17. (This issue is erroneously labeled as Vol. 17, No. 4, but a later erratum corrected the mistake.)

Culbertson, J. L., & Willis, D. J. (1989, Summer). Schroeders to receive Nicholas Hobbs award. *Division of Child, Youth, and Family Services Newsletter, 12,* 10.

Diane Willis: 1993 Nicholas Hobbs award recipient. (1993, Summer). *Child, Youth, and Family Services Quarterly, 16,* 15.

Directory of the American Psychological Association. (1993). Washington, DC: American Psychological Association.

Division of Child and Youth Services Newsletter (1977, October).

Division 37 announces candidates for 1995 election ballot. (1995). *Child, Youth, and Family Services Quarterly, 18*(2), 17–18.

Division 37 candidates for 1989 election ballot. (1989, Spring). *Division of Child, Youth, and Family Services Newsletter, 12*, 8–9.

Division 37 distinguished contribution to child advocacy. (1988, Summer). *Division of Child, Youth, and Family Services Newsletter, 11*, 8.

Division 37 members-at-large. (1990, Winter). *Child, Youth, and Family Services Quarterly, 13*, 6.

Downs, S. W., Costin, L. B., & McFadden, E. J. (1996). *Child welfare and family services: Policies and practice.* (5th ed.). White Plains, NY: Longman.

Dr. Suniya Luthar to receive Division 37 student award. (1990, Summer). *Child, Youth, and Family Services Quarterly, 13*, 12.

Drotar, D. (1995a). About our president . . . *Child, Youth, and Family Services Quarterly, 18*, 11.

Drotar, D. (1995b). *Consulting with pediatricians: Psychological perspectives.* New York: Plenum Press.

Elkind, D. (1984). *All grown up and no place to go: Teenagers in crisis.* Reading, MA: Addison-Wesley.

Elkind, D. (1987). *Miseducation: Preschoolers at risk.* New York: Knopf.

Elkind, D. (1988). *The hurried child: Growing up too fast too soon.* Rev. ed. Reading, MA: Addison-Wesley.

Elkind, D. (1990). *Grandparenting: Understanding today's children.* Glenview, IL: Scott, Foresman.

Elkind to receive Nicholas Hobbs award. (1991, Summer). *Child, Youth, and Family Services Quarterly, 14*, 16.

Gary B. Melton [Award citation, APA 1985 Award for Distinguished Contribution to the Public Interest] (1986). *American Psychologist, 41*, 405–408.

"Gentle advocate" to receive Nicholas Hobbs award. (1986, Summer). *Division of Child, Youth, and Family Services Newsletter, 9*, 9.

Gerald P. Koocher [Award citation, APA 1992 Award for Distinguished Professional Contributions] (1993). *American Psychologist, 48*, 361–363.

Haggerty, R. J., Sherrod, L. R., Garmezy, N., & Rutter, M. (1994). *Stress, risk, and resilience in children and adolescents: Processes, mechanisms, and interventions.* New York: Cambridge University Press.

Harris to receive distinguished contribution award. (1992, Summer). *Child, Youth, and Family Services Quarterly, 15*, 16.

Hartup, W. W. (1976). [Letter to Milton F. Shore, June 30]. Copy in possession of the authors.

Henggeler, S. W. (Ed.). (1994). Task force report on innovative models of mental health services for children, adolescents, and their families. *Journal of Clinical Child Psychology, 23* (Suppl.), 1–58.

Hilgard, E. R. (1987). *Psychology in America: A historical survey.* San Diego, CA: Harcourt Brace Jovanovich.

Hobbs, N., Perrin, J. M., & Ireys, H. T. (Eds.) (1985). *Chronically ill children and their families.* San Francisco: Jossey-Bass.

Hodges, K. (1989, Summer). Minutes of the meeting of the executive committee, Division of Child, Youth, and Family Services, February 18 and 19, 1989. *Division of Child, Youth, and Family Services Newsletter, 12,* 12–13, 17, 19.

Interdivisional Committee on Adolescent Abortion. (1987). Adolescent abortion: Psychological and legal issues. *American Psychologist, 42,* 73–78.

Introducing the president. (1987, Winter). *Division of Child, Youth, and Family Services Newsletter, 10,* 2, 16.

Introducing the president. (1988, Winter). *Division of Child, Youth, and Family Services Newsletter, 11,* 9.

Introducing the president. (1989, Fall). *Division of Child, Youth, and Family Services Newsletter, 12,* 9.

Introducing the president. (1990, Winter). *Child, Youth, and Family Services Quarterly, 13,* 8.

Introducing the president. (1991, Winter). *Child, Youth, and Family Services Quarterly, 14,* 12.

Introducing the president. (1992, Winter). *Child, Youth, and Family Services Quarterly, 15,* 13.

Introducing the president. (1993, Winter). *Child, Youth, and Family Services Quarterly, 16,* 17.

Ira M. Schwartz: Advocate for children, youth and families. (1990, Summer). *Child, Youth, and Family Services Quarterly, 13,* 14.

James Garbarino. (1990). Award citation, APA 1989 Award for Distinguished Professional Contributions. *American Psychologist, 45,* 469–471.

Keith-Spiegel, P. (1978, July). Report from the program chair. *Division of Child and Youth Services Newsletter, 3,* 3.

Knitzer, J. (1976). Child advocacy: A perspective. *American Journal of Orthopsychiatry, 46,* 200–216.

Knitzer, J. (1982). *Unclaimed children: The failure of public responsibility to children and adolescents in need of mental health services.* Washington, DC: Children's Defense Fund.

Knobeloch, H., & Pasamanick, B. (1966). Prospective studies on the epidemiology of reproductive casualty: Methods, findings, and some implications. *Merrill Palmer Quarterly, 12,* 27–43.

Koocher, G. P. (1979, July). 1979 program report. *Division of Child and Youth Services Newsletter 6,* 3.

Koocher, G. P. (1980). Pediatric cancer: Psychological problems and the high costs of helping. *Journal of Clinical Child Psychology, 9,* 2–5.

Koocher, G. P., & Keith–Spiegel, P. C. (Eds.). (1990). *Children, ethics, and the law.* Lincoln: University of Nebraska Press.

Krugman to receive distinguished contribution award. (1993, Summer). *Child, Youth, and Family Services Quarterly, 16,* 15.

Lipsitt to receive Nicholas Hobbs award. (1990, Summer). *Child, Youth, and Family Services Quarterly, 13*, 12.

Luthar, S. S. (1991). Vulnerability and resilience: A study of high risk adolescents. *Child Development, 62*, 600–616.

Luthar, S. S. (1995). Social competence in the school setting: Prospective cross domain associations among inner-city teens. *Child Development, 66*, 416–429.

Manegold, C. S. (1992). Dr. Lee Salk, child psychologist and popular author, dies at 65. *New York Times Biographical Service, 23*, 570.

Mark Weist to receive Division 37 student award. (1991, Summer). *Child, Youth, and Family Services Quarterly, 14*, 17.

Marsden, G. (1974). Minutes, Section I Executive Committee Meeting August 27, 1973–Montreal, Quebec Section 1, Division 12, APA. *Journal of Clinical Child Psychology, 3*, 50–51.

Maryland v. Craig, 497 U.S. 836 (1990).

Massimo, J. L., & Shore, M. F. (1963). The effectiveness of a comprehensive, vocationally oriented psychotherapeutic program for adolescent delinquent boys. *American Journal of Orthopsychiatry, 33*, 634–642.

Melton, G. B. (1983). *Child advocacy: Psychological issues and interventions*. New York: Plenum Press.

Melton, G. B. (Ed.). (1986). *Adolescent abortion: Psychological and legal issues*. Lincoln: University of Nebraska Press.

Melton, G. B. (1987). Legal regulation of adolescent abortion: Unintended effects. *American Psychologist, 42*, 79–83.

Melton, G. B. (Ed.) (1989). *Economics and regulation of children's services*. Lincoln: University of Nebraska Press.

Melton, G. B. (1990). Giving psychology away systematically: Division 37's task forces. *Child, Youth, and Family Services Quarterly, 13*, 4–5.

Melton, G. B. (1994). Building safe environments for children and families: The integration of research, teaching, and public service. In P.A. Keller (Ed.), *Academic paths: Career decisions and experiences of psychologists*. (pp. 135–147). Hillsdale, NJ: Lawrence Erlbaum.

Melton, G. B. (1995). Bringing psychology to Capitol Hill: Briefings on child and family policy. *American Psychologist, 50*, 766–770.

Melton, G. B., Lyons, P. M., Jr., & Spaulding, W. (Eds.). (in press). *No place to go: Civil commitment of minors*. Lincoln: University of Nebraska Press.

Melton, G. B., & Russo, N. F. (1987). Adolescent abortion: Psychological perspectives on public policy. *American Psychologist, 42*, 73–78.

Melton, G. B., & Small, M. R. (Eds.). (in press). *Following the money: Financing and regulation of child and family services*. Lincoln: University of Nebraska Press.

Milonas v. Williams, 691 F.2d 931 (1982).

Mnookin, R. H. (1975). Child-custody adjudication: Judicial functions in the face of indeterminacy. *Law and Contemporary Problems, 39*, 226–290.

Mnookin, R. H. (1978). Children's rights: Beyond kidder libbers and child savers. *Journal of Clinical Child Psychology, 7,* 163–167.

New student award created. (1988, Fall). *Division of Child, Youth, and Family Services Newsletter, 11,* 12.

Nicholas Hobbs award presented. (1988, Fall). *Division of Child, Youth, and Family Services Newsletter, 11,* 8.

Pellegrini, D. S. (1984). Mnookin addresses division on abortion. *Division of Child, Youth, and Family Services Newsletter, 7,* 1.

Rie, H. E. (1975). [Letter to the Editor]. *Journal of Clinical Child Psychology, 4,* 53–54.

Roberts, M. C., Erickson, M. T., & Tuma, J. M. (1985). Addressing the needs: Guidelines for training psychologists to work with children, youth, and families. *Journal of Clinical Child Psychology, 14,* 70–79.

Rosenberg, M. (1987). [Psychological maltreatment] *American Psychologist, 42.*

Routh, D. K. (1984, Spring). On advocacy. *Division of Child, Youth, and Family Services Newsletter, 7,* 1, 4.

Routh, D. K. (Ed.). (1988). *Handbook of pediatric psychology.* New York: Guilford Press.

Routh, D. K. (1994). *Clinical psychology since 1917: Science, practice, and organization.* New York: Plenum Press.

Routh, D. K., Patton, L., & Sanfilippo, M. D. (1991). Celebrating 20 years of the *Journal of Clinical Child Psychology:* From child advocacy to scientific research and back again. *Journal of Clinical Child Psychology, 20,* 2–6.

Salk, L. (1992). *Familyhood: Nurturing the values that matter.* New York: Simon & Schuster.

Sarason, S. (1988). *The making of an American psychologist: An autobiography.* San Francisco: Jossey-Bass.

Schellenbach, C. (1992, Spring). Draft minutes of the meeting of the executive committee, Division 37 Child, Youth, and Family Services, APA, February 22–23, 1992. *Child, Youth, and Family Services Quarterly, 15,* 20–23.

Schroeder, C. S. (1979). Psychologists in a private pediatric practice. *Journal of Pediatric Psychology, 4,* 5–18.

Schroeder, S. R. (1987). *Toxic substances and mental retardation: Neurobehavioral toxicology and teratology.* Washington, DC: American Association on Mental Deficiency.

Schwartz, I. M. (1989). *(In)justice for juveniles: Rethinking the best interests of the child.* Lexington, MA: Lexington Books.

Seibert, J. M., & Olson, R. A. (1989). *Children, adolescents, and AIDS.* Lincoln: University of Nebraska Press.

Shore, M. F. (Ed.). (1965). *Red is the color of hurting.* Washington, DC: U.S. Government Printing Office.

Shore, M. F. (1976). [Letter to John J. Conger, July 13]. Copy in possession of the authors.

Shore, M. F., & Massimo, J. L. (1979). Fifteen years after treatment: A follow-up study of comprehensive vocationally-oriented psychotherapy. *American Journal of Orthopsychiatry, 49*, 240–245.

Smith, M. B. (1985). Nicholas Hobbs (1915-1983). *American Psychologist, 40*, 463–465.

Sobel, S. B. (1978, May). Report from Suzanne B. Sobel, treasurer. *Division of Child and Youth Services Newsletter, 2*, 1–2.

Soler recipient of "distinguished contribution award." (1987, Summer). *Division of Child, Youth, and Family Services Newsletter, 10*, 7.

Sugarman to receive distinguished contribution award. (1991, Summer). *Child, Youth, and Family Services Quarterly, 14*, 17.

Takanishi, R. (1978). Childhood as a social issue: Historical roots of contemporary child advocacy movements. *Journal of Social Issues, 34*(2), 8–28.

Task Force on Pediatric AIDS (1989). Pediatric AIDS and HIV infection: Psychological issues. *American Psychologist, 44*, 258–264.

Terr, L. (1990). *Too scared to cry: Psychic trauma in childhood.* Grand Rapids, MI: Harper & Row.

Wald, M. S. (1976). Legal policies affecting children: A lawyer's request for aid. *Child Development, 47*, 1–5.

Weithorn, L. A. (1987). *Psychology and child custody determinations: Knowledge, roles, and expertise.* Lincoln: University of Nebraska Press.

Wertlieb, D. (1989, Summer). 1989 Advocacy award to William W. Harris. *Division of Child, Youth, and Family Services Newsletter, 12*, 11.

Williams, G. J. (1975). Visions and division/sections and reflections. *Journal of Clinical Child Psychology, 4*, 50.

Williams, G. J. (1976). The Division on Children and Youth: Visions . . . divisions . . . revisions. *Journal of Clinical Child Psychology, 5*, 7–9.

Willie M. et al. v. James B. Hunt, Jr. et al., Civil No. C-C-79-294 (W.D.N.C. 1980).

Willis, D. J. (1987a). Obituary: Gertrude J. Rubin Williams, 1927–1986. *Journal of Clinical Child Psychology, 16*, 168–169.

Willis, D. J. (1987b, Winter). In [memoriam]: Gertrude J. Williams 1927–1986. *Division of Child, Youth, and Family Services Newsletter, 10*, 11.

Willis, D. J., Holden, E. W., & Rosenberg, M. (Eds.). (1992). *The prevention of child maltreatment.* New York: John Wiley & Sons.

Wooden, K. (1976). *Weeping in the playtime of others: America's incarcerated children.* New York: McGraw-Hill.

Wooden, K. (1981). *The Children of Jonestown,* New York: McGraw-Hill.

Wright, L. (1983, Spring–Summer). In memoriam: Nicholas Hobbs 1915–1983. *Division of Child, Youth, and Family Services Newsletter, 6*, 2.

8

A HISTORY OF DIVISION 39 (PSYCHOANALYSIS)

MURRAY MEISELS and ROBERT C. LANE

Psychoanalysis has long been an important psychology, and today, approximately 10% of the members of the American Psychological Association (APA) are students of the field. Although there had been discussion of founding a division of psychoanalysis in the 1940s when the APA was reorganizing, and again in 1969 (see Meisels, 1994a), it was not until 1979 that the division actually formed.

BACKGROUND

Psychoanalysis was founded in the late nineteenth century and has developed and grown throughout this century. Unless outlawed (as it was in Eastern Europe by the communists and earlier by the Nazis), it has spread to almost all developed countries and has sometimes had a dramatic impact on those countries, as in France after Charles De Gaulle. The num-

In 1994, in honor of the American Psychological Association centennial, Division 39 published *A History of the Division of Psychoanalysis of the American Psychological Association* (Lane & Meisels, 1994), which presented, from a positive perspective, the history of the division through 1991 or 1992. This chapter is a selective review of some of the material of that book, brought up to date through early 1996 but cast in a more objective and critical format. The interested reader is referred to the original book for more detail.

ber of practitioners has grown steadily and sometimes even spectacularly, as is now occurring in Russia; the number and total pages of journals have grown, as have the numbers of books, conferences, training institutes, and societies. *Psychoanalytic theorizing*—meaning theories that are regarded by their advocates as psychoanalytic—has grown as well.

Most psychologists are familiar with some of Sigmund Freud's opus and are aware that psychoanalytic theories were also formed by Alfred Adler, Carl Jung, and, in the postwar years, by culturalists and existentialists. In fact, the theoretical diversity is great, and the current, active perspectives in psychoanalysis may be listed as follows, roughly in order of historical origin: Freudian, Adlerian, Jungian, Rankian, Interpersonal, Kleinian, Horneyian, British Object Relational, Existential, Lacanian, Ego Psychological, Modern Psychoanalytic, Self Psychological, Relational, and Intersubjective. Controversies and schools of thought often exist *within* these main theories as well, such as followers of Erikson or Hartmann among ego-psychologists, or students of Winnicott or Fairbairn among the British object relationists. It is also the case that different theoretical perspectives have been dominant in different countries, so that in the post-World War II era Americans were largely ego-psychological, the French were Lacanian, and the Argentineans were Kleinian. Object relations perspectives currently dominate psychoanalysis in the United States.

Early in this century Freud founded the International Psychoanalytic Association (IPA) to organize and develop his vision of psychoanalysis, and the IPA in turn founded national associations for the dissemination of psychoanalytic ideas. By the mid–1920s, these national societies formed free-standing psychoanalytic training institutes and began formally educating individuals in psychoanalysis, making the IPA the worldwide oversight body for psychoanalytic training in the Freudian tradition. The Freudian tradition gradually underwent theoretical change, but most of the new theorists, including many of those previously listed, asserted that the changes derived directly from Freud's ideas. Thus, American ego psychologists such as David Rapaport argued that they were elaborating on Freud's opus, yet Melanie Klein and Jacques Lacan, among others, put forth similar claims regarding radically different theoretical changes. Amid the fractiousness, Lacan was ejected from the IPA because of his theories, and Karen Horney was denied teaching privileges at the New York Psychoanalytic Institute after she developed her ideas.

In the United States, the IPA's national society was the American Psychoanalytic Association (APsaA), which dominated American psychoanalysis until recent decades, and which, unlike the IPA or most other national societies, regarded psychoanalysis as a province of medicine. APsaA was an organization made up of mostly of psychiatrists and designed to train other psychiatrists. It grew rapidly and established a network of institutes around the country, but it refused admission to almost all psychologists. Indeed, the APsaA leadership, which believed that psychoanalysis was a medical procedure, prevailed on the IPA to enact a rule that no U.S. citizen could train in any IPA institute in the world without its permission, this despite Freud's view, one widely endorsed by non-Americans in the IPA, that psychoanalysis was not a part of medicine (see Schneider & Desmond, 1994).

APsaA's exclusionary policies were effective in most of the United States, and psychoanalytically oriented psychologists of the Freudian orientation—the predominant orientation—suffered years of frustration in seeking and failing to gain admission to APsaA institutes. In the New York City area, however, psychologists began forming their own institutes in the late 1940s, and by the time Division 39 was founded in 1979, there were many training institutes (mostly interdisciplinary) in greater New York and a few in other urban areas. In 1979 psychologists in the New York area had never been part of a national organization, and few psychologists outside of New York had ever been part of any psychoanalytic organization, local or national. As a result, the formation of the Division of Psychoanalysis triggered a period of dramatic, rapid growth. The healthy growth of the division is therefore related to both the prior lack of a national psychologist psychoanalytic organization and the APsaA's suppression of psychoanalytic activity among psychologists. Once these barriers were removed, psychologists vigorously expressed their psychoanalytic commitments through Division 39 and its activities, especially through the formation of a national network of local societies. Along with this, they also brought to the division their history of theoretical animosity and fractiousness.

THE DIVISION OF PSYCHOANALYSIS

Reuben Fine, a noted psychologist–psychoanalyst who had founded several major psychoanalytic institutes in New York and who also helped launch Division 29 (Psychotherapy) a decade earlier, decided in 1978 that psychologists in psychoanalysis needed a division in the American Psychological Association (APA). He, along with Robert C. Lane, George D. Goldman, Samuel Kutash, and Max Rosenbaum, proceeded to send a mailing to members of Divisions 12 (clinical) and 29 (psychotherapy), and received 869 expressions of interest. Fine and his associates then petitioned the APA for divisional status. Following the first day of the APA Council of Representatives session, at which time the vote was delayed, the organizing committee held an emergency meeting to elect pro-tem officers. Division 39 was granted official status a few days later, on September 1, 1979 (see Lane, 1994c). During the first year Division 39 was governed by pro-tem officers and a steering committee of 44 members, after which bylaws were developed that defined the division board as comprising a president, president-elect, past-president, secretary, treasurer, and nine members-at-large. These bylaws were later changed to include on the board one representative from each section established by the division.

Since its establishment in 1979, the division's membership has grown greatly, and it has developed a central office and a large and effective committee structure. The division has also developed eight subdivisions, called sections, which are national organizations that have a delimited area of interest within psychoanalysis. Perhaps the division membership's most remarkable accomplishment was the development of a network of 30 local chapters, which are lively centers for psychoanalytic education and activity all over the country. For a broad overview of the division's growth, see Table 32, which presents a list of the division presidents, the dates they served, and a capsule description of the major events during their administrations.

The division is actually a network of sections and local chapters with their own officers, committees, and meeting schedules, as well as division-level officers, committees, and conferences. In this chapter, we will first examine the division's Central Office, followed by the division-level committees, and then the sections and local chapters. Next we will explore some of the allied organizations that the division developed for specific purposes, including the free-standing psychoanalytic training institutes and the lawsuit against the APsaA.

CENTRAL OFFICE

Reuben Fine's psychoanalytic institute, the New York Center for Psychoanalytic Training, provided secretarial services for the division from 1979 through 1980. Then George D. Goldman, the division's first secretary, provided these services at his home institution, Adelphi University. Because subsequent secretaries lacked the facilities to provide administrative functions, the secretarial work has since been provided by the Central Office, and the secretary has functioned largely as a recording secretary. The Central Office remained at Adelphi, under George Goldman's direction, until 1984, and was then moved to the Postgraduate Center for Mental Health in New York City, where it was overseen by Zanvel Liff. These two facilities provided low-cost services and free oversight by two dedicated colleagues and were suitable for the division in its early phase. By 1990 the increasing complexity of the division's commitments, and its enhanced treasury, led the leadership to a professional group to manage its secretarial affairs. Thus, from 1992 onward the Central Office functions have been under contract with The Administrators in Phoenix, Arizona.

TABLE 32
Presidents of Division 39

Year	Name	Highlights
1979–1980	Reuben Fine	Committees, bylaws, local chapters form, newsletter begins
1980–1981	Gordon Derner	First spring meeting; Qualifications Committee
1981–1982	Robert C. Lane	Section I formed; Journal editor appointed
1982–1983	George D. Goldman	ABPP committee formed; Section I conflict
1983–1984	Ernest S. Lawrence	Sections II & III; Journal starts publication
1984–1985	Helen Block Lewis	White Conference; antitrust lawsuit filed
1985–1986	Nathan Stockhamer	Sections IV & V; *PsycSCAN: Psychoanalysis* published
1986–1987	Fred Pine	Clark Conference; 15 local chapters admitted
1987–1988	Murray Meisels	3 local chapters; intense lawsuit negotiations
1988–1989	Zanvel A. Liff	Lawsuit settled; membership directory
1989–1990	Ruth Jean Eisenbud	Sections VI & VII; criteria for psychoanalyst
1990–1991	Bertram P. Karon	*Clark Conference* book; 6 local chapters
1991–1992	Jonathan H. Slavin	Membership at 3,000; contact with Russia
1992–1993	Leopold Caligor	The Consortium; 4 seats on APA council
1994	James Barron	History book of Division 39; managed care
1995	Harriette Kaley	ABPsaP grants diplomates; 30th chapter
1996	Morris Eagle	Section VIII
1997	Marvin Hyman (elected)	—

COMMITTEES

The Division of Psychoanalysis rapidly evolved a potent and wide-ranging committee structure. It has attracted a large number of devoted members who have been stalwart in developing and enlarging its functions, activities, and productivity. The committees have generally operated with great autonomy, and the initiatives of the chairs and the task requirements produced a great deal of work.

Committee Structure

The standing committees now mandated by the bylaws are APA Liaison, Education and Training, Ethics, Executive, Fellows, Finance, Membership, Nomination and Elections, Professional Issues, Program, Public Information and Social Responsibility, Publications, Qualifications and Standards and Research. The ad hoc committees for 1996 were Adult Development and Aging; Awards; Health Care Reform; Multicultural Concerns; Family Therapy; Continuing Education; Convention Management and Site Selection; Graduate Students; Historian, International Relations; Infant Mental Health; Long Term Planning; Psychoanalytic Consortium;

Social Responsibility, Specialization, and Accreditation; and Spring Meeting. There are also two task forces, on prescription privileges and managed care. It is not entirely obvious why some committees are standing and others ad hoc— as it was different in the past and will likely change again in the future—but such was the structure in 1996.

Of the numerous committees that have existed over the years, many have evolved into the current structure, many were temporary and no longer exist, and still others developed to section status. The six committees that became sections were Childhood and Adolescence, Women, Local Chapters, Psychoanalysis and Groups, Research, and Family Therapy. Some of the more important committees that performed time-limited functions were the American Board of Professional Psychology, Clark Conference, National Program, Psychoanalytic Education, and Peer Review. Some committees appear and reappear as needed, such as Bylaws or Structure and Function.

According to Lane and Meisels (1994, pp. 59–60), the five major achievements of the division's committee structure were as follows:

- The development of an effective program of publications that has expended great effort in providing the division with a journal, a journal of abstracts, a newsletter, and a forthcoming book series.
- The Program Committee for running the annual spring meeting of the division, one of the major annual psychoanalytic conventions held in the United States.
- The Qualifications Committee and the Division Board for developing criteria for qualification in psychoanalysis, in the face of enormous diversity in the membership.
- The Local Chapter Committee for laying the foundation for the chapter movement.
- The Division Board, serving as a Committee of the Whole, in supporting, financing, championing, advocating, and overseeing the lawsuit against APsaA.

Lane and Meisels (1994) noted that although these five committees produced the most visible successes so far in the division's history, other committees and individuals have made great contributions as well. These include the time-consuming work of the treasurer and the editors of its publications, as well as great efforts by many committees, most notably the publication, program, qualifications, and membership committees.

Publication Committee

Psychologists had long published in the psychoanalytic literature, and with the advent of the division they quickly developed a wide variety of publications.

The Newsletter

At the first meeting of the Steering Committee, Reuben Fine, president pro tem, appointed Marvin Daniels and Robert C. Lane coeditors of what was to become the *Psychologist–Psychoanalyst*, the division's newsletter. It is published four times a year, with occasional special supplements (see Lane, 1994b). Usual features of the newsletter are the president's column, news from sections and local chapters, feature articles, book reviews, and abstracts of papers given at division meetings. One interesting topical supplement, edited by James W. Barron, who was also the newsletter editor, was published shortly after the Gulf War on the theme "Psychoanalytic Perspectives on War."

The Journal

Robert C. Lane, the division's third president, was responsible for moving the issue of journal publication forward. As president, he appointed Helen Block Lewis to a 5-year term as editor, and she established a name for the journal, *Psychoanalytic Psychology*, negotiated suitable publishing agreements with Lawrence Erlbaum Associates, and produced the first issue in 1983. Lewis hoped the journal would present the finest clinical and experimental work in psychoanalytic psychology, publish original articles that would broaden and enhance information exchange between psychoanalysis and psychology, and contribute to the development of both (Marshall, 1994). She established standards of excellence for the journal and was mindful of minority and gender problems.

In 1987 the current editor Bertram J. Cohler, was appointed. His 6-year term has been extended for 4 additional years. Under his guidance, the journal has grown and its quality has continued to improve. Because of a backlog of papers, the annual number of journal pages was increased in the early 1990s from approximately 356 to 576. The number of scholarly articles submitted has also increased, from approximately 40 the first year to from 70 to 90 in recent years. The percentage of rejections remains around 70%, and blind review by at least two reviewers has always been in effect. Cohler, like Lewis, has requested the right of first refusal of papers presented at the division's scientific programs, but this thorny issue is still being debated. Despite much negotiation with many different publishers, the journal continues its affiliation with Lawrence Erlbaum Associates (see Cohler, 1994, regarding journal policy and activity).

The Journal of Abstracts

Robert C. Lane also envisioned developing a journal of psychoanalytic abstracts. When he became president of Division 39, he negotiated with the APA Publications and Communications Board about details involved in creating *PsycSCAN: Psychoanalysis*. Lane then appointed Edward

Penzer and Ruth Formanek cochairs of a committee to work with Psyc-INFO, the department of APA that publishes psychological abstracts, and come up with a plan for a journal of abstracts. In 1987, 5 years after the original negotiations, the first issue of *PsycSCAN: Psychoanalysis* appeared. In March 1993 it was renamed *Psychoanalytic Abstracts* in an attempt to increase circulation and gain international readership.

Psychoanalytic Abstracts is a quarterly publication that provides abstracts and summaries on psychoanalytic topics from three major sources of information: books, chapters, and serials. It includes indexes in the first three issues each year, and offers an annual index in the fourth issue of the year. The March issue contains summaries of books and chapters, the September issue contains abstracts of psychoanalytic topics from nonanalytic journals, and the June and September issues contain abstracts and index articles from 45 psychoanalytic journals (see Lane, 1994b).

The Directory

Another publication of the division has been the membership Directory. This project also had growing pains, and it was not until 1987, when Murray Meisels became president, that a Directory Committee was appointed, with Carol Butler as chair. Earlier efforts to publish a directory were derailed by fears that a directory might suggest qualification in psychoanalysis, and the actual publication stirred up the Section I–Section V controversy (discussed later in the chapter), which concerned Section I receiving special or privileged status if sectional membership were included in the directory (see Meisels, 1994b). These issues fortunately have been resolved. The most recent Directory was published in 1994 and contains a foreword, the division bylaws, an alphabetical listing of division members followed by student members, a geographical roster of division members, rosters of all the sections, and a listing for language fluency.

The Publication Committee

The initial chairs of the division's Publication Committee were uncertain of their tasks, and the publications were developed primarily because of the initiatives of the division presidents, especially Lane, but also Fine and Meisels. Eventually, when Robert Marshall held the position from 1986 to 1991, an effective committee structure was established that spelled out the purposes and goals of the Publication Committee (see Marshall, 1994). Marshall was followed by Charles Spezzano, who proved to be a very active division chair. Under Spezzano, the division sponsored two centennial books (including the history book so often referenced in this chapter), and he is planning a series of edited, multiauthored books to provide a forum for a broad range of division members to contribute to the psychoanalytic literature. The first will be *The Handbook of Psychoanalytic*

Psychology (Reppen, Tucker & Spezzano, in press) intended to be a literate, accessible, and definitive account of the evolution and current status of psychoanalytic theory and practice, a volume aimed at younger clinicians and graduate students.

Other Division Publications

The publications and committee activities just detailed were all at the divisional level. However, the sections and local chapters also publish literature, albeit mostly of the newsletter variety. Sections I, III, V, and VI all publish newsletters, as did 15 of 26 local chapters in 1991 through 1992. *The Round Robin*, the newsletter of Section I since 1985, well illustrates the genre, with columns like "Distinguished Member's Commentary," "Psychoanalysis and Contemporary Life," and "Being an Analyst in Different Places." The newsletter of the Washington Society of Psychoanalytic Psychology, one of the local chapters, is of journal quality. In 1991 through 1992, the sections published 12 newsletter issues and the local chapters published 68 issues for a grand total of 80 newsletter issues in one year—a high level of activity indeed.

Program Committee

Just as psychologist psychoanalysts quickly developed a series of publications, so too did they organize programs and meetings, especially at the local chapter level. Here, we shall only discuss division-level programs.

APA Convention

Summaries of some features of Division 39 presentations at APA conventions for 1980 through 1991 are presented in Table 33 (from Callan, 1994) and include a listing of the invited speakers and titles of presidential addresses. Division 39 is generally allocated about 28 hours for presentations, up from 18 hours in its first year, and this is supplemented by a hospitality suite that features additional discussion hours. However, because August is a vacation month, divisional attendance at the APA convention is not particularly high.

Division 39 Annual Meeting

Division 39 also holds an annual midwinter/spring meeting. Initially organized as a winter vacation conference in a resort area, the first three conferences were held in Mexico or Puerto Rico. These vacation-type conferences had attendance in the low hundreds and board members were dissatisfied that students and younger colleagues might not be able to afford the expense. They also considered the possibility that holding conferences in major U.S. cities might invigorate both psychoanalysis and the local

TABLE 33
Division 39 APA Programs (1980–1991)*

Year	Invited Speakers	Presidential Address
1980	M. Mayman	Reuben Fine
1981	H. J. Schlesinger, R. Ekstein	Gordon F. Derner, "The Psychoanalysis of Human Experience: Love, Grief, and Parataxes"
1982	H. B. Lewis, S. R. Smith	Robert C. Lane, "The Language of Dreams"
1983	S. J. Blatt, H. Shevrin, G. Mandler	George Goldman, "Psychotherapy and Psychoanalysis: Are the Two So Different?"
1984	R. R. Holt, J. L. Singer	Ernest S. Lawrence, "The Object in Intrapsychic Conflict: Strategic and Clinical Considerations"
1985	R. Schafer, J. R. Greenberg, L. Breger	Helen Block Lewis, "Psychoanalysis as Therapy Today"
1986	E. Fromm, M. Eagle, M. Brenman-Gibson	Nathan Stockhamer, "Psychoanalysis From Any Point of View"
1987	B. Karon, R. Fine	Fred Pine
1988	Z. A. Liff, B. J. Cohler	Murray Meisels, "A Critique and Redefinition of Resistance in Psychoanalysis"
1989	A. Carotenuto, R. M. Jones, R. C. Lane	Zanvel A. Liff, "On, Off and Beyond the Couch: Fifty Years After Sigmund Freud"
1990	K. K. Novick, J. Novick, H. Bolgar, C. Gilligan	Ruth-Jean Eisenbud, "Ego Dream Transformations During Psychoanalysis"
1991	M. Slavin, I. Fast, C. Spezzano	Bertram P. Karon, "The Fear of Understanding Schizophrenia"

*Adapted from Callan, 1994, p. 85.

chapters in those areas. The conferences were therefore shifted to U.S. cities in the springtime, attendance grew dramatically, and local chapters were in fact energized by the task of organizing a major meeting for psychologist–psychoanalysts. The pattern now established is that two conferences are held at varying urban locations and every third meeting takes place in New York City, where a thousand or more colleagues attend and the division's coffers are well replenished. To date, spring meetings have been held in San Diego, New York, San Francisco, Boston, Chicago, Washington, D.C., Philadelphia, and Los Angeles, and future meetings are scheduled for Denver and Dallas.

The spring meeting has become one of the premier psychoanalytic conferences in the United States. It is a 5-day affair with scores of speakers, and sessions are scheduled simultaneously. This is also the primary site at which members of the sections and divisional committees transact their business, so these conferences are veritable beehives of organizational, theoretical, and scientific activities. The content of the presidential addresses in Table 33 illustrates some of the substantive issues of the spring meetings.

A summary of some statistics from the 1995 spring meeting and the 1995 APA convention document the vigor of the division's conference program. In 1995, 299 colleagues presented 127 symposia and paper sessions totaling 227 hours at the spring meeting. At the APA convention, 85 psychologists presented 29 symposia and paper sessions lasting 48 hours, with some of the presentations made at the division's hospitality suite. Organizational meetings also abounded at the conferences, with meetings of the division board, of section boards, and of numerous division or section committees. In all there were 24 such meetings lasting a total of 53 hours at the spring meeting, and there were 11 meetings lasting a total of 29 hours at the APA convention. Social receptions were held, six at the spring meeting and two at the APA convention, for a total of 12 hours for celebrants.

Special Conferences

The division has held three special conferences to address particular issues in psychoanalysis. The first was the National Conference on Psychoanalytic Training, held in December 1984, which started the local chapters on the road to becoming a section (discussed later in the chapter). The second meeting was the Clark Conference on Psychoanalytic Education, held at Clark University in October 1986, to discuss psychologists' perspectives on training (see Meisels & Shapiro, 1990). The most recent conference was held in Washington, D.C., in May 1990 to develop an overarching organization to include all American psychoanalytic organizations, especially the newly evolving, independent psychoanalytic training institutes that were offshoots of the local chapters. This last conference led to the formation of the International Federation for Psychoanalytic Education (discussed later).

Qualifications Committee

Immediately after Division 39 was formed, the members addressed the problem of determining the education and experience requirements for someone to be identified as a psychoanalyst, and a Qualifications Committee under the leadership of Ernest S. Lawrence was appointed to the task. The issue of qualification in psychoanalysis has a long and stormy history because of theoretical divergencies, and these controversies were played out within the division. The traditional viewpoint was the one held by members of the future Section I, Psychologist-Psychoanalyst practitioners, which was that psychoanalysis was an intensive procedure that required frequent contact, such as the IPA standard of at least 4 treatment hours a week. The Qualification Committee considered, however, that a number of psychoanalytic institutes actually treated analysands three times per week, and the committee members eventually decided that three times a week was sufficient (see Lawrence, 1994).

During 1980 through 1982, the Qualifications Committee members recommended that the division be an interest group open to all members of the APA but that it also identify those psychologists who met the qualifications for psychoanalysis by developing a section of psychoanalysts. They defined a psychoanalyst as someone who had undergone at least 300 hours of personal analysis at a frequency of at least three psychoanalytic sessions per week (the personal analysis requirement), had received at least 200 hours of weekly supervision on at least two cases that were being treated in psychoanalysis at a frequency of at least three sessions per week (the supervision requirement), and who had also had 4 years of course work (the course work requirement). These criteria are mostly standard at psychoanalytic training institutes, and they fundamentally indicated that three meetings a week was the division's criterion for psychoanalysis. The Qualifications Committee membership took pains to include as qualified those psychologists who had not graduated from institutes (largely because of the APsaA's rules) but who had successfully completed these requirements in a program of self-directed training (i.e., personal analysis, supervision, and course work completed outside of a formal psychoanalytic training institute). The Qualifications Committee members also adopted the position that all schools of psychoanalysis were welcome to meet the qualifications of the division (i.e., neither the division nor Section I has ever been of Freudian or Jungian or any specific theoretical persuasion but always included all who were interested or qualified). Lastly, it noted that even though APA divisions may not grant credentials, they may nevertheless set membership requirements more stringent than the APA's and recommended a bylaws change to enable sections to be formed (Lawrence, 1994).

The Division 39 board members approved all of these recommendations and then formed Section I using the division's qualification criteria (including thrice weekly treatments) as the admission requirement. This meant that members of Section I were thereby identified as meeting the criteria for qualification in psychoanalysis. Section I leaders considered that psychologists could now identify themselves as psychoanalysts.

The Conflict Over Standards

Concern about the requirement of three weekly sessions eventually led less traditional members to organize. The less traditional view—which would result in the formation of Section V—held that intensity of the treatment was not measured by the number of weekly treatment hours (see Lawrence, 1994; Marlan & Trachtman, 1994; Meisels, 1994a; Slavin, 1994). These psychologist–psychoanalysts argued that some psychoanalytic training institutes required only two weekly sessions and further that at least some Jungians received only one treatment session per week. They considered the three-times-a-week requirement arbitrary and presumptuous, and the series of strained, strife-laden board meetings that ensued featured serious conflicts between Section I and the future Section V. Section V was finally formed in 1985. As proposed, the members wanted to call the section the Psychologist–Psychoanalyst Clinicians, but Section I objected to this designation so, as a compromise, Section V was named the Psychologist–Psychoanalyst Forum. When, in 1994, Section V members renamed the section Psychologist–Psychoanalyst Clinicians—the name they originally intended—the move provoked Section I leaders into recriminations against both Section V (for reneging on an agreement) and the division board (for not disciplining Section V). Prior to this latest clash, the senior members of Section I, who constituted many of the most active and important psychologist–psychoanalysts, had largely removed themselves from active participation in the division's life, except for their involvement in presenting papers and symposia at the national meetings.

It is perhaps because of the withdrawal of the active Section I leadership that, in 1990, the board members, accepting the idea that all constituencies had a place in the division, revised their definition of psychoanalysis and deleted any reference to the number of treatment hours. The personal analysis, supervision, and course work requirements of psychoanalytic training were redefined as comprising "a substantial personal analysis," "intensive supervision" of "two patients, each carried two years in psychoanalysis," and didactic work that is "the equivalent of 12 courses in a traditional two-semester program" (see Meisels, 1994a, p. 17). No numbers were given detailing the frequency of any of these analyses, albeit the training programs of 11 psychoanalytic institutes were presented to provide concrete examples of ways to implement the criteria. Although the Division 39 board members had done a stellar job of keeping these divergent positions contained in one organization—even at the cost of the withdrawal of Section I leadership—the tension regarding these two deeply held positions nonetheless persists.

Membership Committee

Table 34 summarizes the division's membership history. From 926 members at its inception, the 1995 Division 39 membership stands at 3,641, a 293% increase. The double-digit growth during the early years, which was likely due to the time it took for psychologists to learn of its existence, slowed to single-digit growth and has now stabilized, perhaps as a result of managed care. There has also been a gender shift. From 1980 to 1995 male membership increased from 679 to 1,675, but female membership increased more impressively from 247 to 1,966. For those years, the percentage of males in the division decreased from 73% to 46%, whereas the percentage of females increased from 27% to 54%. From 1991 to 1992, the only time period for which data were collected, the 3,433 members of the division were supplemented by 1,929 members of 26 local chapters who were not division members, thus producing a psychoanalytic organization made up of a total of 5,362 people.

The geographic distribution of the membership is available from the biannual division directory and documents the overwhelming influence of the New York City area. The number of division members living in Manhattan increased from 344 in 1980 (Meisels & O'Dell, 1994) to 906 in 1994, fully 25% of the current membership, and the overall number of members in New York and New Jersey now stands at 1,665 of 3,667, or 45% of the membership. This is down from 54% of the membership in 1980, as reported by Meisels and O'Dell (1994), and is even less, at 30%, when the 1,929 nondivision local chapter members are included in the calculation.

In December 1994 the APA had 70,821 associate members and members. With 3,667 Division 39 members in December 1994, this means that 5.2% of the APA membership were members of the Division of Psychoanalysis. In view of the fact that only approximately 50% of APA members belong to divisions, it appears that approximately 10.4% of APA members who join divisions have joined Division 39. This also suggests that 10.4% of APA members are interested in psychoanalysis. Further information about members, collected in two surveys, is discussed later in the chapter.

TABLE 34
Membership in the Division of Psychoanalysis (APA statistics)

Year	N	Male	Female	% Male	% Female	% Change
1980	926	679	247	73	27	
1981	1,175	806	369	69	31	27
1982	1,355	888	467	66	34	15
1983	1,544	981	563	64	36	14
1984	1,748	1,059	689	61	39	13
1985	1,949	1,112	837	57	43	11
1986	2,177	1,205	972	55	45	12
1987	2,294	1,230	1,064	54	46	5
1988	2,435	1,277	1,158	52	48	6
1989	2,583	1,333	1,250	52	48	6
1990	2,773	1,397	1,376	50	50	7
1991	3,279	1,613	1,666	49	51	18
1992	3,433	1,653	1,790	48	52	5
1993	3,694	1,729	1,965	47	53	7
1994	3,667	1,711	1,956	47	53	-1
1995	3,641	1,675	1,966	46	54	-1
TOTAL CHANGE	293%	146%	695%	-37%	100%	

THE SECTIONS

The description Lane and Meisels (1994) gave of the roles of the sections and local chapters in Division 39 is still applicable and is repeated in the following excerpt, with updated material in brackets:

> The Division of Psychoanalysis has achieved its remarkable organizational success in part by identifying and utilizing the best features of its two parent disciplines, psychology and psychoanalysis. The APA structure is that of a large central organization (which deals with broad psychologist issues such as membership, journal publication, national conventions, etc.) and a host of divisions, such as ours, which represent narrower substantive areas. The Division of Psychoanalysis has adopted this model, and it too is composed of a central organization that represents broader issues for psychologist–psychoanalysts (practically the same list applies, i.e., membership, journal publication, meetings, etc.) and subdivisions, called sections, which represent narrower substantive areas. The sections are national and even international in scope, have great autonomy, raise dues, hold meetings, publish newsletters and organize committees. It is surely the case, for example, that the Board of Section II, Childhood and Adolescence, will do more to develop this area of psychoanalysis than the Division Board could ever have time for, or that a Division committee could ever have authority for. Most sections have derived from committees when it appeared that the scope of a committee was too limiting for the purposes at hand.
>
> Note that other national and international psychoanalytic organizations do not have such a structure. Rather, those organizations are comprised of a central body and a network of local institutes. The Division has emulated this model as well, and has developed a network of [30] local chapters. In the end, we are the only division in APA with a network of local chapters, just as we are the only psychoanalytic organization with a substructure of sections.
>
> Organizationally, all of the sections and local chapters are semiautonomous associations that operate under the auspices of the Division, just as Division 39 is a semi-autonomous group in APA. APA and Division 39 policies provide defining parameters for sections and local chapters, but within those parameters the sections and local chapters have great autonomy and scope for action. It is noteworthy that what is being discussed here is a totality of [39] organizations—[30] local chapters, [eight] sections and one Division. Each has a Board and committee structure, and most produce newsletters and hold scientific meetings, so that in the aggregate there must be literally hundreds of psychologists who are involved in some way in the governance of the Division. If each of the [39] organizations has 20 active participants in its governance, then [780] psychologists, or 21% of the total Division membership, are involved in sharing Division 39 authority. Add to this the colleagues who chair and present papers and symposia (there were

about [300] presenters at the [1995] Spring Meeting in [Santa Monica]) and who participate in our offshoot institutes, and the number probably doubles. It appears that part of the success of the Division has been to share its authority (with sections and local chapters), and that by so doing it has given the opportunity for hundreds of its members to be active participants in its growth. Further differentiation, and further empowerment of colleagues, is to be expected in the future.

It is also noteworthy that even though psychoanalysts are usually identified by theoretical perspective (e.g., ego-psychologists, interpersonalists, or object-relationists), the sections are not so organized. Rather, they are organized by substantive areas. (Lane & Meisels, 1994, 165–166)

The current sections, along with the number of 1994 members, the last year for which information is available, are as follows: Section I, Psychologist–Psychoanalyst Practitioners, 440 members; Section II, Childhood and Adolescence, 137 members; Section III, Women and Psychoanalysis, 234 members; Section IV, Local Chapters, 30 members, one for each chapter; Section V, Psychologist–Psychoanalyst Clinicians, 261 members; Section VI, The Psychoanalytic Research Society, 262 members; and Section VII, Psychoanalysis and Groups, 152 members. Section VIII, Psychoanalysis and Family Therapy, was not established until early in 1996 and had no members then. In total, in 1994 the division had 1,515 section memberships. In addition, industrial/organizational psychoanalysis is now in the process of preparing for section status. Of the current eight sections, we shall comment here first on Sections I and V, next on the Section of Local Chapters, and then on the remaining sections.

The Section I Versus Section V Controversy

This conundrum was introduced during the discussion of the Qualifications Committee. At issue here is the nature of psychoanalytic treatment and its defining characteristics. In terms of extrinsic characteristics, Freud saw analysands 6 days a week for 60-minutes on the couch, Sullivan practiced vis-à-vis (sitting) three times a week, Jung saw analysands once a week vis-à-vis, and Lacan might precipitously end a session after just a few minutes. More, the 2-day weekend has eroded the practice of six sessions a week, the "hour" is no longer an hour but is usually a 45- or 50-minute session, and financial considerations lead at least some potential analysands to psychotherapy instead. In terms of intrinsic defining characteristics, there is widespread agreement on the roles of transference, child development, and unconscious processes, but here theoretical divergencies lead to vastly different views of what is psychoanalytic (in development, the unconscious, the structure of personality, motivation, technique, interpretations, etc.). Added to these extrinsic and intrinsic factors are social issues such as government policy, public interest in psychoanalysis, availability of analysands, insurance reimbursements, managed care, medication, licensure, and so on, all of which have an impact on actual practice in the field.

Despite various possible combinations of these extrinsic, intrinsic, and real-world considerations, psychoanalysts of most schools of thought have abided by an adaptation of Freud's original procedures, and the IPA position of at least four sessions a week is widely endorsed in the psychoanalytic community. Thus, the most widely accepted practice of psychoanalysis is for an analysand to talk on the couch for about 50 minutes perhaps three or four or five times a week—this despite widely divergent, even antithetical—theorizing about what the analysand's productions mean, what interventions the analyst should use, and how the analysis works. Hence, when the Qualifications Committee proposed a three-times-a-week criterion in 1981, it was a compromise designed to satisfy both the traditionalists (because three meetings is still frequent) and the less traditional (because it thereby includes such groups as the interpersonalists). However, it should be clear that the traditionalists were not comfortable with the laxity of this compromise, and the less traditional were sufficiently aroused—for example, the policy excluded some Jungians—to eventually form a new section. This bifurcation has influenced the division in numerous ways. It was the major agenda item for three or four intense board meetings in the early 1980s. It caused repeated overt conflict until the organizational solution of forming a new section, Section V, eased tensions. And it so hampered the American Board of Psychoanalysis in Psychology (ABPsaP, part of the American Board of Professional Psychology) that it took 12 years, from 1983 to 1995, for the first diplomate examinations in psychoanalysis to take place. The controversy affected numerous other issues as well, such as the emerging local chapters, the directory, the Clark Conference, elections, and committee appointments.

At the present time, some Section I leaders are considering forming a new division in the APA, one that more accurately reflects their more traditional vision of psychoanalytic practice. Part of the issue is that ever since the successful completion of the lawsuit (see The Lawsuit Against APsaP) permitted psychologists' psychoanalytic institutes to join the IPA—and four such institutes have done so—there has been a movement to add more institutes to this cadre and to reaffirm the IPA position in reference to training requirements. To many in Division 39, including the writers, the IPA definition is persuasive. It appears that this issue is far from resolved.

The Section of Local Chapters

As Meisels (1994a, p. 13) wrote, "This intense emotional issue of standards, which preoccupied the Division Board and Section I Board for years, was almost irrelevant to non–New Yorkers." The qualifications issue was a New York area issue, but because colleagues from New York made up most of the division's membership and leadership, this agenda item became the division's issue as well. A variety of New York area institutes with vastly different theoretical persuasions and definitions of qualifications had long disagreed with one another, but now, sitting together on the division board, they were forced to interact with one another, hence the internecine warfare. In contrast, "The focal emotional issue for psychologists outside of greater New York City was the lack of training opportunities because of the successful exclusionary policy of APsaA" (Meisels, 1994a, p. 13).

Local groups began to organize immediately after the division was established. Inspired by the determination of Oliver J. B. Kerner, chair of the Local Chapters Committee, a series of proposals was placed before the division board regarding possibilities for developing training opportunities around the United States (see Slavin, 1994). By 1984 Helen Block Lewis, the presiding president, joined with Murray Meisels, Robert C. Lane, and George D. Goldman in orchestrating the first Nationwide Conference on Psychoanalytic Training, often informally called the White Conference because it was held at the White Institute (perhaps the most outstanding institute in the United States). This was the first convening of local chapters, "a very significant and transformative event" (Slavin, 1994, p. 105). Slavin described it well:

> The atmosphere in the meeting was electric. People who had been on the periphery of the Division, but thinking in some embryonic way about local chapters or psychoanalytic training were energized by the opportunity to meet colleagues from around the country who shared similar passions, fantasies, hopes and concerns. . . . [S]ome representatives returned to their home areas almost manic with energy and enthusiasm. (p. 106)

A series of conferences followed, leading, on the one hand, to the formation of the Section of Local Chapters in 1985 and, on the other, to the Clark Conference on Psychoanalytic Education in 1986, which has been the division's only venue for the discussion of that important issue (see Meisels & Shapiro, 1990; also see the discussion presented later in the chapter). The local chapters, and their offshoot institutes, will be considered further later in this chapter.

Other Sections

The five remaining sections, Child and Adolescence, Women, Research, Groups, and Family Therapy were not controversial. These were all originally division-level committees, but committees have an uncertain position in the organizational hierarchy. It appears that once a policy position is established, such as holding a national meeting or publishing a journal, the corresponding committee then operates relatively independently of the division board, except for major policy changes or for increases in funding. When a committee is first organizing its activities, however, it must frequently report to the board. Board members, however, often do not have time to hear new proposals; when they do, they seem frequently to disapprove of new ideas. The advantages of becoming a section are manifold, for the committee becomes a national organization, raises dues, appoints committees, and takes action without division-level oversight. In addition, Division 39 grants each section an unjuried 2-hour symposium both at the APA annual convention and at the annual spring meeting, and this provides the sections with a vehicle to express their views.

These sections have particular foci. Psychoanalytic work with children and adolescents, or with groups or families, do not receive much attention in mainstream psychoanalysis, and these sections provide a venue for psychologists interested in these issues. The same applies to the Research Section, which perennially requests research funding from the division leadership and is perennially denied. The section on Women and Psychoanalysis parallels similar groups in the APA and other APA divisions, but it has been noteworthy because of an ongoing controversy about the nature of psychoanalytic thought in reference to women's issues. These sections, along with a possible new section on industrial–organizational psychoanalysis, indicate the breadth of the application of psychoanalytic thinking.

LOCAL CHAPTERS

In 1992, Lane and Meisels wrote,

The local chapter movement is one of the premier results of the formation of the Division of Psychoanalysis. At first, it was largely a grassroots movement among psychologists who had been long-frustrated by the psychiatry prerequisite in APsaA. Often enough, these new founders and leaders in the field of psychoanalysis were not qualified psychoanalytic practitioners. Still, their dedication and intensity led them to form local chapters, and after that, even institutes. It is noteworthy that the most senior and traditional psychologist–psychoanalysts in a given area usually did not participate in these organizational successes. Those psychologists who had been trained by APsaA were largely involved with APsaA, and the new creative leaders in the field came from elsewhere.

Two examples may illustrate this. The first example is Charles Spezzano, who almost single--handedly organized the Colorado local chapter and then the offshoot Colorado institute; the latter so that he could be formally trained in psychoanalysis, which is what he proceeded to accomplish. A second example is Arnold Schneider, who had received limited training at . . . [APsaA's] Topeka Institute—limited training means that he completed coursework and a personal analysis, but that his petition for a waiver to receive supervision had been rejected—and who was so upset by APsaA's refusal to allow him full training that he joined the psychologists' lawsuit as one of the plaintiffs. He was then ostracized at Menninger's and found a position in Tampa, where he . . . [organized] a local chapter. It is exhilarating to think that Spezzano and Schneider are now having a far greater impact on the field of psychoanalysis than they would have, had APsaA admitted them to full training. Stated differently, the era of helpless frustration with APsaA had passed, and psychologists now bent their energies to creative forms.

Once the Section of Local Chapters was formed in 1985, it exerted a great deal of energy to defining the requirements to become a local chapter, and actively recruited local Division 39 members to form new organizations. It continues to do so. (1994, pp. 213–214)

Each local chapter has its own particular history, its own founders, bylaws, committee structure, conflicts, education program, relationship to Division 39, and, importantly, its attitude toward the formation of a free-standing psychoanalytic institute. This last issue refers to a goal common among local chapters, and that is the formation of a formal training program. The local chapters may educate, but under APA rules they may not organize a formal training program that would lead to a certificate in psychoanalysis. Many local chapter leaders, however, have organized such free-standing institutes. In 1992 there were 26 local chapters, and each of their histories, most of which were written by their founders, is presented in Lane and Meisels (1994).

Most of the local chapters have experienced growth and integration, but several have experienced conflict and dissension—not unlike the division itself—and in Chicago, Denver, and Washington, D.C., this has led to multiple chapters. Note that most of the chapters are in urban areas, but some are dispersed in more spearsely populated areas (e.g., Appalachia, Vermont). The division now has 30 local chapters in 27 geographic areas, with possible new chapters forming in Kansas City, Chapel Hill–Durham–Raleigh, Memphis, and Milwaukee. Several attempts to launch chapters in other areas have failed for lack of interest, internal conflict, or lack of leadership.

Table 35 presents a summary of some information collected in 1991 and 1992 about the local chapters, the only time period for which such data were collected. The data are for the 26 chapters then in the division (Minnesota, Pacific Northwest, Rhode Island, and western Florida had not yet been admitted). Table 35 indicates that the size of the chapters varied greatly, from 16 in the Potomac Society to 500 in Massachusetts. About a third of the local chapter members were also division members, whereas nondivision psychologists comprised another 26%. The 1992 local chapter memberships consisted of 1,705 psychologists (59%), 577 social workers (20%), 366 students (13%), 120 psychiatrists (4%), and 119 others (4%). Thus, the local chapters may be fairly described as interdisciplinary societies that are psychologist-dominated but that have made impacts on other disciplines as well.

The total local chapter membership in 1992 was 2,887, a figure slightly inflated because of multiple memberships. Still, subtracting the 958 division members from the 2,887 total membership means that, in 1992, 1,929 colleagues were affiliated with the division even though they were not members of the division. Thus, the total membership of the division and its local chapters in 1992 consisted of the 3,433 division members plus the 1,929 nondivision local chapter members, a total of 5,362 individuals. The 1,929 nondivision local chapter members have no direct contact or formal status with the division. At the present time, the division leadership is taking steps to develop a more formal connection to these colleagues, one aspect of which may be to invite them to subscribe to division publications. One further point: the division is the largest psychoanalytic organization in the United States, with APsaA in second place with 3,052 members (in June, 1995).

Table 35 also presents information on the educational activities of the local chapters. For 1991 through 1992, these chapters held an aggregate of 130 paper sessions of about 1 hour in duration, 66 workshops of at least 3 hours in duration, 27 study groups that met for one semester or one academic year, and 38 courses, each of which had a median of ten students and lasted either one semester or one academic year. In addition, the offshoot institutes also provide educational experiences.

The column on institutes in Table 35 refers to the presence of a psychologist institute in the geographical area. Local chapter members have founded free-standing institutes in Chicago, Colorado, Connecticut, Massachusetts, Michigan, Minnesota, Northern California, Ontario, Philadelphia, Seattle, and southeast Florida, but other institute training opportunities have developed as well. Thus, Washington, D.C., has a branch of the New York Freudian Society, and Oklahoma City has a branch of the Colorado Institute. New York and Los Angeles have long had independent institutes.

Lastly, the very existence of organizations with their own educational activities leads members to develop ideas, present clinical material, and write—as witnessed by the 84 newsletter issues produced in a year. By having their own organizations, psychologists have stood forth and produced psychoanalytic literature; they have also developed a network of

TABLE 35
Local Chapter Membership and Educational Activities*

	Year Founded	Year Local Chapter	Membership		Educational Activities				Newsletter Issues	Institute?
			In Division	Nondivision 39	Paper Sessions	Workshops	Study Groups	Courses		
Appalachia	1989	1989	23	60	4	1	—	2	4	—
Austin	1988	1988	16	70	7	2	1	—	—	—
Baltimore	1991	1991	10	95	—	6	3	—	—	Yes
Chicago CAPP	1980	1986	80	234	6	2	2	—	3	Yes
Chicago Open	1985	1986	8	45	4	—	2	—	4	Yes
Cincinnati	1991	1991	7	26	5	—	—	—	—	—
Colorado	1984	1986	58	152	2	—	—	—	—	Yes
Connecticut	1985	1986	60	140	—	4	3	—	3	Yes
Dallas	1982	1986	33	123	7	2	1	—	10	—
Georgia	1990	1991	10	35	4	2	—	—	4	—
Massachusetts	1983	1986	170	500	9	5	—	12	4	Yes
Michigan	1980	1986	50	150	8	2	1	1	3	Yes
New Mexico	1991	1991	9	63	1	2	—	—	—	—
New York	1986	1986	10	10	—	—	—	—	—	Yes
N. California	1986	1986	137	350	4	8	1	9	4	Yes
Oklahoma	1990	1990	5	29	11	1	—	—	—	Yes
Ontario	1991	1991	10	15	10	1	—	—	—	Yes
Philadelphia	1985	1986	50	140	5	4	3	—	3	Yes
Pittsburgh	1986	1986	10	28	10	8	1	3	—	—
Potomac	1980	1986	11	16	3	5	—	1	—	Yes
SE Florida	1987	1988	25	96	4	—	2	—	4	Yes
S. California	1984	1986	50	186	7	1	2	—	—	Yes
Vermont	1983	1986	3	68	—	1	—	2	2	—
WPSP, Wash,DC	1980	1986	73	121	10	2	3	—	10	Yes
WSPP, Wash,DC	1981	1986	25	80	—	4	—	6	2	Yes
W. MA & Albany	1986	1986	15	55	9	3	2	2	8	—
TOTALS			958	2,887	130	66	27	38	72	

*Adapted by permission of the publisher from R. C. Lane and M. Meisels (Eds.), (1994), *A History of the Division of Psychoanalysis of the American Psychological Association.* Hillsdale, NJ: Laurence Erlbaum.

psychologist experts who are in demand to speak at both local chapter and division meetings. Since the end of 1991, the division's board of directors has unfortunately turned its attention away from psychoanalytic issues to organizational, APA, and political struggles, but still the sections and local chapters have become centers for theoretical, clinical, and applied initiatives in psychoanalysis. The effects of having 39 different organizations have been profound, divergent, and largely generative.

WHO ARE THE MEMBERS OF DIVISION 39?

The Division has conducted two membership surveys, in 1980 and 1987 (Goldberg, Shapiro, & Trachtman, 1994; Meisels & O'Dell, 1994). Results of the 1980 survey, completed by 327 members, showed that members of Division 39 are intensely involved in psychoanalysis: 51% graduated from psychoanalytic institutes and only 13% had not had some postdoctoral psychoanalytic training. Fully 84% of respondents had been psychoanalyzed, 83% had been supervised on psychoanalytic cases, 25% were doing training analyses, 43% supervised analytic candidates, and more than 76% were practicing psychoanalysis in their work, predominantly independent practice. Only 3% had not been in psychoanalysis or psychotherapy (see Meisels & O'Dell, 1994).

The 1987 survey produced 593 scoreable replies and showed highly similar results (see Goldberg et al., 1994). The psychologists surveyed had attended 50 different postdoctoral psychoanalytic training institutes; 95% had been in analysis 3 or more years; and they reported a median of 4.9 years of postdoctoral supervision. In terms of their practices, 94% saw patients once or twice a week, 60% saw patients three times a week, and 32% saw patients four or more times a week, and the respondents generally regarded about a third of their cases as psychoanalytic. Division members work in other modalities as well: one third worked with groups, 45% worked with families, and two thirds worked with couples.

Division 39 membership is largely composed of clinicians in independent practice who are educated in, and dedicated to, a psychoanalytic perspective. They work intensively with individuals in prolonged treatments, use psychoanalytic ideas in their work, and write, publish, and educate in the field.

ALLIED ORGANIZATIONS

Associations often develop allied organizations to perform particular tasks. In the case of the Division of Psychoanalysis, these have included the offshoot institutes, the International Federation for Psychoanalytic Education, ABPsaP, the psychoanalytic lawsuit and the Group for the advancement of Psychoanalysis and Psychotherapy in Psychology, and the Psychoanalytic Consortium.

Institutes

As previously mentioned, psychoanalytic training typically occurs in free-standing institutes, albeit some few universities (e.g., Adelphi University in Garden City, New York, New York University, and Nova Southeastern University in Fort Lauderdale, Florida) have postdoctoral programs. Many Division 39 leaders initially thought that local chapters could house institutes, but it eventually became clear that, under APA rules, local chapters could engage in educational activities but could never grant a certificate. Only the APA may accredit, so if local chapter members wanted an institute—that is, a formal training program leading to certification—they would have to form separate organizations to accomplish that purpose. The offshoot institutes do precisely that.

The development of local chapters proceeded from the White Conference in 1984, through the formation of the Section of Local Chapters in 1985, and through further local chapter meetings in Ann Arbor and Washington, D.C., all of which culminated in the Clark Conference for Psychoanalytic Education in October 1986. Slavin described the impact of the Clark Conference on psychologists generally and on Massachusetts psychologists particularly:

> What may be most important . . . is that Helen Block Lewis, with the assistance of Shapiro and Meisels, was able to use the the event to sponsor the articulation and legitimation of new visions of psychoanalytic education and training, especially in the symbolic context of holding the meeting at Clark University, where Freud had spoken decades before. Indeed, the conference program tackled just about everything. Views about psychoanalysis and psychoanalytic training from the most traditional to the most radical were represented and discussed. Those who attended, and there were many from chapters around the country, found a heady air of excitement, ferment and open debate that few had expected to characterize a psychoanalytic conference. Questions were raised about the traditional models of psychoanalytic training, forms of training, the interface of psychoanalysis with other approaches to treatment, the educational and symbolic role of the training analyst and training analyses, the nature of the curriculum, the role and nature of supervision and other issues. The quality and openness of this debate proved very inspiring to those who were thinking not only of establishing training programs in their areas but especially to the possibility of doing things differently. . . . Many members of the Massachusetts local chapters were in attendance and for many

whose only contact with psychoanalytic issues was through the traditional medical institutes, it was the first glimpse that fundamental questions about psychoanalytic training could be asked and discussed in this way. There is no question that it enabled the individuals involved in forming a training program in Massachusetts to begin to take these fundamental questions as their own, instead of feeling that they had to begin with the forms and models of training that already existed. (Slavin, 1994, p. 109)

As mentioned previously, (see Table 35) a number of institutes were launched by members of various local chapters, and although they all retained the basic tripartite educational model of personal analysis, supervision, and course work, they also varied and arranged these features in new combinations. For example, the Michigan Psychoanalytic Council has a strong gender-issues component in training, the Chicago Center and the Colorado Center for Psychoanalytic Studies use weekend seminars featuring noted visiting speakers, and the Boston and San Francisco groups developed special programs for advanced candidates.

The International Federation for Psychoanalytic Education (IFPE)

These new institutes were not a part of Division 39 or the APA, and it soon became apparent that they could form a home for themselves by establishing a federation of psychoanalytic educational programs. Murray Meisels proposed such a federation to the division board members, and they supported the idea and funded a first meeting with a grant for $10,000. This first meeting of the future International Federation for Psychoanalytic Education (IFPE) took place in Washington, D.C., on May 5, 1990, but became bogged down around the perennial issues of qualifications and accreditation, of who should be admitted, and whether the future IFPE should set standards and perhaps even accredit institutes. Despite this unfortunate but perhaps inevitable beginning, in subsequent meetings it became apparent that the participants wanted to transcend narrow professional issues and move the whole field of psychoanalysis forward. Barron wrote:

[T]he raison d'etre of the federation would be to enrich psychoanalysis by pursuing the following broad goals: Supporting the educational and training endeavors of analysts from different disciplines, geographical regions, and theoretical perspectives; not leveling, or obscuring differences among us in a kind of mindless anything goes eclecticism, and not trying to legislate uniformity, but rather sharply delineating those differences in constructive dialogue and learning from them; articulating the theory, practice, and application of psychoanalysis to the larger community and working to overcome popular distortions, misconceptions, anti-analytic bias; and fostering teaching and research. (Barron, 1994, p. 346)

In the end, IFPE organized as a broad-based enterprise to encourage psychoanalytic education of all sorts, from institutes to undergraduate colleges, from study groups to graduate schools, and from individuals to psychoanalytic societies, both national and international. The concept was to move psychoanalytic education forward for all who are interested, and to avoid credentialing and disciplinary issues. So far, it is working: In October 1995 IFPE held its sixth annual conference. Its membership in July 1995 consisted of 218 individuals and 50 organizations, the latter mostly psychoanalytic institutes and societies.

The American Board of Psychoanalysis in Psychology (ABPsaP)

Early in its history, the Division 39 leadership applied to the American Board of Professional Psychology (ABPP) to offer the diplomate in psychoanalysis. When ABPP approved this proposal on March 4, 1983, the division leaders proceeded to appoint a liaison committee to ABPP, but they filled the committee with adherents of both the traditional/Section I position and of the less traditional/Section V position. After an initially productive meeting in 1983, there was no further progress. Indeed, no more meetings were held until May 12, 1986, when the committee reformed itself as ABPsaP and held its first organizational meeting—a conference call (much of the material in this section comes from Lane, 1994a).

Immediately thereafter, controversy arose regarding the division's qualification criteria, which then stood at three sessions a week. Donald S. Milman, from the Adelphi Postdoctoral Program in Psychotherapy, stated, "It is presumptuous, constrictive, and non-creative to allow any narrow set of numbers to designate a professional" and added that the thrice-weekly criterion impinged on Adelphi's academic freedom (Lane, 1994a, p. 337). In 1986 two of the less traditional ABPsaP board members resigned in protest. An effort ensued to develop different criteria for classicists, self-psychologists, and interpersonalists, and then, in 1987, the seats that had been vacated were again filled with less traditional members.

In 1988 it was the traditionalists' turn to resign, and three of them did so. In 1990 the division membership reconsidered its criteria for qualification in psychoanalysis and redefined them without the numerical criterion, but this had little impact. In 1991 Bertram Cohler, also editor of the division's Journal, called for tolerance of the diverse positions in psychoanalysis and pressed ABPsaP to move forward. It is interesting to note that over the years a number of committees had completed assignments and a broad outline of the form of an examination had developed. The individuals who drafted this outline accepted the division's nonnumerical criteria, and the outline stated that applicants must meet ABPP standards, submit evidence of their psychoanalytic education, and present a psychoanalytic case. They would then be examined by four examiners—at least two of whom shared their theoretical orientation—regarding their theoretical and technical knowledge, their case, and someone else's case (see Lane, 1994a). Still, there was no action until 1995, when the first group of seven board members was examined. By mid-1996, the diplomating process was finally launched.

The Lawsuit Against APsaA

Whereas psychologist–psychoanalysts of an earlier era were left helpless and frustrated by APsaA's psychiatric requirements, colleagues of more recent vintage were more aggressive, and by early 1984 several psychologists were developing lawsuits in various local areas to force APsaA to train psychologists. APsaA would no longer be the final word in psychoanalysis, for it too must answer to the law. Bryant Welch organized this movement at the national level, and on March 1, 1985, in the U.S. District Court for the South District of New York, Bryant Welch, Toni Bernay, Arnold Schneider, and Helen Desmond filed a class action lawsuit against the IPA, APsaA, and two APsaA institutes in New York (Schneider & Desmond, 1994). The other developing lawsuits did not materialize.

This was not the division's lawsuit in a legal sense, nor was the division a plaintiff. Fund-raising for the lawsuit was under the Group for the Advancement of Psychotherapy and Psychoanalysis in Psychology (GAPPP), not Division 39. Despite this, the lawsuit was a class-action suit, and the class that was being represented was the division's membership. It *was* the division's lawsuit emotionally, and *was* widely experienced by the membership as their civil rights case—they would finally get their just due after years of discrimination—and *was* mostly financially supported by the division, its sections, and its members. From a legal standpoint, however, it was not a civil rights case; it was a case of restraint of trade (see Schneider & Desmond, 1994, for a detailed discussion of the lawsuit).

The division membership always supported the lawsuit, and the division board members always voted for it unanimously. At first, there were some dissenting concerns that the successful prosecution of the lawsuit might weaken the local chapters and fledgling institutes, but these fears were cavalierly dismissed: Psychologists' institutes would then fairly compete with theirs, it was said, and would win in the competition. As a result, local chapters strongly supported the lawsuit. For many New Yorkers, who long had their own institutes and did not need APsaA to be trained, the possibility of access to IPA, from which they had been barred, was particularly desirable. The IPA was the home of most of the world's psychoanalytic organizations and important thinkers, and psychologists wished to participate in its life. Indeed, when the division first began, several of its leaders met with IPA representatives in an attempt to gain access, but nothing came of it. Now, however, IPA was a defendant in the lawsuit, and the successful result of that lawsuit would enable many to gain the long-awaited admission to IPA. Overall, the lawsuit was widely supported.

The prosecution of the lawsuit generally went favorably, albeit with some difficulties. Although APsaA's leadership always insisted during the lawsuit that psychoanalysis was a medical enterprise, it proceeded to alter the rule that barred its members from teaching in non-APsaA institutes, developed a new policy to enable more psychologists to gain admission, and agreed to let psychologist institutes join the IPA. It did commit a blunder in threatening to make the plaintiffs' personal analyses public, to see if they were actually emotionally qualified to be analysts, but the division responded aggressively to this threat and the matter was dropped.

The plaintiffs blundered into a secretly proposed settlement that caused a great deal of distress when made public. To resolve this distress, the proposed settlement was dropped and the division board became the Oversight Committee to the Group for the Advancement of Psychotherapy and Psychoanalysis in Psychology for future negotiations. Indeed, eventually APsaA agreed to negotiate, and the division board members did discharge their oversight responsibilities and, to the surprise of many, APsaA in fact met practically all of the plaintiffs' demands. The court approved the settlement agreement on April 17, 1989. Psychologists had won.

But what precisely was won? Schneider and Desmond (1994) argued that there were six benefits. First, psychologists are being trained in APsaA institutes—68 psychologists as of 1992. Second, some institutes joined IPA. Third, fighting and winning the lawsuit "increased the sense of self-esteem and feeling of first-class citizenship that had been developing since the birth of Division 39" (Schneider & Desmond, 1994, p. 333). Fourth, it provided APsaA institutes with more students. Fifth, it was another blow to psychiatry's hegemonic imperative. And sixth, it provided a lever that had the potential to end the stultification of psychoanalysis in APsaA.[1]

To critique these alleged benefits, it is certain that the 68 psychologists attending APsaA institutes in 1992 were not attending psychologist institutes, and although the division has not conducted a survey on the matter, discussions between Murray Meisels and psychologists in Chicago, Denver, and Michigan indicate that these three groups are losing candidates to APsaA. That is, the successful prosecution of the lawsuit has hurt psychologists' institutes and local chapters. The second benefit, that of

---

[1]APsaA was comprised predominantly of male psychiatrists who had graduated from an APsaA training institute and whose theoretical persuasions were mostly Freudian and ego-psychological. Many manifested little interest in the social sciences, biological psychiatry, feminist scholarship, or other schools of psychoanalytic thought.

joining IPA, was not widely pursued, in part because IPA policy would allow only some members of an institute to be admitted but exclude others, and in the process perhaps destroy the institute; only five psychologist institutes applied and only four were admitted (of perhaps 100 non-APsaA institutes countrywide). The third benefit, an increase in self-esteem and winning psychologists' civil rights, was certainly desirable. The remaining three alleged benefits were unrelated to the purposes of the lawsuit. In the end, whatever hegemonic imperatives psychiatry may have were not much affected, and helping APsaA decrease its stultification and increase its candidates were not the reasons to pursue the lawsuit. Indeed, however, those benefits are accruing to APsaA, which has become invigorated by losing. Critical evaluation of the Schneider–Desmond list of benefits suggests that APsaA may have profited from the lawsuit more than psychologists did: Psychologists won their civil rights, and APsaA won an institutional rebirth.

Stated differently, the timing of the lawsuit was off. The lawsuit was developed in 1984, prior to the consolidation of the local chapter movement, and it was settled in 1989, at the time that psychologists were spawning their own training institutes and no longer needed APsaA's training facilities. The success of the lawsuit had the effect of strengthening psychologists' competition at a time when managed care was harming psychoanalytic practices. The timing was off.

The Psychoanalytic Consortium

In 1972 an interdisciplinary group formed that is now called the National Association for the Advancement of Psychoanalysis (NAAP). It represents a network of institutes in the United States, many of which are Adlerian, Jungian, and Modern Psychoanalytic. NAAP asserts that psychoanalysis may be practiced by individuals who have not been trained in a mental health discipline.

In the early 1990s NAAP, through its accrediting arm, the American Board of Accreditation in Psychoanalysis (ABAP), filed a petition to be recognized as an accrediting body in psychoanalysis with the Commission on Recognition of Postsecondary Accreditation (CORPA). CORPA is the national accreditor of accrediting bodies, and recognition of ABAP would give it and NAAP great clout. In an effort to develop concerted opposition to ABAP/NAAP, Leopold Caligor, then president of the division, organized the Psychoanalytic Consortium, which is composed of the American Academy of Psychoanalysis (a psychiatric group), APsaA, the National Membership Committee on Psychoanalysis in Clinical Social Work, and Division 39. Once formed, the consortium provided strong opposition to ABAP and has also moved in the direction of addressing other issues of mutual concern, such as managed care and national health. It remains, however, constituted of three disciplines, and disciplinary prerogatives will likely influence its development.

On July 1, 1994, the state of Vermont passed a law that, in agreement with NAAP, licenses psychoanalysts solely on the basis of training in psychoanalysis, making a background in mental health irrelevant (i.e., not part of the criteria for licensure). Psychoanalysts throughout the country may now apply to Vermont for licensure in psychoanalysis for a fee of $300—to the consternation of the established mental health professions. The designation of qualification in psychoanalysis is thereby made a state licensing matter, no longer the sole province of psychoanalytic organizations or the mental health professions. The consortium has moved to change this law.

CONCLUSION

The growth of Division 39 indicates the importance of psychoanalytic thought to psychologist practitioners. The division rapidly attracted a large following—one that further differentiated into sections and local chapters and even into new institutes and other organizations. Intense conflicts and disagreements are part of that history. Still, in a decade or so, to quote Bertram Karon (1994, p. 365), a former division president, "We, in the Division of Psychoanalysis, have developed a national psychoanalytic association of psychologists. It is the largest and most important organization in psychoanalysis, scientifically and professionally, in the United States."

REFERENCES

Barron, J. W. (1994). A brief historical perspective on the International Federation for Psychoanalytic Education. In R. C. Lane & M. Meisels (Eds.), *A history of the Division of Psychoanalysis of the American Psychological Association* (pp. 344–348). Hillsdale, NJ: Lawrence Erlbaum.

Callan, J. E. (1994). Division 39 programs: Annual convention, Midwinter/Spring Meetings, and continuing education. In R. C. Lane & M. Meisels (Eds.), *A history of the Division of Psychoanalysis of the American Psychological Association* (pp. 84–94). Hillsdale, NJ: Lawrence Erlbaum.

Cohler, B. J. (1994). *Psychoanalytic Psychology.* In R. C. Lane & M. Meisels (Eds.), *A history of the Division of Psychoanalysis of the American Psychological Association* (pp. 70–77). Hillsdale, NJ: Lawrence Erlbaum.

Goldberg, F. H., Shapiro, D., & Trachtman, J. P. (1994). The 1987 survey of psychoanalytic training and practice. In R. C. Lane & M. Meisels (Eds.), *A history of the Division of Psychoanalysis of the American Psychological Association* (pp. 36–57). Hillsdale, NJ: Lawrence Erlbaum.

Karon, B. P. (1994). The future of psychoanalysis. In R. C. Lane & M. Meisels (Eds.), *A history of the Division of Psychoanalysis of the American Psychological Association* (pp. 351–365). Hillsdale, NJ: Lawrence Erlbaum.

Lane, R. C. (1994a). A history of the American Board of Psychoanalysis in Psychology. In R. C. Lane & M. Meisels (Eds.), *A history of the Division of Psychoanalysis of the American Psychological Association* (pp. 336–341). Hillsdale, NJ: Lawrence Erlbaum.

Lane, R. C. (1994b). *PsycSCAN: Psychoanalysis* and the *Psychologist–Psychoanalyst*. In R. C. Lane & M. Meisels (Eds.), *A history of the Division of Psychoanalysis of the American Psychological Association* (pp. 78–81). Hillsdale, NJ: Lawrence Erlbaum.

Lane, R. C. (1994c). The first five years. In R. C. Lane & M. Meisels (Eds.), *A history of the Division of Psychoanalysis of the American Psychological Association* (pp. 3–10). Hillsdale, NJ: Lawrence Erlbaum.

Lane, R. C., & Meisels, M. (Eds.). (1994). *A history of the Division of Psychoanalysis of the American Psychological Association.* Hillsdale, NJ: Lawrence Erlbaum.

Lawrence, E. S. (1994). Section I: Psychologist–Psychoanalyst Practitioners: A history, 1982–1992. In R. C. Lane & M. Meisels (Eds.), *A history of the Division of Psychoanalysis of the American Psychological Association* (pp. 167–175). Hillsdale, NJ: Lawrence Erlbaum.

Marlan, S., & Trachtman, J. P. (1994). Section V, Psychologist–Psychoanalyst Forum: A history (1986–1991). In R. C. Lane & M. Meisels (Eds.), *A history of the Division of Psychoanalysis of the American Psychological Association* (pp. 197–205). Hillsdale, NJ: Lawrence Erlbaum.

Marshall, R. J. (1994). A history of the Publications Committee. In R. C. Lane & M. Meisels (Eds.), *A history of the Division of Psychoanalysis of the American Psychological Association* (pp. 61–69). Hillsdale, NJ: Lawrence Erlbaum.

Meisels, M. (1994a). A history of the Division of Psychoanalysis. In R. C. Lane & M. Meisels (Eds.), *A history of the Division of Psychoanalysis of the American Psychological Association* (pp. 11–20). Hillsdale, NJ: Lawrence Erlbaum.

Meisels, M. (1994b). The Membership Directory. In R. C. Lane & M. Meisels (Eds.), *A history of the Division of Psychoanalysis of the American Psychological Association* (pp. 82–83). Hillsdale, NJ: Lawrence Erlbaum.

Meisels, M., & O'Dell, J. W. (1994). The 1980 membership survey of the Division of Psychoanalysis. In R. C. Lane & M. Meisels (Eds.), *A history of the Division of Psychoanalysis of the American Psychological Association* (pp. 21–35). Hillsdale, NJ: Lawrence Erlbaum.

Meisels, M., & Shapiro, E. (Eds.). (1990). *Tradition and innovation in psychoanalytic education: Clark conference on psychoanalytic training for psychologists.* Hillsdale, NJ: Lawrence Erlbaum.

Reppen, J., Tucker, J., & Spezzano, C. (in press). *The Handbook of Psychoanalytic Psychology.* Washington, DC: American Psychological Association.

Schneider, A. Z., & Desmond, H. (1994). The psychoanalytic lawsuit: Expanding opportunities for psychoanalytic training and practice. In R. C. Lane & M. Meisels (Eds.), *A history of the Division of Psychoanalysis of the American Psychological Association* (pp. 313–335). Hillsdale, NJ: Lawrence Erlbaum.

Slavin, J. H. (1994). Professional identity in transition: Psychoanalytic education and training in the Division of Psychoanalysis. In R. C. Lane & M. Meisels (Eds.), *A history of the Division of Psychoanalysis of the American Psychological Association* (pp. 95–120). Hillsdale, NJ: Lawrence Erlbaum.

9

A HISTORY OF DIVISION 48 (PEACE PSYCHOLOGY)

MICHAEL G. WESSELLS

The history of Division 48 (Peace Psychology) is the story of American psychology changing in response to changes in the nation and the global arena. It is also the story of psychologists who were concerned about peace and who worked to make a difference in the world and to encourage social responsibility in their profession. Although Division 48 has existed for slightly more than 5 years, its roots extend back to early in the century. Furthermore, its history illuminates what it takes to form a new division of the American Psychological Association (APA) as well as the growing pains that any new organization must undergo.

I want to thank the many dedicated people who participated in the construction of Division 48. Special thanks go to Alan Nelson, who launched the effort to establish the division and who provided much vision and energy in petitioning for the division. In preparing this history, I drew extensively on recorded minutes of the Division 48 executive committee and other key documents, which I currently store in the Division 48 archive. In addition, I sought the advice and historical recollections of many people who participated in the formation and start-up of the division as well as its actual operation. I want to thank Anne Anderson, Daniel Christie, Morton Deutsch, Paul Kimmel, Susan McKay, Bianca Murphy, Alan Nelson, Linden Nelson, Marc Pilisuk, Janet Schofield, Milton Schwebel, Gregory Sims, M. Brewster Smith, Richard Wagner, and Deborah Winter for their very helpful comments and recollections. I also want to thank Rodney Baker and Donald Dewsbury for their useful reviews of the manuscript. Of course, the responsibility for any errors in this history is mine.

Readers who are unfamiliar with peace psychology will benefit from a definition of the field. Because peace psychology is relatively new, however, it is best to offer only a working definition of the field, along with the caveat that it is important to avoid excessively narrow definitions that will limit future growth and evolution. *Peace psychology* may be defined as the use of psychological concepts, tools, and perspectives for the construction of peace and for the understanding, management, and prevention of destructive conflict at all levels, from the family to the international. *Peace* refers not only to the absence of organized violence but also to the presence of equity and social justice, tolerance and respect for human rights, reconciliation, and sustainable development. Among the many people who call themselves peace psychologists are scholars who study the origins and psychological effects of wars such as those in Vietnam and Bosnia, clinicians who seek to heal the psychological wounds of war and urban violence, educators who teach for peace and develop school-based mediation programs, and professionals who work on prevention-oriented intercultural understanding, nonviolent conflict resolution, gender equity, cooperation, and ecological health.

As Smith (1986) noted, American psychology reflects the dominant values, themes, and currents at work in the society. Although the United States has a long history of action for peace and nonviolence, the nation has pursued military preparations and engagements in armed conflict on a much larger scale. Reflecting this fact, American psychology has had much greater involvement in war and war preparations than in war prevention and the construction of peace. It was APA's participation in World War I that put the association on the map through the construction of widely used, if culturally biased, tests for selecting military personnel (Cattell, cited in Samelson, 1979, p. 106), and American psychology also made significant contributions to the U.S. military in World War II and the following decades (Capshew & Hilgard, 1992). Among the first divisions of the APA was the Division of Military Psychology (Division 19), established in 1945 and 1946. Yet it was not until 1990 that the APA established a Division of Peace Psychology. Because Division 48 is the product of social forces outside psychology and has been shaped by events that long antedated its existence, this chapter will focus equally on the context surrounding the establishment of the division and on its first 5 years.

HISTORIC CONTEXT

A significant historical question is, what changes enabled the formation of the Division of Peace Psychology? No doubt an important factor was the growth of a respectable body of psychological research and analysis (Jacobs, 1989). Early in this century, William James (1910–1995) published

MICHAEL G. WESSELLS

an insightful essay on "The Moral Equivalent of War," which continues to have relevance to contemporary problems (Deutsch, 1995; Smith, 1992). In subsequent decades prominent social psychologists such as Urie Bronfenbrenner (1961), Morton Deutsch (1973, 1983), Herbert Kelman (1965), Otto Klineberg (1956, 1984), Thomas Milburn (1961), Charles Osgood (1962), and Ralph White (1970, 1984, 1986) made significant scholarly contributions to the study of war and peace. The Society for the Psychological Study of Social Issues (APA Division 9, or SPSSI) was particularly active early on, as in 1945 when it published Gardner Murphy's *Human Nature and Enduring Peace*. SPSSI established a Committee on International Relations and a Committee on Arms Control and Disarmament, and SPSSI members were active in publishing on issues such as deterrence (Deutsch, 1961), the military-industrial complex (Pilisuk & Hayden, 1965), and public opinion and foreign policy (Kelman, 1954). In 1961 SPSSI devoted an entire issue of its *Journal of Social Issues* to policies regarding nuclear war, and in 1962 it published a special issue of its newsletter entitled "Psychologists and Peace."

Expanding the Research Base

In the 1960s clinical and developmental psychologists had begun investigating the developmental and mental health implications of young people's fears of nuclear war (Escalona, 1963; Schwebel, 1963, 1965), and in the 1970s social psychologists such as Kelman (1972) had begun doing applied work in protracted international conflict. Psychiatrists such as Frank (1967) and Lifton (1967) analyzed the psychological origins and consequences of nuclear war. In the early 1980s there was an expanding literature on psychological analysis of international issues and events, and the International Society of Political Psychology launched its multidisciplinary journal, *Political Psychology*. Furthermore, some of the most distinguished psychologists, most notably Carl Rogers and B. F. Skinner, did much public speaking on peace. Most of these pioneers in peace psychology recognized that psychological factors played a rather small part in international conflict, which by its nature required the insights of many different disciplines. Nevertheless, it was apparent that psychologists had important things to say about issues of peace.

If World Wars I and II had activated large numbers of psychologists concerning war, it was the nuclear threat that activated large numbers of psychologists for peace (Jacobs, 1989; Morawski & Goldstein, 1985; Smith, 1986). The Soviet invasion of Afghanistan in 1979 slammed the door on détente and ignited new Cold War passions. Fears of U.S. military weakness, stirred by the Iranian hostage crisis and the failed rescue attempt in the mid-1970s helped to usher in a highly conservative Reagan administration dedicated to increasing U.S. military strength. With superpower tensions increasing and both the United States and the Soviet Union building and deploying new generations of nuclear weapons, including those having significant first-strike capabilities, public concerns about nuclear war reached unprecedented levels. By 1982 nearly 75% of the U.S. public supported a freeze on the development, production, and deployment of nuclear weapons (Yankelovich & Doble, 1986).

With professional organizations such as Physicians for Social Responsibility making connections between health and nuclear war, growing numbers of psychologists began to make connections between mental health and the nuclear threat. Psychologists increasingly questioned whether they had a responsibility to work as professionals and as citizens to prevent nuclear war, and the APA Council of Representatives voted to support a nuclear freeze in 1982 (Jacobs, 1989), the same year in which it voted to support the establishment of a United States Institute of Peace. By 1983 momentum was building for the establishment of a United States Institute for Peace (USIP), and the APA board of directors voted in 1985 to support the USIP legislation (Kimmel, 1985). As in the earlier part of the century, many psychologists assisted the military, but this group was now increasingly balanced by the growing numbers of psychologists who worked to develop nonmilitary options for handling conflict.

Organizing for Peace

In the cauldron of concerns about nuclear war prevention, new psychological organizations were forged, extending the organizational work of previous decades (see Jacobs, 1989). By 1982 Doris Miller and Bernice Zahm had established state chapters of Psychologists for Social Responsibility in New York and California, respectively. Independently, in 1982 Alex Redmountain was establishing in Washington, D.C., a national, nonprofit organization that would have a national representation of prominent psychologists. These three groups joined forces to form the national Psychologists for Social Responsibility (PsySR, pronounced "sigh-ess-are"). Through the energies of people such as Anne Anderson, Carmi Harari, Helen Mehr, Doris Miller, Robert Moyer, M. Brewster Smith, Brett Silverstein, Ralph White, and Neil Wollman, PsySR followed George Miller's advice on "giving psychology away" by launching public education programs on the psychology of nuclear war and war prevention, enemy imaging and misperceptions, nonviolent conflict resolution, and peace education. The members of PsySR formed a National Steering Committee of prominent psychologists representing diverse constituencies and areas of expertise. They also created local chapters that served as vehicles for activating psychologists around the country.

Present in the nation's capital and independent of the APA, PsySR developed a rapid response capability for applying the best psychological insight on key peace issues and for making its voice heard in the public arena. From its inception, PsySR was an activist organization, yet its action was informed by scholarship and by extensive dialogue among diverse constituencies about what the role of psychologists should be and about what psychologists could legitimately say, based on their professional expertise, regarding particular issues. PsySR members encouraged scholarship on issues of peace, giving an annual Research Award for outstanding research on peace and conflict resolution. In addition, PsySR membership played a leading role in organizing panels, discussions, and other events on peace for the annual APA convention. It not only assisted in organizing events on the official APA program but also created beginning in the mid-1980s its own program in the PsySR hospitality suite, which became the convention "home" for many psychologists who worked on issues of peace and conflict resolution. These programs often featured well-known psychologists and drew overflow audiences in cities such as New York, making it clear that peace had an audience at the APA convention.

Within and outside of the APA, diverse organizations worked alongside PsySR on issues of peace during the 1980s. Division 9, SPSSI, had a long and distinguished history of involvement in peace (Jacobs, 1989) and had worked with APA groups such as the Board for Social and Ethical Responsibility in Psychology (BSERP) to formulate policy analyses and resolutions regarding war. In 1982 SPSSI formed a Task Force on Peace, which, under the leadership of Theodore Landsman, Richard Wagner, Robert Moyer, and Daniel Mayton, organized symposia and peace-related events for the APA convention and helped to produce a special issue of the *Journal of Social Issues* on positive approaches to peace (Wagner, de Rivera, & Watkins, 1988). In the same way, the Association for Humanistic Psychology published a special peace issue of its *Journal of Humanistic Psychology* in the summer of 1984 (Greening, 1984). In affiliation with the Harvard Medical School, in 1982 John Mack founded the Nuclear Psychology Program (which in 1985 was renamed the Center for the Psychological Studies in the Nuclear Age), which organized scholarly symposia and produced a variety of publications on peace.

These organizations were as much a product of the times as was Division 48, and they cannot be credited with having established the division. The combined impact of these organizations and their activities, however, should not be underestimated. These organizations built credibility and legitimacy, they promoted the exchange of ideas, advanced research, education, and practice, gave peace psychology a voice in the wider professional and public arenas, and supported the work of individuals who might otherwise have felt isolated and marginalized. These organizations carried forward the work begun much earlier of transforming psychology in directions of peace and social justice, and they constituted part of the foundation on which the Division of Peace Psychology was built.

THE FORMATION OF THE DIVISION

The formation of any APA division requires the existence of a favorable Zeitgeist, appropriate levels of credibility, a demonstrated need for a division, and a constituency willing to make its voice heard. Although necessary, these factors are not sufficient. In the case of peace psychology, the other key factors were leadership, persistence, and political savvy (see Wagner, 1992, for a useful discussion of the formation of the division).

Much of the initial leadership came from Alan Nelson, who coined the term *peace psychology*. Following a SPSSI-sponsored symposium chaired by Nora Weckler at the 1981 APA convention, Nelson initiated the plan to establish a Division of Peace Psychology (A. Nelson, personal communication, January 30, 1996). Working with Nora Weckler, Nelson spoke widely on the importance of having an APA division of peace psychology, convinced distinguished psychologists such as Carl Rogers to support the division's formation, and collected more than 200 petitions (proposals to establish a new APA division must be supported by signed petitions from 1% of the APA membership). Soon, other participants entered the effort to form the division. Helen Mehr and Gregory Sims, working through the California State Psychological Association and Northern California PsySR, organized symposia on psychology and nuclear war and generated enthusiasm for having the APA work on nuclear war prevention. Mehr, a skillful networker, sparked the interest of prominent psychologists such as M. Brewster Smith in working on issues of peace. The APA-related work of Mehr and Sims was influenced by Mehr's association with Alan Nelson since late 1981 (A. Nelson, personal communication, January 30, 1996). Mehr initially had been concerned that an APA division might weaken existing organizations such as SPSSI or PsySR (Sims, 1995). But at a 1983 meeting of Northern California PsySR convened by Sims and moderated by Mehr, there was considerable enthusiasm for an APA division of peace psychology, and Mehr and Sims soon joined in the petitioning effort (Sims, personal communication, December 19, 1995).

The Petitioning Process

By 1985 several hundred valid petitions had been collected, but the APA membership was increasing, elevating the bar to be crossed ever higher (eventually to the point of requiring more than 600 signatures). When Alan Nelson suffered a debilitating back injury at the 1985 APA convention, a brief hiatus occurred in the petitioning effort, leading Gregory Sims to turn the task over to James Polyson and Michael Wessells. This expanding team, which called itself the Steering Committee to Form an APA Division of Peace Psychology and which was aided by many dedicated peace psychologists, collected petitions by writing letters, making telephone calls, and requesting signatures at state, regional, and national psychological meetings.

Although many divisions have grown out of existing organizations or elected formative committees, the founders of the Division of Peace Psychology eschewed formal structure and organization. In keeping with values present in the wider community of peace activists outside psychology, the steering committee operated in a consensual, participative, informal mode. Discomfort over adopting formal roles such as "chair" led Polyson and Wessells to define their roles as "co-coordinators," although more formal terminology was to be adopted later in an attempt to match the more traditional APA structure.

The steering committee members encountered numerous obstacles such as lack of funding available for mailings and travel expenses, sharply diminishing returns from mass mailings, and a chicken–egg problem (i.e., many of the petitioners' signatures were invalid because the signers did not belong to the APA, yet they had avoided the APA precisely because of its relative inactivity on issues of peace). But the greater obstacles were psychological. The early and mid-1980s were times of intense Cold War fears, and U.S. society was saturated with concerns that well-intentioned peace activities would inadvertently weaken the position of the United States. Numerous members of the APA council expressed concern that a peace division might politicize psychology or create a forum in which psychologists spoke out inappropriately on issues that were not specifically psychological or said things in public that would damage the APA's credibility. Many mainstream psychologists wondered what peace psychology was and doubted whether it was "real" psychology. In short, peace psychology was marginalized. This situation sparked minor disagreements within the peace community about the name of the proposed division, as some believed that the name Division of Peace and Conflict Resolution would widen the appeal of the division and diminish some of the concerns associated with the word *peace*.

No orderly process existed for addressing these concerns, and because they were emotional as well as intellectual, they could not be settled through scholarship and public debate. What turned the tide in favor of the petitioners was a cumulative process of education, both personal and professional, in a context of progressive relaxation of Cold War tensions. Throughout the period during which petitions were collected, most peace psychologists did what good psychologists do—they conducted research, taught, and practiced, applying their methods to real-world problems and educating their colleagues about peace as they went. In talks with colleagues, petitioners pointed out the many points of intersection between psychology and peace, noting areas such as posttraumatic stress among Vietnam veterans, the psychology of conflict resolution in levels ranging from the family to the international system, war and the abuse of women, aggression, and enemy imaging, among many others. Furthermore, the organizers did not look or act in ways that embarrassed traditional psychologists. Within the budding community of peace psychologists, there was agreement on the importance of respect and civility, for it seemed unfair to ask the world to move toward peace if the group behaved in intolerant, belligerent ways toward its critics. Although peace psychologists did not always adhere to these lofty ideals, they created a sustainable, constructive dialogue internally and externally, taking the edge off many of the doubts that had been expressed. As distinguished elders such as Skinner and Rogers expressed support for forming the division, the relevance of psychology to peace and the acceptability of working on peace increased.

These gains notwithstanding, in August 1987 the APA Council of Representatives rejected the first official petition by the steering committee to establish a division of peace psychology. This failure taught valuable if painful lessons on the importance of learning to work within the APA political process. Put simply, most of the steering committee members were young psychologists who had not been very active within the APA and did not know how to move motions through the council effectively. In 1987 there had been no systematic education and dialogue with council members in advance, and there had been no designated leader on the council floor to answer criticisms and move the petition ahead.

Gaining the Approval of the APA Council of Representatives

Following the 1987 setback, the steeering committee members learned and adjusted their tactics accordingly. Seeking additional wisdom and more gender and age balance, the steering committee membership invited Janet Schofield and Milton Schwebel, both well-known scholars, to join the committee, and Schofield agreed to serve as one of three co-chairs (with Polyson and Wessells). By telephone, members of the steering committee contacted many APA council members not only to lobby for the division but also to hear the main reservations and sources of resistance. Whereas the peace advocates were accustomed to analyzing concerns about the nuclear threat and the Soviets, they now had to learn to talk about concerns over the proliferation of divisions within the APA and about whether psychologists should get involved on issues of public policy and national security. This enlargement of the dialogue over whether to form a peace psychology division created an environment in which members of the peace community could voice doubts about the desirability of having a division dedicated to peace. Some within the peace community were concerned about the possible negative impact a division of peace psychology might have with regard to membership, convention program hours, and resources on other APA divisions such as SPSSI and on non-APA organizations such as PsySR.

Because the APA council had imposed a 1988 moratorium on the formation of new divisions, in order to consider issues of reorganization, members of the steering committee had 2 years to prepare their next formal application for divisional status. This afforded much needed time for dialogue and education. There was increasing agreement internally that an APA division of peace psychology should have a scholarly rather than an activist emphasis, thereby creating an appropriate division of labor with PsySR, the activist arm of psychology. In addition, comfort grew around the idea that the proposed peace division would complement SPSSI, with the proposed division focusing directly on peace and SPSSI addressing a very broad spectrum of social issues and helping to establish the wider connections between peace and social justice. Beyond the peace community, supporters argued that the proposed division could help the APA meet its stated goal of advancing human well-being and could act for peace in the same way that leading professional organizations outside psychology had done (for example, Physicians for Social Responsibility). Advocates also argued that the proposed division would provide a home within the APA for psychologists who might otherwise hold the APA at arm's length.

With these dialogues in progress, profound and unforeseen events—the Gorbachev reforms, the Reagan–Gorbachev summits, nuclear arms reduction treaties welcomed by both East and West, and the dismantling of the Berlin Wall—reshaped the international arena and melted the ice of the Cold War. Suddenly, work on peace no longer seemed idealistic or inimical to U.S. security interests. More than any other single factor, the winding down of the Cold War created an environment conducive to the establishment of a division of peace psychology.

In August 1989 the steering committee members submitted their second petition to the APA council. The petition had been revised to address directly the concerns that had been heard from various corners and to reflect the increased scholarship in the field. In hopes of continuing the educational process and building credibility, it listed references from many prominent psychologists. This time around, the committee members had recruited M. Brewster Smith—a distinguished social psychologist, former APA president, and someone often referred to as the conscience of the APA—to serve as captain on the floor of the APA council meeting in New Orleans. Providing just the right mixture of force of argument, leadership, and humor, Smith defused the concern over the proliferation of APA divisions by pointing out that a peace division would not even constitute a noticeable difference in an Association that already had 45 active divisions. On August 13, 1989, The APA council members approved the motion to establish the division, thereby giving peace psychology an entry into the central house of the profession. Continuing the numbering practice already begun, the Division of Peace Psychology was designated as Division 48.

MAKING THE TRANSITION

Under APA rules, a new division is not officially established until it conducts an official business meeting at which at least 10% of the petitioners, approximately 70 people in the case of Division 48, are present. Because it would have been counterproductive to schedule this meeting on the spur of the moment following the council's decision in 1989, the steering committee members decided to hold the inaugural business meeting in 1990 as part of the APA convention in Boston. Following the suggestion of numerous senior peace psychologists and seeing few alternatives, the steering committee membership decided that it should continue on an interim basis until the division's first officers and executive committee members had been elected and installed. The steering committee members, however, were acutely aware of being in an ambiguous, if not precarious position. Although they were not elected officials, they were nevertheless charged with acting on behalf of the division, and they knew that the steps they took and the process they created would set precedents. In addition, they had proposed bylaws that took into account APA requirements and that used the bylaws of several extant divisions as models. But these bylaws had never been reviewed and approved by the petitioners. Under the circumstances, the committee members agreed that no small part of their work would be to build participation, to work as openly as possible, and to seek advice widely and from diverse constituencies.

Work of the Steering Committee

With the aid of Sarah Jordan of the APA Division Services Office, the steering committee members worked to get the division up and running for the inaugural business meeting. Because the division had received 8 hours of program time for the 1990 convention, the steering committee members designated Polyson as program chair and decided that the program should emphasize invited symposia and events because no mechanisms existed for handling and reviewing large numbers of proposals. There was also a need to elect the first set of officers for the division. Although the proposed bylaws had not been officially approved, it seemed important to elect official leaders of the division who could then guide the events at the first business meeting. The steering committee accordingly created an interim elections committee (with Wessells as chair). Because the steering committee had no funds available, money was also needed to cover the costs of mailings.

Having obtained support via the APA Division Services Office, the steering committee members arranged a fall mailing to everyone who had petitioned for the division. This initial mailing (dated October 1, 1989) notified supporters of the APA council's action, reiterated the complementarity of the new division with PsySR and SPSSI, urged attendance at the inaugural business meeting, invited suggestions regarding the 1990 convention program, and requested nominations for officers as well as contributions to support the transition effort. The mailing succeeded in stimulating many nominations, program ideas, and discussions about the directions of the new division. Early on, the spirit of participation was visible. Following the fall mailing, the steering committee members learned the good news that, as a result of the APA apportionment ballot from the fall of 1989, the division had won a seat on the APA Council of Representatives. From the outset, the division would have a voice on the central policy-making body of the association.

Having no scheduled winter meeting but wanting to work in a collegial manner, the entire steering committee membership held a telephone conference February 10, 1990. This was the first meeting of the entire steering committee, which had previously conducted its business informally by mail or by a chain of individual telephone conversations, and it established important precedents for divisional operations. During the meeting, committee members decided that (a) the nominees for officers should be those who received the highest numbers of nominations and who expressed a willingness to serve if elected; (b) it was desirable for purposes of building credibility and legitimacy to have the first candidates for president be senior, highly distinguished peace psychologists, whereas younger, less well-known nominees might run for president-elect; (c) the officers' terms should begin when the election returns were in, whereas the terms of office would normally begin in August at an annual business meeting; (d) the nominees for president and president-elect would provide a written statement of their vision and main goals for the division; (e) nominees whose names did not appear on the ballot but who had received multiple nominations should be invited to run for the two positions of members-at-large on the executive committee; (f) the division should work to achieve gender balance on the executive committee and in all of its activities; and (g) everyone who petitioned for the formation of the division, whether an APA member or not, would be entitled to vote. In the conference call, the steering committee membership decided to nominate Milton Schwebel and Richard Wagner for the Division 48 seat on the APA council.

In discussing the planning for the 1990 convention, Polyson reported that Janet Schofield would chair an invited symposium on "Peace Psychology—Past, Present, and Future" and that he was working with Anne Anderson, the national coordinator of PsySR, on having PsySR and Division 48 share a hospitality suite. It was agreed that 2 hours of program time should be allocated for the inaugural business meeting, and Alan Nelson and Michael Wessells agreed to review the proposed bylaws in preparation for the meeting. The ideas of starting a division newsletter and scholarly journal generated considerable enthusiasm, though it was recognized that these tasks must await the official constitution of the division and be guided by elected officers. This initial meeting, for which there are no official minutes, helped to set a tone of cooperation and participation that would carry on through the first 5 years.

In April 1990, the steering committee membership conducted the first divisional elections. Because several members of the steering committee were candidates and Helen Mehr was the only candidate identified for the office of secretary–treasurer, Mehr received and oversaw the counting of the ballots. These elections brought into office Morton Deutsch as president, Wessells as president-elect, and Mehr as secretary–treasurer (see Table 36). Because the election was not conducted using the Hare system, in which voters rank the nominees and the cumulative rankings are used to decide the outcome of ties in—for example, the number of "1" votes—there was a three-way among Joan Gildemeister, Marc Pilisuk, and James Polyson for the two positions of executive committee members-at-large. On the view that a greater number and diversity of voices is better, the incoming officers decided that all three should serve. In the vote for the APA council representative (conducted by the APA because only APA members and fellows were eligible to vote in it), a tie had also occurred, and a decision was made to invite Wagner and Schwebel to share the term. Division 48 now had its first elected leadership team, one that bridged the generations of active peace psychologists, and it gained stature by having as its first president a senior peace psychologist whose work was well known and highly respected internationally, who blended skills of scholarship and practice, and who had exercised leadership within the APA and in other organizations for decades. For purposes of continuity and the construction of norms of cooperation, it was decided that the executive committee should work with the members of the soon-to-dissolve steering committee in planning the inaugural business meeting.

The First Meeting of the Executive Committee

The executive committee held its first meeting August 10, 1990, in Boston as part of the annual APA convention. That the meeting took place in a hospitality suite shared equally by the division and PsySR indicated the spirit of partnership between these two organizations. In an atmosphere of informality and participation, the executive committee affirmed the importance of increasing division membership, building diversity, and defining peace psychology in a broad manner that would enhance the development of the field.

Among the main agenda items was the bylaws, the evolution of which provided significant insights about how peace psychologists defined their nascent field and the directions that would be most appropriate for the

TABLE 36
Officers and Executive Committee of Division 48

Year	Officers	Members-at-Large	APA Council Representative
1990–1991	Morton Deutsch (President) Michael Wessells (Pres. Elect) Helen Mehr (Sec.–Treas.)	Joan Gildemeister Marc Pilisuk James Polyson	Richard V. Wagner (1991)
1991–1992	Michael Wessells (President) Richard V. Wagner (Pres. Elect) Morton Deutsch (Past Pres.) Dorothy Ciarlo (Sec.–Treas.)	Joan Gildemeister Marc Pilisuk James Polyson	Milton Schwebel (1992)
1992–1993	Richard V. Wagner (President) Paul Kimmel (Pres. Elect) Michael Wessells (Past Pres.) Dorothy Ciarlo (Sec.–Treas.)	Susan McKay Linden Nelson	Janet Schofield (1993)
1993–1994	Paul Kimmel (President) Susan McKay (Pres. Elect) Richard V. Wagner (Past Pres.) Petra Hesse (Sec.–Treas.)	Leila Dane Linden Nelson	Janet Schofield (1994)
1994–1995	Susan McKay (President) Daniel Christie (Pres. Elect) Paul Kimmel (Past Pres.) Petra Hesse (Sec.–Treas.)	Hector Betancourt Thomas Milburn	Janet Schofield (1995)
1995–1996	Daniel Christie (President) Marc Pilisuk (Pres. Elect) Susan McKay (Past Pres.) Margaret Houlihan (Secretary) Petra Hesse (Treasurer)	Hector Betancourt Thomas Milburn	Deborah Winter (1996)

new division. The bylaws that had accompanied the petition to form the division had been concise but rather general:

> The purposes of this Division shall be: (a) to encourage scholarly psychological research on issues concerning peace and conflict resolution; (b) to provide an organization that fosters communication among researchers, teachers and practitioners who are working on these issues; and (c) to apply the knowledge and the methods of psychology in the cause of peace and nonviolent conflict resolution. (Petition for an APA Division of Peace Psychology, 3)

In spring of 1990 Alan Nelson had suggested revising the proposed goals to emphasize *nonviolent* conflict resolution and also processes of reconciliation. At the executive committee meeting, additional changes seemed necessary because Morton Deutsch and others expressed concern that the field would be narrowed prematurely by focusing on war rather than on destructive conflict at all levels. Following the distinction between positive and negative peace (Galtung, 1969), peace researchers recognized the problems of defining peace as the absence of war when international tensions continued to run high or when strong racial hatreds and conflict continued.

At the same time, it seemed important to include psychological work on the causes and consequences of war. To be proactive rather than reactive, the executive committee wanted to emphasize the prevention of war. For these reasons, the proposed bylaws were modified in July 1990 to read as follows:

> The purposes of this Division shall be: (a) to encourage psychological research on issues concerning peace, nonviolent conflict resolution, and the causes, consequences and prevention of war and other forms of destructive conflict; (b) to provide an organization that fosters communication among researchers, teachers and practitioners who are working on these issues; and (c) to apply the knowledge and the methods of psychology in the advancement of peace, nonviolent conflict resolution, reconciliation, and the prevention of war and other forms of destructive conflict. (Revisions to the Proposed By-laws in the Petition for an APA Division of Peace Psychology, 3)

These were no small semantic changes—they embodied a proactive, systemic approach to peace that could accommodate under a single roof work on family violence, the causes of war, and international conflict resolution. Division leaders hoped that these changes would encourage psychologists of diverse stripes to conceptualize their work as part of peace psychology, thereby diversifying the field and increasing the division's membership.

The executive committee members also set about forming and activating the committees (membership, program, fellowship, and elections) called for by the provisional bylaws and that seemed necessary for the development of the division. In view of the importance of the convention program in defining the field and inviting participation, the executive committee members decided that the president-elect should serve as the program chair for the convention in the following year, thereby establishing a practice that continued throughout the first 5 years. Out of a lively discussion of how to encourage psychologists in traditional areas to see the connections between their work and issues of peace came the suggestion to establish a committee on interdivisional relations, to be chaired by Marc Pilisuk and James Polyson. Morton Deutsch also suggested the need for a committee on public relations to help peace psychologists work effectively with the media and for a finance committee to assist in raising funds. To encourage participation in the division, members agreed that the initial dues should be kept at the modest figure of $15 annually. Amid the spirit of new beginnings, the meeting was punctuated with humor over the fact that the executive committee was meeting when it did not yet exist officially. All of the decisions that had been made were provisional and would be presented in the constitutional meeting the following day.

THE INAUGURAL MEETING

The official birthdate of Division 48 was August 11, 1990, on the occasion of the inaugural business meeting, with Morton Deutsch presiding. It was, of course, a historic occasion because the division's existence signified the legitimacy of peace psychology and created a channel through which peace psychologists could move their work into the mainstream. The excitement associated with the meeting was tempered, however, by world events. Despite the end of the Cold War, everyone recognized that the war system remained deeply entrenched, and Saddam Hussein's forces had recently invaded Kuwait, causing war fever to rise swiftly in the United States. These events charged the atmosphere, added new urgency to work for peace, and raised questions right from the start about how the new division would define its role.

The meeting was historic also because it represented a coming together of diverse generations and constituencies. Approximately 75 people participated in the 2-hour meeting, although movement into and out of the room made it difficult to determine the exact number of participants. With little sense of hierarchy, young peace psychologists joined in dialogue with some of the senior, best-known people in the field. Significant numbers of women participated in the meeting, and their voices were welcomed, as were those of people who had long associations with PsySR and SPSSI. New faces also appeared, testifying to the interest in peace beyond the group of known peace psychologists and presenting the opportunity for new voices and leadership. In addition, several members of the APA staff were present, and the meeting opened with a warm expression of thanks to Sarah Jordan and the Divisional Services Office. Later in the meeting, Jacqueline Gentry invited Division 48 members to become active within the Public Interest Directorate and to comment on a proposal from the Board of Social and Ethical Responsibility regarding the APA's position on weapons of mass destruction. In a quiet manner, the meeting helped to build links between the division and the APA Central Office, allaying some of the lingering doubts in the peace community about working through the APA.

The president set a participatory tone for the meeting by announcing at the outset that the division was in need of input and help from as many members as possible. As he read the list of committees that needed leadership, several members suggested their willingness to help, strengthening the norm of participation.

The main agenda item—the bylaws—was not to be so easy and free of conflict. To appreciate the salience of this subject, it must be remembered that the Cold War had recently ended, and the immediate threat of nuclear war had subsided, even if the longer-term nuclear threat had not (Polyson, 1992; Wessells, 1992a, 1995). Unlike the Cold War era, there was no central galvanizing issue. Moreover, the post–Cold War era provided the opportunity to address a much wider spectrum of interconnected issues—such as militarism, poverty, sexism—than could have been addressed effectively during the Cold War. Although there was a generally recognized need to enlarge the scope of peace psychology and to avoid premature narrowing of the field, it was no longer clear what peace psychologists should do. Perhaps more than at any other time since work had begun on forming the division, there was significant uncertainty about the definition and mission of peace psychology. Added complexity arose from the ambiguities surrounding the respective roles of Division 48 and of extant organizations such as PsySR. To complicate matters further, the executive committee had made the changes noted in the proposed bylaws, but because many of these changes had been made the day before, the membership was hearing the revised (proposed) bylaws for the first time.

In this climate, there was need of extensive dialogue about the purposes of the new division. Much of the initial discussion examined whether to expand peace psychology to include environmental issues. It was well understood that the Cold War had masked a host of environmental problems, many of which stemmed from military preparations and armed conflict (McKenzie-Mohr & Winter, 1992; Sivard, 1991), and that resource scarcity was a major source of war and destructive conflict. But there were concerns that peace psychology might be weakened by making environmental issues central. The ranks of peace organizations nationally were shrinking significantly as the environmental movement gathered steam. Several members pointed out that the APA already had a division (34, Population and Environmental Psychology) that worked on environmental issues, that the phrase "causes and consequences of war" in the bylaws created an umbrella for work on environmental issues as they intersected with peace, and that it would be unwise to make the stated purposes of the division so specific as to appear noninclusive. No real agreement was reached on how centrally environmental issues ought to be situated within peace psychology, making it a topic for future work by the division.

The need to expand the stated purposes also became apparent in regard to a question as to whether interpersonal conflict was within the division's scope of work. The general sentiment of those present was that the division should work on conflict at all levels, making connections with wider, macrosocial issues. Having noted that the stated purpose placed too strong an emphasis on research, particularly when psychological work for peace already encompassed education and training in areas such as conflict resolution and cultural sensitivity, Paul Kimmel suggested that part of the purpose was "to encourage psychological research, education, and training on issues concerning peace." By general agreement, this phrase replaced the phrase "to encourage scholarly psychological research on issues concerning peace" in item (a) regarding purposes. With this modification, the members present accepted the expanded statement of purpose crafted by the executive committee. In this manner, the members enlarged the scope of peace psychology, avoided specific definitions of a field that was evolving rapidly, and strived to create a broad umbrella that would accommodate diverse orientations and kinds of work for peace. It was revealing that there had been no powerful impetus for orienting the new division toward activism. The membership generally agreed that PsySR, being independent of the APA, was in a better position to pursue activist work. Most division members implicitly appreciated that it would take time for the division to formulate its goals and strategies in regard to work in the policy arena.

Animated discussion arose over the requirements for amending the bylaws. The proposed bylaws allowed amendment only if two thirds of the members who voted in a mail ballot approved. Numerous members stated that this requirement was too stringent and had the effect of enshrining the bylaws at a time when the field was young and in need of openness to change, particularly in regard to the purposes of the division. Linden Nelson suggested and Milton Schwebel formally proposed that amendments to the bylaws be made by a majority vote, but others maintained that the bylaws ought to have the support of more than a simple majority. Marc Pilisuk proposed that the bylaws could be amended by a majority vote during the first 2 years and by a two thirds vote thereafter. With the discussion becoming labored and with no consensus in sight, Schwebel withdrew his motion, and the group voted to accept the Pilisuk compromise. In addition to approving the first set of divisional bylaws, the business meeting achieved its unstated purpose, that of Division 48 becoming a group not on paper but in human process. This process, characterized by norms of dialogue, inclusiveness, and informality, was instrumental in enabling the division to take on its major tasks and issues of the first 5 years.

MEMBERSHIP

New divisions have a fragile existence, making membership recruitment and retention high priorities. Recognizing that communications is a key element in attracting and retaining members, Morton Deutsch approached the cochairs of the publications committee, Alan Nelson and Gregory Sims, regarding the publication of a division newsletter, and Sims agreed to serve as the interim editor. Despite the lack of precedent, established format, or logo, Sims managed to produce two issues of the *Division 48 Newsletter* from 1990 to 1991. They contained presidential columns, reports on the executive committee and business meetings, a call for proposals for the 1991 Division 48 convention program, and perspective pieces on issues such as the Persian Gulf crisis. When Daniel Jordan became newsletter editor in the fall of 1991, the newsletter title changed to *The Peace Psychology Newsletter*, it took on a more professional appearance, and tripled in length to 18 pages. Its content expanded to include reports from committees and newly established task forces, as well as reports and announcements regarding meetings well beyond the circle of the division. These improvements owed much to the hard work of Daniel Jordan and Julie Carvalho (associate newsletter editor) from 1991 to 1994 and also to their successors, Sheldon Levy (editor), Phyllis Turner and J. Carvalho (assistant editors). Renamed *The Peace Psychology Bulletin* in April 1992, and *Peace Psychology Newsletter* in 1995, the newsletter has become the communications lifeline for the division.

In addition, the executive committee members developed early on the practice of making regular mailings to the membership, particularly each fall, for purposes of soliciting input on key issues, inviting participation in divisional activities and elections, and announcing important events. This practice reflected a strategic decision to use more personal means of communication (i.e., letters) than a newsletter could provide.

The task of attracting new members required significant leadership, and the division turned first to Linden Nelson (1990–1992) and then to Daniel Mayton (1992–1994, with Deborah Winter as cochair in 1992–1993) to serve as chair of its membership committee. Nelson cleaned up a mailing list that was far from accurate, having evolved over 8 years without careful maintenance, and he also developed regular procedures for contacting members regarding renewal, handling inquiries about membership, conducting recruitment drives, and so forth. Nelson collaborated extensively with a highly efficient secretary–treasurer, Dorothy Ciarlo, to create accurate records of dues-paying and APA dues-exempt members, of which affiliates had paid dues, and of who was remiss in payment.

To build membership, the executive committee members worked to keep the annual dues at a modest level. The dues for Division 48 members and affiliates started at $15 annually, climbed to $17 in 1992, and increased to $20 in 1994. In 1995, with the publication of the divisional journal, dues for members and affiliates rose to $25. To attract student members as the next generation of peace psychologists, the executive committee set the dues for student members at $5 per year, and this level continued through 1995.

A key task in building membership was to provide a point of entry and a home for people doing diverse kinds of work on peace. To invite the participation of all members and enlarge the scope of peace psychology, then-President Wessells proposed the creation of various task forces, called working groups beginning in 1994. The executive committee leadership established six task forces: Children, Families, and War; Ethnicity and Peace; Feminism and Peace; Peace and Education; Peace and Sustainable Development; and Public Policy and Action. During the next several years this list expanded. In 1993 the executive committee added a working group on international alliances and ventures and one on militarism, disarmament and conversion to replace an inactive task force on the continuing nuclear threat. In 1994 it added a working group on conflict resolution. The chairs of these groups have participated regularly in dialogues with the executive committee. Moreover, these groups have organized convention programs, written newsletter articles, reviewed new books and work in their areas, assisted in long-range planning for the division, and undertaken projects such as encouraging the inclusion of material on peace in psychology texts.

As a result of these efforts, the division had approximately 850 members (including affiliates and student members) by July 1992. It is a positive sign that membership continues at a level near this figure today, for during the early 1990s, peace organizations nationwide experienced membership declines of approximately 40%. By 1992, the division had attracted 25 international members, most from developed nations. This small number was troubling for a division that had strong international aspirations, that wanted to nurture the growth of peace psychology worldwide, and that wanted to include people with many different backgrounds and value systems (Wessells, 1992b). To address this problem, in 1994 the division established an International Affiliates program that provided sponsored membership in the division for approximately 20 psychologists working in developing areas around the world.

An early problem encountered in building membership was accurate record keeping, a task made difficult by the fact that petitions had been collected for years, and many of the petitioners had been kept on the division mailing list even if they had dropped out of sight. This problem was corrected on June 30, 1992, when those who had not paid dues at least once in 1991 or 1992 were removed from the list. Further, nearly 20% of Division 48 members were affiliates (including students) who do not belong to the APA and therefore did not show up in APA membership records. It made little sense to have APA offices keep membership records for the division, particularly because the division needed a directly accessible database for purposes of membership research and communication. Keeping the membership database was too much for a membership chair already immersed in frequent correspondence and membership drives. A third difficulty was that membership chair is, by design, a rotating position. Some members feared that transferring the Division 48 membership database would create problems of computer incompatibility and long response times while learning a new system. To address these problems, the executive committee members decided in August 1993 to contract the maintenance of the membership database to the PsySR office, giving the database a stable home. Recognizing that the job of treasurer had become quite time intensive, the executive committee members proposed to split the office of secretary–treasurer into two parts, with the secretary overseeing all membership functions and serving as chair of the membership committee. This proposal required a bylaws revision, which the Division 48 membership approved in a mail ballot in spring 1995. That spring, the division membership elected Margaret Houlihan as its first secretary, and Petra Hesse continued as treasurer.

ONGOING ACTIVITIES

Despite increasingly widespread activity via electronic mail within the division, the annual APA convention remains the hub of interaction. Following its initial "grant" of 8 hours of program time in 1990, the division held its first full convention program of 26 hours in 1991, and comparable numbers of program hours have been maintained since then. This figure contrasts sharply with those of the 1980s, when it was considered a success to have even 10 hours of formal convention program time devoted to peace. Here, then, is a very tangible accomplishment of the founders of Division 48—the institutionalization of peace in the APA convention program. No longer are peace issues to be relegated to the convention sidelines.

Convention Programs

Three trends are evident in the division's convention programming. Perhaps the most important is the progression toward gender balance. From 1990 through 1992, there was a 2:1 ratio of men to women among presenters and discussants and a 3:1 ratio favoring men as session chairs. This situation has improved considerably through the efforts of the working group on feminism and peace. At the 1994 and 1995 conventions, Division 48 programs had no dominance of men as session chairs or as presenters and discussants (Boyer & Swain, 1995). The now established practice of ensuring gender balance among invited speakers has also supported movement toward gender balance on the division convention program.

Second, the convention program has become more diverse and wider in scope. Owing in part to the Gulf War and to the residual influence of the Cold War, international issues and war dominated the early programs, with few sessions on issues of ethnicity, community violence, or sustainable development. By 1994 and 1995 the latter themes had become much more visible, thereby enabling the division to fulfill its initial commitment to developing a systemic, multilevel approach to peace and to integrate issues of peace and social justice. This trend also owed to the third development, increased collaboration with other groups in the creation of cross-fertilizing programs. Particularly noteworthy have been productive programs jointly constructed with SPSSI on the United Nations, programs on women's issues cosponsored with Division 35 (Psychology of Women), regular dialogues and joint events with Division 19 (Military Psychology), and an extensive array of events cosponsored with PsySR. In 1995, recognizing that the office of president-elect has too many responsibilities to carry the burdens of program chair, the executive committee members decided to appoint a talented person (Hector Betancourt) who held no office as program chair for the 1996 convention. By separating the jobs of president-elect and program chair, the division leadership has given the program chair additional latitude and time for constructing collaborative programs.

Even the best planned conventions, however, cannot possibly stay abreast of peace-related events in the world. The 1990 convention took place on the eve of the Gulf War, and participants in the 1991 convention were shaken by news that an attempted coup had occurred in the Soviet Union. In dealing with these events, members of Division 48 have learned to be rather quick on their feet. In 1991, for example, the division membership arranged on very short notice a dialogue session on the Soviet coup attempt, and this turned out to be one of the most energetic, provocative peace-related events at the convention. In 1995, in the face of mounting pressures to send U.S. troops to Bosnia and in the aftermath of the bombing of the federal building in Oklahoma City, Ralph White led a session on Bosnia, while Morton Deutsch led one on dealing with militia groups. These sessions brought forward diverging views, and they served well the larger functions of educating, raising new questions, and stimulating the additional inquiry needed to construct informed analyses and policy stances.

Usually at the APA convention, the division has given a variety of annual awards to honor and encourage excellent work and outstanding commitment. In 1992 the division instituted a Presidential Award for Lifelong Contributions, the recipients of which have been Ralph White (1992), Jerome Frank (1993), Milton Schwebel (1994), and Morton Deutsch (1995). In 1992 the division copresented with PsySR a National Service Award to Helen Mehr, the first secretary–treasurer of the division, shortly before her death. The division then instituted an annual Outstanding Service Award, the recipients of which have been Dorothy Ciarlo (1994), Linden Nelson (1994), and Daniel Mayton (1995).

Long-Range Planning

A significant and ongoing activity of the division is the construction of its first long-range plan, which owes much to the leadership of Susan McKay during her term as president. Regular executive committee meetings with their packed agendas did not permit the longer-term, more creative orientation that planning required. In spring 1994, McKay began the planning dialogue via e-mail but was cognizant that not everyone used e-mail and that there is no substitute for face-to-face interaction, particularly on difficult issues. During the August 1994 APA convention, McKay brought together a group of Division 48 leaders for the initial planning meeting. Meeting informally in Paul Kimmel's home, the group members generated many ideas concerning the vision, goals, and strategies for the division as it headed toward the next millennium. As a result of this meeting and subsequent discussions held in conjunction with the winter 1995 executive committee meeting, the division adopted a sweeping statement of vision that called for "the development of sustainable societies through the prevention of destructive conflict and violence and the amelioration of its consequences, the empowerment of individuals, and the building of cultures of peace and global community"(Appendix to the Minutes of the 1995 Winter Executive Committee Meeting). In addition, the executive committee membership adopted six broad program goals that reflected the perspectives from various working groups, which commented on and refined the proposed operational goals and strategies at the 1995 APA convention.

By design, this planning effort lacks a distinct end point, because the intent is to create an ongoing dialogue about planning and a rolling plan adjusted to meet changing needs and realities. Already, the effort has helped the division members to think consciously about the division's priorities and strategies, and it has bolstered the norm of participation that has been so conspicuous throughout the life of Division 48.

UNRESOLVED ISSUES

Like any new organization, Division 48 has experienced a variety of growing pains associated with difficult issues. The nature of these issues reflects the division's values and identity, and the process through which it addresses them says much about its character.

Relationship With Psychologists for Social Responsibility

As mentioned, the relationship with PsySR was an issue for peace psychology well before the establishment of the Division 48. At the 1990 APA convention, an open discussion in the PsySR–Division 48 hospitality suite evoked general agreement that PsySR and Division 48 are sister organizations, with PsySR being more activist and Division 48 being oriented more toward scholarly pursuits. Although tidy in concept, this strategic positioning is not so orderly in reality. Many Division 48 members have wanted the division to become more active and vocal in regard to the key issues of the day (e.g., Pilisuk, 1994), raising the possibility of duplicating the functions traditionally performed by PsySR. Indeed, at the 1990 APA convention, the Division 48 executive committee voted to support a resolution from the APA Board of Social and Ethical Responsibility to condemn nuclear, chemical, and biological warfare. At the 1995 APA convention, members of PsySR and Division 48 agreed to collaborate in drafting a resolution condemning France's plan to continue nuclear testing that could undermine the negotiations for a comprehensive test ban.

Through the leadership of its working group on public policy and action (Kimmel, 1992, 1995; Kimmel & Dane, 1993), members of Division 48 have worked to define the division's role in regard to public policy. As articulated by Paul Kimmel, the division's fourth president, the division's work should be more proactive than reactive, it should reflect a collectively constructed vision informed by a careful analysis of the values underlying its programs, and it should link peace and social justice concerns in the pursuit of a sustainable world. Within this framework, the working group membership proposed educational programs for policy makers, media programs to educate the public, and the construction of a proactive code of ethics supportive of public interest science. Many of these ideas informed and have been incorporated into the division's long-range plan. As this deliberate, long-range approach spawns tangible programs, additional dialogue about the relationships between Division 48 and PsySR will be necessary.

Fortunately, these two organizations have developed a mutually supportive relationship that enriches peace psychology and heightens its impact. Their overlap in leadership has enabled mutual understanding, and both organizations have benefited from cooperation on various projects and a constructive, ongoing dialogue about their roles and future. In 1993 this relationship was cemented when Division 48 entered a cooperative office arrangement wherein it contracted out to PsySR tasks such as maintaining the membership database. Nevertheless, PsySR, like all peace activist organizations, has experienced declines of membership and finances since the 1980s, leading some of PsySR's prominent elders, notably M. Brewster Smith and Ralph White, to voice strong concerns about the sustainability of activism on very small budgets. This issue of how to sustain responsible activism within peace psychology remains a central, if unanswered, question.

Diversity, Inclusiveness, and Equity

A second unresolved issue, one that goes to the heart of issues of peace and justice, is that of diversity within Division 48. This is not a single issue but a package of interrelated issues having to do with inclusiveness of and equity among people and ideas from diverse cultures. Recognizing the impossibility of achieving peace without social justice, the fundamental question is whether the division will be a U.S. enterprise dominated mostly by White males or a multicultural, international enterprise that contributes to peace by embodying diversity and by stimulating collaboration and learning across lines of race, class, gender, ethnicity, and nationality (Wessells, 1992b).

In addressing issues of diversity, the division membership encounters significant obstacles associated with the history and practices of the society, the academy, the discipline, and the peace movement. For example, the division membership has worked to include African Americans in its executive committee, its membership, and its projects. Yet the pool of African American psychologists working on issues of peace is rather small, in part because of issues associated with the U.S. history of discrimination and the economic and educational underprivileging of people of color. As a result, it has been difficult to build African American membership within the division. In the same way, both the national peace movement and psychology have a long history of male domination. This pattern also exists within peace psychology, where men have been much more visible than women and have held most of the leadership positions (McKay, 1992, 1995). In the first 2 years of the division's history, it was apparent that women needed to have a stronger voice within the division.

That the division has imported much baggage from society on issues of diversity is less important than how the division has attempted to handle this baggage. To begin with, the division membership set up working groups to focus on such topics as ethnicity and peace, feminism and peace, and international alliances and ventures in hopes of integrating diverse perspectives and people into the division's projects and leadership. Thanks to the efforts of determined people such as Curtis Branch, Jeanette Diaz-Veizades, and Hector Betancourt, the division offered in its early years numerous important convention programs on issues of ethnicity and conflict, and the international alliances and ventures working group has regularly arranged sessions that feature psychologists from developing nations. Space limitations preclude a detailed description of the division's efforts to address diversity issues. It is instructive, however, to examine the case of gender balance more closely because it reveals much about the division's work and the current situation.

To activate women in the division, Susan McKay and Bianca Cody Murphy, cochairs of the Task Force on Feminism and Peace, sent out a mailing in Spring 1992 to all female members of the division, inviting their participation and encouraging them to develop programs for the APA conventions. This mailing stimulated lively responses from many people, and by August 1992, the Feminism and Peace group had become the most active of all the Division 48 task forces and had established subgroups working on book reviews, writing newsletter articles, and networking. Over the next several years, women became much more prominent in the division, and Susan McKay became the division's first woman president in August 1994. At the same time, women became more active in the Division 48 convention program, with the imbalance between men and women presenters and session chairs having been corrected by 1994. In planning the journal, gender balance received significant attention, as two of three associate editors (Susan Fiske and Ethel Tobach) are women, and women comprise one third of the editorial board, a figure that compares favorably to APA journals (Boyer & Swain, 1995). Owing to the hard work of people such as Judith Van Hoorn and Michele Stimac, current cochairs of the working group on feminism and peace, women maintain a high level of activity within the division, and significant dialogue occurs via a feminism and peace e-mail group, which includes Daniel Christie, the current division president.

Nevertheless, a tremendous amount of work remains in this key area. In a recent survey of active APA divisions, Division 48 ranked 41st in the percentage of female officers and 21st in the percentage of women fellows (Boyer & Swain, 1995). Indeed, the continued use of the term *fellows* indicates the pervasiveness of the problem. Nor has gender balance been achieved on a steady basis within the executive committee (see Table 36), despite much effort by the elections committee, which is chaired by the current past president, to bring forward strong female candidates and a gender-balanced slate. Perhaps the largest imbalance occurs in regard to the journal, in which a significant majority of authors (particularly first authors) are men.

Much more work also needs to be done in regard to ethnicity and international activity. Although the division has developed convention programs jointly with Division 44 (Society for the Psychological Study of Ethnic Minority Issues), too little has been done to build the necessary bridges between peace and ethnic conflict at the community level and international levels. Partly for economic reasons, key divisional activities such as the convention program include few people from cultures outside the United States, making it difficult to stimulate the multicultural dialogue on the origins of conflict and peace and to build peace psychology in diverse countries. In this sense, the division is a microcosm of the APA, and true multiculturalism and international perspective remain areas for significant work in the future.

STARTING THE JOURNAL

Many of the charter members of Division 48 had long wanted a scholarly journal of peace psychology that would help to legitimate the field, encourage new scholarship, provide a home for work that might not fit into more traditional psychological journals, and communicate the insights and methods of peace psychology to a wide audience within and outside of psychology. Establishing a journal was to be the central task as well as the major accomplishment of the division in its first 5 years.

Testing the Waters

To explore the feasibility of establishing a division journal, the publications committee in Spring 1991 invited Richard Wagner, the president-elect, to interview journal editors, publishers, and division members. Wagner's (1991) written report examined issues such as the need and possible niche for the journal, the problem of attracting manuscripts of high caliber, and costs and publishing arrangements. Wagner also arranged discussions at the August 1991 executive committee meeting with Gary VandenBos, executive director of APA Publications, and Terry Hendrix of Sage Publications, who explained that the start-up costs for a quarterly journal were in the neighborhood of $20 per member for a small division, that even under the best of conditions it took several years to break even on an initial investment of more than $100,000, and that the current environment was not very favorable for efforts to initiate a journal. Their suggestions started the executive committee along a rather protracted learning process regarding journal publications.

At the August 1991 business meeting, members expressed considerable enthusiasm for starting a journal, and Milton Schwebel accepted the executive committee's invitation to oversee the planning for a journal. Questions arose over a dues increase of $20 per person to subsidize the journal and the importance of avoiding duplication with existing publications. Members agreed that it would be useful to poll the Division 48 membership regarding a journal, and this participatory method was subsequently employed. In keeping with a suggestion from Gary VandenBos to the executive committee, participants at the meeting decided to create a new publication, the *Peace Psychology Bulletin and Newsletter* (subsequently called *The Peace Psychology Bulletin*), which would be divided evenly between newsletter material (edited by Daniel Jordan and Julie Carvalho) and scholarly articles (edited by Milton Schwebel). The new publication was a stepping stone toward a journal. Ideally, the publication of scholarly papers would provide an interim outlet for research, help to define the field of peace psychology, establish peer review processes, and test the waters in regard to manuscript volume and the feasibility of starting a journal.

The *Peace Psychology Bulletin* fulfilled its promise and by fall 1992 was being published three times a year at a length of approximately 35 pages. Both the newsletter and scholarly articles were increasingly diverse and reflected work being done around the world. The *Bulletin* attracted articles from well-recognized scholars such as Ralph White (1992) and Ervin Staub

(1992), increasing the credibility of Division 48 publications. Equally important, it helped to expand the scope of peace psychology by publishing high-quality papers in diverse areas such as feminism and peace (McKay, 1992), environmental issues (Winter & McKenzie-Mohr, 1993), and ethnicity (Branch, 1992). In a tangible way, the division was now helping to move the field beyond its initial Cold War frame. Early in this initial foray into scholarly publishing, the division developed a policy, endorsed by the executive committee, of providing a constructive, humane review process that would employ rigorous standards but that would help authors to bring their work into publishable form.

Economic Support and Planning for the Journal

The year 1992 was a watershed in the movement to establish a journal. Because limited finances posed the main obstacle to forming a journal, it was no small accomplishment when Milton Schwebel brought home a major gift of $30,000 from a private donor—the first in the division's history—to be used in establishing a journal. The donor was Luella Buros, widow of Oscar Buros (of the *Buros Mental Measurements Yearbook*), who had worked with Schwebel at Rutgers University. Luella Buros had a passion for peace. In her April 22 letter of gift, she wrote, "I consider it a very special privilege and honor to be a founding contributor to such a highly significant and noble cause in behalf of world peace and understanding." In appreciation of her contribution, the members of the executive committee subsequently established (January 1994) a category of founding contributors to the journal for people who had contributed $25,000 or more. The committee members also decided to recognize Luella Buros in perpetuity by designating her as founding contributor in writing near the front of each issue of the journal. In January 1994 Buros gave an additional $20,000 in support of the journal. Luella Buros lived to see the start of the journal, and shortly before her death in June 1995 she endowed the journal through yet another major gift of $50,000. It was thus Buros' generosity that enabled the establishment of a journal.

The August 1992 business meeting occasioned a lively discussion regarding the journal, which as a result of the initial Buros gift suddenly seemed to be more than a distant dream. It was suggested that the journal should be multidisciplinary, because issues of peace transcend the boundaries of any single discipline. Members also expressed a desire to publish a richer diversity of work than was characteristic of most psychology journals, including applied work on conflict resolution and peace education, reviews and classic contributions now seldom read, and work by clinicians, counselors, peace activists, and people in developing countries. Later that year, Schwebel (1992a, 1992b) published two important concept papers in which he argued that psychology has a responsibility to use its knowledge and tools to prevent violence at levels ranging from the interpersonal to the international and that no existing peace journals reflected primarily the work of psychologists. Having noted the historic proportions of starting the first full psychology journal devoted to peace, he suggested that the journal should include theoretical, empirical, historical, and interpretive work and contributions from all corners of psychology and the world. This was not to be an academic journal having little relevance to the world. Also in 1992, the division launched an international search for the first editor of the planned journal.

On August 1, 1993, the publications committee consisting of Wessells (chair), Wagner, and Schofield brought forward a written framework of proposed policies, policy issues, and a set of financial models for the journal. Accepting the main elements of this document and making necessary revisions, at its August 1993 meeting the executive committee membership adopted an editorial policy that welcomed contributions from diverse peoples and nations, encompassed diverse kinds of work on peace, and invited work from related disciplines. It also adopted policies regarding the review process, the responsibilities of the editor, and the composition of the editorial board, which would include representatives from diverse geographic areas. The executive committee members unanimously selected as editor Milton Schwebel, who was invited to name several associate editors. The committee members also decided that the editor should receive a minimum of $3,000 in financial support annually and that the dues increases associated with the establishment of the journal should be incremental rather than large steps that might be aversive to members.

Much less agreement existed, however, on the proposed journal's title, a key factor in defining the journal's identity, niche, and stature. Several publishers had suggested having a broad title that would be inviting to audiences outside psychology, and there were concerns about limiting the scope to war or to conditions of peace. Committee members agreed that peace psychology had much to say about the origins of conflict and the conditions that promote peace, and the title should reflect this. From among suggested titles such as *Journal of Peace Psychology* and *Peace, Conflict, and Psychology*, the committee members settled eventually on Wagner's suggestion, *Peace and Conflict: Journal of Peace Psychology*.

Following the 1993 APA convention, the publications committee began the process of preparing a formal proposal for a Division 48 journal and ushering it through the APA, which required approval by the Publications and Communications Board, the Board of Directors, and then by the Council of Representatives. Having received valuable advice from Susan Knapp, director of APA Publications, and having conducted a survey of the literature, Michael Wessells wrote the proposal, which made the case that a respectable but scattered literature on peace psychology existed, that there ought to be a psychology journal focused specifically on peace and conflict, and that the division had laid an appropriate foundation for the journal by means of the *Bulletin*. The case would have been difficult to refuse in light of the growing literature on peace and the fact that the division membership had followed nearly all of the suggestions made by Gary VandenBos 2 years earlier. In February 1994, the APA council members approved the establishment of the journal—the door was open for institutionalizing peace psychology in the scholarly literature.

Selecting a Publisher

With the start-up date of January 1995, the division needed to find a suitable publisher. Although many possibilities had been explored, the two top prospects were the APA and Lawrence Erlbaum. The publications committee opened the dialogue with each publisher via a list of elements that the division wanted and then by means of an official request for proposals. In the subsequent negotiations, which extended throughout the spring, differences surfaced in the strengths and the arrangements offered by the two publishers. The APA (via its subsidiary, the Educational Publishing Foundation) was attractive because of its prestige, extensive journals list, and the strength of its publications office. Lawrence Erlbaum was attractive because it published and marketed in multiple disciplines, published major international journals in psychology, required a very low cash outlay by the division, and had a president (Lawrence Erlbaum) who showed a strong personal commitment to peace. Following extended exchanges between Wessells and the prospective publishers and a careful review of the financial implications of the decision (via a report from the publications committee of June 6, 1994), the executive committee members reviewed the offers by means of two telephone conferences and decided to sign with Lawrence Erlbaum. The incoming publications committee chair, Richard Wagner, obtained the final contracts, and Petra Hesse, as division secretary–treasurer, signed them on July 28, 1994. Concerned about rising costs to members, the executive committee members decided to use the Buros gift to subsidize the journal, thereby reducing members' expenses for the journal.

Through Milton Schwebel's stewardship, the new journal officially began publication in February 1995. With the front page listing a diverse and distinguished editorial board, 20% of whose members came from outside the United States, it was clear that the journal would have both prestige and international scope. Among other items, the initial issue included pieces by Federico Mayor, the secretary–general of the United Nations Educational, Scientific, and Cultural Organization, an analysis of women in peace psychology (McKay, 1995), an examination of when armed intervention is justified (White, 1995), and a classic on the need for a morally condonable substitute for war by William James (1910–1995) with a companion piece by Morton Deutsch (1995). Subsequent issues contained articles on topics such as peace education (Nelson & Christie, 1995), the Gulf War (Kelman, 1995), urban drug policy (Kahan, Rydell & Setear, 1995), sustainability (Kimmel, 1995), and political conflict resolution in the Philippines (Montiel, 1995), underscoring the wide scope of work within peace psychology. Several articles were written by scholars from disciplines outside psychology. To be sure, this is only the beginning, and much work remains to be done in areas such as attracting more female authors and including work done at the community level.

CONCLUSION

No one would argue that the world would be a better place if peace were a permanent condition and peace psychology were obsolete. In the post-Cold War era, however, bitter conflicts such as those in Bosnia and Rwanda show that the need has never been greater for psychological analyses and interventions that contribute to peace, which is an essential component of human well-being. The very existence of the Division of Peace Psychology is a significant accomplishment, because it institutionalizes and legitimates work for peace. The establishment of the division signals that what psychologists do pertains to peace—peace psychology is *real* psychology, not a political activity to be pursued after hours.

Because Division 48 is still in its formative stage, it is too soon to tell what its long-term contributions and status will be. Yet its early accomplishments, particularly establishing the first journal in the field and developing a full convention program on peace, bode well for the future. Equally important is the value orientation and the process that Division 48 has established. There is concerted attention to issues of diversity, to the inclusion of people from local communities around the world, and to the need to enlarge the dialogue and the scope of work for peace. It will take many years for psychological work on peace to reach maturity. But peace psychology now has a strong and appropriate foundation, thanks in no small part to the work of Division 48.

REFERENCES

Appendix to the Minutes of the 1995 Winter Executive Committee Meeting. In Division 48 Archives, M. Wessells, Department of Psychology, Randolph-Macon College, Ashland, VA 23005.

Boyer, D., & Swain, J. F. (1995, August). *Women's voice in peace psychology*. Poster presented at the 103rd Annual Convention of the APA, New York.

Branch, C. (1992). Communities at peace: The same and different? *The Peace Psychology Bulletin, 1*(2), 4–5.

Bronfenbrenner, U. (1961). The mirror image in Soviet–American relations: A social psychologist's report. *Journal of Social Issues, 17*(3), 45–58.

Capshew, J. H., & Hilgard, E. R. (1992). The power of service: World War II and professional reform in the American Psychological Association. In R. B. Evans, V. S. Sexton, & T. C. Cadwallader (Eds.), *100 years: The American Psychological Association, a historical perspective* (pp. 149–175). Washington, DC: American Psychological Association.

Deutsch, M. (1961). Some considerations relevant to national policy. *Journal of Social Issues, 17*(3), 57–68.

Deutsch, M. (1973). *The resolution of conflict: Constructive and destructive processes.* New Haven, CT: Yale University Press.

Deutsch, M. (1983). The prevention of World War Three: A psychological perspective. *Political Psychology, 4*(1), 3–31.

Deutsch, M. (1995). William James: The first peace psychologist. *Peace and Conflict: Journal of Peace Psychology, 1*(1), 27–35.

Escalona, S. (1963). Children's responses to the nuclear war threat. *Children, 10,* 137–142.

Frank, J. (1967). *Sanity and survival: Psychological aspects of war and peace.* New York: Random House.

Galtung, J. (1969). Violence, peace and peace research. *Journal of Peace Research, 3,* 176–191.

Greening, T. (1984). Commentary by the editor. *Journal of Humanistic Psychology, 24*(3), 3–4.

Jacobs, M. S. (1989). *American psychology in the quest for nuclear peace.* New York: Praeger.

James, W. (1910–1995). The moral equivalent of war. *Peace and Conflict: Journal of Peace Psychology, 1*(1), 17-26.

Kahan, J. P., Rydell, C. P., & Setear, J. (1995). A game of urban drug policy. *Peace and Conflict: Journal of Peace Psychology, 1*(3), 275–290.

Kelman, H. C. (1954). Public opinion and foreign policy decisions: Some problems for research. *Bulletin of Research Exchange on Prevention of War, 2*(4), 2–8.

Kelman, H. C. (Ed.). (1965). *International behavior: A social psychological analysis.* New York: Holt, Rinehart & Winston.

Kelman, H. C. (1972). The problem-solving workshop in conflict resolution. In R. L. Merritt (Ed.), *Communication in international politics* (pp. 168–204). Urbana: University of Illinois Press.

Kelman, H. C. (1995). Decision making and public discourse in the Gulf War: An assessment of underlying psychological and moral assumptions. *Peace and Conflict: Journal of Peace Psychology, 1*(2), 117–130.

Kimmel, P. R. (1985). Learning about peace: Choices and the United States Institute of Peace as seen from two different perspectives. *American Psychologist, 40*(5), 536–541.

Kimmel, P. R. (1992). Peace psychology, public policy and action. *The Peace Psychology Bulletin, 1*(1), 14–16.

Kimmel, P. R. (1995). Sustainability and cultural understanding: Peace psychology as public interest science. *Peace and Conflict: Journal of Peace Psychology, 1*(2), 101–116.

Kimmel, P. R., & Dane, L. (1993). Peace psychology and public interest science. *The Peace Psychology Bulletin, 2*(1), 10–12.

Klineberg, O. (1956). The role of the psychologist in international affairs. *Journal of Social Issues* (Suppl. IX), 3–17.

Klineberg, O. (1984). Public opinion and nuclear war. *American Psychologist, 39*(11), 1245–1253.

Lifton, R. J. (1967). *Death in life: Survivors of Hiroshima*. New York: Random House.

Mayor, F. (1995). How psychology can contribute to a culture of peace. *Peace and Conflict: Journal of Peace Psychology, 1*(1), 3–9.

McKay, S. (1992). Feminism and peace psychology: Establishing connections. *The Peace Psychology Bulletin, 1*(3), 16–19.

McKay, S. (1995). Women's voices in peace psychology: A feminist agenda. *Peace and Conflict: Journal of Peace Psychology, 1*(1), 67–84.

McKenzie–Mohr, D., & Winter, D. (1992). The case for approaching global issues systemically: International security and environmental security. *The Peace Psychology Bulletin, 1*(1), 4–6.

Milburn, T. W. (1961). The concept of deterrence: Some logical and psychological considerations. *Journal of Social Issues, 17*(1), 3–11.

Montiel, C. J. (1995). Social psychological dimensions of political conflict resolution in the Philippines. *Peace and Conflict: Journal of Peace Psychology, 1*(2), 149–159.

Morawski, J. G., & Goldstein, S. E. (1985). Psychology and nuclear war: A chapter in our legacy of social responsibility. *American Psychologist, 40*, 276–284.

Murphy, G. (Ed.). (1945). *Human nature and enduring peace*. Cambridge, MA: Houghton-Mifflin.

Nelson, L. L., & Christie, D. J. (1995). Peace in the psychology curriculum: Moving from assimilation to accommodation. *Peace and Conflict: Journal of Peace Psychology, 1*(2), 161–178.

Osgood, C. E. (1962). *An alternative to war or surrender*. Urbana: University of Illinois Press.

Petition for an APA Division of Peace Psychology. In Division 48 Archives, M. Wessells, Department of Psychology, Randolph-Macon College, Ashland, VA 23005.

Pilisuk, M. (1994). An agenda for peace psychology. *The Peace Psychology Bulletin, 2*(1), 22–36.

Pilisuk, M., & Hayden, T. (1965). Is there a military-industrial complex which prevents peace? Consensus and countervailing power in pluralistic systems. *Journal of Social Issues, 21*(3), 67–117.

Polyson, J. (1992). Psychology and nuclear holocaust: The task before us. *The Peace Psychology Bulletin & Newsletter, 1*(2), 6–7.

Samelson, F. (1979). Putting psychology on the map: Ideology and technology in intelligence testing. In A. R. Buss (Ed.), *Psychology in social context* (pp. 103–168). New York: Irvington.

Schwebel, M. (1963). Students, teachers and the bomb. *National Education Association Journal, 52,* 46–48.

Schwebel, M. (1965). Nuclear cold war: Student opinions and professional responsibility. In M. Schwebel (Ed.), *Behavioral science and human survival* (pp. 210–223). Palo Alto, CA: Science and Behavior Books.

Schwebel, M. (1992a). A journal of peace psychology: A concept paper. *The Peace Psychology Bulletin & Newsletter, 1*(2), 4–7.

Schwebel, M. (1992b). A journal of peace psychology: A concept paper II. *The Peace Psychology Bulletin, 1*(3), 26–30.

Sims, G. M. (1995). *One part of the story as to how peace psychology found a place of its own in the American Psychological Association.* Unpublished manuscript.

Sivard, R. L. (1991). *World military and social expenditures 1991* (14th ed.). Washington, DC: World Priorities.

Smith, M. B. (1986). War, peace and psychology. *Journal of Social Issues, 42*(4), 23–38.

Smith, M. B. (1992). Nationalism, ethnocentrism, and the new world order. *Journal of Humanistic Psychology, 32*(4), 76–91.

Staub, E. (1992). Turning against others: The origins of antagonism and group violence. *The Peace Psychology Bulletin & Newsletter, 1*(2), 11–14.

Wagner, R. (1991). Report on establishing a journal of peace psychology. *The Peace Psychology Newsletter, 1*(3), 12–13.

Wagner, R. (1992). Psychologists in pursuit of a division of peace psychology. *The Peace Psychology Bulletin, 1*(1), 9–12.

Wagner, R. V., de Rivera, J., & Watkins, M. (Eds.). (1988). Psychology and the promotion of peace. *Journal of Social Issues, 44*(2), 1–219.

Wessells, M. G. (1992a). The Cold War has ended but the nuclear threat has not. *The Peace Psychology Bulletin & Newsletter, 1*(2), 18–20.

Wessells, M. G. (1992b). Building peace psychology on a global scale: Challenges and opportunities. *The Peace Psychology Bulletin & Newsletter, 1*(3), 31–44.

Wessells, M. G. (1995). Social-psychological determinants of nuclear proliferation: A dual-process analysis. *Peace and Conflict: Journal of Peace Psychology, 1*(1), 49–65.

White, R. K. (1970). *Nobody wanted war: Misperception in Vietnam and other wars.* New York: Doubleday/Anchor.

White, R. K. (1984). *Fearful warriors: A psychological profile of U. S.–Soviet relations.* New York: Free Press.

White, R. K. (Ed.). (1986). *Psychology and the prevention of nuclear war.* New York: New York University Press.

White, R. K. (1992). The fear motive in twentieth century wars. *The Peace Psychology Bulletin, 1*(3), 1–13.

White, R. K. (1995). When does intervention make sense? *Peace and Conflict: Journal of Peace Psychology, 1*(1), 85–95.

Winter, D., & McKenzie-Mohr, D. (1993). Toward a sustainable future: The role of psychology. *The Peace Psychology Bulletin, 2*(1), 16–19.

Yankelovich, D., & Doble, J. (1986). The public mood: Nuclear weapons and the USSR. In R. K. White (Ed.), *Psychology and the prevention of nuclear war* (pp. 38–54). New York: New York University Press.

NAME INDEX

Harlow, Margaret, 80
Harper, Robert A., 163
Harris, Albert J., 106
Harris, Dale B., 67n, 69, 71, 72, 73, 78
Harris, Irving, 217, 221
Harris, William W., 216, 221
Hartrup, Willard, 69
Hartshorne, T., 118
Hartup, Willard W., 74, 77–78, 79, 80,
    82, 197, 198
Harzem, Peter, 168
Hasher, Lynn, 17, 18
Haugaard, Jeffrey J., 212, 223
Hayden, T., 267
Hayes, Linda J., 168, 181
Hayes, Steven C., 157n, 164, 165,
    167–168, 169, 174, 175, 176,
    179, 180, 181, 182, 184, 187
Hebb, Donald O., 46, 54, 56–57, 80, 94
Heiby, E., 187
Heidbreder, Edna, 12, 23, 30, 33
Held, Richard M., 52
Helson, Harry, 13, 14, 15, 33, 34
Hendrix, Terry, 290
Henggeler, Scott, 222
Hensley, T. L., 129
Herrnstein, R. J., 161
Hesse, Petra, 277, 284, 293
Hetherington, E. Mavis, 69, 72, 80, 83,
    89
Hildreth, Harold M., 139, 140, 142, 143
Hildreth, J. D., 104–105
Hildreth, Jane, 11, 24, 32, 45
Hilgard, Ernest R., 3, 5, 11, 21–22, 26,
    27, 28, 42, 54, 70, 102, 105, 157,
    159, 162–163, 165, 266
Hill, John P., 78
Hinde, Robert A., 80
Hineline, Philip N., 161, 164, 181
Hoagwood, Kimberly, 125
Hobbs, Nicholas, 71, 204, 218
Hobson, James R., 106, 108
Hodges, Kay Kline, 202, 219
Hodges, W., 75
Hodos, William, 55
Hoebel, Bertley G., 52, 56
Hoedt, K. C., 115
Hoffman, Lois Wladis, 69
Holden, E. Wayne, 204, 211
Holland, James G., 164, 169–170
Hollander, Edwin P., 11, 15, 16, 34
Hollis, Karen L., 53

Holmes, Edward J., 57
Holsopple, J. Quinter, 138, 139, 140
Holt, Robert, 46, 242
Honzik, Majorie, 80
Horai, J., 122
Horney, Karen, 234
Horowitz, Frances Degen, 69, 78, 85, 89,
    90
Houlihan, Margaret, 277, 284
Hovland, Carl I., 13, 33
Hubel, David, 54–55
Hughes, Jan N., 107
Hull, Clark, 74, 158–159
Hulse, Stewart H., 52
Hunt, James McV., 47, 80
Hunter, Carol P., 108
Hurlock, Elizabeth B., 72, 78
Hussein, Saddam, 279
Huston, Aletha C., 69, 91
Hutt, Max L., 138, 140
Hyman, Irwin A., 106, 108, 121, 124
Hyman, Marvin, 237
Hynd, George W., 125

Illback, R., 127
Ingle, David, 55
Inouye, Daniel K., 211
Ireys, H. T., 218
Irwin, Orvis C., 80
Isaacson, Robert L., 53
Iscoe, Ira, 213
Isquisth, Peter K., 221
Itkin, William, 106, 108
Ives, Margaret, 138, 139, 144

Jackson, John H., 124
Jacobs, Durand F., 139, 140, 144, 150
Jacobs, M. S., 266, 267, 268, 269
Jacobson, J. W., 185
Jacob-Timm, S., 118
Jacobvitz, Robin, 72
James, William, 266–267, 293
Jersild, Arthur T., 69, 70–71, 78
Johnson, Lyndon, 74–75
Johnson, Neal F., 18
Johnson, R., 121
Jones, Harold E., 68, 69, 70, 78
Jones, Mary Cover, 69, 80
Jones, R. M., 242
Jordan, Daniel, 281–282, 290
Jordan, Sarah, 11, 274, 279
Jung, Carl, 234, 248

Levine, Murray, 221
Levy, Jerome, 139
Levy, Sheldon, 282
Lewin, Kurt, 201
Lewis, Helen Block, 237, 239, 242, 250, 256
Liben, Lynn, 72
Liff, Zanvel A., 236, 237, 242
Lifton, R. J., 267
Lindsley, Donald B., 41n, 42–43, 44, 51, 52, 54, 55
Lindzey, Gardner, 14, 15, 30, 34
Lips, Orville J., 139
Lipsitt, Lewis P., 67n, 69, 78, 85, 87–88, 89, 219, 221
Liss, Marsha B., 209, 217–218
Little, Kenneth B., 15, 16, 17, 24–25, 33, 36
Lockard, Robert, 56
Loucks, Roger B., 43, 53
Lovinger, Sophie, 202, 209
Luckey, Bertha M., 106
Lundin, R. W., 181
Luthar, Suniya, 220–221
Lutzger, John R., 168, 173
Lynch, Mervin, 15, 16, 24
Lynn, Elizabeth, 16, 17, 18, 33
Lyons, C. A., 181

Maccoby, Eleanor, 69, 76–77, 78, 79, 80, 81, 93
Mace, F. Charles, 177
MacFarlane, Jean W., 70, 80
MacGregor, Mary Jo, 106
Mach, Ernst, 158
Machado, Armando, 177
Mack, John, 269
Macmann, Gregg, 125
MacPhee, Halsey M., 13, 33
Maddi, Salvatore R., 16, 17
Magary, James F., 106
Mahut, Helen, 46
Malmo, Robert, 53
Mandler, George, 15, 16, 17, 37, 242
Maples, Ernest, 57
Marlan, S., 244
Marquis, Donald G., 43, 51, 52
Marsden, G., 196
Marshall, Robert J., 239, 240
Martens, Brian, 125
Martin, Roy P., 106
Martin, William E., 69, 78

Maslow, Albert P., 139
Mason, Emanuel J., 125
Mason, William A., 52, 58
Massimo, J. L., 197–198
Masters, John C., 72, 87
Maurer, Adah, 196, 220, 221n
Mayman, M., 242
Mayor, Frederico, 293
Mayton, Daniel, 269, 282, 285
McCall, Robert, 86
McCandless, Boyd R., 69, 70, 71, 75, 78, 82, 85, 106, 117, 124
McCarthy, Dorothea, 69, 72, 78
McClannahan, Lynn E., 177
McCullough, Milton W., 140, 144
McFadden, E. J., 200
McGraw, Myrtle, 70, 92–93, 94
McKay, Susan, 265n, 277, 285–286, 288–289, 291, 293
McKeachie, Wilbert J., 11, 14, 15, 16, 30
McKenzie-Mohr, D., 280, 291
McNeill, Harry. See McNeill, Henry V.
McNeill, Henry V., 138, 139
Meacham, Merle L., 106
Meck, Warren H., 57
Medway, Frederic J., 125
Meehl, Paul, 46
Meenes, Max, 14, 33, 34
Mehr, Helen, 268, 270, 276, 277, 285
Meisels, Murray, 7, 233, 237, 238, 240, 242, 243, 244, 245, 246, 247–248, 249–250, 251–252, 255, 256, 260
Mello, Nancy, 55
Mellon, M., 123, 129
Melton, Gary B., 144, 195n, 199, 202, 203, 205, 210, 211, 212, 213, 219, 221, 222, 223
Meyer, Adolf, 46
Meyer, C. Edward, 124
Meyer, Donald R., 52, 56, 61
Meyer, George, 106
Meyers, Joel, 106
Meyers, Judith C., 195n, 199, 206–207, 209, 213
Michael, Jack, 164, 165, 175
Milburn, Thomas, 267, 277
Miller, David, 58
Miller, Doris, 268
Miller, George, 268
Miller, James G., 17, 144
Miller, Neal, 46, 56

Polyson, James, 270, 271, 272, 274, 275, 276, 277, 278, 279
Popplestone, John, 10, 157n
Postman, Leo J., 15, 32
Poulson, Clair, 164
Prentice, W. C. H., 13, 24, 33, 34
Pressey, Sidney, 218
Pribram, Karl, 52, 55, 56
Price, Helen G., 140
Primoff, Ernest, 138
Pronko, N. H., 13, 33
Prue, Donald, 169
Pryzwansky, Walter B., 106, 108, 121, 124, 129

Raab, David, 47
Radke-Yarrow, Marian, 69, 72, 78, 80, 85, 86
Rae, William, 222
Ramage, Jean, 108, 120
Randolf, Suzanne M., 72
Rapaport, David, 234
Ray, Barbara, 173
Rayburn, Carole A., 198, 209
Razran, Gregory, 13, 14, 33, 34
Reagan, Ronald, 273
Rebelsky, Freda, 46
Reed, E., 159
Reese, Ellen P., 157n, 164, 167, 179
Reicken, Henry W., 148–149
Reiser, John, 92
Reisinger, James, 222
Renner, Michael J., 57
Reppen, J., 240–241
Repucci, N. Dickon, 212
Reschley, D. J., 121
Resnick, Robert J., 89
Reuder, Mary E., 15, 16, 17, 30
Rexroad, Carl N., 12, 13, 33
Reynolds, Cecil R., 125
Rheingold, Harriet L., 67n, 69, 70, 77, 78, 80
Ribes, E., 181
Richards, T. W., 72
Richardson, Elliot, 76–77
Richardson, Marion W., 138, 139, 140
Richmond, Julius, 75
Rie, Herbert E., 197
Riecken, Henry W., 144
Riesen, Austin H., 52, 53, 56
Risley, Todd R., 164, 165, 168, 174, 175, 176

Roberts, Michael C., 213, 222
Roca, J., 181
Rogers, Carl, 218, 267, 270, 272
Rogers, Lawrence S., 139, 140–141
Rogoff, Barbara, 91
Roitblat, Herbert L., 57
Ronca, April, 57
Rose, Jerzy, 54–55
Rosebrook, Wilda Mae, 105, 106, 108, 109
Rosenbaum, Max, 235
Rosenberg, M., 204, 222
Rosenblith, Judy, 67n
Rosenfarb, Irwin, 169
Rosenfield, Sylvia A., 106, 108, 124
Rosenthal, Susan, 202
Rosenzweig, Mark, 55, 56
Ross, Barbara C., 17, 29
Ross, Helen Warren, 10, 15, 16, 17, 18, 19, 33, 36
Routh, Donald K., 7, 101n, 195n, 196–197, 199, 202, 204, 213, 220, 221
Routh, Marion W., 195n
Rowland, L. W., 77–79
Rumbaugh, Duane M., 16, 17, 52
Rushton, J. Philippe, 59–60
Russell, Roger W., 13, 14, 15, 24, 33, 34, 55
Russo, N. F., 68
Rutter, M., 216
Rydell, C. P., 294

Saffir, Milton A., 106, 108
Sales, Bruce, 144, 176
Salk, Lee, 199, 202, 203, 204
Salzinger, Kurt, 164, 165, 181, 182, 183, 184
Samelson, F., 181
Sameroff, Arnold, 69, 78, 88, 90
Sample, Rick A., 10
Samuelson, F., 266
Sandoval, Jonathan H., 106
Sanfilippo, M. D., 197
Saper, Bernard, 139, 149
Sarason, Seymour, 124, 201
Sather, K. J., 56
Satinoff, Evelyn, 52
Saywitz, Karen, 209
Scales-Taylor, Tia, 11
Scarr, Sandra W., 69, 72, 78, 79, 81, 84–85, 93

Schafer, R., 242
Schaffer, Marcia B., 106
Schellenbach, Cynthia, 209, 221
Schlesinger, H. J., 242
Schlitt, P., 123, 129
Schneider, Arnold Z., 235, 252, 259, 260
Schneider, Stanley, 144
Schneidman, Edwin S., 139, 140, 144
Schoenfeld, William N., 164, 165
Schofield, Janet, 265n, 272, 275, 277, 292
Schofield, William, 140
Scholnick, Ellen, 72
Schroeder, Carolyn, 198, 199, 202, 203, 213, 219, 221
Schroeder, Patricia, 211
Schroeder, Stephen R., 219, 221, 222, 223
Schuster, Charles R., 184
Schwartz, A. A., 185
Schwartz, Ira M., 216–217, 221
Schwebel, Milton, 265n, 267, 272, 275, 276, 277, 281, 285, 290, 291, 292, 293
Schwitzgebel, R. K., 169–170
Scott, John P., 14, 15, 56
Scott, Winifred S., 106
Scott-Jones, Diane, 222
Scrivner, Ellen M., 139
Seagoe, May V., 106, 107n, 116
Sears, Pauline, 69, 74, 78, 81
Sears, Robert R., 68, 69, 70, 71, 74, 78, 79, 80, 81
Seashore, Robert H., 12, 22, 23, 30
Sechrest, Lee, 144
Segal, Evalyn E., 165
Seibert, Jeffrey M., 223
Senders, Virginia L., 11, 15, 16
Setear, J., 294
Sexton, Virginia S., 2, 17, 18, 30, 42
Shalala, Donna, 211
Shantz, Carolyn U., 69, 72, 89, 90
Shapiro, D., 255, 256
Shapiro, Edward, 125, 243, 250
Shepard, R. H., 172
Sheridan, Susan, 125
Sherif, Muzafer, 15
Sherrod, L. R., 216
Sherrod, Lonnie, 91
Shevrin, H., 242
Shock, Nathan, 47
Shonkoff, Jack, 217, 221

Shore, Milton F., 82, 195, 196, 197–198, 199, 202, 203, 211, 213, 218, 221
Short, R. J., 128
Short, Rick, 120
Sidman, Murray, 177
Siebert, Jeffrey, 222
Siegel, Alberta E., 67n, 69, 77, 78
Sigel, Irving, 69, 72, 82–83, 90
Silver, Barbara J., 209
Silverstein, Brett, 268
Sims, Gregory, 265n, 270, 281
Singer, J. L., 242
Sivard, R. L., 280
Skeels, Harold M., 70, 79, 80, 140
Skinner, B. F., 6, 43, 54, 74, 157–158, 159, 160, 161, 162–163, 164, 168, 178, 179, 181, 182–183, 184, 267, 270, 272
Skinner, Christopher, 125
Slaby, Ronald, 77
Slater, Barbara R., 106, 121
Slavin, Jonathan H., 237, 244, 250, 256–257
Slavin, M., 242
Smith, L. D., 158
Smith, M. Brewster, 11, 218, 265n, 266, 267, 268, 270, 273, 287
Smith, S. R., 242
Smotherman, William P., 53
Smuts, A. B., 68
Sobel, Suzanne B., 140, 195n, 196, 198, 199, 202, 203, 211, 214
Soler, Mark, 216, 221
Solomon, Richard L., 13, 14, 33, 34, 52
Sondregger, T., 222
Spaner, Fred E., 139
Spence, Janet, 60
Spence, Kenneth W., 54
Spencer, Metta, 56
Sperry, Roger, 55
Spezzano, Charles, 240–241, 242, 251–252
Spiker, H. H., 75
Squier, Larry, 56
Stamm, John, 47, 55
Stark, Kevin, 125
Staub, Ervin, 290–291
Stendler, Celia, 71
Stenger, Charles A., 144
Stern, John, 49
Stern, Judith, 56

SUBJECT INDEX

National Education Association (NEA), 102
National Institute of Child Health and Development, 74–75
National Institute of Mental Health, 77
National Medal of Science, 93
National Research Council, Division of Anthropology and Psychology, 3

Office of Child Development (OCD), 76

Peace Psychology. *See* Division 48 (Peace Psychology)
Portraits of Pioneers in Psychology (Kimble), 3, 39
Principles of Psychology (James), 38, 39
Psychoanalysis. *See* Division 39 (Psychoanalysis)
Psychoanalytic Consortium, 261–262
Psychological Bulletin, 11
Psychological Review, 11
Psychologists in Independent Practice. *See* Division 42 (Psychologists in Independent Practice)
Psychologists in Public Service. *See* Division 18 (Psychologists in Public Service)

Psychology in America: A Historical Survey (Hilgard), 11, 162–163

Rockefeller, Laura Spellman, Memorial, 68

School Psychology. *See* Division 16 (School Psychology)
Skinner, B. F., Young Researcher Award, 183–184
Society for Research in Child Development (SRCD), 68, 70, 86, 90–91
Society for the Advancement of Behavior Analysis, 185
Society for the Experimental Analysis of Behavior (SEAB), 159, 160, 161
  and ASP's Human Capital Initiative, 185
  and Hake Award, 177
Society for the Study of School Psychology, 122
Society of Experimental Psychologists, 2
Society of Pediatric Psychology, 202

Teaching of Psychology. *See* Division 2 (Teaching of Psychology)
Trainers of School Psychologists, 122

Witmer, Lightner, Award recipients, 125

ABOUT THE EDITOR

Donald A. Dewsbury was born in Brooklyn, New York, grew up on Long Island, and received an AB degree in psychology from Bucknell University in Lewisburg, Pennsylvania. After completing his PhD in psychology at the University of Michigan with Edward L. Walker, he spent a year as a post-doctoral fellow at the University of California, Berkeley, with Frank A. Beach. Through much of his career he has been a comparative psychologist with a special interest in the evolution of reproductive and social behavior. In recent years, his interests have shifted so that he now works primarily in the area of the history of psychology, with a secondary interest in comparative psychology. He is the author or editor of eight books, including *Comparative Animal Behavior* (1978) and *Comparative Psychology in the Twentieth Century* (1984). In addition, he has published more than 260 articles and book chapters. He is a fellow of the American Psychological Association's Divisions 1, 2, 6, and 26, the American Association for the Advancement of Science, the American Psychological Society, and the Animal Behavior Society. He has served as president of the Animal Behavior Society and APA's Division 6 and is currently president-elect of APA's Division 26.